The Tenth Minnesota
Volunteers, 1862–1865

The Tenth Minnesota Volunteers, 1862–1865

A History of Action in the Sioux Uprising and the Civil War, with a Regimental Roster

MICHAEL A. EGGLESTON

McFarland & Company, Inc., Publishers
Jefferson, North Carolina, and London

LIBRARY OF CONGRESS CATALOGUING-IN-PUBLICATION DATA

Eggleston, Michael A., 1937–
The Tenth Minnesota Volunteers, 1862–1865 : a history of action in the Sioux Uprising and the Civil War, with a regimental roster / Michael A. Eggleston.
          p.   cm.
Includes bibliographical references and index.

ISBN 978-0-7864-6593-4
softcover : acid free paper ∞

1. United States. Army. Minnesota Infantry Regiment, 10th (1862–1865) 2. United States. Army. Minnesota Infantry Regiment, 10th (1862–1865) — Registers.   3. United States — History — Civil War, 1861–1865 — Regimental histories.   4. Minnesota — History — Civil War, 1861–1865 — Regimental histories.   5. Dakota Indians — Wars — 1862–1865.   6. Indians of North America — Wars — 1862–1865.
I. Title.
E515.510th.E44 2012   973.7'476 — dc23   2012020557

BRITISH LIBRARY CATALOGUING DATA ARE AVAILABLE

©2012 Michael A. Eggleston. All rights reserved

No part of this book may be reproduced or transmitted in any form or by any means, electronic or mechanical, including photocopying or recording, or by any information storage and retrieval system, without permission in writing from the publisher.

On the cover: The Union attack on the second day of the Battle of Nashville (December 16, 1864) led by the United States Colored Troops (Library of Congress)

Manufactured in the United States of America

*McFarland & Company, Inc., Publishers
Box 611, Jefferson, North Carolina 28640
www.mcfarlandpub.com*

To my wife, Margaret.
Her hard work and infinite patience
made this book happen.

Acknowledgments

This history relies upon the letters, diaries, and reminiscences of many of the participants quoted within. I am indebted to the Minnesota Historical Society for the endless amount of information they provided to me. They always gave me a prompt response and provided many photos that the reader will see in this history.

I owe a special thanks to Professor Robert J. Wilensky of George Mason University who provided excellent input in order to help me improve this book.

I am also indebted to Mary G. who shared many books from her library to help me get at the facts. Whenever I was missing a piece, I seemed to find it in the books she sent me.

Many excellent histories of Minnesota are available, but one stands out as a superior work. *A History of Minnesota*, written by William Watts Folwell, is exceptionally well documented and was the source that I used to check facts. I was never disappointed.

Table of Contents

Acknowledgments	vi
Preface	1
Introduction	5
1. Sibley's Campaign Against the Sioux	11
2. Vengeance on the Plains	50
3. Moving South	76
4. The Battle of Nashville	87
5. The Last Battle	98
Epilogue: The Key Participants After 1865	103
Appendices	
A. Treaty with the Sioux—Sisseton and Wahpeton Bands, 1851	111
B. Narrative of the Tenth Regiment	114
C. Tenth Regiment Roster	131
D. The Casualties	164
E. Eating on the March	177
F. The Tribes	178
G. The Trials	181
H. Lincoln's Report to Congress	188
I. The Executions	197
Chapter Notes	213
Bibliography	223
Index	227

Preface

This is the story of the Tenth Minnesota Volunteer Infantry Regiment told in the words of the participants and their opponents. Many died along the way. Most members of the Tenth Regiment served from the organization of the regiment in August of 1862 until its final muster in August of 1865. The experience of this regiment is unique. Its members fought in two wars over a period of three years. Because this regiment shared an experience with few other Civil War units and only a summary of its service was published in 1890, its story needs to be told. Volunteers who signed up to fight the Confederacy suddenly found themselves fighting the Sioux in the Minnesota Indian War instead. After two years of fighting the Sioux, they moved south to fight the Confederate Army in a series of battles in the West. In telling this story, it was necessary to address the Sioux war and the battles with the Confederate Army from a broad perspective. The narrative includes what was going on in sister units and the enemy camp since a discussion that focuses only on the actions of the Tenth does not present the complete picture. As an example, I have provided the details of the Fifth Minnesota Regiment's battle against the Sioux in August of 1862 although only a handful of the Tenth Regiment's soldiers participated. The events that month set the stage for what would happen to the Tenth later. On the other hand, when the Tenth left Minnesota to fight against the Confederacy in 1863, there were other campaigns against the Sioux that were yet to be fought. These are omitted because they had nothing to do with the Tenth and they were, in many respects, reruns of the earlier campaigns.

This book focuses on compilations of the records written at the time of the war, such as *The War of Rebellion: A Compilation of the Official Records of the Union and Confederate Armies*. These provide thousands of first hand reports by commanders engaged in the fighting and other valuable information. The Minnesota Board of Commissioners' *Minnesota in the Civil and Indian Wars*, published in 1890, was the best effort by the Civil War survivors to document the histories of their Minnesota regiments. Research also concentrated on newspaper articles written at that time. The reader will find the newspaper accounts very helpful in understanding why there was so much hatred on the Minnesota frontier for both Indians and the Confederacy. Many of these newspaper articles have not been subsequently published since they were originally written during the Civil War period. The account of the executions of the Sioux (Appendix I) is quite remarkable in that correspondents interviewed the condemned Indians the night before they were hanged. As far as is known, this newspaper account has not been published since its first appearance and gives readers a rare opportunity to find out what the Sioux said the night before they were hanged as well as the thoughts of those waiting to watch the executions. Research at the National Archives also provided details of pension and service records that are relevant to this history. Most important, the letters, reminiscences, and diaries of the participants provide an enormous insight into what was going on at the time and what the soldiers were thinking. For example, it is difficult to imagine what was going through Minnesota soldiers' minds as they faced Lee at Gettysburg and were reading daily newspaper accounts of Indian raids on their homes in Minnesota. We find some of this in the diaries of these soldiers. That makes this book different from other works in that I have presented the history in the words of the participants.

Many important accounts of this period have been written and there are numerous good books that have been published in Minnesota. Unfortunately most deal with the Civil War or the Indian wars, but not both. As an example, there have been several excellent histories of the First Minnesota Volunteer Regiment that fought against the Confederate Army, but no mention is made of the Indian wars. This makes sense since the First did not fight against the Sioux, yet there are unaddressed common threads between these two wars. For example, Alfred Sully, an early commander of the First Minnesota, led the campaign against the Sioux in 1863 at the same time as his former regiment was facing Lee at Gettysburg. As noted herein, there were delightful idiosyncrasies of Sully that were noticed by his soldiers in the West that do not appear in the history of the First Minnesota.

Throughout this book, I use the words Indian, Santee, or Sioux to identify Native Americans. These were the terms used at the time of the Indian war. I use the term Indian when a conflict involved Sioux or other tribes. Dakota (or Lakota) is the name that Native Americans of that nation would prefer to be called rather than Sioux. Unfortunately the histories were flooded with the term Sioux so I have used that term. See Appendix F for more information about the tribes.

I was born and raised in Minnesota. While I was growing up after World War II, my parents purchased a cabin in northern Minnesota as a summer place. Many Chippewa lived nearby. We traded with them and I got a very small bit of understanding and developed a great deal of interest about the Indians of Minnesota, something that I have carried with me to this day. In the late 1940s I got first hand information about the last Indian war in the United States. This was not Wounded Knee in 1890, but the Chippewa uprising in northern Minnesota in 1898. After spending thirty years in the U.S. Army and as a U.S. Military Academy graduate of 1961, I was interested in how well the members of West Point's Long Gray Line performed in these two conflicts. Of course they did well. They were among the few leaders with any military training (at government expense) when these wars started. "At government expense" was an important factor during the 19th Century. It made the difference between a college education or none. Given his family's circumstances when he was growing up, Robert E. Lee could not afford a college education. Had he not gotten an appointment to West Point, he probably would not have gotten a college degree. In that case he may have spent the Civil War farming a plantation in Virginia. I chose to review the records of many of the Civil War West Point graduates. Many on opposing sides were classmates such as Hood and Schofield at Franklin (see Chapter 4). This is not new, as other writers have done this, but I found that some graduates on opposing sides were also roommates as cadets. It would appear that this gave them an insight to help figure out what the other side was going to do.

What is more interesting is how well those with no military background performed. These included General Henry Hastings Sibley, General Nathan Bedford Forrest, General John McArthur, and General James Heaton Baker, the commander of the Tenth Regiment. These were among thousands of leaders who without military training stepped up to major responsibilities and did exceptionally well.

Preface

There have been many authors over the past 150 years that have presented a biased view of what happened during the Indian war. Until 1970, most authors presented the Indians as bloodthirsty savages who murdered every white that they could lay their hands on. In that year, Dee Brown published his book *Bury My Heart at Wounded Knee*. It presented the Indian point of view that was seldom found in earlier books. Brown's book was long overdue and in keeping with the times when mistrust of government and everything that we had been taught were in question. Unfortunately, the pendulum swung too far and we were told only how bad the whites were and how noble and exploited the Indians were. The myth goes on to this day. It is difficult to find a balanced view of this period, but a few historians stand out as providing this view. The most notable is Folwell in his history of Minnesota written nearly one hundred years ago. His extensive documented research should be a model for historians today. He did not resort to innuendo to seduce the reader to a point of view. He laid out all of the facts in exquisite detail. My hope is that the reader will find that this history presents a balanced view. Folwell was my model.

What we learn from the history of the Tenth Regiment is that there were many heroes or key players in this conflict. The most important were General Henry Hastings Sibley, who had no military experience and opposed military action of any kind, but accepted command of Union forces in Minnesota in the crisis; Little Crow, chief of the Sioux, who opposed war with the whites but when it was forced upon him led the Sioux nation in the war; and John Bell Hood, who accepted command of the Confederate Army in the West when there was no chance of victory. I have done my best to present their dilemmas. Most important, the main characters of this history are the individual soldiers who kept diaries, sent letters or published reminiscences of the war. Some diaries survived the wars, but their authors did not. The Epilogue tells what happened to the participants or their families after the war. For details, please read on. This book tells the story of the Tenth Minnesota Regiment. Unlike Eastern regiments that had to rely on bounties paid for service, the Tenth was composed of volunteers. The Sioux had threatened and some times killed members of their families. As a consequence, the volunteers were unwavering in their commitment to fight and they carried that commitment with them when they moved south to fight the Confederate Army. We see this in their diaries and letters home. They fought and won because they would not give up. That is the theme of this book.

Introduction

It was late afternoon on 16 December 1864 before the attack against the Confederate line at Nashville could begin. The troops had waited in freezing cold since early morning. Colonel McMillen's First Brigade included the Tenth Minnesota Infantry Regiment, which was positioned against the left center of the Confederate position. The Union line moved forward and the Tenth suffered severe casualties when it was caught in a crossfire as it approached the enemy works. Major Cook was mortally wounded as was Captain White, the commander of F Company. The regimental commander, Lieutenant Colonel Jennison, fell wounded within a yard of the enemy works as Color Sergeant O'Neil led the Union charge over the parapet. Captain Sanders took over as regimental commander. The Union overwhelmed the Confederate defenses with the Tenth's bayonet charge. Sixteen cannon and two thousand prisoners were taken. Of the 301 soldiers of the Tenth that mustered that day, sixty-eight were killed or wounded, but the disintegration of the Confederate Army in the West was nearly completed. On this day, the good fortune of the Tenth ended after two years of fighting in the Indian war and against the Confederate Army. Until now, few soldiers had been killed in action, but on this date, more would be killed than any time before or after. The epitaph for the Tenth Regiment published in the press shortly after the end of the war summarizes its contribution.

> The Tenth Regiment, although it had received less notice from the press of the State than any of our other [Minnesota] regiments, perhaps, is as deserving of fame as any. It has done well all that it was ordered to do, and though they have had few chances, compared with some other regiments, its men have made a glorious record. Its charge over the rebel ramparts at Nashville alone was one of the most gallant acts of that memorable field, and every man whose name has been born on the rolls of the Tenth Regiment should feel proud of its record.[1]

Nearly all of the Minnesota volunteers had joined to fight the Confederacy, but that changed when the Sioux Indian War broke out in August of 1862 while six of the new regiments were organizing at Fort Snelling, Minnesota. For two years the Indian war was fought with few battle deaths among the Union regiments that engaged the Indians. With the Indian war ended, the Minnesota regiments were joining the fight against the Confederacy.

This is the history of the Tenth Minnesota Regiment from its formation in August of 1862 until its final muster in August 1865. The regiment completed its organization in the winter of 1862 after the first Indian campaign was completed, but as will be seen, elements of it fought the Sioux from the start of the Indian war while the regiment was being formed. The regiment served throughout the Sioux Indian War of 1863 and was then engaged fighting the Confederate Army at Nashville, Tupelo and other battles in the South. Because of the Civil War in the East, the events of the Sioux War were largely obscured at that time. The Eastern battles, Gettysburg, Antietam and Fredericksburg, captured the nation's attention, then and now. The story of the Tenth is told in the words of the participants, including the Sioux and the Confederate soldiers who fought against the Tenth as well as the members of the Tenth and other Union soldiers who survived the war. In telling the story of the Tenth in this way, we capture and understand what was going on at that time.

Occasionally the reader will see references to the Medal of Honor (frequently called the Congressional Medal of Honor, which is not the correct name)[2] that is, today, our nation's highest military award. Today, few members of the armed forces receive this award. The Medal of Honor originated in the Civil War and at that time was commonly awarded. As an example, all members of the 27th Maine Infantry, all 864 men, received the Medal of Honor because they reenlisted before a battle when their enlistments had expired. Many awards of the Medal of Honor were later rescinded long after the Civil War.[3] An interesting quirk appears. The Grand Army of the Republic (GAR) was a fraternal organization formed after the Civil War. It is similar to modern organizations such as the Veterans of Foreign Wars (VFW). The GAR badge and the Medal of Honor are remarkably similar. Comparing the Medal of Honor to the GAR badge leads the viewer to believe that they are the same and they look that way in old photos, but they are not. There are small differences. Perhaps the old veterans intended it to be that way: whoever served was a hero, and indeed they were. Those who are authentic Medal of Honor recipients can be found on the website http://www.history.army.mil/moh.html.gov. One will find Lieutenant Thomas P. Gere, who defended Fort Ridgley during the Sioux Indian War on this list. Gere won the Medal of Honor at the Battle of Nashville.

In many cases, this narrative includes information not previously published and compiles information from a variety of other published sources. A journal format indicating dates of events is used because many events were compressed into a short time frame. A journal format makes it easier to understand what was going on. Names of participants also cause mischief and confusion. For example, there were two generals named Henry H. Sibley (not related). One fought for the North and one for the South.[4] A reader may recall that at Gettysburg the Union cavalry leader was General Buford, but there was also a Confederate cavalry leader named General Buford fighting in the West. Indian names and tribes are also a cause for confusion because there are multiple names for the same Indian participants and tribes. Appendix F attempts to provide information in this regard. As is usually the case, the rank of the participants changed over time and in this narrative the most commonly quoted rank is used. As an example Henry Hasting Sibley was a Minnesota colonel until he was promoted to Union general by the president and U.S. Congress after the 1862 Indian campaign. He is referred to as General Sibley throughout this narrative. Names are sometimes confusing. Each Indian had at least two names and sometimes more. The same is true of place names. To remove confusion, alternate names are provided in parentheses.

At the sesquicentennial of the Sioux War in Minnesota, it is often difficult to understand the many inaccuracies that appear in the records of the participants. Numbers quoted by the people that were present at the time are often widely different for the same event. Usually, it is because of the time period involved. For example, one reference may refer to General Thomas's unit strength at Nashville to be one number, but that number was constantly changing over time as casualties occurred or reinforcing units arrived. All one can gather from this is the general strength of opposing forces as the battles progressed. A different commander viewing the same battle may tell us numbers of killed and wounded that are far different from another commander at the same battle. If they were referring to their own unit, the numbers can usually be trusted, but if they are referring to enemy casualties, the numbers were generally inflated. The reader may see much hatred in the records of the time because of the hundreds of white women and children murdered by the Sioux. While it is true that hundreds were murdered, the stories of rape and mutilation (except for scalping of the dead, which was done with relish by both sides) were wildly exaggerated. As an example, Lincoln's review of the trial records of 303 convicted Indians sentenced to be hanged showed only two convicted of rape. See Appendix H.

In 1851, the treaty of Traverse de Sioux (See Appendix A) was signed at the village of the same name in central Minnesota. This treaty turned over 24 million acres of land in southwestern Minnesota to the Federal government. In return, the treaty provided $2.075 million to the Sioux. Most of this was in the form of an annuity ($71,000) to the Sioux that could be used to provide food and supplies. The Sioux would live on reservations, farm, and survive on the annuity. Loss of the land caused crowding, resentment and a change to the traditional way of life for the Sioux. This was the underlying cause of the Sioux war. The Sioux chief Big Eagle summarized: "It seemed too sudden to make such a change."[5] Most of the funds provided by the treaty went to the annuity and nearly all of the remainder was claimed by Indian agents; only $30,000 reached the Sioux. In the words of Little Crow, the Santee chief, "We had no corn crops and could find no game to speak of; well, the white settlers came in and showered down their houses all over our country. We did not really know whether this country any longer belonged to us or not.... Why, we have neither our lands where our fathers' bones are bleaching, nor have we anything. What shall we do?"[6]

Other dynamics were introduced. Earlier in the history of the West, the settlers were English-Scotch-Irish and inclined to cooperate with the Indians in order to survive in a less than friendly environment. If an Indian stopped at your door and asked for food, you shared it with him. He would help you later. A new element of white settlement entered the mix shortly before the Sioux War. The Scandinavian immigrants who started to arrive had a different ethic: if you did not earn your livelihood do not ask me for help.[7] The era of cooperation on the frontier was ending.[8] More important, settlers were flooding in and devouring resources needed by the Sioux such as fish and game. Further, the Sioux discovered that the whites were not invincible when they killed soldiers in August of 1862. Finally, when the Sioux annuity did not arrive on time, the stage was set for war.

By 1862, the war in the East had slowed the annual payments to the Sioux. Food and supplies were stockpiled at the Lower Agency warehouses and Fort Ridgley (spelled Ridgely in some documents) was built near the Redwood Agency to protect it. Federal funds had not arrived and the Indian agents would not release the supplies. The Sioux were hungry. Fort Ridgley was commanded by Captain John Marsh. The troops at Fort Ridgley were members of the Fifth Minnesota Infantry Regiment. They frequently visited the Lower Agency (also called the Redwood Agency) to maintain order and protect government property. Marsh's lieutenants included Timothy Sheehan, an immigrant from Ireland, and Thomas Gere, at nineteen, the youngest officer in the regiment. Both would show uncommon coolness in very tense situations such as the showdown at the Lower Agency.

In the East, the Civil War raged in the summer and fall of 1862. In August the Union Army under McClellan was beaten before Richmond. The Union Army fell back as Lee moved north to threaten Washington. The Union would lose again to Robert E. Lee at Second Manassas. The Union commander at Second Manassas, John Pope would be replaced and sent west. Pope would take over command of the campaign against the Sioux.

The Civil War would produce over six hundred thousand deaths: two out of three would be from disease and accident with the death toll among those fighting in the West higher since medical care was less available. Three out of four deaths in the Minnesota regiments were from disease and accidents. The sad thing is that many of the deaths were preventable. In the East, wounded soldiers had resources to fall back on. Friendly homes provided care while there were reasonably close supporting medical facilities. It was different in the West. There were no friendly homes on the prairie (the occupants had been either killed or fled). Anyone who straggled or was left behind would be killed by Indians. As a consequence, a wounded or ill soldier had only himself and his buddies to rely on to survive. Each regiment had a surgeon and two or three orderlies and these were overwhelmed by casualties and the sick. We see some of this in the diaries and letters left behind. Appendix D provides a listing of Tenth Minnesota casualties.

On the supply side, the story of support is far from good. Even after the war in the East settled down, there were shortages of all types that hampered the war effort for the Union. In the Confederacy and for the Union forces fighting in the West, the problems were unimaginable. A number of factors played into all of this. Priority for the war effort went to units fighting in the East, and units in the West had to wait until the supply system caught up with demand.[9] The Harper's Ferry .69 caliber musket was issued in 1842. This was replaced in the 1850s by modern .58 caliber rifled muskets so the Union was producing large quantities of .58 caliber rifles and Minié bullets (conical rounds for rifled muskets) to fit them, not the older .69 caliber muskets and balls. As a consequence, soldiers were fighting with antique muskets and sometimes the wrong sized bullets which were the only thing between them and the tomahawk. Many would die because of this.

During the Indian war, fighting involved a few thousand people on each side, but that would change when the Minnesota regiments moved south to fight the Confederate Army as the Indian war subsided in 1863 and 1864. The tactics used by each side during the Indian war favored the Union. While the Indian warriors were skilled and very brave, they favored individual combat rather than the massed formations used by the Union Army. When faced with a siege such as New Ulm (Chapter 1), the individual Indians would become bored and depart for more lucrative endeavors such as raiding farms. Little Crow, the Indian chief, would later ridicule the Union tactic of forming a line of troops shoulder to shoulder since it made it easy for the Sioux to shoot them down. True in some cases, but this tactic also enabled the soldiers to fire massed volleys with devastating effect on the Indian attackers. The Union lines supported by artillery and cavalry would defeat the Sioux in every battle. The Sioux were masters of the ambush and could win when this tactic was successful, but in most cases, the ambush was discovered and a bayonet charge or cavalry attack would rout the Indians. When the Tenth and other regiments moved south to fight the Confederacy everything changed. These regiments were now a part of huge armies composed of tens of thousands of troops. They were fighting a seasoned Confederate Army with plenty of artillery and possibly the best cavalry in the world. It was here that the Tenth sustained most of its losses.

The Civil War in the East was always the focus of attention as armies moved back and forth between Richmond and Washington and beyond. Lincoln's first general in chief, Winfield Scott, devised the Anaconda Plan shortly after the war started. This provided a plan to strangle the Confederacy through a naval blockade of the South and cutting it in two by controlling the Mississippi River. The Anaconda Plan was never a top priority strategy, but warfare in the West along the Mississippi continued at a slow pace and finally started to succeed at the time when the Minnesota regiments began to arrive along the Mississippi.

Jefferson Davis, the president of the Confederacy, had different motives and a different situation. He decided early in the war to adopt what could be called a fixed defense. This involved spreading Confederate troops over his entire nation to repel any incursion by the Union. As an example, thousands of Confederate troops were deployed along the Confederate coastline and while there were a few Union incursions along the coast, the fact is that tens of thousands of Confederate troops were tied up along the coast doing nothing. They could have been used better elsewhere and ultimately were. A mobile defense would have worked better as this would allow troops to concentrate and move to repel Union troops after they had invaded. Davis was forced to use the fixed defense for several reasons. First, the fragile institution of slavery could not survive if Union armies were occupying Confederate territory (which ultimately happened). Second, the South could simply not allow loss of ground when they were faced with a vastly superior economy in the North. The more territory they lost, the less they had to wage war. They needed to keep all that they had if they were to have a chance to survive. Finally, the South could not expect recognition from other nations such as Great Britain if their land was being flooded by advancing Union forces.[10] When the Confederacy started to crumble in 1864, the war was lost in the West when vast amounts of Confederate territory were occupied by the Union.[11] The following chapters describe how the Confederacy in the West was dismembered and the Minnesota regiments played a key role in this.

In 1860, the population of Minnesota was 172,000. Minnesota would send over 10 percent of its population to war. This was not 10 percent of eligible males, but 10 percent of the total population meaning that nearly every male from teens to forties was fighting in the Civil War or would be diverted to fight in the Indian war. Those who served from Minnesota joined eleven Minnesota infantry regiments, artillery units and cavalry units. Additionally, many Minnesotans joined units from other states such as Wisconsin and Iowa. A review of the roster of the Tenth Regiment shows soldiers ranging in age from sixteen to middle forties and beyond. The ages of the younger soldiers are suspect. They were probably far younger than the record indicates. Drummer boys, as we now call them, were listed as musicians on the rosters. The last surviving soldier of the Civil War (North and South)[12] was Albert Woolson. Woolson enlisted in the 1st Minnesota Heavy Artillery Regiment as a musician in 1864. He died in 1956. Early records indicate that he was sixteen years old when he enlisted, but later research indicates that he was thirteen or fourteen years of age which is typical of younger volunteers in the Civil War. The Grand Army of the Republic was disbanded shortly before Albert Woolson died in 1956. An image of Woolson honoring him and the GAR was issued by the U.S. Postal Service as a stamp after Woolson's death.

Judge Flandrau in his history of Minnesota states that of the 22,970 men that Minnesota sent to war, 2,254 lost their lives.[13] The frontier was stripped of troops and eligible males in order to fight the Confederacy. It must have occurred to Ramsey and others that they were divesting the state of most of their eligible fighting men in order to fight Lincoln's war in the East. If the Sioux became a major problem Ramsey would not have forces available to react. The Sioux were also aware of the white man's war in the East and the reduction in the number of troops near them. Big Eagle, a Sioux chief, summarized. "The war with the South was going on then, and a great many men had gone down there to fight. We understood that the South was getting the best of the fight, and it was said that the North would be whipped."[14]

When the Indian war started, there were rumors that the Confederates were inciting the Sioux to violence or even supplying arms. Some historians are convinced that these stories were true, but there is no evidence to support them, then or in the years since.[15] The notion that the Sioux were too stupid to prosecute the war and needed Confederate advisors to tell them what to do is absurd. In every council the Sioux leadership showed intelligence, clever planning, and insight into their problems and solutions to them. The point is that the Sioux had more than adequate reasons to go to war and did not need any incitement from the Confederacy. There were reports throughout the conflict that French and Anglo whites were with Little Crow. This is hardly surprising in view of the number mixed bloods among the Santee Sioux.

Canada was blamed for deaths on the frontier since it provided a safe haven for the Sioux who often fled to Canada and then drifted back across the border to continue raids. This was true and as will be seen, Union soldiers needed to cross the border in order to deal with the Sioux. Most of the blame rested on traders in Canada who supplied food and ammunition to the Sioux, but the same blame applied to traders in the United States. The British were less than thrilled with a large number of Sioux consuming resources in Canada, and they were well aware of the fact that they did not have sufficient military forces to eject the Sioux from Canada. For the troops in Minnesota, it was a matter of coaxing Sioux across the border with offers of food and then arresting them once they were back in the United States. In this way, Chief Little Six (Shakopee) and Medicine Bottle were apprehended in 1864 and later hanged.

Minnesota's Hatch's battalion of cavalry entered the scene in December of 1863. Major Hatch moved north to the Canadian border near Pembina where temperatures were down to forty degrees below zero and would drop to sixty degrees below zero by 1 January 1864.[16] Hatch crossed the border and engaged the Sioux in the only battle fought by his battalion in the war. Some concluded that the battle was more like a massacre of sleeping Sioux who were trying to stay warm. A few Sioux were killed and in what can best be described as the act of an impressive entrepreneur, Hatch opened after-the-fact negotiations with the governor in chief of Rupert's Land, A. G. Dallas, Esq. The headline in the Minnesota newspaper read: "MAJOR HATCH PERMITTED TO CROSS THE BOUNDARY LINE IN PURSUIT OF THE SIOUX." Dallas then asked his council to endorse his actions (share the blame for his illegal decision), which they did. To the Sioux in Canada he suggested that "they make peace with the Americans, or be prepared for a prosecution of the war with renewed vigor next summer."[17] The Sioux did not make peace and the war was prosecuted with vigor the following summer. While this incident put a damper on Sioux flight to Canada, it continued to a lesser degree.

Various maps are included in this history to show approximate distances between battle sites. Most of the fighting occurred on the frontier in Western Minnesota. The land is prairie in the West with valleys carved by rivers in the East especially the Minnesota and Mississippi rivers.

In this book we recognize the soldiers of the Tenth Minnesota Infantry Regiment who fought in obscure and forgotten battles such as Tupelo, Spanish Fort and Dead Buffalo Lake. Like hundreds of thousands of soldiers in the Civil War, they served faithfully with very little thought of money or other rewards. They were volunteers. They had a cause that they felt was worth serving. They did it and then went home to make a new life. We are all beneficiaries of that. Thomas Jefferson Hunt of the Tenth Regiment in his reminiscences summarizes best: "Now at the age of nearly seventy-nine years, with a retrospective view of all that has passed, I can truthfully say that I have never seen the hour that I regretted entering the service of my beloved country, and as I see its greatness and its glory, I am thankful that God allowed me to take a humble part in its salvation."[18]

CHAPTER 1

Sibley's Campaign Against the Sioux
17 August–14 November 1862

The white men are like the locusts when they fly so thick that the whole sky is a snowstorm. You may kill one — two — ten; yes, as many as the leaves in the forest yonder, and their brothers will not miss them.[1]

— Little Crow

On the Verge of War, Monday, 4 August 1862

While the Civil War raged in the East, the Sioux Indian War broke out in Minnesota. It was the bloodiest Indian war waged in the United States. In August 1862, on the Western frontier in Minnesota, the situation of the Sioux was tense. The 1851 Treaty of Traverse de Sioux between the U.S. government and the Sioux nation included an annuity for the Sioux in return for the land that the tribe agreed to relinquish (see Appendix A). The annuity was used to purchase supplies that the Sioux needed, and it was late in arriving from the East that summer. In southwestern Minnesota Fort Ridgley (also spelled Ridgely in some documents) was near the Redwood Agency (or Lower Sioux Agency as it was also called) and the annuity would be sent there.[2] The Sioux were starving and chief of the tribe, Little Crow, was losing control of his people. The young warriors wanted a war because they perceived that the whites had violated the treaty. In St. Paul over a hundred miles away, Minnesota governor Alexander Ramsey was struggling to produce the six new infantry regiments for the war in the East that he had promised Lincoln. The new regiments were organizing at Fort Snelling, next to St. Paul. Minnesota had achieved statehood only four years earlier, had a small population and a very long, virtually unprotected frontier.

In July, the situation on the frontier was becoming desperate. The annuity still had not arrived from Washington[3] and to make matters worse there had been a crop failure. Lieutenant Sheehan of the 5th Minnesota Infantry with one hundred troops was ordered to proceed to the Lower Sioux Agency to maintain order and protect U.S. property. At this time, over 2,300 Sioux resided at or near the Lower Sioux Agency[4] while another 4,000 were at the Upper Sioux Agency (or Yellow Medicine as it was also called).[5] The Sioux sent word through an interpreter named Quinn that they wanted a council with Sheehan at the Upper Agency, which was granted. The meeting was recorded by Lieutenant Thomas P. Gere, 5th Minnesota Regiment. The Sioux request was clear. "We are the braves. We have sold our land to the Great Father. The traders are allowed to sit at the pay table and they take all our money. We wish you to keep the traders away from the pay table, and we desire you to make us a present of a beef."[6] This enraged the traders because they claimed that the amount of goods already provided to the Indians equaled the amount of the annuity.[7] Trader math could always be expected to equal several times the value of goods provided to the Indians. Trader claims[8] were always outrageous and were one of the causes of the Sioux war. Since the arrival of the annuity was expected soon, the Indian agent, Thomas Galbraith, decided to start the counting of Sioux and then send them back to their camp to await the arrival of the money. Gere continued this report.

> Early on the morning of August 4th, the Indians sent two messengers to the camp, saying they were coming down to fire a salute ... and make one of their demonstrations; soon some eight hundred warriors, mounted and on foot, came down with wild yells, firing their guns in the air, completely surrounding the camp ... Lieut. Sheehan favored an issue of provisions and after much parleying an issue of pork and flour was made on condition that the Indians return to their camp.[9]

Lieutenant Sheehan had averted a massacre, but the issue of rations was not resolved. A series of councils continued after the August 4 confrontation. Word reached Little Crow and he rode to the Lower Agency from his camp, two miles away. The council was held outdoors with hundreds of Sioux present. The annuity had not arrived and Little Crow perceived that he could use this situation to enhance his reputation as a leader. At the meeting the next day, Thomas Galbraith, the Indian agent, John P. Williamson, a young missionary, and the trader, Andrew Myrick, listened as Little Crow rose to speak. Little Crow summarized that the annuity was overdue and something needed to be done. "We

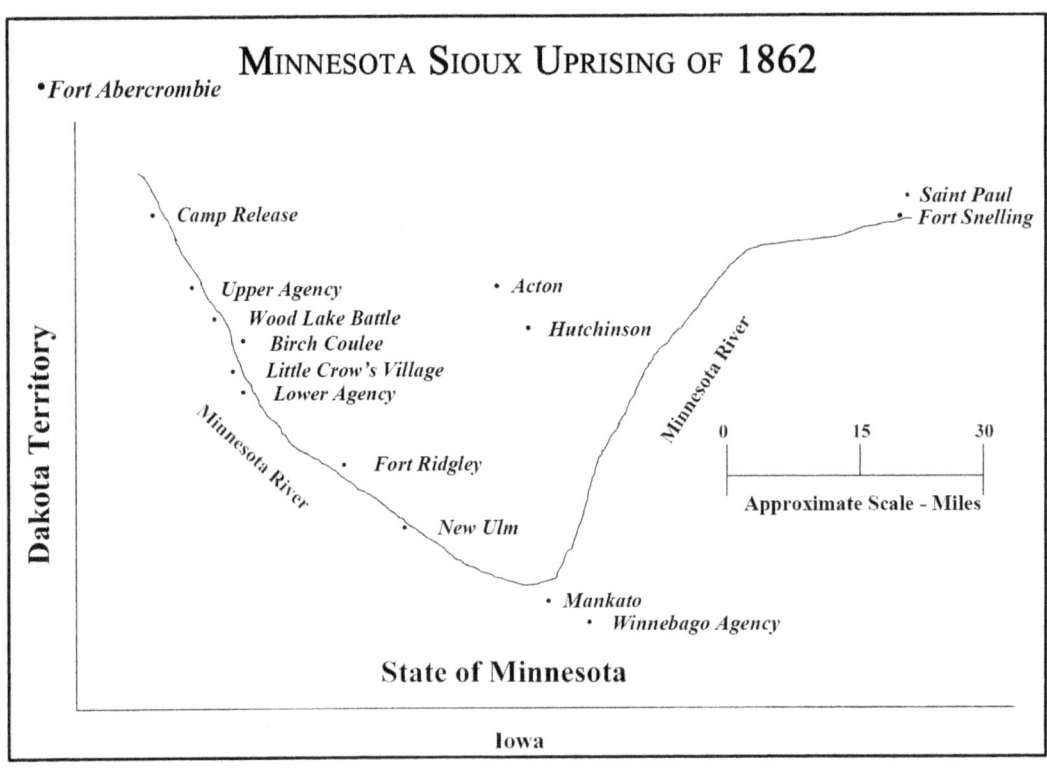

Important sites of the Sioux War.

1. Sibley's Campaign Against the Sioux 13

Alexander Ramsey, Minnesota governor during the Sioux War (Library of Congress).

Timothy Sheehan, the "Fighting Irishman" who took over the defense of Fort Ridgley (Minnesota Historical Society).

Thomas Gere, the Medal of Honor winner who held Fort Ridgley with few troops (Minnesota Historical Society).

Thomas Galbraith, the Indian agent (Minnesota Historical Society).

have waited for a long time. The money is ours, but we cannot get it. We have no food, but here are these stores, filled with food. We ask that you, as agent, make some arrangement by which we can get food from the stores, or else we may take our own way to keep ourselves from starving. When men are hungry, they help themselves."[10] While Galbraith's warehouse was nearly empty, the traders had an abundance of supplies. Could not something be done to arrange for a release of the trader's supplies until the annuity arrived and they could be paid? After discussion, Myrick was prodded to speak: "So far as I am concerned, if they are hungry, let them eat grass."[11] Williamson acted as interpreter because the interpreter who was present appeared to be too frightened to translate the insult. The Indians either could not hear or understand what Myrick had said and when Williamson translated, the Sioux spontaneously shouted "weird and savage war-whoops" before they disappeared.[12]

Captain Marsh arrived from Fort Ridgley that afternoon. He realized that Myrick had created a major problem and called for a council with the Sioux. It was time for damage repair. The discussion led to the issue of food—130 barrels of flour and 30 barrels of pork and this appeared to placate the Sioux.[13] On Sunday, 17 August 1862, Little Crow attended church services at the Lower Agency and shook hands with the Reverend Hinman before departing for his lodge. At about the same hour, the gold annuity had arrived in St. Paul and had left for Fort Ridgley.[14] It appeared that war had been averted.

Calls of the President: The Tenth Regiment Is Organized, Tuesday, 12 August 1862

> *In the midst of the organization of companies for these new regiments the Sioux Indian War unexpectedly broke out [August 18] on the Western frontier of the state, and threw regular organization into confusion.*[15]
> — James H. Baker

Andrew Myrick, who triggered the war (Minnesota Historical Society).

The Tenth was formed from towns in southeastern Minnesota and many of the men of the Tenth fought and some were killed or wounded before the regiment was fully organized. Colonel James Baker would command the new regiment. Baker was an attorney who had served as the secretary of state for Minnesota. Several members of the first Minnesota Legislature (1857–1858) also joined the Tenth Minnesota Regiment. While organizing the regiment, there were some cases where men on their way to Fort Snelling (near St. Paul) to enlist in the Tenth were diverted in order to assist other units already engaged in combat against the Sioux. During the period of August and September 1862, the organization of the regiments was confused and constantly changing. People and companies were moved back and forth among the regiments to fill them out and prepare them for battle. As an example, on the 25th of August, Captain Alonzo J. Edgerton appeared at the Winnebago Agency in Blue Earth County with a company that he had raised. He reported to the authorities in St. Paul that the Winnebago tribe might join in an alliance with the Sioux.[16] This did not happen and Edgerton's company was folded into the Tenth as Company B. The recruits for the Eleventh Regiment were diverted to fill the Tenth Regiment.[17] The Eleventh was not organized until 1864. Some volunteer units such as the Le Sueur Tigers made their appearance, fought, and then disappeared as they were absorbed into the new regiments.

At Fort Snelling, the organization of the six new regiments continued. Colonel Baker summarized. "The first order received for military service of the 10th Regiment was one directed to Col. Baker to prepare his regiment to go to New York.... The Sioux outbreak was followed by the immediate countermanding of this order, and the regiment was directed to report to Gen. H. H. Sibley, commanding against the hostile Sioux."[18]

James Baker, the attorney who commanded the Tenth Regiment (Minnesota Historical Society).

The Tenth Regiment continued its muster at Fort Snelling. The companies of the regiment would be stationed as follows after the organization: A Company at Garden City; B and F Companies at Winnebago Agency; C Company at Fort Ridgley, D and E Companies at Henderson; G and I Companies at Le Sueur; H Company at Swan Lake; and K Company at Norwegian Lake. The companies would provide security to the towns where they were assigned and would spend their winter there waiting for the Indian Campaign of 1863. In 1890, a short history of the regiment was published and is included in Appendix B. The regimental roster is in Appendix C.

Alonzo Edgerton of the Tenth Regiment (Minnesota Historical Society).

Fort Snelling, where Minnesota regiments were organized and the Sioux were later imprisoned (Minnesota Historical Society).

The War Begins, Sunday, 17 August 1862

> *You are like dogs in the Hot Moon when they run mad and snap at their own shadows. We are only little herds of buffaloes left scattered ... [but] the white men are like the locusts when they fly so thick that the whole sky is a snow-storm. You may kill one — two — ten; yes, as many as the leaves in the forest yonder, and their brothers will not miss them.*[19]
>
> — Little Crow

At the same time that Little Crow was chatting with the Reverend Hinman after church services and the gold annuity had left St. Paul for Fort Ridgley, fate intervened. The war started by accident rather than a plot. Twenty Indians from Shakopee's camp left their village to hunt in the Big Woods. Shakopee was a sub-chief of Little Crow.[20] The Indians divided into several groups and at 11:00 A.M. on Sunday, 17 August, a group of four warriors stopped at the home of Robinson Jones near Acton in Meeker County looking for food. Big Eagle tells the story.

> These young fellows all belonged to Shakopee's band. They said they went over into the Big Woods to hunt; that on Sunday, Aug. 17, they came to a settler's fence, and here they found a

1. Sibley's Campaign Against the Sioux

Little Crow, Chief of the Sioux, who led them in the war (Minnesota Historical Society).

Shakopee, the Sioux leader who fled to Canada and was later hanged (Minnesota Historical Society).

hen's nest with some eggs in it. One of them took the eggs, when another said: "Don't take them, for they belong to a white man and we may get into trouble." The other was angry, for he was very hungry and wanted to eat the eggs, and he dashed them to the ground and replied: "You are a coward. You are afraid of the white man. You are afraid to take even an egg from him, although you are half-starved. Yes, you are a coward, and I will tell everybody so." The other replied: "I am not a coward. I am not afraid of the white man, and to show you that I am not I will go to the house and shoot him. Are you brave enough to go with me?" The one who had called him a coward said: "Yes, I will go with you, and we will see who is the braver of us two." Their two companions then said: "We will go with you, and we will be brave, too." They all went to the house of the white man (Mr. Robinson Jones), but he got alarmed and went to another house. The four Indians followed them and killed three men and two women (Jones, Baker, a Mr. Webster, Mrs. Jones and a girl of fourteen).[21]

Mrs. Baker's testimony, below, is from the inquest.

> About 11 o'clock A.M. four Indians came into our house, staid [sic] about 15 minutes, got up and looked out, had the men take down their guns and shoot them off at a mark, then bantered for a trade with Jones. About 12 o'clock two more Indians came and got some water; our guns were not reloaded; the Indians loaded their guns in the dooryard; I went back into the house, did not suspect anything at the time; supposed they were going away; next I knew I heard the report of a gun and saw Webster fall; he stood and fell near the door; another Indian came to the door and aimed at Howard Baker and shot; did not kill him at that time; he shot the other barrel of his gun at Howard and he fell. My mother walked to the door and another Indian shot her; she turned to run and fell into the buttery; they shot at her twice as she fell.
>
> I tried to get out of the window, but fell down [into the] cellar; saw Mrs. Webster

pulling her husband into the house, don't know where she was prior to this. Indians immediately left the house; while I was in the cellar I heard firing out of doors. Jones said they were Sioux Indians and that he was well acquainted with them. Two of the Indians had on white men's coats; one quite tall, one quite small, one thick and chubby and all middle aged Indians, one had two feathers in his cap and one had three.[22]

The warriors returned to Shakopee's camp, which they reached late that night. They explained what had happened and without delay Shakopee took the men to Little Crow's camp, which was reached in the early hours of Monday, the 18th of August. Little Crow was awakened by some very agitated people in his lodge. They argued strongly that Little Crow should lead them in a war against the whites. The warriors were crazed with excitement and resentment against the whites. They also knew that the murders at Acton would bring a terrible retribution. An all out war against the whites was their only way out. Little Crow resisted. "You are full of the white man's devil-water [liquor].... You are like dogs in the Hot Moon when they run mad and snap at their own shadows. We are only little herds of buffaloes left scattered ... [but] the white men are like the locusts when they fly so thick that the whole sky is a snow-storm. You may kill one — two — ten; yes, as many as the leaves in the forest yonder, and their brothers will not miss them."[23]

Big Eagle and many of the other warriors realized that the Civil War had divested Minnesota of most of the troops, but Big Eagle was still opposed to the war: "Though I took part in the war, I was opposed to it and I had been to Washington and knew that they would finally conquer us. We might succeed for a time, but we would be overpowered and defeated at last."[24]

Now was the time to strike a blow against the whites. Little Crow responded, "Do you hear the thunder of their big guns?" he asked. "No; it would take you two moons to run down to where they are fighting, and all the way your path would be among white soldiers."[25] Big Eagle recalled. "Wabasha, Wacouta, myself and others still talked of peace, but no one would listen to us, and soon, the cry was 'Kill the whites and kill these cut-hairs [Indians who had taken up farming] who will not join us.'"[26]

Little Crow's arguments did no good. The young warriors wanted war and could not be persuaded. They accused Little Crow of cowardice. Finally, angry and tiring of the argument, Little Crow relented.[27] "You are fools. You cannot see the face of your chief; your eyes are full of smoke. You cannot hear his voice; your ears are

Big Eagle, the Sioux chief who was later pardoned by Lincoln (Minnesota Historical Society).

full of roaring waters.... You are fools. You will die like rabbits when the hungry wolves hunt them in the Hard Moon. Taoyateduta [Little Crow] is not a coward. He will die with you!"[28]

The Lower Agency Is Attacked, Bloody Monday, 18 August 1862

Indians are raising hell at the Lower Agency. Return as soon as possible.[29]
— John Marsh

The 18th of August was a bloody day with a Sioux attack on the Lower Agency that left many dead. A line of Sioux entered the compound and small parties broke from the main group. At a prearranged signal, the Sioux opened fire. James A. Lynd, a clerk, was the first to die.[30] All traders and agency personnel were targeted to be killed. Myrick was killed while he tried to escape from the second floor window of his store. Grass was stuffed into his mouth after he was killed with arrows and a long scythe. Of the eighty white people at the Redwood Agency (Lower Agency), twenty were killed immediately, ten were taken captive and the remainder fled to Fort Ridgley.[31]

Captain Marsh at Fort Ridgley sent the following dispatch to Lieutenant Sheehan who was forty miles away at Glencoe, Minnesota: "Lieutenant Sheehan: It is absolutely necessary that you should return with your command immediately to this post. The Indians are raising hell at the Lower Agency. Return as soon as possible."[32] By the time that Sheehan arrived, Marsh would be dead with most of his command.

Lieutenant Gere would then command at Fort Ridgley.

10:30 A.M.

Captain Marsh mustered everyone that could be spared in order to move to relief of the Lower Agency.

Cyrus G. Wyckoff, a clerk for the superintendent of Indian Affairs, arrived in a coach with four guards and $71,000 in gold annuity money for the Sioux. A week ago he would have been hailed as a savior. Now the gold was just one more problem to take care of.[33]

DARK

Indian massacres were occurring up and down the Minnesota River Valley. Sergeant John S. Bishop arrived at Fort Ridgley with more bad news: Captain Marsh and his command were ambushed at the Redwood Ferry. Only a few escaped the massacre with Sergeant Bishop, who was wounded. Bishop was certain that Marsh had drowned in the Minnesota River when he got cut off and tried to escape the Sioux by swimming across the river.

8:30 P.M.

The following note was sent to Fort Snelling. Private Sturgis carried the note by fastest horse, but it took him hours to travel the 125 miles in the dark.[34]

To: Commanding Officer, Fort Snelling
Captain Marsh left this post at 10½ this morning to prevent Indian depredations at the Lower Agency. Some of the men have returned — from them I learned that Captain Marsh is killed and

only thirteen of his company remaining. The Indians are killing the settlers and plundering the country. Send reinforcements without delay.

Thomas P. Gere
2nd Lieutenant
5th Minnesota Volunteers
Commanding Post

Please hand this to Governor Ramsey, immediately.[35]

MIDNIGHT.

The following dispatch was sent to Lieutenant Sheehan.

Force your march returning. Captain Marsh and most of his command were killed yesterday at the Lower Agency. Little Crow and about 600 Sioux warriors are now approaching the fort and will undoubtedly attack us. About 250 refugees have arrived here for protection. The Indians are killing men, women, and children.[36]

Gere

EARLY MORNING.

Defenses were improved at Fort Ridgley. No attack was made on the fort but there was at least one false alarm. Pickets were out and the women and children were moved to the stone barracks.[37]

AFTERNOON

Still no sign of the Sioux, but work continued to improve the fort's defenses. The attack at the Redwood Agency set off an orgy of murder by the Sioux in the Minnesota River Valley. Since killing a man, a woman or a baby gave the Sioux warrior the right to wear an eagle feather, no one was spared.[38] In the four days following the Redwood Agency attack, over 400 settlers were killed and 100 captured.

The whites were outraged and some of the Sioux chiefs spoke out against the violence. Akipa, a Wahpeton chief, spoke eloquently about the violence.

There is no bravery in killing helpless men, women, and little children, who have no means of defense. That is simply cowardice, and it is only cowards who would boast of it. If I had found that any of my relatives had been harmed by such cowards, I would tomahawk your whole camp. I would slaughter such braves as you are, as I might kill beavers on dry land. When the sun arose that witnessed the horrors of indiscriminate massacre of the whites in this valley of the Minnesota, regardless of sex or age, by you Lower Sioux, the upper bands were peacefully attending to their crops on their own reservation, or out on the distant prairies hunting buffalo. The report of that awful bloody day's work fell on our ears with more astounding force than the voice of the Great Spirit issuing from the black clouds of the West.[39]

Fort Ridgley was a stronghold and gateway to the Minnesota River Valley. It needed to be taken by Little Crow if he was to move and threaten Mankato and all of the settlements to Fort Snelling.[40] At Fort Ridgley, the fort commander, Lieutenant Thomas Gere, was powerless to do anything to help the settlers in the valley who continued to arrive at the fort in large numbers. Gere was ill in bed with the mumps at this time and he had a total of twenty troops to defend the fort, but help was on the way. Lieutenant Sheehan returned to Fort Ridgley with forty more troops and took over command. Troops continued to arrive, including the Renville Rangers. By evening Sheehan had 180 troops in the fort and settlers who had no weapons were also armed as they arrived with any weapon that could be found within the fort.[41]

Little Crow delayed any attack on Fort Ridgley while he waited for more warriors to arrive and others to return from raids. This was a colossal mistake. Had he attacked on the 19th with the forces that he had he could have easily taken the fort.

The Yellow Medicine Agency Is Attacked, Tuesday, 19 August 1862

It was some of those who came that night and drove away the storekeepers and plundered. They also reported that all of the whites at the agency had made a stand in the [Yellow Medicine] Agency buildings.[42]

— Gabriel Renville

The Yellow Medicine Agency or Upper Agency as it was also called was thirty miles north of the Lower Agency. Rumors reached the Upper Agency of the bloodshed but were not believed until refugees began to arrive. Yellow Medicine was home to the Wahpeton and Sissetons, who took no part in the massacres of 18 and 19 August. A council was held, but the Indians would not agree to join the uprising.[43] Nevertheless, some of the young warriors slipped away to join Little Crow. On the night of the 18th, attacks by the Lower Agency Sioux caused the burning of four traders' stores and two employees were mortally wounded.[44] Another, Peter Patoile, was shot through the lungs. An Indian turned him over and declared him dead, but Peter managed to crawl away. He was nineteen years old at the time and had been left in charge of his uncle's story. His uncle, Francis Patoile, was killed while trying to escort three settlers to safety.[45] With every breath Peter gushed blood but as he continued to move the bleeding stopped and he managed to crawl and walk an incredible journey with the help of friendly Indians. After two weeks he reached what is now St. Cloud, Minnesota, a journey of nearly two hundred miles. The townspeople prepared to hang him because they thought he was Sioux, but his English sounded a little too good to be that of an Indian so with suspicion, they shipped him to St. Paul where the authorities could figure out who he really was.[46] His story was verified. Young Peter had risen from the dead. He would go on to fight in Sibley's campaign of 1863 as a member of the H Company, First Regiment of the Minnesota Mounted Rangers, a unit that fought with great bravery in the battles along the Missouri in 1863.[47]

The sun rose on the 19th as the hostile Sioux gathered before the agency and the realization at the Upper Agency set in that all whites would soon be killed. While the Indians plundered the stores. John Other Day, who had a white wife, agreed to lead fifty-four whites to safety, and after three days they arrived at Shakopee, Minnesota. Major Galbraith, the Indian agent, would later make this journey more epic than it really was. "Led by the noble Otherday [sic], they struck out on the prairie, literally placing their lives in this creature's hands and guided by him and him alone. After intense suffering and privation, they reached Shakopee on Friday, August twenty-second, Otherday never having left them for an instant; and this Otherday [sic] is a full-blooded Indian, and was not long since one of the wildest and fiercest of his race."[48] Galbraith had reason to eulogize Other Day: Galbraith's wife and children were among the fifty-four that were saved. John Other Day would be honored for this rescue. He would say later "I am a Dakota Indian.... I have been instructed by Americans, and taught to read and write. This I found to be good ... with fifty-four men, women, and children, without moccasins, without food, and without blanket, I arrived in the midst of a great people, and my heart is now glad. I attribute it to the mercy of the Great Spirit."[49]

While the whites escaped, the Sioux got down to the business of plundering the warehouses at the Upper Agency before they moved on, seeking other targets. Several miles above the agency two missions had been established by the Reverend Thomas S. Williamson and the Reverend Stephen R. Riggs. Both missions were in danger and the missionaries had to flee. While Other Day led the fleeing group from the Upper Agency, a separate group left the missions guided by another friendly Indian. Gabriel Renville provided an eyewitness account many years later. Renville was the son of parents of mixed blood. He was raised as a Dakota and married three sisters in 1847, 1858 and 1860, so he apparently got along quite well with the family. He never spoke English and his account was translated and published in 1903 after his death in 1892. His story follows.

> It was some of those who came that night and drove away the storekeepers and plundered. They also reported that all of the whites at the agency had made a stand in the Agency buildings. They who reported this were not enemies to the whites. I went as fast as I could towards the Agency, and stopped suddenly in front of the warehouse building. I did not see a person, but heard very much thumping noises. I then went around to the east door, and saw that they [the hostiles] had gone in that way and were plundering inside.... I came out of the house, rode swiftly away, and fording the river, reached my home. I found the horses already hitched to the wagon, and we started to hurry, going toward a ford which was a good crossing for wagons. I saw at that time the Doctor's [Williamson] children and others with them, who were crossing the river and fleeing towards the East under the guidance of an Indian who was friendly to the whites.[50]

The Reverend Stephen R. Riggs would recall that the problem of the tardiness of Sioux annuity was the primary cause of the outbreak.[51] Riggs was warned by friendly Sioux and

Left: Other Day, the friend of the whites who saved many at the Upper Agency. *Right:* Gabriel Renville, the Indian guide who saved many whites (both photographs, Minnesota Historical Society).

these guarded the mission but urged Riggs to leave: "It was after midnight before we thought of leaving.... And they [the friendly Sioux] evidently began to feel that *we* might not be safe, and that our staying would endanger them."[52] Riggs and the other whites fled joining up with members of the Reverend Williamson's family for the flight to Fort Ridgley. A young photographer, Adrian J. Ebell,[53] captured faces from the past when he took a photograph of the fleeing group as they stopped to rest on 21 August 1862. The group had stopped, killed a young cow, roasted meat, baked bread and dried their soaked clothing. The Reverend Riggs is in front of the woman at the wagon wheel.[54]

The party now numbered over

Above: The Reverend Stephen Riggs, who escaped his mission with his family. *Below:* The only surviving photograph of the war in August 1862. The Riggs mission stopped during their flight (both photographs, Minnesota Historical Society).

forty people but had few firearms. As they approached Fort Ridgley they discovered that it was under attack, so the party detoured to St. Peter and the town of Shakopee. In this way, through the help of friendly Sioux and early warning nearly all of the whites escaped from the Upper Agency and missions. The slaughter that had occurred at the Redwood Agency was avoided.[55]

Sibley Takes Command, Tuesday, 19 August 1862

The outbreak must be suppressed, and in such a manner as will forever prevent its repetition.[56]

— Alexander Ramsey

Word of the massacre of five civilians at Acton reached St. Paul quickly. On 19 August, Governor Ramsey rode from Fort Snelling to Mendota to meet with Henry Sibley. After much discussion, Ramsey promised Sibley a free hand in fighting the war and Sibley accepted command of all forces. His objectives were to defeat the Indians in a decisive engagement, gain release of captives, punish the guilty murderers and criminals and drive the Sioux from Minnesota.[57]

Henry Hastings Sibley , the first governor of Minnesota and Ramsey's predecessor, resided at Mendota, across the Mississippi River from Fort Snelling. Sibley had not run for a second term. After war broke out in the East, Sibley saw many of his friends lead regiments headed there, but he never sought a commission. He foresaw that a river of blood would run through the states because of the Civil War and he wanted no part of it.[58] He was an expert attorney and politician, not a soldier, but he had many years of experience as a trader with the Sioux and he was confident of a positive outcome in the war against the Sioux. His wife, Sarah, would later say that his aversion toward the military seemed to change after he was promoted to general and he became enamored with military life.[59] Ramsey issued a proclamation to the people of Minnesota on 21 August announcing the war and calling for volunteers.

Henry H. Sibley, the first governor of Minnesota and the commander of Minnesota troops during the Indian War (Minnesota Historical Society).

TO THE PEOPLE OF MINNESOTA
PROCLAMATION OF THE GOVENOR
Executive Chamber
St. Paul, August 21, 1862

The Sioux Indians upon our Western frontier have risen in large bodies, attacked the settlements and are murdering men, women, and children. The rising appears concerted and extends from Fort Ridgley to the Southern boundary of the state.

In extremity I call upon the Militia of the Valley of the Minnesota, and the counties adjoining the frontier, to take horses, and arm and equip themselves taking with them substance for a few days, and at once report, separately or in squads, to the officer commanding the expedition now moving up the Minnesota River to the scene of the hostilities. The officer commanding the expedition has been clothed with full power to provide for all exigencies that may arise.

Measures will be taken to subsist the forces so raised.

The outbreak must be suppressed, and in such a manner as will forever prevent its repetition.

I earnestly urge upon settlers of the frontier that while taking all precautions for the safety of their families and homes, they will not give way to any unnecessary alarm. A regiment of infantry, together with 300 cavalry, have been ordered to their defence, and with the volunteer troops now being raised, the frontier settlements will speedily be placed beyond danger.

ALEXANDER RAMSEY[60]

The Siege of Fort Ridgley, Wednesday, Thursday, and Friday, 20, 21, and 22 August 1862

The soldiers fought us bravely we thought that there were more of them then there were. The cannon disturbed us greatly, but did not hurt many.[61]

— Big Eagle

2:00 P.M.

The attack on Fort Ridgley started. Little Crow had over four hundred warriors. The plan was to make several false charges followed by a frontal attack on the fort.[62] Little Crow rode out to the West of the fort to distract the troops while a party attacked the opposite side and drove in the troops reaching the rear of the barracks. Sheehan was not fooled by the maneuver and ordered his troops to take cover and fire at will.[63] Sheehan would later say that the Indian penetration of his perimeter was a serious problem. They drove off the horses, mules and cattle, seized the outbuildings and fired on his troops from all directions. Sergeant John Jones of the Fifth Regiment, Company B, with his three gun sections brought the cannon into action and drove off the Indians.[64] He became the hero of Fort Ridgley: "Sergeant Jones saved the Fort."[65] As always throughout the Indian war, when the artillery arrived the Indians departed. They knew that artillery was bad for them. Little

Sergeant (later Captain) Jones, whose artillery saved Fort Ridgley (Minnesota Historical Society).

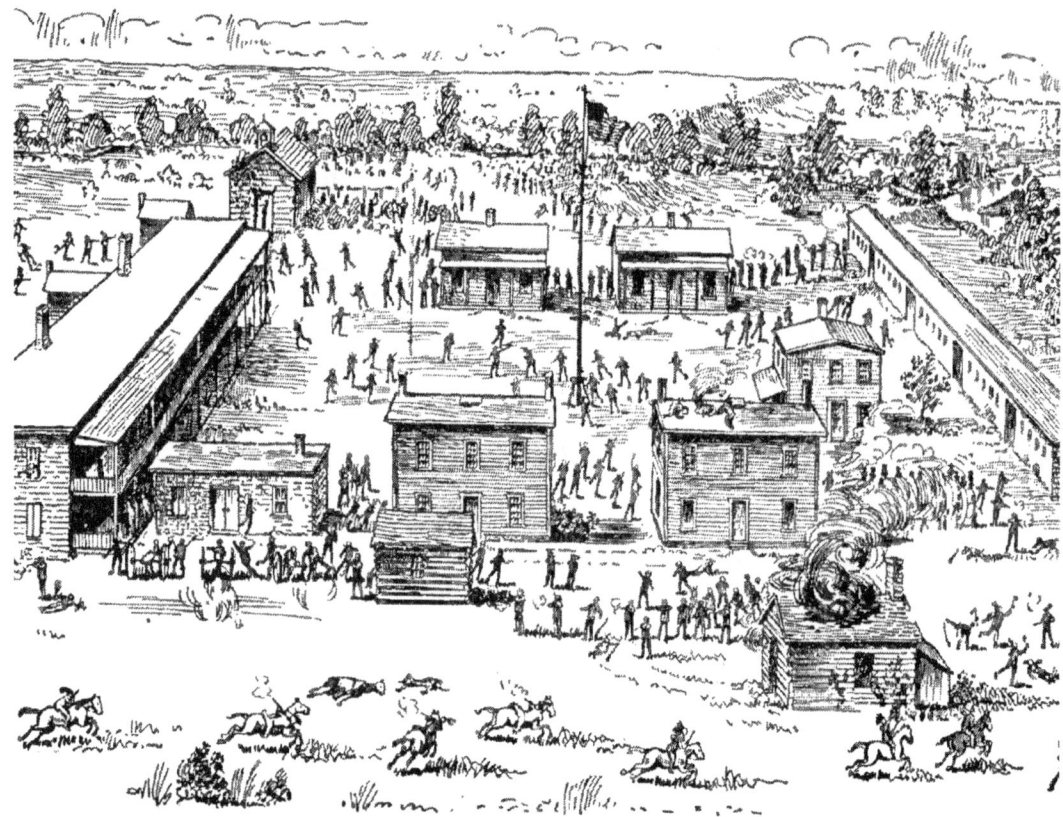

Firsthand sketch of Fort Ridgley under attack on the first day of the battle (20 August 1862) — from A.P. (Alonzo P.) Connolly, *A Thrilling Narrative of the Minnesota Massacre and Sioux War of 1862–63* (Chicago, 1869).

Crow had to content himself with sniping at the fort from a safe distance, which had no effect. All attacks had failed and a heavy rain set in that night.

Little Crow was not discouraged by Wednesday's defeat and decided to make the next attack "a grand affair."[66] Only scattered firing occurred on Thursday since the Sioux had withdrawn and Little Crow was building up the number of his warriors. On Friday, Little Crow continued the attack. Again, he deployed his warriors in the ravines near the fort. Big Eagle was there and provided the following account.

> The fight commenced about noon on Friday after the outbreak. We had a few Sisseton and Wahpeton with us, and some Winnebago under the Little Priest were in this fight and at New Ulm. I saw them myself. But for the cannon I think we would have taken the fort. The soldiers fought us bravely we thought that there were more of them then there were. The cannon disturbed us greatly, but did not hurt many. We did not have many Indians killed. I think that the whites put the number too large, and I think that they overestimated the number killed in every battle. We seldom carried off our dead. We usually buried them in a secluded part of the battlefield when we could. We always tried to carry away the wounded. When we retreated from Ridgley I recrossed the river opposite the fort and went up on the South side. All our army but scouts fell back up the river to our villages near Redwood Agency, and then on up the Yellow Medicine and the mouth of the Chippewa.[67]

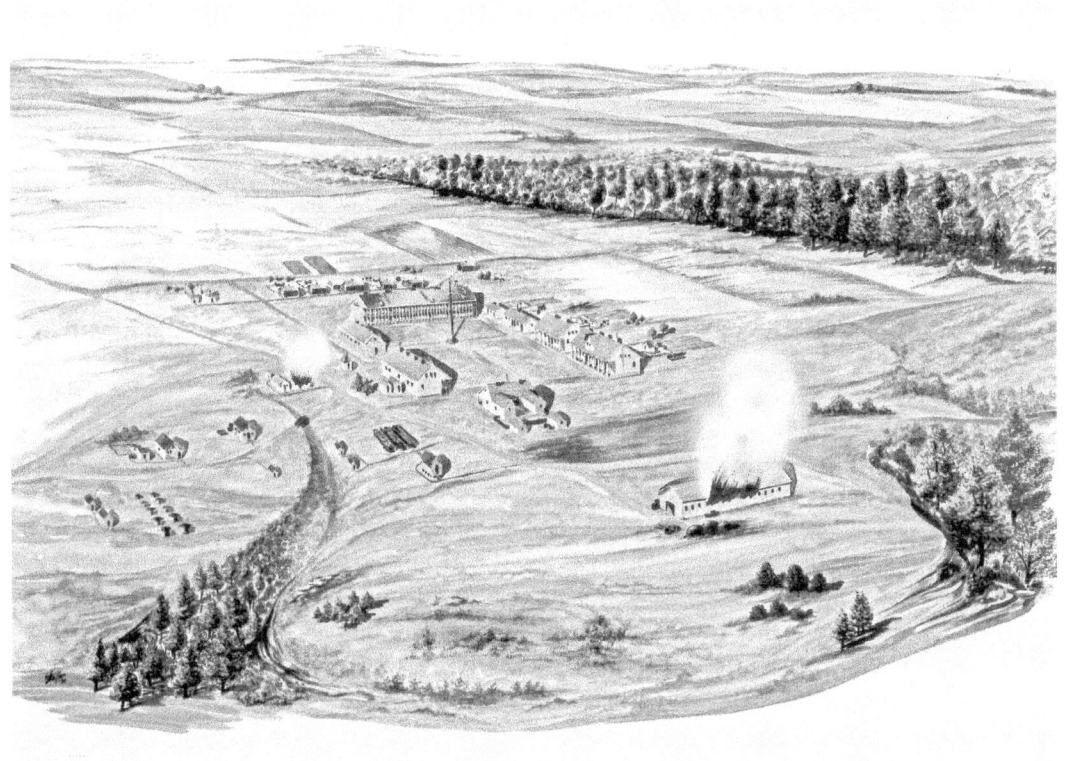

Little Crow's second attempt to take Fort Ridgely on 21 August 1862, when the barracks were burned (Minnesota Historical Society).

1:00 P.M.

Little Crow mounted an all out attack on all sides with the main attack from the South. Artillery again dispersed the attack, which failed. Firing continued from all sides.

4:00 P.M.

The southeast corner of the fort was attacked, but the effort was repulsed by a double charge of canister fired by Sergeant Jones[68] and the attack failed. This ended the siege of Fort Ridgley. Total losses in the battle were reported as three killed and thirteen wounded while Indian losses were estimated at not less than one hundred by Lieutenant Gere. This last number was probably a bit above the true number. Years later the Indians could only recall two dead.[69] Big Eagle would remember, "We thought the fort was a door to the valley as far as to St. Paul, and that if we could get through the door nothing could stop us this side of the Mississippi. But the defenders of the fort were very brave and kept the door shut."[70] Lieutenant Gere was later awarded the Medal of Honor for capturing a Confederate flag at Nashville. Big Eagle recalled: "Our scouts brought word that our old friend Wapeton honska (The Long Trader), as we called Gen. Sibley, was coming up against us, and in a few days we learned that he had come to Fort Ridgley with a large number of soldiers."[71]

The Siege of New Ulm—Turning Point of the War, Monday to Monday, 18–25 August 1862

The Indians are coming.... They have murdered the Recruiting Party.[72]

New Ulm is sixteen miles below Fort Ridgley on the Minnesota River. In 1862 it was a fair-sized village of about nine hundred citizens, mostly of German ancestry. It held a large amount of food and supplies, a great attraction to the Sioux. While Fort Ridgley was under attack, other Sioux raiding parties were sweeping through the Minnesota River Valley murdering settlers and plundering homes. Soon, it would be New Ulm's time for terror. The siege would last a week.

On the morning of 18 August, while Captain Marsh was mustering his troops at Fort Ridgley, a recruiting party left New Ulm for Milford, a small town eight miles from New Ulm, to begin a recruiting effort. The Sioux ambushed the first wagon as it approached the bridge near Henle's Inn in Milford. Three men in the wagon, Fenske, Dietrich, and Schneider, were killed in the first volley and following wagons picked up the wounded and fled back to New Ulm. The Sioux now realized that the frontier was alarmed. A large number of refugees were fleeing to New Ulm for safety.[73] Shortly after this incident, Theresa Henle at Milford found herself surrounded by Sioux as she returned from her mother's home. She fled and hid in the forest to escape. She related her experience. "Toward evening I heard the voice of my husband in the direction of the house calling me, and I came forth from my hiding place.... One of his [our] children, a girl of four, they found dead, and a servant girl of eighteen, beheaded."[74] She continued. "Martin, a lad twelve years old, was found by Conrad Zeller. He had seventeen wounds upon his body, but was still alive. He died two weeks later. This boy related that when he was running away a mounted Indian kept galloping at his side, striking him with a tomahawk, until at last, being completely exhausted by pain and loss of blood, he fell to the ground; and the Indian, believing him to be dead, rode away."[75] Twenty-one of Henle's relatives were killed that day.

The next day, August 19, while the battle was raging at Fort Ridgley, the Sioux probed New Ulm killing six people and ambushing a relief party. Three buildings were burned in New Ulm on the 19th, but a violent thunderstorm intervened at 4:30 P.M. and the Sioux were driven off. The townspeople now had a respite and as reinforcements rolled in, barricades were erected in the streets and the defense of the town was organized. After the engagement on 19 August, the defenders were ready. The ranks of the defenders were swelled by the arrival of about 200 volunteers including Captain Sanders, later commander of G Company of the Tenth, with a group known as the Le Sueur Tigers. Sanders had organized his company on 20 August. Problem: there still was no artillery at New Ulm, a vital ingredient in defeating the Sioux. While the rest of the Tenth was organizing at Fort Snelling, Sanders would be fighting for his life at New Ulm.

Judge Charles E. Flandrau (also called Colonel Flandrau) had organized the defense of New Ulm, and he sent an urgent message to Sibley as the Sioux were moving to attack. "I think that I can hold the town until you come, if not attacked by a very large force. I hear Indians all around me, but see none. I am making some entrenchments, etc. I am sure that everything above [the town] is lost, and all the people killed.... Bring powder, lead, and caps. We are short."[76] Flandrau was clearly rattled but hopeful that help would arrive soon. Unfortunately, it would be days before Sibley would arrive and Flandrau was on his own. The issue at New Ulm would be decided long before Sibley could help.

After the failure to take Fort Ridgley, the Sioux returned in strength to destroy New Ulm, attacking at midmorning, 23 August. Judge Flandrau continued to organize the defense of the town and had about 250 armed men. Flandrau would later claim that he was attacked by 650 Sioux, but the judge overestimated the number of attackers.[77] Chief Mankato would lead the attack because Little Crow had been slightly injured in the attack on Fort Ridgley. Flandrau made a near fatal blunder. He saw smoke from the direction of Fort Ridgley and thought that the fort had been taken. It was an Indian ruse and Flandrau fell for it sending every man he could spare, about seventy-five people under Lieutenant Huey, forward to investigate. Huey crossed at the nearby ferry and formed a line with the river at his back. When the Sioux attacked, Huey's line broke and he was cut off from New Ulm, so he fled to St. Peter. Flandrau had now lost a third of his command, but Huey would return the next day.[78]

Colonel Flandrau, who organized the defense of New Ulm (Minnesota Historical Society).

As the Sioux approached the town, they fanned out in an arc planning to envelop the town. They successfully surrounded the town and fired the buildings on the windward side. Flandrau later wrote: "Their advance upon the sloping prairie in bright sunlight was a very fine spectacle and to such inexperienced of soldiers as we all were, intensely exciting."[79] Flandrau's men rallied and a long, bitter battle ensued, fought in the streets and houses of the town with the Sioux attacking barricades erected by the citizens. Captain Sanders and his troops were mounted and he led a charge as fast as he could ride down the main business street of New Ulm attacking the Sioux who were busy scalping men, women and children as fast as they could. His attack so surprised the Sioux that they mounted their ponies and fled.[80] Sanders was severely wounded and several of his men were killed: Sergeant William Maloney, Private Ahern, and Private Kulp. Corporal Hazard was wounded in the hip.[81] Sanders would recover and serve to fight at Nashville, taking over the command of the Tenth Regiment when the commander was shot down while leading the attack against the Confederate line. Also, about eighteen men of the Tenth's Company I, under Lieut. M. R. Merrill of Henderson, voluntarily proceeded to New Ulm to join the company of Capt. Cox and reported to Flandrau, who was in command of the defense of that place.[82] Judge Flandrau explained the decisive event. "At about 2 P.M. a great conflagration was raging on both sides of the main street in the lower part of the town, and destruction seemed inevitable. A squad of about fifty men was collected, a charge made down the burning street, and the Indians driven out beyond the houses. We then burned everything behind us, and the day was won."[83]

By nightfall, the town was in flames and the Sioux departed without a victory.[84] Losses on both sides were heavy. The Sioux losses were estimated at over one hundred while

Flandrau lost thirty-six killed and sixty wounded. The Sioux losses were probably inflated as was usually the case during the Indian war. Flandrau must have been a gambler who knew when to fold because he did what might appear to be a very risky thing. He decided to evacuate the town and move all of the civilians to Mankato, thirty miles away. He had no choice. By this time the population of New Ulm had swelled to over two thousand civilians with the influx of refugees from all over. Flandrau had a very small force to protect the civilians. He had volunteers that had arrived, but the town was mostly in ashes so there was very little to support the population. On 25 August, two thousand civilians loaded into 153 wagons for the trip to Mankato. A Sioux attack on the wagon train was expected at any moment, but nothing happened. A very relieved group of over two thousand civilians entered Mankato unharmed several hours later. What happened? This was an opportunity for Little Crow to slaughter civilians on a biblical scale, but nothing happened: the Sioux warriors, disheartened by the twin failures at Fort Ridgley and New Ulm simply faded away, seeking more lucrative targets to plunder. The end of the battle was summarized by a participant and can best be labeled as ingenuity.

> New Ulm had only eight dead and sixty wounded. Many of the latter died on account of its being impossible to give them the necessary care. One hundred and forty-nine residences were destroyed. Between nine and ten o'clock, Captain Cox managed to get into town with seventy-five men. Soon after that all the Indians retreated and held a council, whereupon they left altogether. Their main camping ground was in the neighborhood of the present Catholic cemetery. It is said that their sudden retreat was partly caused by a piece of strategy. It is well known that nothing can terrify the Indians so much as artillery. An inventive genius placed a stovepipe upon a cart, and two anvils were used for making the necessary noise. The Indians were thereby made to believe that a cannon had arrived during the night.[85]

It is difficult to perceive how a clanging anvil could be mistaken by anyone as a cannon firing, but some claimed that it did, especially by the clangors who thought that they had saved the town. A great deal of controversy existed after the war as to who had saved New Ulm. The anvil trick was also reported by T. J. Hunt in his reminiscences: in Dodge County they mounted a stove pipe between two wagon wheels and beat an anvil. Hunt claimed that it scared off the Sioux.[86] These were called Quaker guns in the 18th and 19th centuries, but it is unlikely that people on the Minnesota frontier had heard of that term. In Minnesota soldiers merely applied a practical solution to the problem when they realized that the Sioux were terrified by artillery. In the East during the Civil War, a Quaker gun was usually a tree trunk cut to the size of a cannon and painted black. This was rolled into defenses to deceive the adversary into thinking that they might have to attack a heavily defended position supported by artillery. At New Ulm phony cannons were not needed. Little Crow knew he had lost the war and Flandrau knew it was a safe bet to leave the town before they started the long train of wagons. The Sioux had departed.

This ended the Siege of New Ulm, the most publicized battle of the Sioux War. Since then at least three books have focused on the battle and many articles have been published about the event. One historian summarized: "The failure of the Dakotas to take these two strongholds [Fort Ridgley and New Ulm] made it necessary for them to evacuate their camp near Little Crow's village. The flight up the Minnesota River toward Lake Traverse was a turning point in the war."[87] After a week at war, Little Crow and the Sioux knew that they had lost. A peace party within the Sioux started to form.

General Sibley Arrives at Fort Ridgley, Thursday, 28 August 1862

... for a greener set of men were never got together.[88]
— H.H. Sibley

As soon as he was appointed to command all Minnesota state forces, Sibley started organizing and prepared to move to Fort Ridgley to reinforce the garrison moving by way of St. Peter where he stopped. Recruits were flocking to join Sibley as refugees poured into St. Peter. The full extent of the Sioux uprising became clear: the Sioux had fanned out across the Minnesota River Valley attacking and murdering any whites that they could find. Seeing the hacked bodies, Sibley wrote to his wife, Sarah: "Oh, the fiends, the devils in human shape! My heart is hardened against them beyond any touch of mercy."[89] Needing rifles and knowing that the U.S. quartermaster had a supply he sent a note to Ramsey telling him that if red tape got in the way, "Cut it with the bayonets of a corporal's guard."[90] By the 25th, Sibley had gathered nearly twelve hundred men, many unarmed and mostly untrained. Over five thousand refugees crowded St. Peter and the road to Mankato. Isaac Heard would later become a member of Sibley's staff and would serve as recorder during the Indian trials. Heard related the scene in St. Peter.

> Oxen were killed in the streets, and the meat, hastily prepared, cooked over fires made on the ground. The grist mills were surrendered by their owners to use of the public, and kept in constant motion to allay the demand for food. All thought of property was abandoned. Safety of life prevailed over every other consideration. Poverty stared those who had been affluent in the face, but they thought little of that. Women were to be seen in the streets hanging on each other's necks, telling of their mutual losses, and the little terror-stricken children, surviving remnants of once happy homes, crying piteously around their knees. The houses and stables were all occupied, and hundreds of fugitives had no covering or shelter but the canopy of heaven.[91]

Sibley needed artillery and cavalry, but there was little of that available. He was commanding an untrained mob, the only force between the Sioux and population centers such as St. Paul. Panic had set in on the frontier. In addition to the Sioux that were rampaging in the valley, there was great fear that the Chippewa (or Ojibway as they are also called), traditional enemies of the Sioux, would join the uprising. The Winnebago were also possible joiners. While they did not join the Sioux in strength, these tribes kept this fear alive in order to gain advantage with the whites. Ramsey was still committed to provide six regiments to fight in the East. He had these half formed regiments, such as the Tenth at Fort Snelling, and this amounted to several thousand soldiers. They could be diverted from the Civil War in the East to fight on the frontier. He cabled Lincoln, "Half the population of the state are fugitives. It is absolutely impossible that we should proceed [to provide the regiments].... No one not here can conceive the panic in the state."[92] Lincoln cabled back, "Yours received. Attend to the Indians. If the draft cannot proceed of course it will not proceed."[93]

On the 27th of August, Sibley was at Mankato and ready to move. He sent Colonel Samuel McPhail with 150 cavalry ahead to relieve Fort Ridgley. McPhail quickly covered the forty-five miles to Fort Ridgley and the wary defenders saw approaching horsemen uncertain if they were Indians or the relief force. Sheehan prepared his defenders for another attack and was relieved to see that it was U.S. Army cavalry. Colonel McPhail took over command of Fort Ridgley from Sheehan and all awaited the arrival of Sibley and the main force.[94] Sibley started his column toward Fort Ridgley the next morning. He could live off the land from abandoned farms as he moved and he arrived with 1200 men on Thursday, the 28th of August. The troops set up on the parade field and Sibley put them to work drilling while he sent out scouts and planned his next move. He did not have long to wait. His next move would be decided by Little Crow who would hand him his worst defeat of the war.

The Battle of Second Manassas— General Pope Moves West, Saturday, 30 August 1862

> *I must have McClellan to reorganize the army and bring it out of chaos, but there has been a design—a purpose in breaking down Pope, without regard to consequences to the country.*[95]
>
> —A. Lincoln

By the 30th of August, the Battle of Second Manassas was over: heavy casualties on both sides with the Union suffering more. The problem would continue to be that the South could not replace their losses as easily as the North. The Union commander, General John Pope, was defeated and withdrew from Manassas to cover Washington, D.C., a capital that appeared to be under siege, a fact that further demoralized the North. Lincoln, by now, was resigned to General George B. McClellan as a replacement for Pope. He stated to Welles, the secretary of Navy, "I must have McClellan to reorganize the army and bring it out of chaos, but there has been a design—a purpose in breaking down Pope, without regard to consequences to the country [Pope's subordinates favored McClellan and were sabotaging Pope's efforts to wage war during the battle]. It is shocking to see and know this, but there is no remedy at present. McClellan has the army with him."[96]

McClellan regarded Washington as unsafe, believing that Lee's army stood a chance of taking the capital. McClellan was writing to his wife, "If I can slip over there I will send your silver off."[97]

Lincoln fired Pope and Pope was reassigned and moved West to fight the Indian war in Minnesota. He would establish his headquarters in Milwaukee, Wisconsin, but took no active part in

General Pope, the man sent by Lincoln to command forces during the Indian War (Library of Congress).

fighting the war. His was an intermediate headquarters that passed information between Sibley or Ramsey and Washington. He was at times very annoying to both Washington and the commanders in the field as will be seen.

A Bad Choice—The Battle of Birch Coulee, Sunday to Wednesday, 31 August–3 September 1862

I wish it was within my power to describe the procession as it moved over the prairie. I think that it was five miles in length and one mile wide.[98]
— Sarah Wakefield

Sarah Wakefield was one of 250 prisoners captured by the Sioux and they were on the move after Little Crow's failure to seize Fort Ridgley and New Ulm. The entire Sioux nation at the Redwood Agency, over three thousand people, was fleeing north to join their brothers, the Sissetons and the Wahpetons, at the Yellow Medicine Agency. It was hoped that they could unite to fight Sibley, who had too large a force for Little Crow to engage by himself. It was a long shot because those at the Yellow Medicine Agency had voted against the war. Sarah Wakefield described the move.

The more ridiculous, the better they were pleased. White women's bonnets were considered great ornaments but were worn by men altogether. White crepe shawls were wound around their black heads; gold watches tied around their ankles, the watches clattering as they rode. The squaws were dressed in silk short gowns, with earrings and breastpins taken from the whites. It made my heart ache to see all this. Still, I could not keep from smiling at times to see how ridiculously [these objects] were used by these poor savage creatures....

Everything was ornamented with green boughs: horses, men, women, and children. United States flags were numerous, and many times it looked like "Uncle Sam's" camp. The noise of that [wagon] train was deafening: mules braying, cows (poor animals) lowing, horses neighing, dogs barking and yelping as they were run over or trodden upon, children crying, kittens mewing, for a squaw always takes her pets with her; and then, to increase the confusion, were musical instruments played by not very scientific performers, accompanied with the Indians singing the everlasting "Hi! Hi!" All these noises, together with the racket made by Little Crow's soldiers, who tried, but in vain, to keep things in order, was like the confusion of Babel.[99]

The army was moving behind the Sioux. Shortly after arrival at Fort Ridgley, Sibley sent burial details out to locate and bury the dead. He ordered Major Joseph R. "Old Joe" Brown, a former Indian agent, to move with 150 men to the Redwood Agency to look for survivors and bury the dead. Brown buried 41 victims and then moved north and east. He was seen by the Sioux.[100]

On the second day out, one of Brown's men selected Birch Coulee as a campsite area. This was about fifteen miles from Fort Ridgley and at the head of a wooded ravine. There was no water and no cover. It was the worst possible location for a campsite and

Joseph R. Brown, who allowed a bad choice of bivouac at Birch Coulee (Minnesota Historical Society).

Birch Coulee, the last Sioux victory of the war, where Joe Brown made a very bad choice for his camp site (courtesy M. J. Eggleston).

the Sioux were moving up the ravine. A.P. (Alonzo P.) Connolly who later became the adjutant of the Sixth Regiment, recalled the arrival at the campsite. "Old Joe said: 'Boys, go to sleep now and rest; you are as safe as you would be in your mother's house; there is not an Indian within fifty miles of you.' At that very moment five hundred Indians were in the immediate vicinity watching us and impatient for the ball to open as they intended it should be at the proper time, which, with the Indians is about four o'clock in the morning."[101] Big Eagle was there and picks up the story. "It was near sundown [on 1 September], and we knew they would go into camp, and we thought the camping ground would be somewhere on the Birch Coulee, where there was wood and water. [The soldiers picked the wrong spot. There was no water.] The women [Indian] went to work loading the wagons."[102]

Dawn

The sentries at Fort Ridgley heard firing in the distance. It was from Birch Coulee. Connolly described the action.

After the guard was placed one of them thought that he saw something moving in the grass. It proved to be an Indian, and they were slowly moving in upon us, their intention being to shoot the pickets with arrows, and noiselessly as possible rush in and destroy us in our confusion. The sentry fired at the moving object, and instantly our camp was encircled by fire and smoke from the guns of five hundred Indians, who had hemmed us in. The guard who fired escaped the bullet intended for him. He said he thought the moving object might be a hog or it might be an Indian, and, hog or Indian, he intended to kill it if he could. The fire was returned by the pickets as they retreated to the camp, and although there was confusion, there was no panic. Quicker than I can write we were out, musket in hand, but the captain's command to "fall down" was mistaken for "fall in," which makes a vast difference [usually fatal] under such circumstances.[103]

A.P. (Alonzo P.) Connolly, whose writing has provided an insight into the war in 1863 not found elsewhere (Minnesota Historical Society).

The fight was on and Brown had every problem imaginable. He was outnumbered by nearly ten to one with the Sioux in excellent positions on high ground looking down on his command. Brown could locate only one shovel, so the troops had to dig in with bayonets and spoons. There was no cover except for the wagons and bullets whizzed through these. Big Eagle relates part of the story. "Faribault, Frazer and another half-breed dug a rifle pit for themselves with bayonets, and Faribault worked so hard in digging that he wore the flesh from inside of his hand."[104] The soldiers had only twenty rounds each and when they opened an ammunition box for more, they found that the bullets were of the wrong size: they were too big for the rifles! The soldiers set to work with the knives cutting down the bullets to size while five hundred Sioux were firing as fast as they could. Brown was steadily losing men. As horses and mules went down, the soldiers used these for cover and started putting down a steady fire from behind the dead animals. One horse survived and was seen prancing around the camp grazing unconcerned about the fate of his comrades as the bullets whizzed past. The horse was either very brave or had not grasped the seriousness of the situation. Resizing bullets was not a satisfactory solution and innovation took hold. Some of the soldiers loaded extra powder in their rifles without bullets and when fired it made a tremendous crash that astonished the Indians and caused them to get down, but did no harm. Old Joe was walking the line encouraging the men when he took a bullet in the back of his neck and went down, but continued to give instructions.[105] At dusk, Old Joe decided to send a man to Fort Ridgley for help. The last surviving horse was saddled, but its luck had run out. As the rider mounted, the Sioux realized what was going on and fired several volleys that riddled the horse. The rider, Corporal James Auge, jumped free, unharmed, as the horse went down. It was an unnecessary gesture, as help was already on the way.

Big Eagle told what he saw from his side.

> Just before dawn the fight began. It continued all day and the following night until late the next morning. Both sides fought well. Owning to the white man's way of fighting they lost many men. Owning to the Indian's way of fighting they lost few. The white men stood up and exposed themselves at first [as seen above, the soldiers thought that they heard the command "Fall in," but it

was really "Fall Down"], but at last they learned to keep quiet. The Indians always took care of themselves. We had an easy time of it. We could crawl through the grass and into the coulee and get water when we wanted it, and after a few hours our women crossed the river and came up near the bluff and cooked for us, and we could go back and eat and then return to the fight. We did not lose many men. Indeed, I only saw two dead Indians, and I never heard that any more were killed.[106]

As soon as firing was heard in the distance, Sibley sent Colonel Samuel McPhail to investigate. He had three hundred mounted volunteers and two cannon. McPhail advanced toward Birch Coulee but was stopped by the Sioux in the gully near Birch Coulee. McPhail sent a rider back to Fort Ridgley for reinforcements.[107] Sibley led the relief column to McPhail, arriving after midnight.

11:00 A.M.

Sibley pushed ahead of the relief column and arrived at the campsite to find a disaster. As his column approached, the Sioux saw the glint of the rifles and fired a few shots before departing. Sibley also raked the woods with cannon fire, which hastened Little Crow's departure.[108] Thirteen dead and forty-seven wounded soldiers were on the scene. The dead included Private Robert Baker and Private Peter Boyer of I Company, Tenth Regiment.[109] The Sioux attack had been a complete surprise. Big Eagle relates what he saw at that time.

> The next morning General Sibley came with a very large force and drove us away from the field. We took our time about getting away. Some of our men said that they remained till Sibley got up and that they fired at some of his men as they were shaking hands with some of the men of the camp.... There was no pursuit. The whites fired their cannon at us as we were leaving the field, but they might as well have beaten a big drum for all the harm they did. They only made a noise. We went back across the river to our camps in the old villages, and then on up the river to Yellow Medicine and the mouth of the Chippewa, where Little Crow joined us.[110]

The troops had dug in for shelter and had used the bodies of ninety dead horses to protect themselves from the heavy fire that came from all sides. In a few hours, Sibley's command had lost nearly all of its horses. There were many close calls. Private James Leyde of Company A of the Sixth Regiment always carried a Bible that his mother had given him. After the battle, he pulled the Bible from beneath his uniform and found that it had been penetrated by a ball that went nearly through the Good Book. To his buddy, Billy Caine, he said: "Hello Billy, my Bible got struck." The ball had gone through Genesis, Exodus and Leviticus until it stopped halfway through Deuteronomy. "God, Billy, it didn't get through Deuteronomy anyway!"[111] At that time, Caine was twenty-eight and Leyde was nineteen. Both Leyde and Caine would survive the war. Sibley wrote to his wife, Sarah: "These Indians fight like devils; no one has seen anything like it."[112] Before departing from Birch Coulee, Sibley left a note on a stick for Little Crow. "If Little Crow has any proposition to make let him send a half-breed to me and he shall be protected in and out of my camp."[113] Little Crow sent a reply to Sibley under flag of truce explaining why he went to war.

Yellow Medicine
Sept. 7, 1862
Dear Sir:

> For what reason we have commenced this war, I will tell you. It is on account of Major Galbraith, we made a treaty with the Government, and beg for what little we do get, and then can't get it till our children are dieing [sic] with hunger. It was with the traders that commence [it] Mr. A. J. Myrick told the Indians they would eat grass or their own dung, then Mr. Forbes told the lower

Sioux that [they] were not men, then Robert he was making with his friends to defraud us [out] of our money if the young braves have push the white men, I have done this myself; So I want you to let the Governor Ramsey know this. I have a great many prisoners, women and children, it ain't all our fault the Winnebagoes was in the engagement, two of them was killed. I want you to give me answer by bearer all at present.

Yours truly,
Friend Little Crow (x)[114]

Little Crow hoped to use his prisoners as a bargaining chip to rescue his war and the lives of the Sioux. This would not work. Too many white civilians had been murdered and genocide of the Sioux was the demand of the settlers on the frontier. The press was calling for a war of extermination.[115] All Indians should be killed. Sibley returned to Fort Ridgley with his wounded to refit and plan the next phase of the campaign. The press and the politicians were criticizing Sibley and demanding faster action. The losses at Birch Coulee were part of the criticism, but more important, 250 prisoners of the Sioux needed to be rescued. Sibley sent Colonel William Crooks to Ramsey to explain the situation and plans. Crooks was well-respected and had attended but did not graduate with his West Point Class of 1854.[116] Crook's visit did little good. Pressure for action continued. The *St. Paul Press* called Sibley "a snail who falls back on his authority and dignity and refuses to march."[117] Fortune would soon smile on his campaign.

The Battle of Acton, Wednesday, 3 September 1862

Crow stationed himself about half a mile to the northwest of Strout's with his trusty Lieutenants around him. Red Dog who was to lead the attack on the north was a tall savage 30 or 35 years old and straight as an Indian's arrow and was wearing a lean and hungry look.[118]

The Battle of Acton (also called Kelly's Bluff) occurred east of Sibley's position. On 24 August, Governor Ramsey had ordered Captain Richard Strout of the Tenth to move to protect the citizens of Meeker County. His company had enrolled between the 14th and 24th of August from Hennepin, Carver, and Wright counties. He had sixty-four men, some of them civilians planning to enlist.[119] Strout was part of the Tenth, but he and his company would later be transferred to the Ninth Infantry Regiment and would become B Company of the Ninth. Strout marched out of Minneapolis headed for Acton in response to Ramsey's order.

Milton Stubbs was with Strout's column. Stubbs was nineteen years old and had enlisted at Fort Snelling on 21 August 1862. Strout reached Acton on 2 September and encamped near the site of the original massacre that started the war. He recalled that volunteers rode in that night to warn

Richard Strout commanded the detachment that fought the Sioux at Acton (Minnesota Historical Society).

Strout that about three hundred Sioux were in his vicinity. Stubbs said that the Indians were commanded by a French half-breed named Campbell, but this claim is disputed by the Sioux who were there. If it was Campbell, this was probably Baptiste Campbell who was hanged for murder the following December.

Little Crow had planned to attack Strout that night (2 September 1862), but realized that Strout had been warned and delayed the attack. One of Little Crow's warriors gave his account to a local newspaper. It is interesting to speculate why no one arrested this hostile after his interview with the press. "We were in the house [in Acton] when the soldiers came in sight, ten of us. We went back into the thick woods. I knew Crow [Little Crow] wanted to fight Strout. I rode a good horse. I sent four men on horses to wave blankets on the high hills which would tell all Indians to come quick.... Crow stationed himself about half a mile to the northwest of Strout's with his trusty Lieutenants around him."[120] In view of the warning, Strout decided to leave Acton and return to Hutchinson, a distance of twenty-five miles. Stubbs recalled that the company arose at daybreak and organized the column into four platoons: two in front and the balance on the flanks and rear. As the column left Acton they noticed the glint of gun barrels in the distance, which they thought was a relief column. It was not: it was Little Crow. Strout was attacked by an overwhelming force of Little Crow's warriors. Strout was outnumbered by about ten to one. It appears that the Sioux were having a very busy day since they were already attacking Sibley's troops at Birch Coulee. The Sioux had an overwhelming number of Indians and many of these were mounted. Strout's soldiers were untrained infantry. The fight that followed is remarkable because they were untrained but fought well. They were fighting for their lives. Milton Stubbs recalled that when they charged the Indians in front, the Indians gave way only to circle around and attack Strout's company, again. The Sioux had horses and those without horses were fleet of foot. Strout rallied his troops and put down a solid rain of fire on the Sioux, one volley after another. The company held until the Sioux sent a mounted band to get behind Strout and cut him off. This move was successful and panic set it when Strout's troops realized they were surrounded. Nevertheless, Strout's company broke out of the ambush and fled toward Hutchinson. A six hour running fight ensued with the Sioux firing on both of the company's flanks. Stubbs saw two friends (Getchell and Gideon) killed and he himself was wounded in the foot. Years later he was awarded a pension of $4.00 a month for his wound. He indicated that firing was heavy coming in from all sides and he looked back to the rear and saw a body of Indians tearing out of the woods like a cyclone.

Strout reached Hutchinson, losing many troops along the way. He placed the number of his wounded at fifteen, but other accounts indicate as high as twenty-three.[121] The Ninth Regiment's history lists the following soldiers dead or who later died of wounds: Alva Gretchell, Abner C. Bennet, Frank J. Beadle, George W. Gideon, and N. E. Weeks.[122] The dead were left behind during the flight. Strout took up the defense of Hutchinson and the Indians withdrew. Strout was dismissed from the army in 1864. Very little information could be found about Strout after his Battle at Acton.

The Attack on Fort Abercrombie, Wednesday, 3 September 1862

> *Their little home was found in ashes, in which were found the bones of the wife and children, murdered and burned by the Indians. Their heads had been split open with tomahawks. The bones were collected and carefully buried by the soldiers that night.*[123]
> — James Hart

As Sibley was fighting at Birch Coulee and Strout was being attacked at Acton, the Indians attacked Fort Abercrombie. Fort Abercrombie was situated on the Red River separating Minnesota and Dakota Territory and located at a place known as Graham's Point. It was established in 1858 to serve as a depot for troops and supplies. For this reason, it was not heavily fortified. When news of the Sioux uprising reached the fort, warnings were sent out to nearby towns and troop detachments scattered in the area were called in. As a consequence people poured into the fort which undoubtedly saved many lives. On the 23rd of August word reached the fort that a large party of Indians perhaps as many as five hundred were on their way to waylay a wagon train that was moving near the fort. The wagon train was warned and it also joined the fort.[124] Intense digging was started to improve fortifications. Captain John Vander Horck of D Company, Fifth Regiment, commanded the fort. By 30 August, fortifications were greatly improved and Captain Vander Horck had entrenched three cannon to protect the fort. That same day a party of Indians was seen near the fort. Requests for reinforcements were sent to St. Paul. In the early morning of 3 September, Vander Horck was inspecting the perimeter when a guard shot him by mistake. The guard thought Vander Horck was an Indian since he thought he saw Indians crawling toward the fort during the night. Why the guard failed to alert the fort that night when he saw the Indians will never be known.

As Vander Horck was being helped to the dispensary to have his arm wound dressed, about four hundred Indians attacked. The fight lasted from 5 to 11 A.M. before the Indians were driven off. The cannons were effective and many Indians were killed. Losses to the garrison were two wounded, one of whom later died, Private Edwin D. Steele. The fort had a total of three hundred and fifty rounds of musket ammunition remaining. Earlier it had been discovered that the supply of cartridges in the warehouse was the new .58 caliber rounds while the garrison had the older Harper's Ferry .69 caliber muskets. This was the reverse of the problem at Birch Coulee where the troops had .58 caliber rifles and .69 caliber bullets. It seems that the ordnance department could never get it quite right. To his great relief, Vander Horck discovered that the canister rounds for the cannon in the warehouse were composed of .69 caliber balls. These canister cylinders were broken open and the balls distributed to the soldiers. The cylinders were refilled with broken glass, pieces of metal and anything else lethal that could be found.[125] A call for supplies had been sent to St. Paul. In St. Paul, the Tenth Regiment was organizing at Fort Snelling and would provide some of the supplies. There were other attacks after 3 September, but the Indians were unsuccessful in taking the fort. The siege was finally lifted on 23 September.[126]

Company D of the Tenth supplied twenty-four men including Private James R. Hart, who was eighteen, and twenty-two-year-old Ira Eggleston, who was the Company D wagoner. E Company of the Tenth also supplied twenty-four men. The distance from Fort Snelling to Fort Abercrombie on the Red River was about 175 miles. Hart wrote a diary of the journey sometime after 1889 from which we learn the details and gain a better understanding of the problems of supply during the Indian war. It was an incredible journey that took thirty-seven days. The supply train consisted of fifty-eight wagons. Each wagon was pulled by six mules for a total of 348, only two of which were broken to harness. Each wagon held two and one-half tons of cargo including ammunition, other supplies, and sixteen barrels of whiskey for a total of 928 barrels. This appears to be an enormous amount of whiskey for a small outpost, but it is likely that Hart sampled a barrel or two and thus lost count. It may be assumed that some of that whiskey was for other than medicinal purposes or in other words, happy times at Fort Abercrombie when the supply train arrived.

The supply train had one howitzer manned by two regulars who would fire as each tree line was approached to frighten off the Sioux. Apparently it worked since the supply train was not attacked during the journey. When swamps were encountered, corduroy roads had to be built to cross them. This took time as the soldiers cut trees to lay side by side so the wagons could cross over. There were accidents and many incidents along the way. Hart tells of a young father named Cobb.

> At the time the train left Fort Snelling it was joined by a man named Cobb, a young man of twenty-seven, six feet tall, straight and handsome. This man with his wife and three little girls had "squatted" on a piece of land intending to make it their home. Mr. Cobb had been obliged to go to St. Paul on business and was glad of a chance to return with the soldiers. His home was in the exact place mentioned where the train camped for the night. Their little home was found in ashes, in which were found the bones of the wife and children, murdered and burned by the Indians. Their heads had been split open with tomahawks. The bones were collected and carefully buried by the soldiers that night.[127]

No record of Cobb could be found. Hart records that when they finally reached Fort Abercrombie they off-loaded the wagons and found twenty-eight soldiers and dependents. By that time, the Indian war was over for Fort Abercrombie and nearly all of the soldiers had been redeployed to fight in the South.[128] The fort now had an ample supply of whiskey.

The Battle of Wood Lake, Tuesday, 23 September 1862

> *I am ashamed to call myself a Sioux. Seven hundred picked warriors whipped by the cowardly whites. Better run away and scatter out over the plains like buffalo and wolves.*[129]
>
> — Little Crow

With precious little time to refit and turn a mob into an army, Sibley finally had to move north after two weeks at Fort Ridgley. He was on a familiar trail headed for the Upper Agency and he intended to free the captives and end the war. Sibley had 1,619 troops in his column including cavalry and artillery.[130] Little Crow tracked his movement and had 740 warriors available to fight.[131] The tide had turned and Little Crow and the Sioux had one last chance for victory. The end came in late September 1862 at Wood Lake near the Upper Agency.

Among Sibley's troops were 270 men from the Third Minnesota Regiment. Theirs is one of the most incredible odysseys of the war. The Third was recruited in the autumn of 1861. Their colonel was Henry C. Lester, who had fought in the East but returned to Minnesota to take command of the newly formed Third.[132] Lester was an attorney by trade and not a soldier, but he had performed well enough in the East as a company commander; however, his lack of military background would lead to disaster for the Third. After training and equipping, the Third moved South to fight the Confederate Army. In July 1862, the regiment was stationed at Murfreesboro, Tennessee, guarding the Union depot and the rail line to Chattanooga when Confederate general Nathan Bedford Forrest arrived. Forrest was one of the best cavalry leaders of the Civil War, and he was raiding to destroy supplies and tear up railroad track.[133] Lester was no match for Forrest. In a masterful job of bluff and trickery, Forrest persuaded Lester that he had overwhelming superiority in numbers although the opposite was true. Forrest threatened to put the soldiers of the Third "to the sword" if they did not surrender and Lester complied virtually without firing a shot beyond a skirmish at his trains. Lincoln would later direct that Lester and others who had voted for surrender be dismissed from the army for cowardice. The Third Regiment surgeon would later observe that Lester was a gentle person who should not have been in command. He literally froze when confronted by Forrest and was unable to do anything but surrender. The soldiers of the Third were outraged when they were forced to surrender without a fight. Madison Bowler in a letter home summarized the sentiment of the troops.

Nathan Bedford Forrest, the South's best cavalry leader (Library of Congress).

> Nashville, Tenn., July 19, 1862
> My Dear Lizzie:
>
> Presuming that you are a little anxious to hear from me, I will just drop you a line to assure you of my safety. Last Sunday morning we were awakened by the report of guns in the Camp of the 9th Mich. We were soon formed in lines and marched into an open field where we got into line of battle just in time to resist a charge from the rebel Cavalry, driving them with considerable loss on their side [This is fiction]. We held our position till three o'clock P.M., repulsing them at every attempt they made upon us, when at last our officers surrendered us amid the tears and curses of the men.
>
> Good Bye
> Madison.[134]

Forrest had no way to care for the large influx of prisoners that outnumbered his force and he was doubtless a bit nervous about the situation. He immediately paroled the soldiers and shipped the officers to Confederate prisons in the East. The Tenth Regiment would later fight and defeat Forrest and at that time it would be sweet revenge for the humiliation of the Third. The soldiers of the Third were shipped to Benton Barracks, a Union

James Madison Bowler in a photograph taken later in life (Minnesota Historical Society).

post near St. Louis. The terms of the parole were that these soldiers would not fight the Confederacy again, but a bungling Union general ordered the Third rearmed to fight the South and the troops mutinied. A violation of their parole could lead to their execution if they were recaptured. After a good deal of negotiation, it was agreed that the Third would be sent north to fight the Sioux. September found the Third encamped near the Upper Agency with very few supplies. One of the troops had heard that an abandoned farm near Wood Lake was a short distance away and included a potato crop. After hitching up several wagons, a detachment of the Third moved out without authority to dig potatoes. They were moving into an ambush. Big Eagle told the story.

> We soon learned that Sibley had thrown up breastworks and it was deemed safe to attack him at the lake [Wood Lake]. We concluded that the fight should be about a mile or more to the northwest of the lake, on the road along which the troops would march.... At the point determined on we planned to hide a large number of men on the side of the road. Near the lake, in a ravine formed by the outlet, we were to place another strong body.... The men in the ravine would then be in the rear of the whites and would begin firing on that end of the column. We expected to throw the whole white force into confusion by the sudden and unexpected attack and defeat them before they could rally.... The night he [Sibley] lay at Wood Lake his pickets were only a short distance from [our] camp — less than half a mile. When we were putting our men into position that night

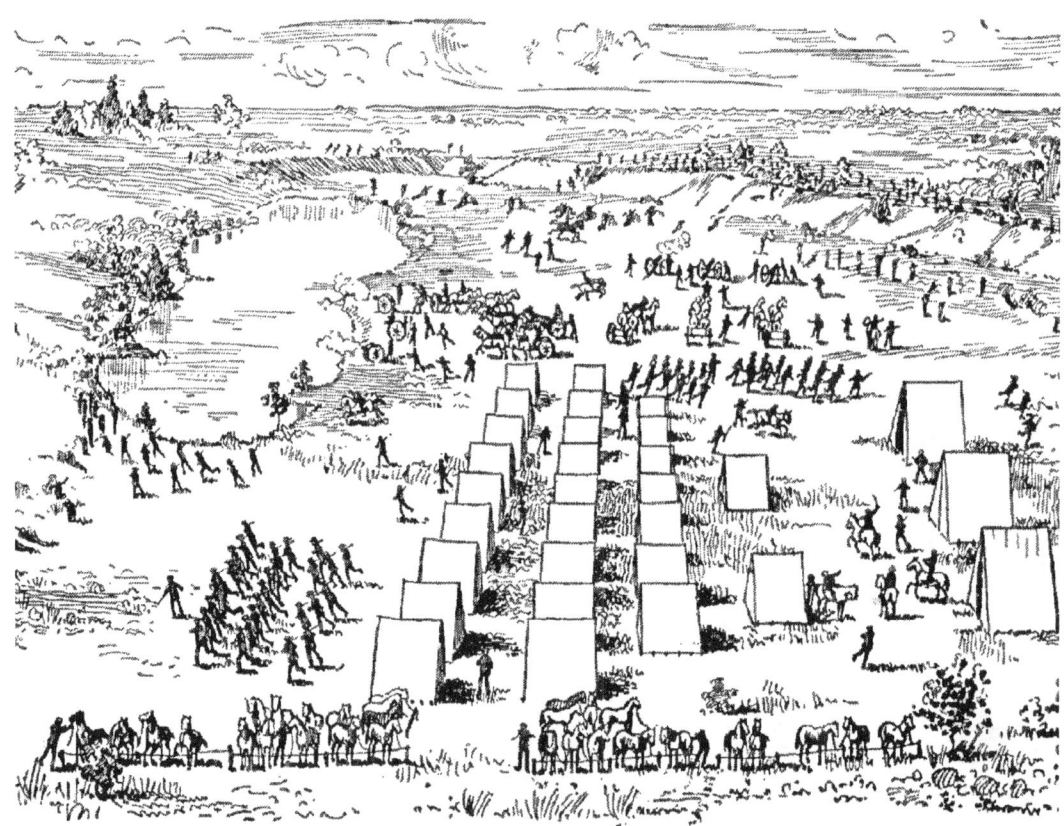

Firsthand sketch of the Battle of Wood Lake on 23 September 1862, which ended the Sioux War in Minnesota (from Connolly, *A Thrilling Narrative...*).

we often saw them plainly ... laughing and singing. When all our preparations were made Little Crow and I and some other chiefs went to the mound or hill to the West so as to watch the fight better when it should commence. There were numbers of other Indians there.[135]

It was early morning as the men of the Third with their wagons moved toward the abandoned farm to dig potatoes. They were about to drive over the Sioux in the ambush site. Big Eagle continued:

> The morning came and an accident spoiled all our plans. For some reason Sibley did not move early as we expected he would. Our men were lying hidden waiting patiently.... It seemed a considerable time after sunup when some four or five wagons with a number of soldiers started out from the camp in the direction of the old Yellow Medicine Agency. They came on over the prairie, right where part of our line was. Some of the wagons were not in the road, and if they had kept straight on would have driven right over our men as they lay in the grass. At last they came so close that our men had to rise up and fire. This brought on the fight, of course, but not according to the way we had planned it. Little Crow saw it and felt very badly.[136]

Several of the Third Regiment soldiers were hit when the Sioux opened fire. The rest took cover behind the wagons and put up a steady fire against overwhelming odds. The remainder of the Third Regiment rushed forward to support their comrades. The Sioux were moving quickly to cut off the Third. Sibley realized what was happening and ordered the Third back so that he could form a line and attack the Sioux. The regimental commander, Major Abraham E. Welsh, continued the fight until he was shot in the leg and went down. As a result, the Sioux took heart and were about to overwhelm the Third as they started their withdrawal to Sibley's line. The Third nearly broke and ran as they were withdrawing, but the Renville Rangers arrived to strengthen the line. By then, the Sixth and Seventh regiments were out of camp and came on line. Sibley attacked with the Third in the center and the Sixth and Seventh on the flanks, supported by artillery and cavalry. The Sioux were beaten back and fled. As the Third moved forward some say that the troops shouted, "Remember Murfreesboro." This ended the Battle of Wood Lake. It had lasted two hours. Sibley lost forty-three killed and wounded, mostly soldiers of the Third. Indian casualties were estimated at twenty-five killed and thirty to fifty wounded.[137] This was the last battle of the Sioux Indian War in Minnesota. The fate of the hostages was now in the balance. Sibley moved forward to the rescue.

In a letter to his wife, Madison Bowler described the action.

Camp near Yellow Medicine, [Minn.,] Tuesday, Sept. 23, 1862
5 o'clock P.M.
My Dear Lizzie

> About 7 o'clock this morning 30 or 40 of our regt. with teams, started off to dig potatoes, and when about a mile from camp were attacked by the Indians." Our boys began to harness up for a free fight, when Major Welch told me that my co. might fall in and go out to the aid of the others, but the firing having considerably increased the whole of our regt.-270-were ordered to fall in; so Co F took its old place on the left flank, and forward we went till within gunshot of the Indians, when Major Welch ordered the left wing to deploy as skirmishers. The Indians retreated before us until we were upwards of a mile and a half from camp; then we commenced firing on the red scamps, when all at once they rose up on our right and left flanks and in front, and at the same time a lot on ponies just round in our rear. Then commenced the fun-Indian yells enough to split the ears, and bullets falling thick and fast around us. Just then an aid of Col. Sibley came up with an order for us to come back, as Major Welch had gone out without orders. Slowly and steadily we retreated, dealing death to the red skins as they pressed upon us, until we were within 100 rods of camp, where we made a final stand. The Indians got into a wide ravine

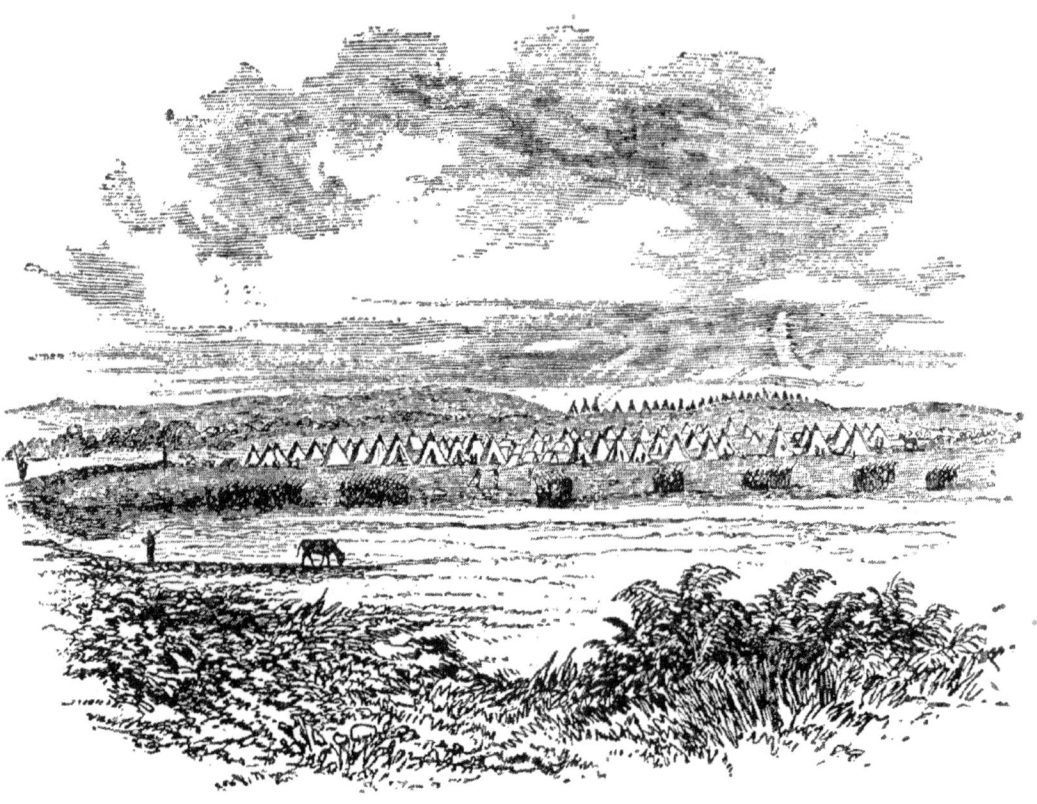

Firsthand sketch of Camp Release, where General Sibley rescued the white prisoners on 29 September 1862 (from Connolly, *A Thrilling Narrative...*).

on two sides of our camp and within about 80 or 100 yards from us. Here we exchanged shots for awhile, the artillery assisting us. Pretty soon the gallant 7th-Am, Wheeler, and Wells among them-charged on the right of the ravine, and our regt on the left of it, completely routing them and peppering them well as they retreated up the bluff on the other side. After they had got away a lot of their dead, which they are always particular to carry off if they can, we picked up and buried 14 of them.

Ever yours
Madison

P.S. If the Indians do not get the messenger, you will get this. I have your good miniature to look at.-Mad[138]

Big Eagle described the action from his side.

Of course you know how the battle was fought. The Indians that were in the fight did well, but hundreds of our men did not get into it and did not fire a shot. They were out too far. The whites drove our men out of the ravine by a charge and that ended the battle. We retreated in some disorder, though the whites did not offer to pursue us. We crossed a wide prairie, but their horsemen did not follow us. We lost fourteen or fifteen men killed and quite a number wounded. Some of the wounded died afterwards, but I do not know how many. We carried off no dead bodies, but took away all our wounded. The whites scalped all our dead men — so I have heard.[139]

After the defeat, Little Crow was despondent and outraged at the performance of his warriors. Little Crow made his way back to his camp and surrendered the hostages to the Sioux peace party before fleeing west into Dakota Territory with two hundred of his followers. Many of these would fight Sibley in the campaign of 1863 in Dakota Territory. Others such as Shakopee fled to Canada. He was later apprehended and hanged. Sibley arrived at the camp on 25 September and saw nothing but white flags and Indians eager to surrender. Two hundred and fifty hostages were released unharmed and two thousand Sioux surrendered. Sibley named the site Camp Release and promised those that surrendered would not be harmed if they had committed no crimes. Big Eagle related what happened to him and many other Sioux: "Soon after the battle I, with many others who had taken part in the war, surrendered to General Sibley. Robinson and the other half-breeds assured us that if we would do this we would only be held as prisoners of war a short time, but as soon as I surrendered I was thrown into prison. Afterward I was tried and served three years in the prison at Davenport and the penitentiary at Little Rock for taking part in the war."[140]

Sibley was now faced with a dilemma: He had defeated the Sioux in Minnesota, but public pressure now demanded revenge and he had two thousand Sioux prisoners that he was now charged to protect from lynch mobs. Sibley set up courts-martial to try those Sioux accused of committing crimes. This would both placate the mobs and see that justice was done. The trials started shortly after the Sioux surrender and were completed on 9 November. They were conducted near Fort Ridgley and 392 Sioux were tried. A total of 303 were sentenced to hang. There were all sorts of problems with these trials that today most consider unjust: see Appendix G for details. With this many lives at stake, the trial records went to Lincoln for review. Lincoln approved thirty-nine death sentences. One death sentence was commuted at the last minute (Tah-te-mi-na or Round Wind) at the request of General Sibley and the executions were carried out on 26 December 1862. See Appendix I for details. Sibley then had the problem of moving the Sioux. Those found guilty were marched to Mankato, Minnesota, while the rest were imprisoned on the bottom land below Fort Snelling where many died that first winter. In the spring they would be moved to Crow Creek in Dakota Territory.

Following Little Crow's defeat at Wood Lake, the companies of the Tenth were garrisoned on or near the frontier. Two companies were stationed at the Winnebago agency in order to prevent the Winnebago from joining the uprising. Two companies were stationed at Le Sueur with the headquarters of the Tenth. Another company was sent to Fort Ridgley and the last three were assigned to locations of lesser importance.[141] With that, the Tenth settled into winter quarters to stay warm while Pope and others planned the spring campaign. The story of A Company of the Tenth is told through the diary of Private George C. Pettie and represents the experiences of all who went into winter quarters in 1862–1863 waiting for the spring campaign. Private Pettie was a member of the first Minnesota state legislature serving during the 1857–1858 period. His photograph was taken while he was in the legislature. When the Sioux war broke out he enlisted in A Company of the Tenth as a private in August 1862. He was thirty-four years old at that time and his diary tells us of life in winter quarters and on the campaign trail later. A Company was stationed at Garden City, Minnesota. This was life on the frontier in the winter of 1862-1863. Pettie's diary started on 1 January 1863 and ended after the campaign into Dakota Territory in October 1863. Below are some of Pettie's diary entries about camp life in Minnesota in the winter of 1862-1863. Winter in Minnesota is always cold and very boring (some call it the "gloom period"). Most of the activity was drill, guard duty and figuring out pastimes to avoid insanity:

Friday, Jan. 9th A.D. 1863

This has been a cloudy day thus far, but not very cold. The day has been spent as usual in drilling and reading or solving algebra's equations as I got time. The southern news are more cheering today Murfreesboro falling and Vicksburg taken by the Federals, and a victory at Cross Roads are among the most exciting news of the day, the flag was drew up as a token of joy for the result. May these late successes, and great victories be soon followed by greater, and may the backbone of Rebellion soon be broken and their flinty heart "made to melt like wax" Lord help the right![142]

Friday, Jan. 21st, 1863

I am again designated as room orderly, a post of neither honor or profit, but of some responsibility. The weather still continues fine which gives us a fine opportunity for drilling. Commenced taking medicine for the blood purchased at Mankato called Compound Syrup of Sazzaparilla but it tastes as though it is mostly molasses.[143]

George C. Pettie, the Minnesota legislator who enlisted as a private (Minnesota Historical Society).

Firsthand sketch of a sentinel on duty in bad weather during the winter of 1862-1863 (from Connolly, *A Thrilling Narrative...*).

Thursday, Feb. 5th.

On guard from one A.M. to three. Two hours. Principal business is to keep fires and sit by them, instead of walking the beat. The prisoner sleeps soundly [Pettie does not tell us who the prisoner was]. Drill is the order of the forepart of the day and signing the payroll the after part as the Pay Master has arrived.[144]

Thomas Jefferson Hunt was a farmer in Ellington, Dodge County, Minnesota. When the Sioux War broke out, he joined B Company of the Tenth and years after the war wrote of his reminiscences. His observations were similar to Pettie's that winter, and Hunt had also been a member of the Minnesota legislature. "Company B was ordered to take station at the Winnebago Agency twelve miles East of Mankato and keep the Indians in subjugation as they were believed to be in sympathy with the Sioux. Here we spent the fall and winter, drilling and erecting log huts for quarters."[145]

Other regiments were similarly deployed to protect the frontier, but all would ultimately be sent South to fight the Confederates including the Third. On 1 December 1862, Lincoln dismissed the officers of the Third who had voted for surrender at Murfreesboro and Madison Bowler was promoted to captain shortly thereafter as the regiment was reorganized.[146] Apparently the reorganization of the Third ended concern about parole violations since Bowler makes no further reference to it in his letters.

Mankato, Minnesota—The Execution of the Sioux, Friday, 26 December 1862

As he cut the rope and they dropped, one Indian facing our company broke his rope. Myself and two others picked him up and hung him again.[147]

— Amos B. Watson

By this time, the Tenth Regiment's organization was at last complete and it played a key role in the execution of the Sioux. The regiment was assigned to maintain order during the execution. Amos Watson of B Company of the Seventh Regiment described the event.

December 5th, Camp Lincoln was abandoned and command moved to quarters in vacant buildings in Mankato. Here on the 26th of December 1862, 38 Indians were hanged from one gallows. They had been found guilty upon trial by court martial of massacring whites. It was a public hang-

T. J. Hunt, the last surviving officer of the Tenth Regiment, circa 1920 (Minnesota Historical Society).

Above: The Executions. Sketch from *Leslie's Weekly*. *Below:* Little Crow's son, Wowinape (Minnesota Historical Society).

ing.... Our company was stationed at the base of the gallows as guards. The Indians came out from the prison and marched up on the platforms and took their places. Some were dancing, some singing, and some were smoking. The gallows was built square, a post through the center with a rope to the platform on which the Indians stood. There was a man, the whole family the Indians had massacred, he alone having escaped and he wanted the privilege of cutting the rope, which the officers granted him. As he cut the rope and they dropped, one Indian facing our company broke his rope. Myself and two others picked him up and hung him again. After the doctors had pronounced them all dead, we took them and placed them in army wagons, hauled them to a sand-bar in the Minnesota River, and buried them about two feet deep in the sand. The next morning I went down to where they were buried, and they were all gone. The doctors had gobbled them up [bodies were needed for research].[148]

Appendix I provides details of the executions.

While Little Crow had escaped justice, he would die six months later in a raspberry patch on Friday, 3 July 1863. When Little Crow fled Minnesota to Dakota Territory in 1862, while many of his colleagues were hanged, some of his followers went with him including the four who had committed the murders in Acton.[149] He later crossed the border into Canada. It was assumed that he was safe but in the spring of 1863, he decided to conduct a raid back into Minnesota to steal horses. With horses, he and all sixteen of his followers could join other Sioux in conflict with troops. At that time, General Sibley was marshalling soldiers for a campaign in Dakota Territory against the Sioux. Citizens in Minnesota were alert and quite willing to shoot any Indian on sight. Understandable, since nearly eight hundred Minnesota civilians were murdered by the Sioux during the uprising. It is not known why Little Crow would concoct such a scheme. Perhaps he just wanted to get back into the action or was hoping to reclaim his reputation, which had been badly damaged in the war of 1862. While the Battle of Gettysburg was being fought in the East, Little Crow and his small band moved South across the border murdering white settlers along the way. These murders alerted the army and troops were sent north to scour the area and deal with the Sioux. What happened next was predictable: a settler and his son fired on Little Crow while Little Crow and his son, Wowinape, were picking berries in a raspberry patch. Little Crow promptly died, wearing the jacket of a white settler who had been murdered the previous week. The other Sioux had already fled and Little Crow's son escaped to Dakota Territory with the others. He was later captured as will be seen in the next chapter.

CHAPTER 2

Vengeance on the Plains

Expedition Against the Tribes in Dakota Territory, 16 June–13 September 1863

> *The Sioux Indians of Minnesota must be exterminated or driven forever beyond the borders of the State. The public safety imperatively requires it. Justice calls for it.... The blood of the murdered cries to heaven for vengeance on these assassins of women and children ... amenable to no law; bound by no moral or social restraints — they have already destroyed every pledge on which it is possible to found hope of ultimate reconciliation. They must be regarded and treated as outlaws.*[1]
> — Governor Alexander Ramsey

Loss of life in the Indian War of 1862 was heavy. Estimates over the years have run from 447 to two thousand.[2] One historian has stated: "Tallies of casualties could not be kept during the killings. Settlers who paused in flight to bury murdered neighbors might themselves be slain before they reported the burials."[3] Also, many bodies would never be found, consumed by prairie fires that frequently occurred. This is a key point. Many participants at the time and some historians since have tried to pin down the exact number of those who perished when the correct answer is that we do not know. We can only provide an estimated number and Lincoln, who had access to all of the information coming in, had the best estimate. Lincoln estimated that eight hundred settlers had been killed.[4] The Sioux lost several hundred including those hanged at Mankato and those from disease while imprisoned below Fort Snelling. No one will ever know the actual total human loss. Material losses were also significant. Efforts to provide relief and reimbursement to settlers for their losses set off a feeding frenzy. Claims poured in to the Sioux Commission set up in 1863. Some may have been extravagant. For example, thousands of dollars were claimed for damages to the rutabaga crops of the settlers. If all of the rutabagas claimed as destroyed by the Sioux were spread evenly over the state of Minnesota, the rutabaga depth would have been one foot.

Over a million dollars were paid to claimants from funds for annuities originally intended for the Sioux and in February of 1863, the United States Congress abrogated treaties with the Sioux, which in effect left them homeless.[6] Proposals started to roll in to the state government in St. Paul on how to get rid of all Indians in Minnesota: 46,880 Sioux, Chippewa, Winnebago, and Menominee.[7] Bear in mind that the Chippewa were traditional enemies of the Sioux and did not take part in the uprising. They killed many of the Sioux in 1862. It appears that things were getting out of control as often happens when a large number of people are killed. In the words attributed to General Philip Sheridan:

"The only good Indian is a dead Indian."[8] One proposal from James W. Taylor, a well known public character in St. Paul, suggested that all Indians be deported to Isle Royale near the north shore of Lake Superior.[9] The government did the obvious thing and started with the Sioux interned below Fort Snelling. They were shipped to Crow Creek in Dakota Territory. The situation settled somewhat and thoughts of deporting all tribes disappeared, but now the settlers wanted to deal with the Winnebago. It is here that possibly the greatest injustice of the Sioux War occurred. The Winnebago were a peaceful tribe, few of whom had participated in the Sioux War.[10] They had been moved to Blue Earth County, Minnesota, from Wisconsin by the government in an earlier deportation to open land for white settlers in Wisconsin. The removal from Wisconsin displaced some of the settlers in Blue Earth County. The Sioux War offered the settlers a way to get rid of the Winnebago and replace their reservation with white farms.[11] This was a land grab. A secret society of whites was formed in Mankato to put political pressure on the Minnesota legislature to remove the Winnebago. It was called the Knights of the Forest and branches sprang up around Mankato.[12] The knights did their job well and the legislature ordered the removal of the Winnebago as well as the Sioux. This was similar to the Cherokee removal from Georgia and the Trail of Tears twenty years earlier. The difference was that the Cherokee and members of the other civilized tribes died on the trail to Indian Territory (now Oklahoma). The Sioux and Winnebago died by the hundreds and perhaps even thousands after they arrived at their new, inhospitable reservations in Dakota Territory and later, Nebraska. G Company of the Tenth Regiment provided guards for the removal of the Sioux and Winnebago by steamboat over a very circuitous route from Minnesota to their new reservations in Dakota Territory. Private John Smith of G Company kept a diary of his experiences during the Civil War including his duty as a guard on the steamboat *Davenport* during the removal. The time taken and route of steamboats was dependent upon weather and the height of the river as seen in the story of Captain LaBarge (see his odyssey below). John Smith's voyage seemed to involve the Sioux deportation, but the same route and comments could be applied to the Winnebago. Smith departed from Fort Snelling and here are samples from his diary.[13]

Friday, May 8th 1863

Arrived at St Louis [Missouri] about 8 o clock this morning and remained there all day. St Louis is an immense shipping emporium for the West and North and South. There was a gun boat came into St Louis this evening. There was a crowd around the boat today to see the Indians. The Missouri comes down from the mouth without mixing with the Mississippi river. Fight with Indians today, several killed.

Saturday May 16th 1863

Had a very pleasant day, a little warm. The *Florence* [steamboat] came back from Leavenworth [Kansas] and took the freight from the island in the river and landed where we were camped. They then took the rest of the freight and Indians and soldiers on board and started for the Fort. The mate on the boat got his leg broke and one of the squaws died on board the boat. The boat tied up at Fort Leavenworth over night.

Monday May 18th 1863

Left St. Joseph [Missouri] at 8 o'clock A.M. with the rest of the Company and about 540 Indians upon board. Passed Mydura Point Kansas came about 75 miles from St Joseph. Buried 2 papooses in one grave one having died last night. A fine day today. Like the appearance of the country here better than the lower Missouri.

Monday May 25th/63

Arrived almost at Sioux City [Iowa] and put up for the night. There has been 13 deaths among the Indians since leaving Snelling.

Over 1300 Sioux and nearly 2000 Winnebago were deported from Minnesota in the spring of 1863.[14] Many farmers in Blue Earth County, Minnesota, today owe their prosperity to the Mankato Knights of the Forest land grab in 1863. The Chippewa would remain in Minnesota and be the basis of the last Indian war fought in the United States. This occurred in Leech Lake, Minnesota, in 1898. See Appendix F for a summary of Indians residing in Minnesota as found in the U.S. Indian Census thirty years after the war. Like the Cherokees deported to Indian Territory as a result of the Removal Act of 1830, many of the Sioux returned to their homeland in Minnesota after the war.

Minnesota governor Alexander Ramsey had a two-fold problem. After the cheers subsided at the hanging of the Sioux murderers at Mankato on 26 December 1862 (see Appendix I), the fact remained that the murders of civilians by marauding Sioux continued in western Minnesota. A review of newspapers of that time provides an account at least once a week of an isolated family murdered by roving bands of Sioux.

South of New Ulm the family of Swenson Roland was attacked and a twelve-year-old son shot to death. In the same area Ole Palmer, Gabriel Elingson, and other Norwegian immigrants were killed. Henry Basche was murdered within two miles of New Ulm. North of the river Gilbert Parker, fishing on Long Lake, was butchered and scalped. In late June the family of Amos Dustin started across the prairie forty-five miles West of St. Paul. In their wagon were six, including three young children and Dustin's widowed mother. In the over-due wagon, when searchers found it, were the lifeless, mutilated bodies of Dustin, his four year old son, and his mother. In a meadow near the road lay Dustin's wife, mortally wounded. James McGannon, homesteader seventy miles West of Minneapolis, was murdered July 1. A gray coat was stripped from McGannon's body, and his horse was taken.[15]

McGannon's coat is the same coat worn by Little Crow when he was shot. Unfortunately, the bounty of $25 offered for Indian scalps had no apparent impact in reducing the level of violence. This bounty would be raised to two hundred dollars by 22 September 1863 with little effect.[16] The result was that settlers were leaving the frontier in alarming numbers because it was not safe. This was not a result of any organized plan by the Sioux, but rather the fact that Sioux individuals and bands wanted plunder and killing whites was a way to get it. Something needed to be done to make the frontier safe. Pope knew that it would take five times as many troops to protect the frontier as to mount an aggressive campaign attacking them.[17] He also knew that a defensive posture would not be effective in stopping the

Cut Nose, who was hanged for murder (Minnesota Historical Society).

bloodshed. As Napoleon said: "A passive defense is deferred suicide." Pope felt that "there are not troops enough in our whole armies to satisfy the people of Minnesota," for they wanted a regiment or at least a company "in the front door of every settler's house in the country."[18]

Ramsey's second problem was that, unlike Cut Nose who (before he was hanged) enjoyed bragging how he had murdered twenty-nine women and children, most of the murderers thought it was a good idea to flee to Dakota Territory and did so. These criminals included their leader, Little Crow. Besides Little Crow, the four Sioux who had started the war when they murdered the settlers at Acton also escaped West along with hundreds of others. The murderers from Acton would never be heard from again. Ramsey needed to answer the cries for justice and hunt down the criminals who had fled to Dakota Territory. Ramsey needed to solve both problems, and quickly. Settlers were abandoning the frontier and leaving Minnesota in increasing numbers. No one thought that both problems could be solved at the same time. Minnesota politicians, of course, pushed for increased security on the frontier at all costs. Others, including Ramsey and the army, wanted a permanent solution by eliminating the hostiles in Dakota Territory. Ramsey and Lincoln tried to do that. Ramsey had already requested that all Minnesota regiments fighting the Confederates be returned to Minnesota. Only the Third Regiment, which had surrendered to Nathan Bedford Forrest at Murfreesboro and been paroled, was returned to Minnesota and fought at the Battle of Wood Lake. That was about it. Other regiments in the East were fully engaged in fighting the Confederate Army and could not be withdrawn. The First Minnesota was nearly annihilated at Gettysburg and there was little left to return to Minnesota. Galvanized Yankees appeared on the scene. These were Confederate soldiers in Yankee prison camps who agreed to fight as long as they would not have to fire on their former Confederate comrades. Killing Indians was a far better existence than living in a Yankee prison camp.

Lincoln's general in chief, Henry Halleck (Library of Congress).

Politically, this campaign was your worst nightmare. Minnesota senators Rice and Wilkinson complained to the Army general in chief in Washington, General Henry Halleck, that the campaign of 1863 into Dakota Territory would leave the state without troops needed to defend Minnesota. It is not clear what the senators feared (other than reelection) since the Sioux had already been driven out of the state, but it is true that Sioux raiding parties continued to harass and kill settlers. The press frequently published reports of these depredations, but the civilians killed or wounded were in the ones and twos, not in the hundreds as in the previous fall. The other main complaint was that the Sioux were very fleet and would easily avoid an army column. The senators forgot or did not know that the Sioux had baggage trains including wives and children that had to be moved and these traveled at a rate nearly as slow as the military once it got started moving. The efforts by the Sioux warriors to defend their families led to enormous Sioux losses in the battles that followed. In the end, those concerned about homeland security would see about two thousand troops kept in Minnesota while fighting shifted to Dakota Territory.

The Campaign Is Launched, Tuesday, 16 June 1863

> *If the devil were permanently to select a residence upon earth, he would probably choose this particular district for an abode, with the redskins' murdering and plundering bands as his ready ministers, to verify by their ruthless deeds his diabolical hatred to all who belong to a Christian race.*[19]
> — Henry H. Sibley

The summer campaign of 1863 as envisioned by General John Pope, the Union commander in the West, included two columns moving into Dakota Territory. This would become known to some as the Sirocco Campaign after the hot, stifling winds blowing from

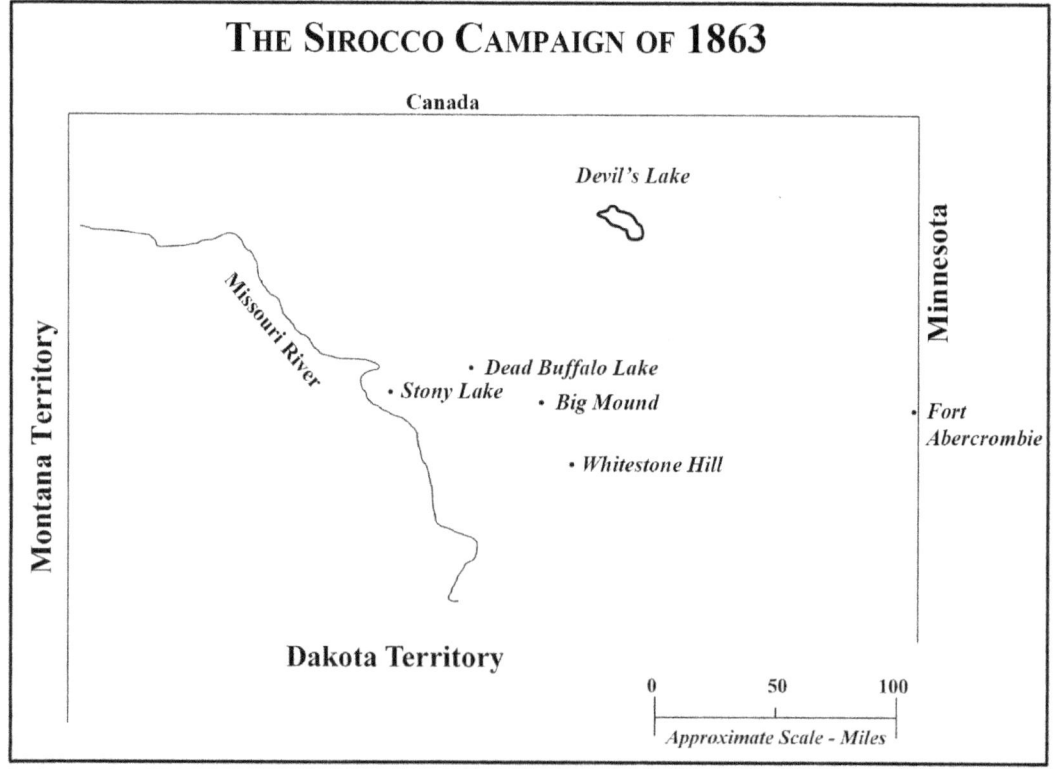

Sibley's Campaign into Dakota Territory.

North Africa into southern Europe. One would be led by Brigadier General Alfred Sully in the West and the other would be led by Brigadier General H. H. Sibley in the East. The purpose of this campaign was to secure the frontier as far West as the Missouri River and to punish those Sioux who had escaped following the Santee Sioux surrender at Wood Lake. Pope's plan was to trap the Indians between the two columns that were to meet at Devil's Lake in Dakota Territory.[20] There were other items on Pope's agenda. He was determined to secure the northern border with Canada where some of the Sioux had fled. He continued to press Washington for permission to cross the Canadian border to pursue the Sioux, but the British government refused. Finally in 1864 the British approved the U.S. pursuit of Indians across the Canadian border.[21] He also found it necessary to make the gold miner trails safe and there were other pressures. Indian traders and Indian agents saw great prospects from lands that would be seized from the Sioux.

General Alfred Sully, the Commander in western Dakota Territory (Minnesota Historical Society).

Perhaps Pope's top agenda items were the need for personal recognition and his hope that he could return to fight in the war in the East where promotion was more promising.[22] These last two would elude him. He had lost badly against Lee at Second Manassas and Lincoln had given him a second chance by sending him West to command forces engaged in the Indian wars. He was never called back to the war in the East. To his credit, Pope was a good planner and from his headquarters in Milwaukee, Wisconsin, and occasionally St. Paul he issued the orders but left the fighting to Sibley and Sully.

Sibley assembled his column in June 1863. By this time, Sibley had a veteran force that had served in the previous campaign against the Sioux in Minnesota in the summer and fall of 1862, but he also had many untried recruits that needed to be trained. Sibley established Camp Pope at the mouth of the Redwood, twenty-five miles beyond Fort Ridgley. It was at Camp Pope that he would start his move west to link up with Sully. Units collected for the great enterprise to come included the Seventh Minnesota, the Sixth Minnesota, the Tenth Minnesota, the First Minnesota Mounted Rangers armed with long range rifles, the Third Battery of Light Artillery, 100 pioneers (engineers) from the Ninth Minnesota, and 70 Indian and mixed-blood scouts. Ration strength was reported at 2,200 infantry, 800 cavalry, 150 artillerymen, 100 pioneers, 70 scouts, for a total of 3,320. To supply and sustain the expedition a train of 225 six-mule-train wagons was gathered, carrying provisions for ninety days.[23] Additionally, another 100 wagons were collected to carry the column's camping gear and other supplies. Sibley's column would be five miles long. As will be seen, the length of his column would prove to be a major problem that Sibley would have to deal with as he moved west.

T. J. Hunt of the Tenth recalled the start of the campaign:

Firsthand sketch of Camp Pope where General Sibley assembled his army in June for the 1863 Indian campaign (from Connolly, *A Thrilling Narrative...*).

Early in June, 1863, four of the five infantry regiments, one regiment of cavalry and a battery, assembled at the mouth of the Redwood River in Redwood County and began the long, weary march of eleven hundred and eighty-five miles. Each infantry soldier's equipment and knapsack weighed some forty pounds. We marched one hour, rested ten minutes, starting at four A.M. and continuing until five or six P.M. or until water was reached that could be drunk. Small lakes were frequent but many of them were so strong with alkali that they were worthless. This was very fatiguing, but the weather was dry and as the supply wagons were emptied, our knapsacks were carried therein, which was a great relief.[24]

Hunt also provided a description of rations and foraging while on the march. See Appendix E.

The artillery and cavalry were vital to the success of the campaign. The Sioux were terrified by the long range and exploding shells of the artillery that could be counted upon to break up any Sioux attack. Most important, the cavalry units mustered in late 1862 provided a match needed against the Indians on horse. This was the largest force ever assembled to fight in the North American Indian wars and these numbers did not include Sully's column moving into the West. The difference between the two columns was that Sully's was predominately cavalry and could move much faster, but Sully had other factors that would slow him down, as will be seen later.

The Indian forces arrayed against Sibley and Sully were enormous. Scattered across over two hundred thousand square miles (over five times the size of the state of Ohio) were over thirty thousand Indians including Teton Sioux as well as other tribes.[25] They were well armed and fierce fighters. Captain Eugene M. Wilson of the First Regiment of Mounted Rangers would later recall shortly before his death in 1890:

> During the campaign the Indians were tolerably well armed with the trade-gun that they used in killing buffalo and the arms that they had taken from troops and settlers. Many still retained the bow and arrows in addition to their guns. At close quarters this was a more dangerous weapon than a revolver. They shot their arrows with rapidity and precision. Although made of light arrowwood, they were tipped with iron and given such a velocity that they would go clear through a man and show the barb on the other side from its entrance.[26]

The Indians were already enraged by atrocities committed by gold miners as well as citizens who had heard of the murders by the Santee Sioux in Minnesota. The Sioux were in no mood to surrender or be herded to reservations. They had seen what had happened to the Santee Sioux at Fort Snelling where they were imprisoned and many died. The chiefs that would fight against the two columns were Inkpaduta, Gall, Sitting Bull,[27] Standing Buffalo and Two Moons as well as others. There was no single chief commanding all of the tribes.[28] Curiously, because of his massacre of civilians at Spirit Lake in 1857, Inkpaduta was often blamed by both sides as the cause of fighting and was thought by some historians to be some sort of commander in chief, which he was not.[29]

The individual tribes could be easily defeated separately as the columns moved west. Both Sibley and Sully knew this. The greatest challenges were weather and terrain. The summer of 1863 was hot and dry, one of the worst on record. Ponds and streams dried up and what was left behind was an alkaline residue that was deadly. Dogs and draft animals that drank would die or go insane. They would need to be shot and the trail west was soon littered with dead animals. Soldiers would later complain in their pension records about the health problems caused by bad water. Ira E. Eggleston of D Company, Tenth Regiment, would complain that he lost all of his teeth "except five old roots" due to the alcholide [*sic*] water.[30] It was a losing campaign for Sibley. The further he moved West, the sicker his column became. Horses died in increasing numbers and more soldiers became sick. The sick were collected and sent back with troops to protect their return. The attrition was enormous. Each night sick horses were shot and their cargo was redistributed among the remaining animals. To the delight of the Sioux following the column, non-essential equipment not burned was left behind. Neither Sibley nor Sully was in stellar health. Both were getting older with the infirmities of old age (judged by 19th century standards). Sibley chose to ride his horse while others (mostly civilians) chose to ride on wagons, although at times he was forced to ride in an ambulance because of a painful wrenching of his knee and hip joint caused by the miring of his horse.[31] At age fifty-two he was among the oldest soldiers in the column.

Despite all of these problems, Sibley called assembly and the column moved out on 16 June 1863 from Camp Pope near present day Redwood Falls, Minnesota, at the juncture of the Redwood and Minnesota rivers. The temperature was 100 degrees in the shade.[32] Sergeant Connolly, the adjutant of the Sixth Regiment, described the departure and the astonishing problem of prairie fires.

> We started out on an exploring expedition to hunt Indians when we left Camp Pope. On the prairies there are enemies of different sorts — Indians, dust, heat, and fire. The latter is a most formidable weapon with the Indian if the grass is plentiful and the weather dry, and they can use

Top, left: Chief Sitting Bull (Library of Congress). *Top, right:* Chief Gall (Library of Congress). *Bottom, left:* Chief Standing Buffalo (Library of Congress). *Bottom, right:* Chief Two Moons (Library of Congress).

it to great advantage if the attacking party is not cool headed. Our sentinels were instructed to report fire at once, no matter how far off it might appear to be. This enemy came in good time — it appeared one night when there was a high wind. The flames spread, becoming one vast sheet, sweeping over the prairies — a very roaring cataract of fire, the bellows of which reached to the clouds. Coming on at this rapid, relentless rate, it would envelop and destroy the whole command. To Arms! To Arms! We are called, by bugle and by drum and in the face of this enemy, at "double quick," we march out to meet it. In case of fire the animals are frenzied, and it was a question at one time whether there would be a stampede. The only way to conquer this sort of an enemy is to fight fire with fire, so we started our fire and as it burned away from us, we took possession of the burnt area as the fire demon in the rear came roaring on high, the dense smoke obscured the moon and the stars, the atmosphere was stifling and thick with coal black dust, and the roar, as the fire fiend rolled on towards us, would have struck terror to the stoutest heart did we not know that the fury would soon be spent.[33]

George Pettie's diary records:

Camp Crooks Tuesday, June 16th Left Camp Pope at 8 A.M., made 8 miles and encamped on the Min River at 2 P.M.

Wednesday June 17th

Left Camp Crooks at 6 A.M. and arrived at Wood Lake at 5 P.M. and pitched tents near the old battle grounds where the 3rd Min fought and routed the Sioux with so much bravery nearly one year ago instance: 14 miles.[34]

The column was five miles long and traveled at a rate of about ten to twenty miles a day. Sibley's column finally reached the Dakota Territory border on 26 June. During this march, 17,500 rations of hard bread had been consumed and the doomsday predictions of the politicians seemed vindicated: it appeared that the column could not support itself very long. Sibley chose the obvious solution and sent wagons to nearby Fort Abercrombie for resupply.[35] The Tenth was the lead regiment behind Sibley and his headquarters troops, but Sibley soon established a rotation of the positions of the regiments in the line of march.

The troops were greeted with grisly sights as they moved west. The unburied bodies of civilians murdered by the Sioux were found along the trail. The troops stopped to bury them. In his diary prior to this campaign, James R. Hart of D Company of the Tenth reported, "Just after leaving the woods the body of a man killed by Indians was discovered beside the road. The body had been terribly mutilated. The abdomen had been cut open, the intestines taken out, and the head cut off and placed in the empty abdomen. A grave was quickly dug and the body was given burial."[36] Some thought that these sorts of finds would lead to atrocities against the Sioux by Sibley's soldiers, but they were not undisciplined and later deaths of Sioux women and children were more the result of collateral damage than murder.

The greatest complaint that the press, government, and citizens had against Sibley was that he was too slow. Sibley, who was never popular with the press, was called by the *Saint Cloud Democrat* "the state undertaker with his company of gravediggers."[37] He fit the description Lincoln applied to General McClellan: "He has a case of the slows."[38] This caused Lincoln to replace McClellan with Pope and Pope was then replaced by McClellan and sent west. The difference between the two was that Sibley would win but "the Indians laughed at Sibley's slow movements, thinking his failure to move ahead was incredible. They concluded that white people did not care much for their women and children."[39] The criticism was less than fair. In spite of the Sioux War of the previous year, Sibley was still faced with the problem of moving 1400 untrained troops that needed to be trained while on the move.

The Tenth had companies engaged at the battles of New Ulm, Fort Ridgley and Big Woods, but most of the troops had not seen action and the regiment had not fought as a single unit. Training was a problem. As an example, Captain Robson of E Company, Tenth Regiment, was killed on 8 November 1862 when a pistol accidentally discharged as Lieutenant McCarty was handing it to him.[40] Apparently, McCarty got over the fact that he had accidentally killed one of his fellow officers since he went on to serve during the Dakota Territory campaign the following year. There were many complaints by the troops. The ammunition did not fit the muskets. As a result there was a scramble to fix the problem. Lead tea pots and other lead items were melted down to mold .69 caliber round bullets. All of this was going on while the new troops were moving and training for a major showdown with the Sioux. Ramsey was starting to feel the pressure and his patience was running thin. In frustration, he cabled Lincoln and demanded three thousand modern rifled muskets and five hundred horses to replace those lost at Birch Coulee. Halleck and Lincoln responded the same day by assigning John Pope as commander in the West. This was not what Ramsey had in mind; however, finally, the supply system started to work. Equipment started to arrive in time for the Dakota campaign.

The cavalry also had its problems. When a trooper of Brackett's battalion tried to spur his pony forward, it would not move. Soldiers observing the trooper told him that his spurs were not touching the pony. The rider was tall and the pony thin. The trooper's spurs were not touching the pony but were shredding the bottom of his pants under the pony. One soldier yelled "Put your spurs on the calf of your legs and that will fetch 'im."[41]

While Sibley was moving so was General Alfred Sully in the West. Pope gave General Sully command of the Union column moving up the Missouri River. Sully was a remarkable officer. He was the son of Thomas Sully, the artist, who painted our early presidents. Alfred graduated from West Point in 1841 and was an experienced officer who had served in the Mexican War and on the frontier in Minnesota before the Civil War. He took command of the First Minnesota Infantry Regiment at the start of the Civil War and served with distinction at the Battles of Bull Run, Antietam, and Fredericksburg, where he was wounded. His career now became entwined with that of General John Pope, Lincoln's commander in the East. Lincoln and General Halleck, his army commander, decided to send both Pope and Sully West to fight the Indian war. Sully was well-disciplined and instilled that in his soldiers. He had also inherited his father's artistic abilities and frequently sketched while on campaign. It is there that the similarity to his father ended. Alfred had a fiery temper and while usually calm and soft-spoken, when aroused, his temper was described by his troops as being similar to that of the wrath of God. Sergeant J. H. Dripps of the Sixth Iowa Cavalry summarized: "General Sully had no superior as an Indian fighter, but he had one enemy he never conquered and that was his ungovernable temper. If he was crossed or criticized he would fairly foam with rage."[42] Many of his outbursts were directed at the gold miners. They slowed Sully down as they wandered into his camp seeking protection from the Sioux. They were also the cause of many of the Indian problems, as Sully would discover as he moved west. The meeting of the two columns never happened due to unforeseen events.

Sibley reached the Sheyenne River near what is now Valley City, North Dakota, on Saturday, 4 July 1863, the day after the Battle of Gettysburg concluded in the East. The regiment halted waiting for a train of supplies from Fort Abercrombie. Upon the arrival of Lieutenant Colonel Averill with a detachment of cavalry and the supplies from Fort Abercrombie, the Tenth moved on. The regiments were being rotated with the Tenth in the front every third day. Position in the column was very important. If a regiment was in the front at the start of battle it would bear the brunt of the fighting (and the casualties). If in the rear, a regiment would be in reserve or digging defensive positions. With a column five miles long, Sibley could not bring up all of his forces to quickly engage the Sioux in a surprise battle. On July 4, the Tenth was the last in the line of march. Colonel Baker reported that for the first time, soldiers saw herds of buffalo. The march was monotonous. Sod was thrown up at night to protect the Tenth. The Tenth had breakfast at 3 A.M. and was on the march by 6 A.M. In the words of Colonel Baker that may fill many with discomfort, "Water in most of the lakes [was] so alkaline as not to be used for drink, or if so used, was followed with dysenteric results more or less aggravated."[43]

George Pettie's diary records:

Saturday July 4th 1863 Camp Hays

A black eagle caught very young. The train was set in motion this morning at 4., the morning being cloudy with a cooling breeze we start off in very good shape, at 12 noon crosses the Sheyenne river and camped upon its right bank pleasantly located upon a beautiful table where we find plenty of grass ready for the scythe, 1000 acres at least and good water by digging only seven feet one well being sufficient for a whole Reg. Distance 10 miles. We heard of about a hundred buffalo were seen near the river today, and one elk. The National Salute of thirty four guns [sic] was fired by the Cavalry. Which constitutes our celebration of our nation's birthday.[44]

Sibley's description of the march was better than any other.

The region traveled by my column between the first crossing of the Sheyenne River and the Coteau of the Missouri is for the most part uninhabitable. If the devil were permanently to select a residence upon earth, he would probably choose this particular district for an abode, with the redskins' murdering and plundering bands as his ready ministers, to verify by their ruthless deeds his diabolical hatred to all who belong to a Christian race. Though the vast desert lakes fair to the eye abound, but generally their waters are strongly alkaline or intensely bitter and brackish. The valleys between them frequently reek with sulphur and other disagreeable vapors. The heat was so intolerable that the earth was like a heat furnace and the breezes that swept along its surface were as scorching and suffocating as the famed sirocco. Yet through all these difficulties, men and animals toiled on until objectives of the expedition were accomplished.[45]

George Pettie's diary records:

Friday July 17th 1863.

This morning we leave camp at 4 o'clock. Marched very slow. Halted at 1 oclock at another very small lake or pond of tolerable good water but the boys chose to dig wells rather than use the lake water. Detailed for poleese [sic] work digging rifle pits and entrenching. The most of the prairie that we passed over today is very rolling and some very beautiful natural mounds are scattered along the route, weather dry and dusty. Distance 15 miles. This morning the officer of the guard reports that a Sentinel belonging to Co. 8 [sic], 10th was found asleep on his post the first of the kind in this reg.[46]

Boredom ended on 24 July 1863.

The Battle of Big Mound, Friday, 24 July 1863

There was not much fighting going on. Sibley immediately followed up; after the killing of Dr. Weiser, the Indians on the other side commenced to run and a few old men that had gone to the front, expecting to have a talk, were caught up by soldiers and killed.[47]

— Chief Little Fish

Firsthand sketch of the Battle of Big Mound, where Sibley defeated the Sioux (from Connolly, *A Thrilling Narrative...*).

A group of buffalo hunters entered Sibley's camp to report that they had seen a large group of Indians with as many as 600 lodges. This was Chief Standing Buffalo's Sisseton band. Standing Buffalo was friendly with the army authorities in Minnesota, but they informed him in 1862 that after all of the murders by the Sioux, all Indians would be shot on sight. This was discouraging news. Standing Buffalo fled Minnesota with his band and eventually found his way into Sibley's path. On 24 July 1863 at Big Mound, near what is now Crystal Springs, North Dakota, Standing Buffalo learned that Sibley's column was approaching and he sent words of peace to Sibley. A parley ensued that did not go well. There was rumor that some young warriors would try to kill Sibley so the general insisted that negotiations be conducted in his camp. Word of this was sent to a small hillock where emissaries were meeting and where discussions had turned to less than friendly. Dr. Josiah S. Weiser, the surgeon of one of the regiments, wandered into the meeting. He saw Indians standing nearby and thought that he recognized them. In an act of stupidity he said, "Let's go out and shake hands with our friends." and with that he rode over to the group. Others instantly realized that this was a bad idea and stayed behind. When Weiser reached the group, he had just started to speak when a Santee named Tall Crown shot him through the heart. Apparently Tall Crown thought that Weiser was Sibley.[48]

Iron Hoop, who was with Standing Buffalo's band, recalled that they were gathered at Standing Buffalo's lodge. All of the old men were standing together and talking. They started to walk toward Sibley's camp when Dr. Weiser was shot. "Sibley immediately followed up; after the killing of Dr. Weiser, the Indians on the other side commenced to run and a few old men that had gone to the front, expecting to have a talk, were caught up by soldiers and killed."[49] The fight was on and history would call it the Battle of Big Mound, the first battle of the Dakota War. T. J. Hunt of the Tenth recalled that on 24 July, a little after noon, the Indians were located about a mile to their front and the troops were eager to advance after the murder of Weiser but were held in check by Sibley. "A stony hill within easy cannon shot was black with hundreds of Indians when our shells began to burst among them, and our skirmish lines advanced to battle. They did not stand our bullets, but precipitately fled while we advanced."[50] The pursuit continued until after dark when a miscommunication caused the troops to turn about and march all the way back from where they had started. "Thus the fifteen miles of our return took the entire night, and no man reached camp before daylight.[51]

Colonel Samuel Jennison, who led the charge at Nashville and was badly wounded (Minnesota Historical Society).

Colonel Jennison had time to get forward because of the negotiations that ended promptly with the demise of Weiser. Thus a part of the Tenth was engaged while Baker dug defensive positions in the rear. Captain Edgerton of B Company, Tenth Regiment, advanced with the artillery and Sibley to a nearby hill where fire could be placed on the Indians. This and supporting rifle fire forced the Indians back to their camp five miles to the rear. Standing Buffalo was fighting a delaying action to allow the women and children to escape. The estimated strength of the Sioux at this time was 1,500 including women and children. Sibley's force with part of the Tenth pursued but miscommunications and a brief thunderstorm delayed and confused the advance. Mistakenly, part of Sibley's force was told to return to camp. In the end it was a victory for Sibley because the Sioux, encumbered by their wives and children, panicked and fled leaving their camp behind. Sibley reported that he chased the Indians for twelve miles, moving a total of forty miles without a rest.[52]

George Pettie's diary records:

Battle of Big Mound Camp Sibley Friday July 24th 1863

Left camp this morning at 4½ A.M. Run on the Indians at 12 P.M., completed our entrenching at 3, at 3¼ P.M. the Indians opened the battle by killing Dr. Wizer [sic]. The 1st general charge was made by Co. D. of the Cavalry. Two only of the Cav being killed by the Indians.... Total loss in killed 5 or six in missing nearly as many. Those of the enemy are known to be 30 at least killed, many wounded. Our wounded amount to about a dozen. They were routed by the artillery and chased by them with Cavalry about 15 miles when darkness put an end to the conflict. Prairie dogs seen today. An Antelope was killed today three others seen. Distance 15 miles.[53]

Sibley claimed losses to the Sioux were eighty killed and wounded. Standing Buffalo would later claim his losses were between fifteen and thirty people. Sibley's force lost several, including the unfortunate Weiser and a private killed by lightning. Lieutenant Freeman also died. He was near Weiser. Lieutenant Beaver (sometimes spelled Beever) was also killed. It was Beaver who had misinterpreted Sibley's order sending troops back to where they had started rather than merely stopping the advance. Beaver had taken a wrong turn and was ambushed and killed along with Private Miller of the Sixth Regiment. Twenty-one of the dead Sioux had been scalped in the last charge. Sibley was outraged: "I am ashamed to say that all were scalped. Shame upon such brutality! God's image should not be thus mutilated or disfigured."[54] Sibley's outrage was genuine. He had reacted in the same manner when he learned that Little Crow's body had been mutilated in Minnesota after he was shot by a settler. In spite of Sibley's orders, the troops took a different view as summarized by Captain L. W. Collins, Seventh Minnesota Regiment: "In all Indian wars, whites have indulged in scalp-taking, more, perhaps, 'as evidence of good faith,' as the newspapers are prone to say, than for any other purpose. No exception to the barbarous practice was made in our command; in fact, it was currently reported that the colonel commanding the cavalry told his men that he had a good deal rather see the scalps than to hear them talk, and probably lie, about the sure-enough dead after the fight."[55]

Captain Loren Collins of the Seventh Minnesota Regiment (Minnesota Historical Society).

Losses to Standing Buffalo's band went far beyond the battle. Supplies left behind or destroyed in the panicked retreat would be needed in the coming winter and lives would be lost because of that. Standing Buffalo fled north and would continue to be haunted by disaster. As darkness fell on the Big Mound battlefield, the troops stopped, totally exhausted. Captain L. W. Collins, gave an account of the sleepless night: "Cold, hungry, thirsty and slightly profane, we stretched ourselves upon the damp earth, realizing that daybreak would find us stiff and sore from the long march of about forty miles and the uncomfortable night to follow."[56] While Sibley was proclaiming a great victory, the Sioux knew that nearly all of Standing Buffalo's band had escaped and many other Indians were moving in to attack. Sibley was moving into an ambush.

Baker had lost none of his troops in this intense battle, but the Tenth lost two days in the confusion and exhaustion following the battle, as did most of the other regiments. They resumed their march on 26 July. As Standing Buffalo fled, hundreds of other warriors were swarming toward Sibley's column. These were Teton Sioux that may have included Sitting Bull. They intended to attack and defeat the whites. About 1,600 warriors were available to fight. Since the start of the campaign and before, gold miners and other whites had been indiscriminately murdering Sioux men, women and children. Part of this was greed, but more of it was retaliation for the settlers slaughtered in Minnesota. The result of this was that as Sibley moved west, losing men daily from disease, death, and wounds, the strength of the hostile force was rapidly building and they wanted revenge. As the column moved through Standing Buffalo's abandoned camp, they encountered the litter of war. Clothing, utensils and even plunder taken in the Minnesota war the previous year were scattered along the trail. Dead animals, including hundreds of buffalo, were everywhere. The fragrance of one dead buffalo was startling. As John Burnham of the Tenth Minnesota's Company C put it, "We did not need sight of it to be aware of its presence."[57] Later when Sibley sent Father Alexis Andre on a peace mission to arrange a surrender, Standing Buffalo and the other Sisseton Chiefs made the following reply.

Captain John Burnham years after the war (Minnesota Historical Society).

> We believe in your words, for you have pity on us, and lies do not cross your lips — It is not the Black Robe who will betray us — but you know how deceitful and [what] liars the Americans are. Your heart is too good to realize how bad theirs is — you are sincere but who can assure us of the sincerity of the Americans. Maybe it is to fool us that they sent you, for we would not have listened to anybody else but you. If traders or others had been sent to talk to us of peace, we would have ignored them as passing little birds, or little dogs barking at our doors, and we would not have paid any attention to their words. We will take council on what you have just told us.[58]

When the chiefs learned that the army had killed several Sisseton women and children, all thought of surrender disappeared.

The Battle of Dead Buffalo Lake, Sunday, 26 July 1863

> *The boys have scalped all that they could get hold of thus far, as nearly as can be ascertained we have 15 scalps today among which is a chief, White Bear, which added to those of the 24th makes about 50 but the probability is that we only get about one half of those we killed, and loss today thus far, 5 P.M. is only one mortally wounded none killed.*[59]
>
> — George Pettie's Diary

Around noon on the 26th, warriors appeared in Sibley's front and flanks. The Battle of Dead Buffalo Lake had started. Because of its position in the column, the Tenth did not participate. The Sixth Minnesota Infantry was in the lead and took the brunt of the Sioux attack. After some prancing around by the Sioux in an attempt to flank the Sixth, the Mounted Rangers drove them back. Artillery was brought forward and fired on the Sioux, and they decided to leave. Late in the day an unusual event occurred as the soldiers prepared to bivouac. The Sioux attacked a group of teamsters gathering hay for their animals. They attacked in earnest and the Sixth and the cavalry responded in full force with flags flying. Because of the dust kicked up by the horses and evening haze, it was difficult to figure out who was doing what to whom. It became a case of everyone on both sides firing all the ammunition that they could lay their hands on when they could not see anything. When the dust settled and as dark moved in, it appeared that two soldiers and two Sioux had been killed and a Teton Sioux chief was seen prancing around taunting the whites to fight. Some say it was Sitting Bull, but this has not been confirmed.[60] The fact was that everyone on both sides was dead tired (or dead) and they decided to go to bed, Sitting Bull or not.

George Pettie's diary records:

Camp Profender, Sunday July 26th 1863

Started this morning at 5 A.M. march 15 miles and found the enemy about 12 o clock. Our teams were immediately corralled and fighting commences by opening upon them with the battery.[61]

This ended the Battle of Dead Buffalo Lake.

Sully's Dilemma, Wednesday, 13 May 1863

Meanwhile in the West, Sully was having his problems arranging the movement of supplies. More bad news was waiting for Sully. The friendly Sioux were guaranteed an annuity as a result of their treaty with the United States. The annuity had not arrived due to the war and bureaucratic reasons. More and more of the friendly Sioux were becoming very unfriendly and joining the Teton Sioux and others. Something had to done because as Sully moved forward converting or killing the Sioux, more were joining the hostiles and he was fighting a losing campaign as was Sibley for similar reasons. A remarkable person now entered history. Captain Joseph Marie LaBarge was a Southerner who opposed slavery.

Captain LaBarge — The man who taught Mark Twain about the Mississippi River (Minnesota Historical Society).

In personal appearance, Captain LaBarge was one of the most distinguished looking men of the West in his time. He stood five feet ten, was well proportioned, weighed about 180 pounds, was erect, muscular, and alert with a sharp, quick eye and a quiet energy in all his movements. He always wore a beard after reaching manhood's estate, and in later years bore a striking resemblance to General Grant.[62]

He was also the owner of a fleet of steamboats and a friend of Samuel Clemens (Mark Twain) who was a riverboat pilot at this time. Mark

Twain would write of LaBarge years later. LaBarge was a Union contractor who moved supplies for the Union Army on the Mississippi and Missouri rivers. Sully needed action and LaBarge appeared to be the solution. With his fleet of steamboats he could solve problems. The Union Army had previously hired LaBarge to move northwest on the Missouri with the supplies for the friendly tribes agreed by treaty: obviously, that meant move as quickly as possible.

The odyssey of LaBarge's ship, the *Robert Campbell, Junior* started as LaBarge cast-off from St. Louis on Wednesday, 13 May 1863.[63] This was not an easy task. He would be confronted by Confederate guerrillas as well as hostile Sioux. Additionally, no one knew where the friendly tribes were, but it was evident that with the annuity on board, they would find LaBarge. Word got around fast on the Missouri.

The *Campbell* carried thirty passengers, including two women and two children. In view of frequent attacks on the river by Confederate guerrillas, a force of thirty Union soldiers and a cannon were on board. The boat was barricaded with cargo on the deck to protect the troops. The soldiers were needed since the Confederates did attack frequently, but LaBarge kept the *Campbell* in the center of the river and anchored there at night rather than tying up on shore.[64] The $75,000 in annuity goods owed to the friendly tribes reached Fort Pierre (now Pierre, South Dakota) on 20 June. The *Campbell* reached Fort Berthold on Independence Day and distributed some of the goods.[65] Since LaBarge had to collect wood for the boilers, he occasionally had to stop and land. This usually meant a fight since the Sioux had followed the *Campbell* for hundreds of miles. The *Campbell* fought off Indian attacks on the 5th and 6th of July.[66] On the 7th of July, a major fight erupted with several hundred hostiles who had lined the shore. Several of the crew were killed when they unwisely rowed to shore in a yawl to parley with the Sioux.[67] LaBarge was able to fight them off although they had boarded his vessel and extinguished his boilers. He finally reached Fort Union several days later to deliver the rest of the goods.[68] While LaBarge's trials were over, the friendly tribes had to return to their camps with their supplies. They were molested along the way by gold miners and hostiles who wanted the supplies. Many lost their supplies and some were killed. Even so, LaBarge's single peace mission probably saved more lives than Sully would ever know.

On 20 June 1863, Sully moved north out of Sioux City with his force of about 1,200 troops. Most of these were cavalry. They were to trap the Indians far to the north at Devil's Lake in Dakota Territory as Sibley's column converged. By the 25th of July, the date established for him to link up with Sibley, Sully was at Fort Pierre, hundreds of miles south of Devil's Lake. The plan was for him to move northwest along the Missouri River with his supplies on steamboats, but at this time, due to the drought, the Missouri River was at record low levels. This meant that supplies had to be off-loaded onto smaller vessels, landed and placed on animals or destroyed. This caused delays as Sully continued his crawl north along the banks of the Missouri. While Sully crawled in the West, Sibley was about to blunder into a major Sioux encampment and would find himself fighting for his life.

The Battle of Stony Lake, Tuesday, 28 July 1863

> *In their courage and earnest desire to clear the enemy from the hill by a double quick charge my officers and men were a unit. Nothing but the imminent peril of the train could induce them to cease the advance they had so gallantly begun.*[69]
>
> — James H. Baker

Firsthand sketch of the Battle of Stony Lake on 28 July 1863, where Sibley defeated the Indians (from Connolly, *A Thrilling Narrative...*).

As the hostile force continued to build after the battle of Dead Buffalo Lake, Sibley resumed his march on 27 July. Predawn reveille sounded on the 28th and the Tenth was the lead regiment. Sibley led his column with a few scouts and small headquarters element with the Tenth close behind and about one-half mile ahead of the rest of the column when all hell broke loose. It was difficult to determine who surprised whom. Sibley's column was approaching Stony Lake and moving up a rise when Sibley's scouts, riding as fast as they could, returned to the column shouting, "They are coming! They are coming!"[70] At the same time two Sioux warriors mounted a crest above the column. "We are too late, they are ready for us," the first one said, but the second yelled, "But remember our children and families; we must not let them get them!"[71] The Sioux quickly mounted an attack against the Tenth with a force of 2,500 warriors. Baker deployed his regiment on either side of the trail as the rest of the column rushed forward to join the fight.[72] History would call this the Battle of Stony Lake. Baker was outnumbered by about three to one, but he, Sibley and the headquarters element put up a determined fight. Two factors saved them all. First, two sections of artillery under Captain Jones (promoted from sergeant after he was credited with saving Fort Ridgley the previous year) and Lieutenant Whipple joined the fight and put steady fire on the Sioux which cooled their ardor. Second, the Sixth and Seventh Minnesota Regiments arrived and joined Baker's line. In his report of 5 August 1863, Baker provided the best summary of the action since his regiment was in the lead and he saw the entire battle unfold.

His account was in line with others and he closed his report with a commendation: "The number of Indians so suddenly charging upon us was estimated at not less than 1,500 to 2,000. They were well mounted, and moved about with the utmost rapidity, and with their characteristic hideous yells. Nothing could exceed the eagerness, firmness and gallant bearing of all the officers and men of my command during this unexpected, and by far, numerically, the greatest, effort the Indians had yet made upon the forces of the expedition."[73]

George Pettie related what he saw after they started the march at 4:30 A.M. They had gone only a mile when they were attacked by 1500 Indians (the real number was closer to 2500). Pettie was in the advance guard, ahead of virtually everyone else in the column, and witnessed the entire battle unfolding close by: perhaps too close. Pettie saw successive Indian attacks on all sides: "The old Chief I think attempted to charge on our front but finding the battery with us, his braves failed him and he shifted tack and tried to get into the rear of the train. Finding a mortar at our rear also, he appeared confused, retreated about two miles, collected his forces and charged on our left flank. There he met with the same treatment and failing to affect anything he struck up a retreat and left the field, leaving a few dead on the ground."[74]

Sergeant Ramer of the Seventh Regiment recalled, "July 28th we struck tents at six o'clock. Soon after starting the Indians pitched into us again. The fight lasted three-quarters of an hour when they fled. The teams formed in lines near together, some five or six lines wide, one infantry regiment marching in front [the Tenth] and one either side forming a square. We marched that way most of the day."[75] Sibley reported "This proof of confidence in our own strength completely destroyed the hopes of the savages, and completed their discomfiture. With yells of disappointment and rage, they fired a few parting volleys, and retreated with expedition. It was not possible, with our jaded horses, to overtake their fleet, and comparatively fresh ponies."[76] The Battle of Stony Lake was over. Incredibly, Sibley's column had lost no soldiers in the fighting. Sibley estimated that the size of the Indian camp was "10,000 souls" composed of Sioux, Sissetons, Cut-heads, and Yank-ton-ais [sic]."[77] Sibley was guessing. Neither Sibley nor any other soldier at that time knew the chiefs or tribes that opposed them. Indian sources later identified the Indian force as Wahpekute and Inkpaduta with some Tetons and Yankton.[78] The Sisseton and Wahpeton had left for Canada after the Battle of Big Mound. Appendix F provides a description of the tribes.

Sibley's column pushed on another eighteen miles beyond Stony Lake in pursuit of the Indians before reaching the Missouri River not far from today's Bismarck, North Dakota. Sibley would later claim that they found eleven Indian bodies, but John Burnham of C Company of the Tenth, in his reminiscences, did not recall seeing any bodies.[79] The Indians would later claim that they lost more people from drowning during their crossing of the Missouri River than during the entire campaign. Frank Jetty, a young half-breed, was there with his mother and he recalled:

> When the Indians arrived between Mandan and Bismarck, N. Dak., below the hills of the river shore, they camped. Sibbly [sic] and his soldiers watched them four miles from the encampment to encircle them the next morning. When the Indians perceived [sic] that they were discovered, they started to improvise boats with small trees on which they tied buffalo hides. All during the night the Indian swimmers guided these boats across the river with ropes held between their teeth. Thus, all who could not swim and the women, children and belongings were carried across. Only a poor old squaw who had died during the night remained behind. The Indians had prepared her well. The next morning, the soldiers found her sitting, waiting for them. When the soldiers waw [saw] they were tricked, they returned [to Minnesota].[80]

Sibley's effective use of his artillery and cavalry, a lethal combination, had defeated the tribes in all three battles and driven them back across the Missouri River.[81] Sibley estimated Indian losses during his campaign at one hundred and fifty dead.[82] He had traveled 585 miles from Fort Snelling to the Missouri River. Sibley decided to turn back to Minnesota. In his report he provided his reasons: "I felt that this column had done everything possible within the limits of human and animal endurance, and that a farther pursuit would not only be useless, as the Indians could cross and recross the river in much less time than could my command, and thus evade me, but would necessarily be attended with the loss of many valuable lives."[83] He was a politician and he knew that he had won three engagements which would look good in the press back home. Why press your luck and try for four? Most important, he had accomplished his mission, which was to drive the hostiles west of the Missouri River. He was not bothered by the fact that he and Sully had failed to link up in the effort to trap the Sioux at Devil's Lake, just north of Sibley's position.

A few days were spent on the Missouri with the Sioux firing out-of-range shots from the west side while Sibley's troops did the same from the eastern bank of the Missouri River. Private James R. Hart recalled that they fired rocket signals but received no reply from Sully's column.[84] Sully's column was hundreds of miles away. Hart's description of the material left behind by the Indians on the east shore of the Missouri River is of interest: "It consisted of many tepees, one hundred seventy-five wagons and buggies, stolen from Minnesota settlers and loaded with household goods stolen from the settlers, thirty tons of dried buffalo

A sketch of Little Crow meditating on the shore of Devil's Lake as imagined in Connolly's *A Thrilling Narrative*....

meat, and strangest of all, a new J.I. Case threshing machine separator which had been stolen in Minnesota, and hauled out there with oxen."[85]

On 31 July, Sibley decided to hold a victory parade and while the soldiers sweated in the hot sun and the Sioux looked down in amazement from the west bank of the Missouri, Sibley gave an address complimenting the soldiers on their great victory over the Indians.[86] There is no record of any Indian comment on this very strange assembly. George Pettie recalled the scene: "The General's address to his command was read at dress Parade, in which he compliments them highly for their good conduct, the patience with which they endured the hardships of the march, and their skill and bravery in action and notified them that in the morning they would be called upon to pack up and start for home."[87] Pettie reported that the mood of the troops was not joy. They knew that they had not conquered the enemy.[88] "Until this is done, our work is not done, while the enemy cuts his pranks and shakes his blankets in our faces in defiance upon the Bluffs upon the other side of the river we cannot wish to meet our friends."[89]

Sully's Luck, Saturday, 1 August 1863

> *I never had the slightest idea that you [Sully] could delay thus along the River, nor do I realize the necessity of such delay ... I never dreamed you would consider yourself tied to the boats if they were obstacles in going up river.*[90]
> — John Pope

Sibley's column turned back on 1 August, and the Sioux recrossed the Missouri to trail and taunt his column. No history of this campaign would be complete without the story of the Mackinaw boat, an incident that may have cost more white and Indian lives than the entire campaign. The name came from the 17th and 18th centuries in the Straits of Mackinac when someone discovered that it was possible to use a retractable centerboard on a canoe hull so a sail could be added. The Mackinaw boat was as long as fifty feet with a twelve foot beam. It was used during the fur-trading era. It had a crew of five, four oarsmen and a steersman, and could carry up to fifty tons of cargo. They ran from fifteen to eighteen hours per day and could make 75 to 150 miles (a very optimistic estimate, probably by the boat builders).[91] On the Missouri River it hauled a great deal of cargo but sails were seldom used. On 3 August 1863 as Sibley was leaving the Missouri River, the tribes re-crossed the river. As the tribes were crossing, they spotted a Mackinaw boat on the Missouri River. This was bad luck for the Mackinaw boat and a windfall for the Indians. On board was a group of miners from Boise, Idaho, with a great deal of gold that they had mined. The party on the Mackinaw included seventeen miners, two half-breeds, one woman and two children. The Indians attacked and in the course of the fighting, all on board were killed but not before ninety-one Indians were killed and an unknown number wounded. The numbers are suspect but it is certain that all of the whites and half-breeds were dead and the boat was sunk. It may still be there. The boat had an estimated $100,000 in gold and paper: an enormous fortune at that time. Value of gold today would place this worth at over seven million dollars. Legend now intervenes. The Indians are said to have joined Little Crow and told him that they had lifted $18,000 to $20,000 from the dead miners to buy weapons. This is very curious since Little Crow was killed a month before the Mackinaw boat attack. The only gold beyond the $18,000-$20,000 is said to have been later found in

Print of the Missouri River Indian attack on the Mackinaw Boat from the nineteenth century print by William de la Montagne Cary (Library of Congress).

a coffee pot and given to a trader named Gerard by the Sioux in return for a horse.[92] It appears that Gerard probably got the better part of the deal. The rest of the gold may still be out there.

On 3 August, Sully was stalled hundreds of miles to the south waiting for supplies. The Missouri was down to a trickle in some places. By this time, Sully was receiving more than his fair share of criticism from Pope and others for his slow progress. Relations between Sully and Pope had never been ideal, and they would get much worse. On 20 August Pope complained to General Halleck in Washington, "General Sully has not made the progress expected of him, and which it is in his power to have made, but the Indians were so badly worsted by Sibley, and are in so destitute a condition, that he has nothing to do except follow up Sibley's success with ordinary energy and the whole of the Indians on the upper Missouri will be reduced to a state of quiet which had not been obtained in some years."[93]

Pope's summary was farfetched. The losses to the Indians as a result of Sibley's campaign were at most 150 Indians killed or wounded and many of these were old men, women and children. The warriors killed or wounded were a small fraction of those engaged. The greatest loss was the supplies abandoned and destroyed as described by Private Hart of the Tenth and Hart's description represented only the material destroyed on the Missouri. Much more had been lost along the way to the Missouri River. These material losses would not be felt until the following winter when the Indians would freeze or starve because of what they lost that past summer. In August of that year, the Indians were still spoiling for a fight and would outnumber Sully if they chose to confront him, but Sully's luck had started to change.

The Battle of Whitestone Hill, Thursday, 3 September 1863

Sully finally left Fort Pierre on 14 August and was able to rendezvous with the steamboat *Belle Peoria* on the 19th. After resupply, he moved forward again toward Devil's Lake. Fortune shone on 28 August when the column came across an old friendly Indian recognized from Sioux City by some of the whites. He had been robbed of his horse by hostiles and was on the verge of starving. He related the victory by Sibley at Stony Lake among other things and then told Sully what he wanted to hear. The Indians had re-crossed the Missouri and were now encamped west of Sully's column. With a cavalry heavy force and recently resupplied, Sully could move with alarming speed, but it still took him five days to locate the Indian camp and prepare his attack. The camp included about three to four thousand people including fifteen hundred warriors. Although down significantly from the previous month because some of the tribes that had left after Stony Hill, the Indian force still outnumbered Sully, and they would be fighting to protect their wives and children. Sully would later learn that he had been followed for days by Sioux hoping to steal his livestock. For some reason they had not warned the Indian camp, so Sully had the element of surprise, but only one battery of artillery. It was late in the day on the 3rd of September when scouts arrived to report that the Sioux encamped at Whitestone Hill were unaware of Sully's presence. As the cavalry horses grazed, the bugler sounded "Boots and Saddles" and the troops mounted for the attack. It took the brigade less than an hour to reach the Indian camp ten miles away.

The advance unit, Major House's Third Battalion, arrived and attempted to surround the Indian camp. It was too big. House was far ahead of the brigade. Sully would be up against a variety of tribes including Blackfeet, Cut-Heads, Santees, Tetons, Yanktonais, and Hunkpapas. The chiefs did the obvious thing and called for a parlay with House while the army cavalry horses cooled down. The Indians were also buying time so that the women and children could evacuate the camp (they had previously been ordered to cook a victory feast). More ominous: warriors were moving to encircle House's cavalry. The Indians were keeping all options open, and it appeared that they had a marvelous opportunity to destroy House's battalion before help could arrive.[94]

The question for Sully as he approached was, "Is this flight or fight?" Sully was an old soldier who had served in the West before the Civil War and he was not easily fooled by any parley. The truce ended as Sully's brigade charged. Sully's focus was to surround the camp and prevent escape. To this end, he ordered two battalions to attack the flanks of the camp while he led a frontal attack. House moved to cut off the Indian withdrawal and at first it appeared that Sully would bag the entire camp, but a miscue allowed the Indians to evade entrapment: Colonel Wilson of the 6th Iowa Cavalry ordered the men fighting on foot to remount. Horses bolted and in the confusion that followed, most Indians made their escape as darkness fell. As Private Milton Spencer put it in his letter home: "Mr. Indian, seeing the gate open, was not long in going out."[95] This ended the Battle of Whitestone Hill. Sully reported:

> I do not think I exaggerate in the least when I say that I burned up over four or five hundred thousand pounds of dried buffalo meat as one item besides the hundred lodges and a very large quantity of property of great value to the Indians. A very large number of ponies were found dead and wounded on the field and besides a large number were captured. By actual count the number of my prisoners is 156 men — 32 women and children. I would beg to say that in the action I had of my command between 600 and 700 men actually engaged. My killed numbered as far as I can ascertain: killed 20, wounded 38.[96]

What Sully did not report was that many of his killed and wounded were from friendly fire when one battalion mistakenly fired into another.[97] The task of destroying Indian supplies was started. Captain R. B. Mason, a wagon master, said that the fat ran in streams from the burning meat.[98] This was a dreadful waste and a loss to the tribes that were engaged. It was their winter supply of meat and represented over one thousand slaughtered buffalo.[99] Samuel J. Brown, an interpreter at the Santee Agency, provided the Indian version of the battle in a letter to his father:

> I hope you will not believe all that is said of "Sully's successful expedition," against the Sioux. I don't think he should brag about it at all, because it was what no decent man would have done, he pitched into their camp and just slaughtered them, worse a great deal than what the Indians did in 1862, he killed *very few* men and took *no* hostile ones prisoners, he took some but they were friendly Yanktons, and he let them go again.... It is lamentable to hear how those women and children were slaughtered it was a perfect massacre, and now he returns saying that we need to fear no more, for he has "wiped out all hostile Indians from Dakota," if he had killed men instead of women & children, then it would have been a success, and the worse of it, they had no hostile intention whatever, the Nebraska 2nd pitched into them without orders, while the Iowa 6th were shaking hands with them.[100]

Sully estimated the number of enemy killed as about one hundred and fifty.[101] It would be a long, hungry winter for the tribes. This ended Sully's campaign and he returned to Fort Pierre arriving on 14 September with his supplies nearly exhausted.[102] While Sully was fighting it out with the tribes at Whitestone Hill, Sibley was travelling back to Minnesota as fast as he could. The first night out two men of the Tenth died and were buried and the next day the Tenth resumed its march to Minnesota. Along the way, a strange episode unfolded as described by Private Hart of the Tenth: "While at Devils Lake Major Birch captured the son of Chief Little Crow. He was surprised and taken prisoner by a party of scouts from Devil's Lake.... From there he was sent to Fort Snelling were he was confined in jail until after the Civil War closed."[103]

Henry Boller, a civilian on board the *Robert Campbell, Junior*, observed: "The army took the field — bugles were blown, the antelope badly frightened ... while from the distant bluffs 'the d--- d redskins' definitely waved their breachclouts [sic]. Some few squaws were captured and the army went into winter quarters, the Indians having gone out of sight, and the safety of the frontiers thus being assured."[104]

Back Home at Last—The End of the Sirocco Campaign, Thursday, 1 October 1863

"Got my papers and started out with several others at 12¼ on foot for New Ulm. There we procured teams to take us through to Mankato and reached Mankato at 3 A.M."[105] Pettie's diary ends with this entry. He kept no diary the following years in the South. For the campaign of 1863, he kept track of miles traveled and calculated a distance of 542 miles from Garden City, Minnesota, to the Missouri River. While Pettie and his comrades headed home for their furlough, the remainder of the Tenth continued its march to Fort Snelling. A rest was made at Fort Abercrombie for four days and the march resumed. At Sauk Center, Minnesota, the Tenth was detached from the main column to follow the string of frontier posts to Fort Ridgley.[106] The Tenth reached Fort Snelling on 1 October, and after a furlough, the regiment would move south. This ended the Minnesota Tenth Infantry Regiment's service in the Indian wars. The Tenth had traveled 1050 miles in eighty-nine days from Camp Pope to the Missouri and the return to Fort Snelling. The Tenth's losses during this period were all from disease or accidents: eleven soldiers. General Baker summarized the Indian campaign of the Tenth: "There is no purpose here of offering criticism upon the campaign. If success was not complete, the hostile Indians were, at least, all driven beyond the Missouri River, and subsequent events would show that their power for mischief was broken."[107] Baker was wrong. While the regiments went into winter quarters, Pope was planning his follow-on campaign in Dakota Territory the following year. The Tenth and other Minnesota regiments would not be involved. They were ordered south to fight the Confederate Army.

While Pope, Sibley and Sully considered the campaigns a success, others did not. Newton Edmunds, the governor of Dakota Territory, considered both Sibley's and Sully's campaigns to be failures.

> Of the two campaigns made against the Indians last summer, one under General Sibley of Minnesota and one under General Sully, starting from Sioux City, Iowa, I am fully convinced that little, if anything, was accomplished towards the subjugation of the Indians. These two expeditions were immensely expensive to the government, and ought, in my opinion, to have brought about more decisive results. I am not prepared to say why they were failures; I leave this subject where it belongs, to the War Department, to make the inquiry; of fact, however, I have not the least doubt.[108]

Edmunds blamed the conflict on "rebel agents and selling whiskey to the Indians."[109] Most would agree with Edmunds that the campaign was a failure. The cost in terms of dollars was enormous, but never fully tabulated. The cost in terms of human lives was significant. While Sully and Sibley reported a small number of dead and wounded soldiers that were casualties of the Indians (fewer than one hundred), the loss from disease was large. The Tenth provides a good example: no soldier was killed or wounded, but eleven died of sickness or accident during this campaign. Sibley and Sully reported a combined total of three hundred dead or wounded Indians while about 150 were captured (mostly women, children and the elderly). The greatest impact was on the Indians. They were highly irritated with Ramsey's "vengeance on the plains" and would not forget. Indian warfare on the prairie would continue for nearly three more decades.[110]

CHAPTER 3

Moving South
18 September 1863–15 November 1864

To Abraham Lincoln, President of the United States:
Sir—I have ordered General A. J. Smith and General Mower from Memphis to pursue and kill Forrest, promising the latter, in case of success, my influence to promote him to major-general. He is one of the gamest men in our service. Should accident befall me, I ask you to favor Mower, if he succeeds in disposing of Forrest.[1]
— Major-General William T. Sherman

After the Tenth Regiment's furlough expired 5 October 1863, the Ninth and Tenth Minnesota Infantry assembled at Fort Snelling for the move south. The Tenth Regiment would move from Minnesota to Benton Barracks near St. Louis, Missouri, reporting to the officer commanding the Department of the Missouri at St. Louis. Most of the companies rendezvoused at Fort Snelling, and on the evening of Wednesday, October 7, on the steamer *Northern Light*, they left for Dunleith, opposite Dubuque. By the time the boat reached La Crosse all the companies were on board. Disembarking at Dunleith they proceeded by rail to East St. Louis, where they arrived on Monday morning.[2] They would stay at Benton Barracks, or Camp Benton as it was also called. It was an encampment for Union troops that could accommodate 30,000 soldiers. It contained a mile of barracks, warehouses, cavalry stables, parade grounds, and a large military hospital that could care for two to three thousand patients. It had a parole encampment and at various times held Confederate prisoners as well as freed slaves. Colonel Baker described the cold winter as severe, and it caused some suffering among the men of the regiment. The river at St. Louis froze over.[3]

The Tenth Regiment was assigned provost duty to guard prisoners and maintain order at Benton Barracks. T. J. Hunt of the Tenth described the assignment.

> At St. Louis, Co. B was soon detailed as provost guard, which duty was akin to police in civil life, but applied mainly to the soldiers, many thousands of whom were stopping there on their veteran furloughs. Our work had to be done mainly at night. Each sergeant with his squad of men paraded disengaged streets, visited every saloon, theater and dance hall, with orders to arrest all soldiers found therein (except those in theaters with written permits). This was to be continued until twelve A.M. and on certain occasions, all night. Scores were arrested in a single evening, sometimes, and locked up to be sent next morning to the proper officers with a report of their offenses. Their uniforms were the means of detection. In the daytime the work was less difficult, but inspection was daily. One evening they dispersed a mob which was smashing the windows and doors of the medical college, instigated by a report that a deceased person from a hospital was being dissected therein. The civil police were powerless, but Company B with fixed bayonets had no difficulty in driving the intruders, and in protecting the building.[4]

The Tenth would spend months at Benton Barracks waiting for the spring campaigns. In October 1863 an order arrived that would change the commanders of the Tenth. Colonel Baker was appointed to serve as commanding officer of the post of St. Louis and Lieutenant Colonel Jennison assumed command of the regiment. Jennison would remain in command of the Tenth for the remainder of the war with some time out when he was recovering from wounds.

With the New Year of 1864 came the realization that the war had tipped in favor of the Union. While thousands were yet to die, the war had little more than a year to run. While the Tenth settled into winter quarters at Benton Barracks, no major battles had been fought since November. The year 1863 saw the Confederacy lose at the Battle of Gettysburg, and in the West the confused Confederate command structure had hastened the loss of the Mississippi River Valley and the occupation of Chattanooga.[5] Ulysses S. Grant had seized Vicksburg and his victory at Port Hudson a few days later had divided the Confederacy in July 1863. Because of these successes in the West, Lincoln brought Grant east and put him in command of all Union forces. Southern dreams of foreign recognition had faded with Lincoln's Emancipation Proclamation. Slaves in the newly conquered Southern territory would be freed. The Confederacy was shrinking and was being cornered and divided by the Union. Jefferson Davis' greatest challenge was manpower and supplies. Discussions had started to enlist slaves into the Confederate Army with the promise of freedom. This would not happen until the end of the Confederacy in 1865, and by then it was too late. Winfield Scott's Anaconda Plan, envisioned in 1861 to blockade and divide the Confederacy, was working as the Confederacy started to fall apart, but there was still plenty of fight left in the South. While Sherman planned his Atlanta campaign and his march to the sea that would divide the Confederacy, John Bell Hood threatened his supply base at Chattanooga. Eighteen sixty-four would become the year of the raids. In February, General Sherman left Vicksburg, Mississippi, to destroy railroads in that state. Sherman was opposed by General Leonidas Pope. Shortly thereafter, one of the few bright spots for the Confederacy occurred on 17 February when the C.S.S. *H. L. Hunley,* which most consider the first successful submarine, sank the U.S.S. *Housatonic* in Charleston Harbor.[6] Sherman's force withdrew after its successful campaign in Mississippi. In the East, action idled with no major battles.

In March, U.S. Grant was promoted to lieutenant general and assumed command of all Union forces. General William T. Sherman replaced Grant in the West. The war would become a war of attrition. While the North could replace losses, the South could not. It was also becoming a total war with the scorched earth policy used by the Union in both the East and the West. Politics became a major driver in 1864 with Lincoln's reelection campaign coming up. Lincoln needed Union victories to secure his reelection. There had been no major action since the fall of 1863 but the killing season was about to start. In the West, General Nathan Bedford Forrest was raiding Union supply lines and on 12 April captured Fort Pillow, Tennessee. The report of a massacre of black troops by Forrest after their surrender has been disputed ever since.

In early April of 1864, the Minnesota regiments were ordered south and left St. Louis for Columbus, Kentucky. The monotony of camp life in Columbus was broken when General Nathan Bedford Forrest attacked Maysville, Kentucky, and the Minnesota regiments were ordered to pursue and cut him off. Forrest escaped and the regiments returned to Columbus after a five day effort. On the 14th of June 1864, the regiment was ordered to Memphis, Tennessee, and arrived there on the 20th. The regiment was assigned to the First Division in XVI Corps, which was commanded by Major General A. J. Smith.[7] General

Andrew Jackson Smith was described as of small stature, with rather brusque, abrupt manners, sometimes verging on irascibility, yet he was popular with his troops because he shared their hardships. General Smith was a Pennsylvanian who graduated from West Point with the Class of 1838. He ranked thirty-six in a class of forty-five.[8]

The First Division was commanded by John McArthur. McArthur was born in Erskine, Scotland, and immigrated to the U.S. at age twenty-three settling in Chicago. He is shown wearing the Scottish tam (cap), the headgear adopted by many of his troops after he took over. He had fought at the battles of Corinth and Shiloh where he was wounded. Other Minnesota regiments were also in the First Division but in different brigades. The Fifth and the Ninth Minnesota were in the Second Brigade and the Seventh Minnesota was in the Third Brigade.[9]

While the Union failed in its effort to cut off Forrest as he withdrew from Paducah, Kentucky, it would soon have another chance to engage him. In May 1864, the war in the East was heating up, including the Battle of the Wilderness, which added 25,000 to the list of dead and wounded on both sides. On 7 May, General Sherman started his march on Atlanta, which made the protection of his supply base at Chattanooga more important. While major battles in the East continued in June, activity increased to prepare for the presidential election in the fall as the casualty lists from the Wilderness and Spotsylvania battles reached homes. The war would have a profound effect on the election. As Sherman sloshed through Georgia in bad weather, Lincoln was nominated for his second term on 8 June. The Tenth was now stationed in Memphis preparing for another campaign against Forrest. On June 16, Sherman telegraphed Secretary of War Stanton: "I

General A.J. Smith, who led A. J.'s Guerrillas on several long campaigns (Library of Congress).

General McArthur, the immigrant from Scotland, wearing his Scottish tam (Library of Congress).

have made the necessary orders through General McPherson ... to send as large a force again as he can on Forrest's trail, and harass him and the country through which he passes. We must destroy him if possible." In a dispatch to McPherson he stated:

> We will not attempt the Mobile trip now, but I wish to organize as large a force as possible at Memphis, with General A. J. Smith or Mower in command, to pursue Forrest on foot, devastating the land over which he has passed, or may pass, and to make the people of Tennessee and Mississippi feel that although a bold and successful leader, he will bring ruin and misery on any country where he may pass or tarry. If we do not punish Forrest and the people now, the whole effect of our vast conquest will be lost.[10]

Total war would now be visited upon Southern citizens in the West as well as those in Georgia. As one of Smith's soldiers said: "We're A. J. Smith's guerrillas. We've been to Vicksburg, Red River, Missouri and about everywhere else ... and now we're going to Hades if old A. J. orders us."[11] The stage was set for the Battle of Tupelo and A. J. Smith's guerrillas, including the Tenth Regiment, would have a major fight on their hands.

The Battle of Tupelo, Mississippi, Thursday to Friday, 14–15 July 1864

> *We were on a smooth, inclined surface. We could not hold our shades over us or lie down, as the water was several inches deep, and running in torrents. We inverted our guns by running the bayonets into the ground, and stood and took it. Many of the boys had only their shirts on and found it difficult or impossible to get into their trousers. Myself and two others made a kind of living tripod and with all our strength held a sheet of canvass around us as if your lives depended upon it and stood or kneeled upon the garments we did not have on, to keep them from being washed away.*[12]
> — Thomas Jefferson Hunt

While Forrest was raiding, Major General A. J. Smith with 14,000 men left Lagrange, Tennessee, on 5 July 1864 to attack Forrest in Mississippi and prevent him from raiding Sherman's lifeline, a single track railroad from Chattanooga to Atlanta. The Tenth was included in Smith's combined force. Smith laid waste to the countryside as he proceeded and reached Pontotoc, Mississippi, on 11 July. T. J. Hunt of the Tenth summarized this excursion:

> Our advance brigade had reached Holly Springs, Miss., and had camped in the beautiful city park for the night. Our train was behind a few miles — its progress having been impeded by bad roads. Early in the night a thunderstorm, the like of which I have never at any other time seen, came upon us. We had no tents and our rubber blankets and shades were not respected by the wind, which blew a gale; and the rain came in torrents. The lightning was incessant.... No man escaped the improvised bath and I doubt that one slept a wink that night.[13]

When Smith reached Tupelo, Forrest was nearby with 6,000 men. His superior was General Stephen Lee, who ordered Forrest to delay until he was reinforced. General A. J. Smith would fight the battle from strong defensive positions facing north. When Lee arrived to reinforce Forrest on 13 July, he ordered an attack against Smith the next morning. This battle matched the best generals on both sides in a desperate fight. T. J. Hunt summarized. "He [A. J. Smith] found Forrest in his rear and, without communication or hope of reinforcements, kept on and into the enemy's country, tearing up railroads and capturing supplies. When he reached a chosen spot he stopped, turned and gave battle."[14] The Tenth had arrived at Tupelo Hill at about dark after a race with Forrest for the position and bivouacked opposing Forrest's line of battle. T. J. Hunt described the night and the opening of the battle.

> As I opened my eyes a cannon-ball struck the ground a few feet in front and to my right, and skipped (as a stone will on water) or jumped over the infantry line, and struck a cavalry horse just forward of its rider's knee. The ball's velocity had been so lowered by striking the ground that it could be seen as plainly as if it had been a hat thrown by hand. The horse was literally knocked from under its rider and he found himself unhurt on the ground where his horse had stood, while the horse lay dead several feet in the rear. I could but laugh at the performance. The cavalry-man with a look of surprise pulled the bridle and saddle from his dead charger, threw them on his shoulder and went to the rear. Another soldier on the same ground was wounded in his head, and carried to the ambulance.[15]

At about 4 A.M., the Tenth was moved to protect the Second Iowa Battery and guarded the battery through the remainder of the first day.[16] In the morning, a lively fight ensued but Forrest could not break the Union line. General A. J. Smith reported.

> The enemy started from the edge of the timber and advanced in three lines. At first their lines could be distinguished separately, but, as they advanced, lost all semblance of lines, and the attack resembled a mob of huge magnitude. There was no skirmish line, main line, or reserve; but it seemed to be a foot-race as to who should reach us first. They were allowed to approach, yelling and howling like Comanches, to within canister range, when the batteries opened upon them. Their charge was evidently made with the intention of capturing our batteries, and was gallantly made, but without order, organization, or skill. They would come forward, fall back, forward again, and fall back with a like result. Their determination may be seen from the fact that their dead were found within thirty yards of our batteries. After two hours of fighting in this manner General Mower advanced his line about a quarter of a mile, driving the enemy before him from the field. This ended the fighting of the day.[17]

Forrest would later claim that the Union defenses were impregnable.

That night while the nearby town of Harrisburg was burned by his troops, General Smith ordered the Tenth to hold a road in the rear where an attack was expected that would be fatal if it were successful. The expected attack was not made on the position held by the Tenth, but to its right. It occurred before daylight and was unsuccessful thanks to the determined defense by the U.S. Colored Troops. The history of the Tenth notes: "Soon after Gen. Smith ... placed it [the Tenth] in position where the enemy were evidently renewing the attack. 'There!' said the general, with the pleasant manner of one doing a favor, 'they may not get through; if they do you can give 'em hell.'"[18]

After Forrest was repulsed, Smith ordered a withdrawal back to Memphis with Forrest in pursuit attacking Smith's rear guard. T. J. Hunt of the Tenth recalled:

> We reached the Tallahatchie River on our counter march and camped, but had hardly broken ranks before our rear was attacked and quite a skirmish followed. I talked with some of the prisoners and wounded in our hands, and they stoutly defended their cause. I noted two old men of more than three score years, both with mortal wounds, who expressed their willingness to sacrifice their own lives for their cause and with a calmness that was heroic. That night another rain caused a freshet that carried off the bridge we had built the previous night, and we spent the next day in rebuilding it and then leisurely continued our march to Memphis, after destroying the bridge behind us.[19]

During the battle, Forrest was in extreme pain from boils and he was on disability leave to treat them shortly before the battle. To add to his medical problems, during the battle, he was shot in the foot, a wound that his surgeon described as "an excruciating wound."[20] When he went down, rumors spread among the troops that he had been killed. John Wythe, a young Confederate soldier at that time, recalled what happened.

> Shortly after Forrest was wounded the rumor spread among the troops that he had been killed, causing the greatest consternation among the soldiers. When this was reported to Forrest, who had been taken some distance to the rear, where the hemorrhage was arrested and his wound dressed, he mounted his horse at once and, without even taking time to put on his coat, rode in his shirtsleeves at a gallop along the line of troopers, cheering them not only by his presence, but with encouraging words, assuring them that it was only a slight flesh wound and he was still able and ready to lead them. Dr. C. W. Robertson, of Somerville, Tennessee, who was then a private soldier under Forrest, says: "The effect produced upon the men by the appearance of General Forrest is indescribable. They seemed wild with joy at seeing their great leader was still with them."[21]

Wythe maintained that over half of Forrest's soldiers did not fire a shot during the battle because of where they were positioned.[22] This was a fate shared with Little Crow at the Battle of Wood Lake, nearly two years earlier. Big Eagle said something similar. It was the luck of the draw: a soldier lives or dies based upon where he is in the line and victory depends upon having troops in the correct place at the correct time. Apparently Forrest had not read his press releases that quoted him as saying, "Whoever gets there first with the most men wins."[23]

The Tenth lost one killed (Private Thomas King of Company G) and twenty-one wounded in the engagement. The attacking forces of Forrest and Lee lost heavily and withdrew. Smith could not hold his position and retreated from the field.[24] He was short of rations, so he returned to Memphis. This decision has been disputed since then, with some stating that he had more than enough to continue. The point is that he beat Forrest and Lee but did not destroy the threat to Sherman's lifeline. The Confederates claimed victory because Smith retreated, but the fact is that Smith inflicted enormous casualties (by Western standards) on the Confederates that they could not replace. The Confederates reported 210 killed and 1116 wounded. Three brigade commanders and all colonels were either killed or wounded.[25] Comparisons were later made with Meade's failure to pursue Lee after Gettysburg and Smith's failure to pursue Lee and Forrest after Tupelo. Hindsight by those who were not there is always exquisite. Revenge for the surrender of the Minnesota Third Regiment at Murfreesboro had started.

The command headed back toward Memphis. General A. J. Smith's corps of about 4,500 troops, including the Minnesota regiments, had been ordered to reinforce Sherman when word arrived that the Confederates under General Price were on the move in Arkansas.[26] Smith was then redirected to counter General Price's advance and T. J. Hunt described the journey.

> We now rested two days, then took steamers for Davall's Bluff, Ark., where a march of more than a thousand miles was commenced, whose length and severity was only equaled by Sherman's from Atlanta, via Savannah, to Washington. The one "through Georgia" was a picnic in comparison.
>
> We passed within twenty-five miles of Little Rock, then nearly to the North line of the state where Price's army had been. Learning that he had gone eastward, we changed in that direction and soon struck his trail, frequently passing his previous night's camping ground before noon. He was heading for Pilot Knob. Our rations ran entirely out and sometimes beeves and corn were not found. Sweet potatoes were at times our only edibles. Corn was too ripe to roast and we grated the corn on improvised graters for the succeeding day, which with beef we killed when we could find it, was our sustenance.

Learning that Price had captured Pilot Knob, Mo., we turned directly East, and reached the Mississippi River at Cape Gerardo, Mo. It was a race of infantry after cavalry and a train of plunder. Here were found a day's rations and were put on steamers for St. Louis. We arrived there early the next morning before daylight, and anchored in mid-river.[27]

This was the start of a long and bitter campaign to defeat General Price. General Baker would later report that the Missouri campaign caused more aliments in later life than any other campaign.[28] Pension requests years after the war usually pointed to this campaign as the cause of disability. Union infantry chasing Confederate cavalry is always hard on the troops, especially in October and November. This was the start of the decisive campaign west of the Mississippi.

Pursuit of General Price in Missouri, 17 September–15 November 1864

> *I find measuring by the scale, the way the bird flies, that we marched, from September 10th to November 6th in the states of Arkansas and Missouri, without tents and pursuing cavalry and living on corn and beef much of the time, more than 1,000 miles. We had marched before and lived equally hard, but it was not so protracted.*[29]
> — Thomas Jefferson Hunt

Sterling Price was one of the most controversial figures in the Civil War. He was born in Virginia on September 20, 1809. He moved to Missouri as a young man in 1833 and settled on a farm near Keytesville in Chariton County. He was a lawer, planter, and politician from Missouri who served in Congress and as the 11th governor of the state from 1853 to 1857. He also served as a brevet brigadier general during the Mexican-Americna War. After Lincoln was elected, Missouri seceded after a great deal of internal strife and bloodshed, such as the Camp Jackson Massacre that occurred in May when federalized Home Guards fired on a mob of Southern sympathizers, killing twenty-eight including two women and a child.[30] Price was then recruited by Missouri governor Jackson to command the secessionist state guard. Missouri could not have been in a more difficult position at that time. It was surrounded on three sides by Union states, the Mississippi River was closed and the largest city, St. Louis, with its arsenal, was a Union stronghold. There was no link to the Confederate states and nearby Arkansas had not yet seceded.[31] Governor Jackson and others pushed for secession while Price recruited his state guard and moved to secure his state for the Confederacy.

A secession ordnance was passed on 30 and 31 October 1861 and Missouri was admitted to the Confederacy as its twelfth state with the state capital in Neosho, Missouri. The Confederate state government was never able to control vast portions of the state. From then until the end of the Civil War, Price fought a series of battles for the Confederacy and those in Missouri who supported the Southern cause. He managed to lose most of his battles, at times needlessly slaughtering his troops. While personally brave he did not quite have a knack for tactics. Some years later when a monument was proposed for Price, a former colleague suggested that the money might be better spent for the widows and orphans that he had created. Nevertheless, he was loved by his troops and affectionately called "Old Pap" because of his grandfatherly appearance.

Following the Confederate loss at Pea Ridge (also called Elkhorn Tavern) which effectively ended the Confederate threat to Union control of Missouri, Price served in Tennessee at Corinth and other battles east of the Mississippi.[32] Price vowed to bring his Army of the West back into Missouri, but other urgent requirements prevented this for the time being. In the spring of 1864, Price continued pressure to invade Missouri to win it back for the Confederacy. The Confederate government in Richmond was well aware of the importance of Missouri. If Missouri could be secured for the Confederacy, the Union forces in the West would be outflanked and the northern states threatened.[33] Although General Kirby Smith, one of the Confederate commanders in the West, was skeptical about Price's abilities, he approved the Price plan to invade Missouri. Price was seen by some as the man who could seize Missouri for the Confederacy. Price, who was known to think big and could not be accused of fretting about details, saw great opportunities: take St. Louis; cause an uprising in Missouri against the Yankees which would cause the loss of Missouri to the Union; help defeat Lincoln in the fall elections, and save the Confederacy through a negotiated settlement of the war.[34]

General Sterling Price, called "Old Pap" because of his grandfatherly appearance (Library of Congress).

In the Confederacy, desperation was setting in. Lincoln's upcoming election was somehow factored in to Kirby Smith's decision since apparently any Confederate victory might disrupt Lincoln's reelection plans. Any other candidate might be more favorably disposed toward making peace with the Confederacy. Originally, the invading army was envisioned as a strong force of infantry, artillery and cavalry, but this got watered down because Richmond directed a transfer of infantry east of the Mississippi to meet more urgent requirements.[35] In either a stroke of genius or a stroke of insanity, depending on one's optimism, Price also took along the secessionist politicians since he hoped to stop long enough in Missouri to hold an election in order to keep alive the legal claim of Confederate Missourians that they had authority in the state.[36] Of course, the politicians might also be killed in the raid and this would not be a plus (for the Confederacy). In this way, Price's Missouri Raid was launched and after evading Federal forces in Arkansas, he crossed the Arkansas River into Missouri on 19 September 1864. Price had at last returned.

PRICE'S MISSOURI RAID

Thanks to Kirby Smith, Price was able to amass nearly twelve thousand cavalry troops and fourteen pieces of artillery.[37] Rather than a full scale invasion, this would become a cavalry raid. This was not a gigantic force compared to the Battle of Gettysburg, but enough to do the job although in many respects the force was a paper tiger. Nearly a third of Price's Army of the Missouri, as he now called it, had no weapons and nearly a thousand lacked mounts.[38] Price was hardly fit to command. By this time his weight had grown to over 300

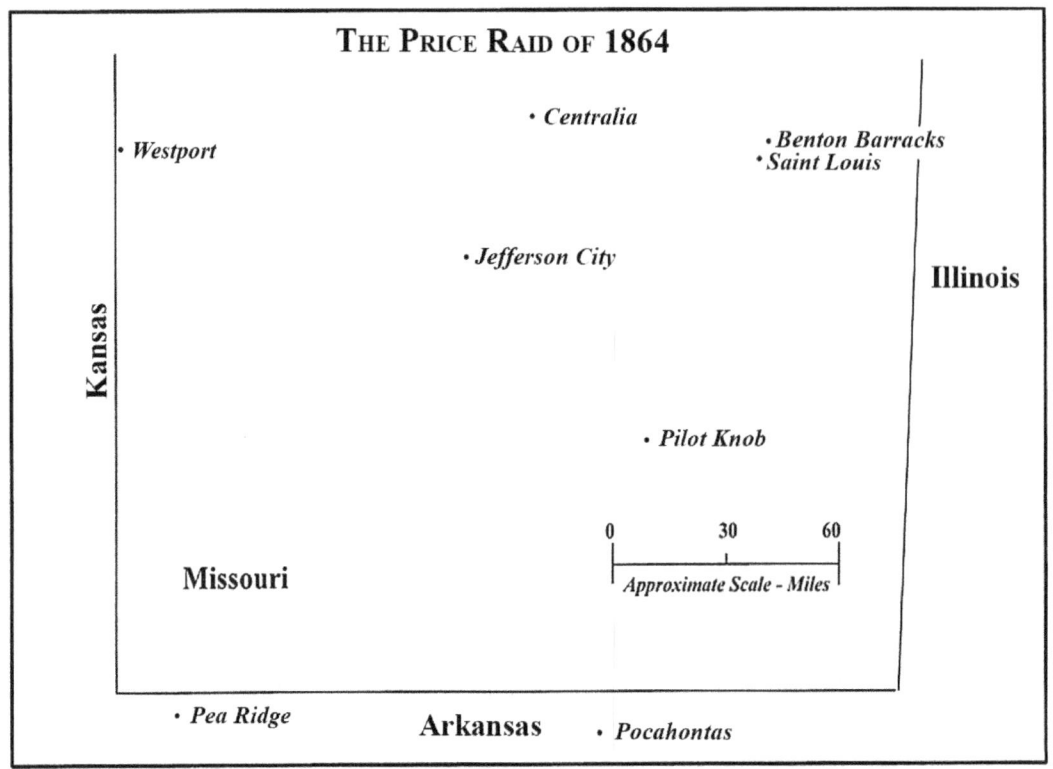

The pursuit of Price in Missouri.

pounds and he spent most of the time riding in an ambulance drawn by four mules.[39] He had an enormous creaking wagon train that would slow down the cavalry. Price underestimated the Union opposition, including General A. J. Smith and his guerrillas.[40]

Price planned to seize St. Louis, which would be a blow to the Union and to Lincoln's reelection campaign. He thought that Pilot Knob, defended by fifteen-hundred Union infantry under General Ewing, would threaten his rear.[41] Actually, Ewing had fewer than one thousand men, and infantry is unlikely to seriously threaten a cavalry unit's flank or rear. Price's scouts had overestimated the force. T. J. Hunt of the Tenth recalled what happened after their arrival at St. Louis from the Battle of Tupelo.

> We were directed to go ashore for clothes and shoes, and need enough there was for them. One of my boot soles was entirely gone. Many were barefoot. I had given a sergeant my last pair of socks the day before, and numbers had only cotton drawers to cover their limbs, others were coatless and all the clothing left on the men carried numerous greybacks [Confederate grey]. The command started next morning with quite a fleet of small steamers for Jefferson City to protect it from Price, whither he was marching. Our steamer [*the War Eagle*] was too heavily loaded for the Missouri River bars, and we made slow progress. It was once snagged and sunk, but in water too shallow to cover the deck. Damage was repaired and finally we were landed on the South shore and took up our march Westward again in the wake of Price.[42]

The Tenth arrived at Jefferson City on 18 October 1864. This was three weeks after the Price attack on Pilot Knob. The raid was turning into a cat and mouse game to see who would surprise whom. So far, Price was ahead of the Union pursuers.

Price's capture of Pilot Knob was a disaster for the Confederacy. General Shelby, Price's subordinate, had argued against the attack on Pilot Knob since it was defended by infantry, which could hardly be a threat to Price's fast moving cavalry. Others favored the attack and it appears that Price was starting to realize that St. Louis was beyond his reach and a victory at Pilot Knob would boost the morale of Confederate sympathizers in Missouri. Price attacked with two divisions abreast on 27 September 1864. They were slaughtered by heavy artillery and rifle fire from the Union positions that included nearby Fort Davidson. General Ewing, the Union commander, subsequently abandoned his position on Pilot Knob and escaped with his command after inflicting enormous casualties on the Army of Missouri. Ewing was fighting from a strong defensive position and estimated that he had killed or wounded about 1,500 of the Confederates. Added to that loss, many of Price's troops deserted and returned to Arkansas after the battle.[43] The campaign was virtually over but Price did not accept defeat. His raid would continue for several more weeks. He abandoned the plan to seize St. Louis: Union forces had blocked his advance on that city. Price was now pursued by Union General Blunt[44] and General Pleasonton's cavalry.

The Price Raid had degenerated into a struggle of roving and undisciplined plunderers killing and looting Unionists and Southerners alike. As an example, William T. "Bloody Bill" Anderson's band (including the James boys)[45] murdered and scalped twenty-three unarmed Union soldiers in the Centralia Massacre. They rode into Price's camp with bloody Union scalps dangling from their saddles. Price's reaction was to tell them to get rid of the scalps and move to the flank of his formation. Guerrillas in Missouri seldom fought with Confederate units but contented themselves with raids, plunder and the murder of civilians. "Bloody Bill" was killed a few days after his arrival at Price's camp. He was beheaded and his head was mounted on a telegraph pole. On the 23rd of October, Price decided to turn on his pursuers and to fight what was later called the Battle of Westport. He was opposed by General Blunt to his front and General Pleasonton closing on the rear of his column. By this time, Price had a train of nearly five hundred wagons and was moving very slowly. Price's plan was to attack and defeat Blunt and then turn on Pleasonton. The history of the Tenth summarized:

> From Jefferson City to La Mine Bridge by railroad and thence on foot, the regiment with its division marched in pursuit of Price through Sedalia, Lexington and Independence. As the command came nearer the game its movement was more and more of the nature of forced marches. One night, about eleven o'clock, after a long and trying march, word came that Gen Smith was advised that Gen. Blunt had Price corralled at the Big Blue, and that Smith promised all who would march at 1 o'clock A.M. a chance at Price before noon the next day. Everyone but those whom the surgeon excused set out and made the march, but Gen. Blunt had not been able to hold the enemy until Smith's arrival. From that time the rebels had no rest. An engagement of even half a day with the Union cavalry would bring the pursuing infantry down upon them. Gen. Price thus endeavoring to make his escape around Gen. Smith's infantry, while Smith was hastening to intercept him, Gen. Pleasonton's cavalry were enabled to strike the enemy in flank while in motion, and at one blow they crushed them so completely that the infantry, camping the following night just across the Kansas line, were allowed to set out on their return to St. Louis the next day. Thither the regiment went on foot, through cold and snow, with a practicable railroad upon one side and a navigable river on the other.[46]

T. J. Hunt provided the soldier's view of this affair.

> Price's army was all mounted and he had an immense train laden with everything his army needed, taken from the country he had passed through for the last four hundred miles. Seeing a foe in front and in rear, he turned South. Our infantry could not out-march him, and we were completely

exhausted; but our limited cavalry, knowing that Price must turn South, had taken a direction southwest and in the early morning of the next day surprised him, attacking his flank and capturing many men and all his train. Here, really, our forced marching ended, but we did march for three more days Southward to Harrisonville, Mo., where we rested three days and began our long tramp for St. Louis.[47]

In Minnesota, the *St. Paul Pioneer* reported the arrival of the Minnesota regiments at St. Louis.

The Fifth, Seventh, Ninth and Tenth Regiments arrived at Saint Louis on Thursday, Friday and Saturday of last week, and they were encamped at Benton Barracks. They were in good health notwithstanding their hard march after Price. They were all literally in rags, however, and some of the men actually barefoot, in which condition, they marched through snow a part of the way. They drew pay and clothing at Benton Barracks, however, and felt "human" once more. After a short rest they are to be sent to the Department of Tennessee. Col. Grant reports great destitution and suffering among the poor of the South, but their pride and spirit, and determination not to submit is as strong as ever. Many of their officers who are prisoners, say that they are sick of the war, and would give up, but dare not do it unless the feeling of the majority changes. Hence they will hold out to the last.[48]

This ended the campaign. Although several other skirmishes were fought on his way out, Price was totally defeated and his raid was a failure. When Price arrived back in Arkansas on 2 December 1864, he had lost half of his force. Only 6,000 survivors returned. Price had moved over 1400 miles in his campaign and had captured and paroled over three thousand Union soldiers. Price had fought forty-three battles during his raid, losing most, but always managing to escape. It was an incredible journey. It was also the last trans-Mississippi campaign of the war. Union control of Missouri would not be threatened again and Lincoln was reelected. The majority of voters in Missouri voted for him.[49] Lee's surrender at Appomattox was now less than four months away. The end was near.

T. J. Hunt recorded the arrival of the Tenth in St. Louis.

I recall how differently we were received by different persons. As we rested a few minutes in the street of St. Louis, a young man began to deride and make fun of us and our condition, when an old, gray-haired citizen turned upon him and grew eloquent in his rebuke, saying, "You bandbox dude, who never done as much for your country as to count the miles they have traveled, you laugh at them; they should put you on the ground for a cushion and sit on you; it would do you good to come in contact with the soil whose defenders you scorn." Men and women onlookers cheered the old man and so did we. Here we rested and cleaned. In a day or two I was detailed with Company A to go aboard a small steamer, anchored in the middle of the Mississippi River, which was loaded heavily with ammunition. A fleet of small steamers was soon assembled and Gen. Smith's 16th corps was put aboard and started for Nashville, Tenn.[50]

One of the last great battles of the Civil War was about to begin.

CHAPTER 4

The Battle of Nashville
Thursday to Friday, 15–16 December 1864

My feet are torn and bloody,
My heart is full of woe,
I'm going back to Georgia
To find my uncle Joe [Johnston].
You may talk about your Beauregard,
You may sing of Bobby Lee,
But the gallant Hood of Texas
Played hell in Tennessee.[1]
— Anonymous

General John Bell Hood was a courageous commander who inspired his troops. Born in Kentucky, he enlisted to fight for the Confederacy from his adopted state of Texas. He was a graduate of the United States Military Academy, West Point, in the Class of 1853, graduating 44th in a class of 52. He was not brilliant as a cadet or soldier as evidenced by his nickname, "Sam Woodenhead."[2] By 1864 he was still a fairly young man thirty-three years of age, but he had lost the use of an arm due to a wound at Gettysburg and his leg was amputated after he was wounded at the Battle of Chickamauga. There were serious concerns about his ability to command due to these injuries, but he had been an excellent brigade and division commander. Most important, he was a fighter, like A. J. Smith. The problem was that by the end of 1864 he found himself commanding the Army of Tennessee and had risen in rank to a level beyond his competence. His carelessness, lack of attention to logistics, lack of reconnaissance (although he had arguably the best cavalry in the world under Forrest) and lack of preparation would doom any adventure that he planned for his army. He was ill-suited to lead an independent command and the fact that he did sealed the fate of the Confederacy.[3]

The fall of Atlanta on 2 September 1864 signaled the end of the war. The South had lost, but President Jefferson Davis and many of his people would fight on. Davis, on a speaking tour in September, told his citizens that he would send Hood and his army west, but he was not clear on exactly what Hood was supposed to do. After much discussion, he ordered Hood to interdict Sherman's supply line. If Sherman attacked, Hood could fall back on Gadsden, Alabama, and fight Sherman there.[4] With Hood heading west as advertised by Davis, Grant and Sherman could now consider their options, and they had many. Sherman decided to cut loose from his supply line, march to the coast and seize Savannah. This would also force Hood to follow since sitting on the Chattanooga to Atlanta railroad would have lost purpose. While Hood was moving at last into Tennessee, Sherman began his march to the sea that would end at Savannah. Sherman and his 60,000 troops marched out of Atlanta on 14 November 1864. They would live off of the land and the supplies that they carried with them. With Hood in the West, there was very little opposition to Sherman's column. The South had surrendered the initiative to Grant and Sherman.[5] On the other hand, a strong Confederate army in Tennessee had endless opportunities to do mischief. Hood preferred to take action without consulting his superiors, which was probably prudent given the caliber of his superiors (Davis and Beauregard). The problem with this was that they were not knowledgeable of his plans and could not support his army although Beauregard tried to keep up with Hood's plans.[6]

General John Bell Hood, whose wounds limited his ability in Tennessee (Library of Congress).

On 19 November 1864, Nathan Bedford Forrest's cavalry led Hood's army into Tennessee. Hood had about 30,000 infantry and 8,000 cavalry. They were headed for Nashville and would find themselves hopelessly outnumbered by the Union Army in Tennessee. Earlier in April, Davis had defined his objectives for Tennessee to General Johnston, at that time commander in the West.

  First. To take the enemy at disadvantage while weakened, it is believed, by sending troops to Virginia, and having others absent still on furlough.
  Second. To break up his plans by anticipating and frustrating his combinations.
  Third. So to press him here as to prevent his heavier massing in Virginia.
  Fourth. To beat him, it is hoped, and greatly gain strength in supplies, men, and productive territory.
  Fifth. To prevent the waste of the army incident to inactivity.
  Sixth. To inspirit it and the country, and to depress the enemy, involving the greatest results.
  Seventh. To obviate the necessity of falling back likely to occur if the enemy be allowed to consummate his own plans.[7]

By November, the weather in Tennessee was bitter and taking a heavy toll on both sides. The Southerners found that they could make an effective shelter by digging a hole in the ground with twigs at the bottom covered by blankets above and below the sleeping soldiers. It reminded one soldier of a grave.[8] Men were detailed to make shoes whenever leather could be found.

The Union had considerable forces available to meet the Hood threat including General John Schofield and General George H. Thomas. Schofield was a West Point graduate with the Class of 1853. He ranked 7th in his class of fifty-two that included Hood. At the time of the battle of Nashville Schofield was thirty-three years of age and had won the Medal of Honor for bravery at the Battle of Wilson's Creek in 1861. Thomas was a Virginian who remained loyal to the Union at the start of the war. He was born in 1816 and at age forty-

Left: General George Thomas — "The Rock of Chickamauga. *Right:* General John Schofield, who defeated Hood at the Battle of Franklin (both photographs, Library of Congress).

eight was one of the oldest generals in the field, but younger than A. J. Smith. Thomas was a West Point graduate with the Class of 1840. His roommate was William Tecumseh Sherman, who graduated 6th in the class. Thomas ranked 12th in the class of forty-two.[9] His previous successes on the battlefield were at Chickamauga, where he held the Union line, and his breakthrough at Missionary Ridge. He was slow and deliberate, the opposite of the impulsive Hood. He never had a good relationship with Grant, and this hurt him especially in the post-war years when Grant was president. Thomas would have 55,000 troops to oppose Hood and this number was constantly changing.

General A. J. Smith's corps including the Minnesota regiments was on the way to Tennessee after chasing Sterling Price out of Missouri. Smith would arrive in Nashville to reinforce Thomas on 30 November 1864, Hood was miles away at Franklin, Tennessee, opposed by Schofield.[10] As the Tenth and the remainder of A. J. Smith's corps arrived at Nashville, Hood attacked Schofield at Franklin on the 30th of November shortly after 4 P.M. in what was later described as the Pickett's charge of the West. He did so over the objections of Forrest and his other subordinates who viewed the attack as hopeless.[11]

Like Pickett at Gettysburg, Hood would lose thousands of troops. It may have been the last grand Confederate attack of the war; certainly it was the last grand hurrah for the Confederate Army in the West. One of Schofield's soldiers described what he saw: "It was worth a year of one's lifetime to witness the marshalling and advance of the rebel line of battle. Emerging from the woods in the most perfect order, two corps in front and one in reserve, nothing could be more suggestive of strength and discipline, and resistless power than was this long line of gray advancing over the plain."[12]

Schofield was dug in south of Franklin. Hood's attack from the south used the only practical approach since Franklin was surrounded on three sides by the Harpeth River. For-

Kurz and Allison 1891 lithograph print showing General Hood's attack on General Schofield's entrenched Union line at Franklin, Tennessee, 30 November 1864 (Library of Congress Prints and Pictures Division).

rest, of course, suggested a cavalry strike, but this would not work because Schofield had cavalry on his flanks. Hood was convinced that if he could defeat or get by Franklin, he had an open path to the Ohio River and the north. He, like Lee at Gettysburg, was also convinced that he could break the Union line. The attack was carried out with all of the flair of the Confederate Army complete with the band playing "Dixie" and "Bonnie Blue Flag" and the rebel yell in the final assault as the soldiers were mowed down by Schofield's entrenched troops. In this very bloody battle, Hood lost about a third of his infantry because he employed frontal attacks against an entrenched enemy. He would later report losses far less than these, but whichever count one wishes to believe, the losses were staggering. The fact that he had lost many of his subordinate commanders made a count more difficult at that time: he lost six of his generals killed, including one of the best, Patrick R. Cleburne.[13] General Thomas Jordan, who served under Forrest, described the Confederate attack.

> The ground of approach to the main position was open, with very slight shelter; but on pressed the Confederates, with little halt, after their first success, though now fully aware of the appalling gravity of the work in hand. They were presently met by a broad, desolating tide of musketry, while shot and canister, both from the entrenchments in front and the redoubts on Figuer's Hill, smote down their gallant ranks from flank to flank. The slaughter, indeed, was now deplorable. The enemy, ensconced behind stout breastworks, with almost a single salvo of their numerous artillery swept away entire Confederate regiments, and thinned all the others to a heartrending degree. But with characteristic, unconquerable resolution the survivors—staggered for a

moment — still moved forward, and many reached the entrenchments, and in attempting to surmount them were slain. In this fearful onset the first line of the Confederates had been almost annihilated. A second and indeed a third line were, nevertheless, brought up, and thrown forward with kindred hardihood to meet, as might be expected, the same sanguinary reception, the same repulse with gaping ranks ravaged of their best officers and men.[14]

An Alabamian had seen the Confederate losses and reported: "I have seen many battlefields, but none equal to this. The ground in front of the works ... is covered with dead bodies and the ditch in front is filled with them." He added that his regiment could muster but thirty men.[15] Hood had limited choices. If he fell back he would be trapped between Thomas and Sherman in Georgia who was completing his march to the sea and could easily double back. Perhaps if he moved to Nashville he could break Thomas's line and push north.

As the winter sun rose on 1 December 1864 Hood looked at the destruction in front of Franklin and technically could claim victory since Schofield had abandoned the field, but Hood knew it was a disaster and now needed to plan his next move. He finally decided to move on Nashville and dig in before the well fortified position of Thomas. He would then see what Thomas would do. If attacked, Hood could defend himself. Hood had apparently not read the maxim attributed to Napoleon: "a passive defense is deferred suicide." It would also be suicide to attack Thomas, who had plenty of time to turn Nashville into a greater fortress than it already was. Also, Thomas was gaining forces daily and would soon outnumber Hood by two to one. Hood had high hopes of reinforcements but would receive none. Hood would later state that he had over 23,000 troops available after the Franklin disaster. Thomas had the IV Army Corps under General Wood, Schofield's XXIII Corps, and A. J. Smith's XVI Corps. Additionally, he had the usual assortment of cooks and bottle washers who could stop what they were doing and man the line if needed. Most important, he had General Wilson's Cavalry Corps which could screen and go Forrest-hunting as required.[16] Thomas started with a few nags as his supply of horses and built that up to a respectable cavalry force of thousands before the Battle of Nashville. Union supply was the decisive factor. As seen by the experience of the Tenth Regiment troops after the pursuit of Price, they were reequipped before moving to Nashville. Hood had no such luxury. He had what he left with before crossing the Tennessee River. For Hood it was a come as you are campaign with no hope of gaining anything later. There were no great supply trains following him to resupply and reequip his army. The Confederacy was on its knees and falling apart. Hood took the only action that he could in this situation and started digging in just south of Nashville. Basically, he was hoping that Thomas would make a mistake as he attacked and provide Hood with an opportunity to destroy Thomas's army. Hood would later justify his decision: "Thus, unless strengthened by these long looked for reinforcements, the only remaining chance of success in the campaign at this juncture was to take position, entrench around Nashville and await Thomas's attack which, if handsomely repulsed, might afford us an opportunity to follow up our advantage on the spot and enter the city on the heels of the enemy."[17]

While the Battle of Franklin was being fought, the Tenth Minnesota and the other Minnesota regiments were arriving in Nashville to reinforce Thomas. T. J. Hunt described the move.

> We passed Fort Donaldson and arrived in Nashville late on Nov. 29th, while the battle of Franklin was being fought. I was still in command of Company A but one of the officers of said company (Lieut. Stowers) was here, so I asked to be relieved of my command; which request was granted

and I resumed my place in Co. B. Our regiment was sent two or more miles South of the city and entrenched, waiting for Hood, the Confederate commander, who had driven Gen. Schofield from the South. I saw the long train of ambulances bringing the wounded from Franklin. Men were placed three abreast, tier above tier, and so rode all night. They were a sorry sight. We did not have to wait long until Hood appeared in our front [at Nashville] and there entrenched within view of us. Here we waited fifteen days. Wood got scarce and daily we lost men who were collecting fuel between the lines. Even shade trees and buildings were consumed.[18]

Hood moved out on the morning of 1 December in pursuit of Schofield, who arrived in Nashville and took up positions selected by Thomas just before noon. On 2 December, Hood's army deployed on the hills south of Nashville and started to dig in. As Thomas was preparing to attack, Hood committed a colossal blunder: he dispatched most of Forrest's cavalry and a division of infantry to besiege a Union force dug-in at Murfreesboro thirty miles south of Nashville. This made no sense at all and some say that Hood was suffering from the use of laudanum (the pain-killer of the day) to treat his old wounds when he made this decision. Hood set up positions on hills several miles south of Nashville. Without Forrest and the infantry with him, Hood was left with 23,000 men in his lines around Nashville and no effective force of cavalry. Forrest took some prisoners at Murfreesboro and seized some supplies but did no serious damage. He then went off raiding and tearing up track as the Battle of Nashville was being fought. He would return to Hood several days after the battle. Hood was now outnumbered by about three to one.[19] Hood did his best to improve his defensive position while Thomas planned and prepared for his attack on Hood. In the meantime, on 13 December, Sherman seized Savannah and Grant was becoming more impatient with Thomas, asking for his removal because he had not attacked Hood. Added to Thomas's problem was the fact that Schofield was a disloyal schemer who was sending cables to Halleck and Grant, distorting information in the hope that Thomas would be fired and Schofield would take over command.[20] Grant continually pushed Thomas to move faster and Thomas, in his slow methodical manner, went at his own pace. He was also hampered by bad weather that delayed everything. Most important, Thomas was building up a superior cavalry force under General James H. Wilson. Wilson was 6th in his 1860 class of forty-one at West Point. He would later serve in the Spanish-American War in 1898. Wilson's cavalry was being equipped with the seven shot Spencer repeating cartridge carbines that were far superior to the muzzle loading single shot rifles used by both the North and the South.[21] By mid-December Wilson had over 12,000 men and they would be used differently from

General James Wilson, whose attack on Hood's left flank and rear were the decisive factor in the battle (Library of Congress).

other cavalry as will be seen in the battle that followed.[22] Finally, Thomas notified Grant on 14 December that he planned to start his attack on Hood the next day and so he was allowed to remain in command.

The Battle of Nashville — The First Day, Thursday, 15 December 1864

> *We approached their first battery and, charging, drove it from the field. Then enveloping their exposed flank, we cleared their line for two or three miles, really fighting two battles alone, as the second brigade — isolated, out of sight and hearing of other troops.*[23]
> — Thomas Jefferson Hunt

The Battle of Nashville opened on the morning of 15 December 1864 after the fog burned off. It was a two day affair. Thomas planned to make a secondary attack on Hood's right flank while the main attack would strike Hood's left flank that was exposed because Forrest had departed. T. J. Hunt offered the best tribute to Thomas: "Thomas still delayed. He was threatened by Grant and others, but would not sacrifice his men.... 'Pap' Thomas, the men called him. He had spared them; he had earned their confidence and they his, as well. Hood was better posted and as well protected as was Lee's army in the wilderness and the fighting was equally severe."[24]

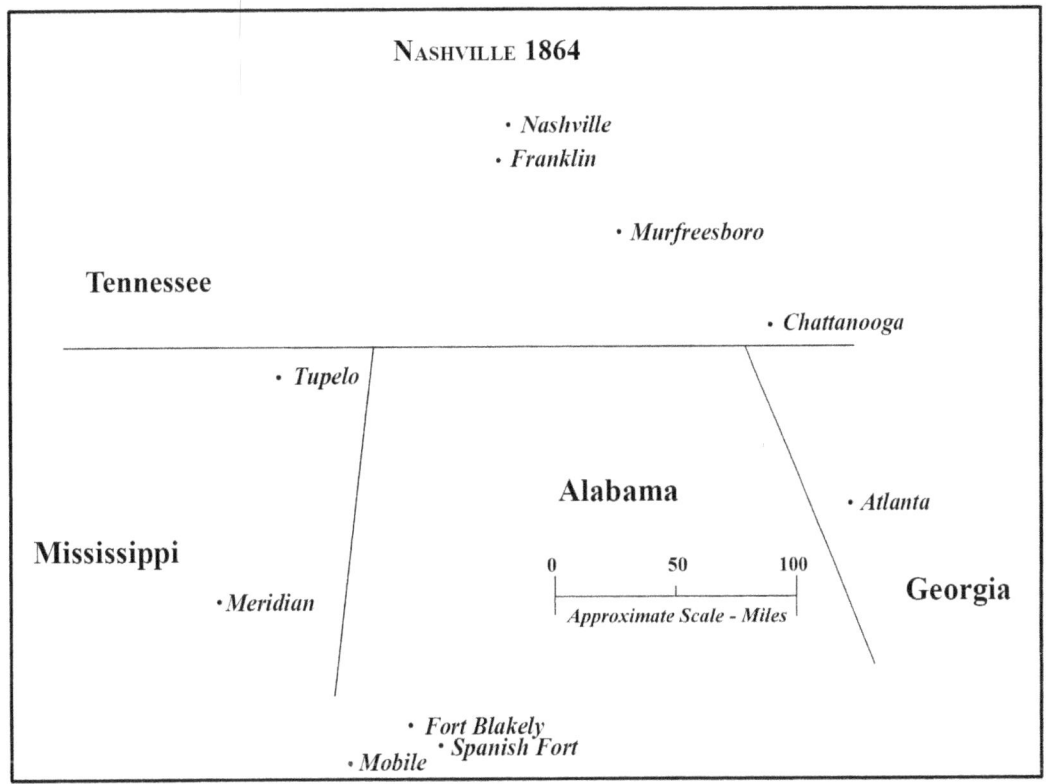

The Battle of Nashville and other battles fought by the Tenth Minnesota Regiment.

Thomas had the superior forces to make this work. General Wood the Union IV Corps commander described the advance against Hood's right flank. The United States Colored Troops led the assault on the right. "The troops were full of enthusiasm and the splendid array in which the advance was made gave hopeful promise of success. Near the foot of the ascent the assaulting force dashed forward for the last great effort.... When near, however, the enemy works, his reserves on the slope of the hill rose and poured in a fire before which no troops could live."[25] The Federals attacking Hood's right flank were driven back in disorder.

On Hood's left, the advancing Union infantry swarmed up the hills and Hood's line started to collapse. A. J. Smith's corps, including the Tenth Minnesota, hit Hood's left flank. Thomas had concentrated overwhelming combat power on Hood's left. As the Union troops overwhelmed Hood's left, Sergeant James R. Maxwell, a Confederate gunner, described the chaos.

> When the charging Federals passed my gun on the left of the redoubt, Lieutenant Hargrove ordered us to leave it. I ran towards Captain Lumsden's section, where Sergeant Jim Jones had turned No.2 to fire canister at the Federals who were near gun NO.4. He called to me "Look out, Jim!." I dropped on hands and knees whilst he fired that canister right over my head.... I went down past Mr. Castleman's house, in front of which Captain Lumsden was reporting to General Stewart, who was congratulating Captain Lumsden for detaining the advance of the Federals so long.... Hilen L. Rosser, one of our gunners had had part of his head shot away. That night as I was pouring some water for Lumsden to wash, he was picking something out of his beard and said: "Maxwell, that is part of Rosser's brains."[26]

On the Federal side, T. J. Hunt of the Tenth recalled:

> We soon were in front of the enemy behind a good breastwork with a four-gun battery. We were ordered to lie down while our brigade battery of six pieces played upon their works. Within rifle range, all our shots hit their works, while theirs from smooth-bores went wild, until one of their guns was turned upon us (lying prostrate) with a grape and canister charge. Their aim was good; our line was torn, men were mangled and dirt flew. Quick as though an iceberg was against my back. I wanted to go, and go anywhere, only go.[27]

Wilson with 12,000 cavalry swung around Hood's left flank and positioned his cavalry to Hood's left rear to prepare for the next day's action.[28] Darkness saved Hood's army from destruction and he backed away from Thomas to establish a new line on the Harpeth Hills a few miles to their rear. A. J. Smith's Corps, including the Tenth, had helped break the Confederate line. The first day of the Battle of Nashville was clearly a Union victory. That night everyone became a fan of George Thomas as he sent out his report of the day's action.

> I attacked the enemy's left this morning and drove it from the river, below the city, very nearly to the Franklin pike, a distance about eight miles. Have captured General Chalmers' headquarters and train, and a second train of about 20 wagons, with between 800 and 1,000 prisoners and 16 pieces of artillery. The troops behaved splendidly, all taking their share in assaulting and carrying the enemy's breast-works. I shall attack the enemy again tomorrow, if he stands to fight, and, if he retreats during the night, will pursue him, throwing a heavy cavalry force in his rear, to destroy his trains, if possible." And, ever the dutiful family man, he telegraphed to his wife in New York: "We have whipped the enemy, taken many prisoners and considerable artillery."[29]

Stanton, the secretary of war, as soon as he received the news, graciously telegraphed Thomas: "I rejoice in tendering to you and the gallant officers and soldiers of your command the thanks of this Department for the brilliant achievements of this day, and hope that it is the harbinger of a decisive victory, that will crown you and your army with honor and do much toward closing the war. We shall give you a hundred guns [a salute, not a firing squad] in the morning."[30] Grant also sent a telegram of congratulations, saying that "I was just on my way to Nashville" when he received the news, but "I shall go no farther." He went on: "Push the enemy now, and give him no rest until he is entirely destroyed. Your army will cheerfully suffer many privations to break up Hood's army and render it useless for further operations. Do not stop for trains or supplies, but take them from the country as the enemy have done. Much is now expected." The next morning President Lincoln telegraphed "the nation's thanks"; and, having seen too many battles start splendidly and then fizzle added: "You made a magnificent beginning. A grand consummation is within your easy reach. Do not let it slip."[31]

Hood had an enormous task on the night of 15–16 December. Thomas thought that Hood would retreat, but that thought apparently never entered Hood's mind. Hood was right: it was probably better to fight it out now, hope for a break, and invade the North than be crushed later by an overwhelming Union force. He decided to reestablish his army on a new line of defense factoring into this the significant losses of the day's battle and the absence of Forrest to screen his flanks. His new line had to be shortened and this was probably his downfall as will be seen. T. J. Hunt had a bad night following the battle.

> During that night I awoke at intervals and heard the groans of Confederate wounded and the picks and axes of those who were constructing defenses we knew we must face the next day. Hood's army had been contracted during the night and lay across two pikes and the only railroad then running South from Nashville. One of his flanks was protected by the river, the other by a precipitous bluff too steep for ascent, from the West, the north end of which formed a right angle and to its right extended a high stone wall to one pike nearly a half mile distant. On the north end of this hill were massed sixteen pieces of artillery and behind its works and the stone wall were four lines of men. Those guns could be used to front or right and sweep for a mile any approaching column. It was the key of the situation.[32]

The Battle of Nashville—The Second Day, Friday, 16 December 1864

It was afternoon on 16 December 1864 before Thomas's attack against the Confederate line could begin. Thomas had to carefully plan (as he always did) and then move forward on Hood's new position. The Union troops had waited in freezing cold since early morning. A. J. Smith was becoming impatient with the lack of action by Thomas on the 16th and one of his division commanders, General McArthur commanding the Minnesota regiments, including the Tenth, decided on his own to attack. Colonel McMillen's First Brigade under General McArthur included the Tenth Minnesota Infantry Regiment which was positioned against the left center of the Confederate position. The second day of the Battle of Nashville was in many respects a rerun of the previous day. Sam Woodenhead was not a fast learner. Again, Wilson's cavalry moved around Hood's left flank, dismounted and delivered a withering fire on the Confederates in Hood's rear. Wilson intercepted a message from Hood to his rear guard commander and reported.

> In the midst of the heaviest fighting, one of our detachments captured a courier from Hood, carrying a dispatch to Chalmers, directing him "for God's sake to drive the Yankee cavalry from our left and rear or all is lost." Regarding this dispatch as of the first importance, I sent it at once to Thomas without even making a copy of it…. I rode around the enemy's left flank to Thomas's

headquarters, which I found on the turnpike about two miles from my own. This was between three and four o'clock, and as it was a cloudy, rainy day, it was already growing dark.... I urged Thomas, with ill-concealed impatience, to order the infantry forward without further delay. Pausing only to ask me if I was sure that the men entering the left of the enemy's works above us were mine, and receiving the assurance that I was dead certain of it, he turned to Schofield and as calmly as if on parade directed him to move to the attack with his entire corps.[33]

As one Confederate soldier said, "The Yankee bullets were coming from all directions passing one another in flight."[34] Colonel Henry Stone on Thomas's staff described the Union attack on Hood's left and its result.

It was more like a scene in a spectacular drama than a real incident in war. The hillside in front, still green, dotted with the boys in blue swarming up the slope; the dark background of high hills beyond; the lowering clouds; the waving flags; the smoke slowly rising through the leafless tree-tops and drifting across the valleys; the wonderful outburst of musketry; the ecstatic cheers; the multitude racing for life down into the valley below—so exciting was it all that the lookers on instinctively clapped their hands as at a brilliant and successful transformation scene, as indeed it was. For in those few minutes an army was changed into a mob, and the whole structure of the rebellion in the southwest, with all its possibilities, was utterly overthrown.[35]

As the Union line moved forward, the Tenth suffered severe casualties when it was caught in a cross-fire as it approached the enemy works. Major Cook was mortally wounded as was Captain White, the commander of F Company. The regimental commander, Lieutenant Colonel Jennison, fell wounded within a yard of the enemy line as Color Sergeant O'Neil led the Union charge over the parapet. Captain Sanders took command of the regiment. The Union carried the works with the Tenth's bayonet charge. Sixteen cannon and two thousand prisoners were taken. Of the 301 soldiers of the Tenth that mustered at the start of that day, sixty-eight were killed or wounded, but the disintegration of the Confederate Army in the West started here.

T. J. Hunt of the Tenth recalled:

On the morning of the second day we approached the enemy's new line with Co. B in front as skirmishers covering the regiment. We drove their skirmish line through a corn field fronting the stone wall mentioned. Being in advance, we received our orders by the bugle which indicated a continued advance; balls were flying thick and the men hesitated. I went in front of the company with hat raised on my sword and said, "Come on, boys," and every man came. When their skirmishers had got back over the wall, up rose a rank of men; their guns told us to lie down. We obeyed and were favored by a depression in the ground, lying as low as we could. Their volley was repeated by rank after rank, and we were literally concealed by stalks and leaves, which were mowed down by bullets. When they ceased firing by rank and only voluntary firing was done, our work began. Each gun was directed just above that wall and when a head appeared more than one ball went in that direction and so it was until our sixty rounds grew low. Two of our boys were ordered to the rear for a supply and ran the gauntlet unharmed.[36]

Hunt's narrative stops here because he received a serious wound in the jaw and had to go to the hospital in the rear. On this day, the good fortune of the Tenth ended after two years of fighting in the Indian war and against the Confederate Army. Until now, few soldiers of the Tenth had been killed in action, but on this day, more would be killed than at any time before or after. The Minnesota regiments helped break the Confederate line and Hood's army collapsed and fled in panic to the rear. Colonel McMillen reported, "We received a volley, which on the right went over our heads, but on the left punished the Tenth Minnesota severely. Nothing daunted, this gallant regiment, together with the others composing the front line, cleared the enemy's works with a bound. The two regiments in the second line were inside almost as quickly, having pushed forward with the highest spirit and determination.[37]

Hunt would write later about what was reported to him.

> Our boys were well drilled with the bayonet and gun breech and well did they use their skill. Though facing more than two to their one, they routed the enemy and turned the sixteen cannon upon the fleeing, and upon the ranks, behind the stone wall we had so long faced. The key of the situation was taken, their rout was complete; the battle of Nashville was won. Our color sergeant's [O'Neil] coat showed seventeen ball holes, his left hand held the colors while his right snatched a gun whose bayonet was thrust at his breast, pulled it from the hand of his opponent and with fist felled his foe and with foot put another out of commission.[38]

As Thomas rode across the battlefield after Hood had been beaten, he saw Union soldiers black and white where they had fallen in battle. To his staff he said, "Gentlemen, the issue has been settled! Negroes will fight!" As the U.S. Colored Regiments marched past him in pursuit of Hood, Thomas turned his horse, removed his hat in a mark of respect and watched as they filed past.[39] Later that night, Wilson was overtaken by Thomas who pulled abreast of him in the dark and said, "Dang it to hell, Wilson, didn't I tell you we could lick 'em."[40] The battle was a disaster for the Confederacy. Five thousand Confederate troops surrendered in one hour. They had had enough. Hood's army was destroyed and Nashville was the last offensive action of the Confederacy in the West. As Hood's army fled south, bad weather and the arrival of Forrest's cavalry covered their retreat.

Since Colonel Jennison was wounded, Captain Sanders was now in command of the Tenth Regiment and wrote the report of the Tenth Regiment in the battle. Sanders' full report is included in Appendix B. T. J. Hunt of the Tenth recalled, "Our army pressed Hood's in retreat to the Tennessee River and halted. The river froze, retarding supplies so the soldiers were forced to live a time on corn issued in the ear."[41]

Both armies struggled through the bad weather and headed south as the year 1864 came to a close. Hood's army was now a disorganized rabble unlikely to fight if cornered. On Christmas Day, the lead elements of Hood's army reached the Tennessee River and crossed in to Mississippi on pontoon bridges. Thomas ended his pursuit on 27 December.[42] This ended Hood's army. It had disintegrated. Hood resigned his command and would never command troops again. Tennessee was secured for the Union. The heroes of the battle were Thomas and, although many would dispute this, Hood. Thomas had the advantage of superior numbers and a supply system that could not be matched, but Hood led his troops in a desperate attempt to save the Confederacy that failed. It was now a little more than three months before the collapse of the Confederacy.

Today, urban sprawl has engulfed the Nashville battlefield and there are few monuments to the battle that may have been the most significant of the Civil War. The battle monument dedicated in 1927 was destroyed by a tornado and construction of the interstate obstructed public view of the site. Union general Joshua Chamberlain, who was present at the surrender of General R. E. Lee, visited Appomattox years after the surrender and found it in ruins. He was quoted as saying, "You could hardly expect the South to build monuments to their defeat." So it was for Nashville.

CHAPTER 5

The Last Battle
Palm Sunday, 9 April 1865

> *After four years of arduous service, marked by unsurpassed courage and fortitude, the Army of Northern Virginia has been compelled to yield to overwhelming numbers of resources.... By the terms of the agreement officers and men can return to their homes and remain until exchanged. You will take with you the satisfaction that proceeds from the consciousness of duty faithfully performed, and I earnestly pray that a Merciful God will extend to you His blessing and protection. With an increasing admiration of your constancy and devotion to your country, and a grateful remembrance of your kind and generous considerations for myself, I bid you an affectionate farewell.*[1]
> — R. E. Lee

As a clear spring sun rose in Virginia, General Robert E. Lee surrendered the Confederate army in Virginia to U.S. Grant at Appomattox Court House. At the same time, in the West, the Tenth Minnesota and the other regiments of McArthur's division were making the final assault on Fort Blakely in Alabama. This was the last major battle of the Civil War.[2] This is what happened to the Tenth and other forces involved in this battle. Colonel Baker described the movement of the Tenth Regiment after Nashville.

> After the battle [Nashville] the regiment joined in the pursuit of Hood to the Tennessee River. It then embarked on boats and ascended the river to Eastport, Miss., where they arrived Jan. 7, 1865. At this place the army went into winter quarters. The regiment built log cabins, and remained in camp without any special incident, except short rations, until February 7th, when they embarked for New Orleans, on the way to attack Mobile. They remained in camp, on Gen. Jackson's old battlefield, about ten days, when they embarked for Dauphin Island, where they awaited the concentration of the Thirteenth Corps and the reorganized Sixteenth Army Corps, now consisting of three divisions under the command of Maj. Gen. A. J. Smith.... After two weeks given to rest, camp duties and collecting and eating the fine oysters of the island waters, the command was transported across Mobile Bay to the mouth of Fish River, about thirty miles South of Spanish Fort, one of the defensive works of Mobile, and about nine miles South of the city.[3]

Grant's objective in January of 1865 was to end the war as soon as possible with minimum loss of life. The Confederacy was defeated and this was clear to people on both sides. Grant had key elements in his plan. He would continue to confront Lee. Sherman intended to invade South Carolina to seize Port Royal. General Sheridan would move in Virginia with the objective of Lynchburg and destroying railroads and locks. General Stoneman's cavalry would raid in Tennessee and move into North Carolina and Virginia. General Canby, who was in New Orleans, was ordered to attack several key objectives including Mobile, one of the few remaining Confederate ports that was also a rail hub. To do all of this, Grant had 900,000 troops including 300,000 reserves that he could call in. The Confederacy could muster only about 160,000 men. The author Shelby Foote labeled this "Grant's Close-Out Plan."[4] Very few Confederates wanted to be the last casualty of the Civil War dying for the lost cause. Absenteeism was about 49 percent in the Army of Tennessee, 60 percent in the Army of Northern Virginia, and Jefferson Davis stated that one-quarter of a million deserters were on the rolls of the War Department.[5] The end was near. Lincoln was very clear: there would be no discussions or negotiations among generals about political matters.[6] Lincoln did not want to fritter away at any conference table of generals what had been won on the battlefield at the cost of hundreds of thousands of lives. The terms would be unconditional surrender. The Union would be reunited. With this backdrop, the last major battle of the Civil War was fought.

The Battle of Spanish Fort in Alabama took place from 27 March through 8 April 1865. After the Union navy victory at the Battle of Mobile Bay, the city of Mobile, Alabama, remained in the hands of the Confederate Army. As a major port and railroad hub, it was necessary to take Mobile, and Union forces including A. J. Smith's XVI Corps under General Canby[7] advanced to take Spanish Fort, a major stronghold defending Mobile. While Grant was trapping R. E. Lee in Virginia, General Canby was preparing for the attack on Mobile, Alabama. This would be trench warfare with the Union troops slowly digging their way to the Confederate Spanish Fort defenses. The battle was fought from 27 March to 8 April 1865. T. J. Hunt described what he saw. As far as is known, Hunt's description of the battle (which goes for many pages) is the only one that survived the war. A few excerpts of his account follow. "During the first night we so entrenched that our casualties diminished. Our line encircling Spanish Fort was three miles long and extended from bay to bay, enclosing the enemy's works, which contained the biggest guns then made. I observed one marked seventeen and one-half tons."[8] Hunt went on to describe the fort. "The ground near the fort was studded with torpedoes; and obstructions made by two rows of stakes sharpened at the top and standing too close together to allow a man to pass between them, added to the difficulty of approaching. The walls of the fort were some six feet across at the top and twenty or more feet at the base with a shelf or walk some six feet wide against the fort wall, of proper height for their men to shoot over the top of the wall and under a headlog which was bolted to strong posts firmly set in the earth walls."[9] This was a formidable defensive position, but the Tenth and the other regiments reduced casualties by digging at night and throwing up dirt and logs to protect them from the enemy fire which followed each morning. The trench followed a zig-zag pattern toward the fort that afforded opportunity to bring in Union artillery, but these guns were unable to penetrate the fort's defenses. By the 7th of April, the Union troops had dug their way to the stronghold of Spanish Fort and were now ready for the final assault. That night a heavy bombardment was started by several hundred Union guns that continued the next day and into the evening of 8 April. Hunt described the scene.

> The cannonading had begun and every piece of artillery on both sides was talking. We were massed at the extremity of our sap and every hood had its sharpshooter aiming and firing where it would be most effective. The enemy had bags of sand suspended from a pole while a man at each end of the pole lifted the bag to fill the notch in the wall through which they discharged their cannon. This protected their men while loading, but not while aiming. Probably fifty of our sharpshooters were directing their fire at each of the bags or guns when the bags were lowered. No man could escape deadly missives; they could not aim their cannon; they shot wild. We feared only their small shells thrown by hand but their fuse was not very good. We were in at the death. Our blood was up; no man thought of the rear; we felt like finishing the work there and then.[10]

The Union troops rushed in and overwhelmed the Spanish Fort defenders only to find that the Confederates had spiked their guns and fled to nearby Fort Blakely seven miles away. When Hunt entered the fort he described the scene. "Our shells had converted the ground into a striking resemblance to a hog yard that had been rooted over and over. We had avoided the torpedoes by having gotten our trench higher than they were. Spanish Fort with its heavy armament was ours."[11]

Fort Blakely was a smaller fort and not well defended. While R. E. Lee was surrendering to Grant at Appomattox on Palm Sunday, 9 April 1865, the Union Army was assembling before Fort Blakely. By the time that the Tenth Regiment arrived that afternoon, the troops that had been investing Fort Blakely had launched their attack. Fort Blakely and two thousand Confederate prisoners were taken. Total cost in Union casualties for this two week campaign was about fifteen hundred dead and wounded or about one in ten of those engaged.[12]

After the surrender of Lee at Appomattox and the last battle at Mobile, service in the army was not over for the Tenth Regiment. Dead time set in as the army figured out what to do now that the war was over. This went on for three months before the regiment could head home to Minnesota. The final days were captured by T. J. Hunt.

> Some of our boys just before the end came, and as they lay fatigued under cover in our trenches, despaired of ever seeing Minnesota again; but I assured them I did not feel so, but expected to raise wheat again in Minnesota and to tell my grandchildren all about this conflict.
>
> April 12, 1865, we commenced the march to Montgomery, Ala., 200 miles distant. Heat became so intense that we threw away our woolen blankets and overcoats.
>
> On April 21st we had a "norther." It rained all day but we had no shelter and kept on the march, wading all streams. It was very cold. At sundown it cleared, and ice was found in the dishes the next morning.
>
> When near Granville, Ala., a troop was sent to us to convey the news of Lee's surrender; well did it stir us. The columns halted, men shouted till they could shout no more, danced and tumbled with joy, sang, "We are going home," and everything else. Just then a warm April thunder shower began. "The artillery of heaven answered back the shouts of men."
>
> On April 30th we heard of Lincoln's assassination. It was well that the war was over; sorrow, gloom or vengeance was seen on every face. Just at that time it would have been hard to respect the uplifted hands of the conquered.
>
> We reached Montgomery and had nothing to do but parade and live on corn until steamers came up the Alabama River. Soon we were ordered Westward, passing through Selma, Ala., and Jackson, Miss.; were camped a few weeks at Meriden, Miss.; then marched to Vicksburg and took steamer north, stopping at Memphis and St. Louis on our way to St. Paul where we were banqueted in the capitol.
>
> While on the steamers (nine days) an epidemic of congestive chills and fever attacked us. About half of the regiment was prostrated when we reached Ft. Snelling, and many died. August 18th, fifty five men were left to be mustered out of Company B of the 10th who served therein. I hastened to my home, then to Vermont where my wife and daughters were.[13]

By this time, most of Minnesota's regiments had been feted and disbanded. It was difficult for the Tenth and a few other regiments, because it had been four months since the war ended. The Tenth Minnesota Regiment was among the last to arrive home. Almost as an afterthought, the *St. Paul Pioneer* posted an article on its arrival. By then, citizens had seen nearly all of their relatives come home and there was little interest for people other than the relatives of the men of the Tenth. The following newspaper article appeared the day after the final muster of the Tenth. It was the epitaph for the Tenth.

5. The Last Battle

The Tenth Minnesota Veterans in 1904. Colonel Baker stands front and center (Minnesota Historical Society).

The TENTH REGIMENT.— Yesterday the Tenth Regiment was mustered out of service, [three years from the day the regiment was formed] and will be paid tomorrow. There are quite a number of the Regiment sick, in this city and elsewhere, but all are improving, we believe and will soon be well again [several would die after the final muster].

The Tenth Regiment, although it had received less notice from the press of the State than any of our other regiments, perhaps, is as deserving of fame as any. It has done well all that it was ordered to do, and though they have had few chances, compared with some other regiments, its men have made a glorious record. Its charge over the rebel ramparts at Nashville alone was one of the most gallant acts of that memorable field, and every man whose name has been born on the rolls of the Tenth Regiment should feel proud of its record.

The Tenth Regiment can boast that its battlefields reach over a greater extent of country than those of any other Union regiment (except our 6th, 7th, and 9th) as it has fought Sioux almost at the British line on the north and fought rebs at Mobile in the extreme South. No other battlefields of this war were so widely extended as that.

In retiring from service, therefore, the men of the Tenth should feel that their gallantry and patience has not been unnoticed or slighted by the people of the state, and that every member of the Regiment will receive its fair share of glorious mention in the future annals of the historian.[14]

Summary

That is the way it was for the Tenth Regiment volunteers. They had enlisted in the midst of the greatest Indian war in the history of the United States. Many had died of heat stroke and disease during Sibley's Dakota Indian campaign in 1863 and before that. Hundreds had died of disease, weather and enemy action pursuing Price, fighting at Nashville, Tupelo, Mobile and in occupation duty after the war when most other veterans were settling into their post-war lives. They were all volunteers: none had been conscripted or paid a bounty to fight. They enlisted because they thought that it was the right thing to do. They served, put war behind them and made a new life. We are all beneficiaries of that. The reunions continued long after the war. The Grand Army of the Republic (GAR) became the fraternal organization that organized activities of the Union veterans and there was a comparable Confederate organization.[15] As seen, Colonel Baker is in front of the Tenth Regiment survivors at the reunion in 1904. As always, he was front and center of his regiment.

Epilogue: The Key Participants After 1865

James Heaton Baker survived the war attaining the rank of brigadier general. He was born in Monroe, Ohio, on 6 May 1829. Following the war he was active in veterans affairs and was the U.S. commissioner of pensions 1871–1875. He was active in the Minnesota Historical Society and wrote articles contained within the society's archives. In 1881 he was elected Minnesota state railway commissioner.[1] He died at Mankato, Minnesota, in 1913.

Big Eagle was imprisoned after the Battle of Wood Lake and was of particular interest to Lincoln because Big Eagle had led the Sioux in most of the battles but had committed no crime. Lincoln pardoned him and ordered his release in October 1864. Despite the presidential order, Big Eagle was not released, and Lincoln issued the order a second time: "Let the Indian Big Eagle be discharged. I ordered this some time ago."[2] In Minnesota, the authorities claimed that they did not believe that Lincoln's first order was authentic because it had notes written on the back.[3] Big Eagle was released and was one of the few Sioux allowed to remain in Minnesota. He was the author who related his story of the war through an interpreter in 1894 entitled "A Sioux Story of the War." His narrative has been quoted extensively in this book. It presented the Sioux side of the war. He would later comment to a reporter in 1894 that if he had known that he would be imprisoned he would never have surrendered.[3] He lived another twelve years before dying on a farm near Granite Falls, Minnesota, on 5 January 1906.

James Madison Bowler of the Third Regiment survived the war. His letters were published in a book. He was born in Lee, Maine, on 10 January 1838. After the war he served in the state legislature in 1878. He was also the state dairy and food commissioner 1899–1901.[4] James Bowler died on May 17, 1916, in St. Paul. Elizabeth Bowler moved to Crow Wing County, Minnesota, in 1920 and resided there until her death in Deerwood Township, January 24, 1931.

Joseph Renshaw Brown, called "Old Joe," was possibly the most colorful and controversial figure of the Sioux War. He was born in Hartford County, Maryland, on 5 January 1805. He had great influence with the Sioux and opposed the war. When he was ordered by Sibley to move forward to collect and bury the dead settlers in August 1862, he approved a place called Birch Coulee to camp overnight. This was the worst possible site to pick as seen in Chapter 1. The battle that followed was a disaster, but he rallied the troops and fought bravely although he was badly wounded. He later provided excellent service to Sibley in the campaigns that followed. Among his many achievements were as publisher of the newspapers *Minnesota Pioneer* and the *Henderson Democrat*.[6] He died in New York City on 9 November 1870.

John Winthrop Burnham, who served with distinction in Sibley's 1863 campaign (Chapter 2) and recorded many events at that time, was born in Derry, New Hampshire, on 19 November 1829. He was a representative in the Minnesota State Legislature, 1858–1859. He later served as captain in a colored regiment.[7] On January 6, 1866, at Cairo, Illinois, he married Ada Lawrence of Plainfield, Vermont. They had four children: Eliza, Benjamin, Ida, and Ella. In 1877, the Burnham family moved to a homestead at Wheatland, North Dakota. There, Burnham served as justice of the peace, land office lawyer, school director, notary public, and in the Territorial Legislature in 1887 and 1889. Ada Burnham died December 21, 1897. In 1900 Burnham married Lydia Reed. He died January 6, 1912, at Wheatland.

Loren Warren Collins, who served in the Seventh Minnesota Regiment, was born in Lowell, Massachusetts, on 7 August 1838. His narrative of the war provided good information not found elsewhere (see Chapter 2). Following the war he was admitted to the bar and settled in St. Cloud, Minnesota, in 1866 where he practiced law. He served in the state legislature, 1881–1883, and was associate justice in the Seventh Judicial District of the Minnesota Supreme Court, 1887–1904.[8] He died in Minneapolis, 27 September 1912.

Alonzo P. Connolly, the prolific author of the Sioux War (see Chapter 2), was born in Sheffield, New Brunswick, Canada, on 15 October 1836. He came to Minnesota in 1857. He served in the Sixth Minnesota Regiment. He organized the militia of the state in 1870 and 1871.[9] His book, *The Minnesota Massacre and the Sioux War, 1862–1863*, was published in 1896. He died in 1915.

Adrian J. Ebell, the Yale student who collided with history when he travelled to Minnesota in August of 1862, produced amazing photographs just before and during the Sioux War. Ebell had a broad range of talents. He also published articles on the war in *Harper's* and the Minnesota press. Sibley recognized his many talents and commissioned him as a lieutenant, assistant commissary, to his campaign. After the Sioux War, he returned to Yale and subsequently graduated from Albany Medical College with an MD in 1869. Ebell died young while on a voyage at age 37 in 1877.

Alonzo J. Edgerton, commander of B Company of the Tenth, would be a brevet brigadier general by the end of the war and later a United States senator.[10] He was born in Rome, New York, on 7 June 1827 and was a graduate of Wesley University in 1850. He died in Sioux Falls, South Dakota, on 9 August 1896.[11]

Ira Eggleston from D Company, Tenth Regiment, came home, got married on Christmas Day in 1866 to Rebecca Susan Fox and fathered many children. He did not write much about his war experiences except in his pension and disability applications. He had a way with animals and would make a living farming and doing such things as making horse collars. He died in 1898 of disabilities associated with hard service during the war such as bad teeth, rheumatism and a bad heart. His wife, Rebecca, would continue to get a pension from the government for his disability until her death in 1929. His great-grandchildren are alive today in Minnesota and Virginia and treasure his service during the Civil War.

Charles E. Flandrau was both a judge and a colonel who commanded forces at the Battle of New Ulm. He was also a gifted writer and historian. He was born in New York City on 15 July 1828 and after the war he practiced law and was an unsuccessful candidate for governor in 1867. Two years later he served as chairman of the state central Democratic committee. He wrote many articles about the war. He died in St. Paul on 9 September 1903.[12]

Nathan Bedford Forrest, "The Wizard of the Saddle," was the Memphis merchant who became a general and is remembered as one of the greatest cavalry leaders of the South. He was also accused of being a war criminal who was never prosecuted for the murder of Black Union soldiers after their surrender at Fort Pillow. This episode has been disputed by historians ever since. He served as the first grand wizard of the Ku Klux Klan. Forrest died in 1877.

Gall, the Lakota chief and a lieutenant of Sitting Bull, survived the Indian campaigns of 1863 and 1864. Gall escaped death in 1865 when he was bayoneted three times in a confrontation with the army near Fort Berthold.[13] He would participate with Sitting Bull and others in the Battle of the Little Big Horn thirteen years later. Chief Gall died at the Standing Rock Agency on 5 December 1894.

Thomas Park Gere, the nineteen-year-old defender of Fort Ridgley, survived the war after winning the Medal of Honor at the Battle of Nashville where he was wounded. Gere was born in Wellsburg, New York, on 10 September 1842. After the war he became the general superintendent of the Eastern division of the Chicago, St. Paul, Minneapolis and Omaha Railroad in 1882. He removed to Sioux City, Iowa, and later to Chicago. Gere died there on 8 January 1912. He was buried in Arlington National Cemetery (Section 1, Grave 361). His wife, Emma, died on 22 November 1929.[14]

James R. Hart enlisted in Company D, Tenth Regiment, at age eighteen on 22 August 1862. He was born in Beaver Dam Wisconsin, May 30, 1845. He survived the war and was mustered out at Fort Snelling, Minnesota, on 19 August 1865.[15] His reminiscences are on microfilm and available on interlibrary loan from the Minnesota Historical Society. His diary has been criticized by some because his dates were off, but the value of Hart's writings is how he related what he saw years later. We get a first hand glimpse of the war. Hart died in Ellendale, North Dakota, April 28, 1927.

John Bell Hood did well as a brigade and division commander but failed when he was promoted to larger independent commands. The decisive defeats that he suffered in the Franklin-Nashville and Atlanta campaigns destroyed his reputation. After the war he retired to New Orleans where he died in the Yellow Fever epidemic in 1879 with his wife and oldest son. His ten orphans were farmed out to other families in Louisiana, Mississippi, Georgia, Kentucky, and New York. A very sad ending for a great hero. If his children ever had a family reunion it must have been a very grand affair with much to discuss. His son Duncan Norbert Hood graduated from West Point with the Class of 1896. Apparently he inherited some of his father's leadership ability. He was a colonel of U.S. Volunteers during the Spanish-American War in 1898.[16]

Thomas Jefferson Hunt of B Company, Tenth Regiment, was born in Vermont in 1831. He enlisted in the Tenth at age thirty-three on 23 January 1864. Hunt was mustered out on 19 August 1865. His reminiscences were extensive and comprehensive providing the reader information not found elsewhere. Hunt's reminiscences were never published but were transcribed to a typed copy that is maintained at the Minnesota Historical Society. His description of the last battle of the Civil War provides a level of detail not found anywhere else.[17] He was the last surviving officer of the Tenth. During his career he served in the Minnesota Legislature and was elected a probate judge. His jaw wound handicapped him for the rest of his life. He was a prohibitionist and author of the first dry laws. He died at age ninety-three in Minnesota.

Inkpaduta fled West after the Indian defeats at the hands of Sibley. He was born in 1815. After the defeat of Custer at the Little Big Horn, Inkpaduta fled with Sitting Bull to Canada. It is said that he died in Sashkatchewan in 1879 from pneumonia contracted while he was out hunting.[18] Like his birth, his death is uncertain. It appears that his only claim to fame is the brutal murder of thirty-nine helpless white civilians at the Spirit Lake massacre in March 1857. Inkpaduta employed a favorite Indian trick as seen in the Acton murders of 1862. Whites were invited to a shooting contest and when their backs were turned, they were murdered by the Indians.[19]

Samuel Pierce Jennison, the Tenth Regimental commander who was wounded at Nashville, was born in Southbridge, Massachusetts, on 9 May 1830. He also served in the Second Regiment and was promoted to brevet brigadier general at the end of the war. After the war he served as Minnesota secretary of state, 1872–1876. He removed to Covina near Los Angeles where he died on 29 November 1909.[20]

John Jones, the hero of the Battle of Fort Ridgley, was born in Middlesex, England, on 5 December 1924. He served in the Mexican War before he came to Minnesota in 1856. After the Fort Ridgley battle, he was promoted to captain of artillery and served with Sibley in the campaign of 1863. After the war he resided in St. Paul where he was chief of police and later a veterinary surgeon. He died in St. Paul on 4 May 1886.[21]

Captain LaBarge, "the man who taught Mark Twain about the Mississippi River," would live on after the Civil War, dying in St. Louis in 1899 at age 84. He was born in 1815 and worked on the river until he was 70. He knew from the start the importance of his annuity mission and would speak often of it afterward. Some of his comments are as vivid today as they were in 1863. When commenting on the hostile attack on his vessel he said:

> I looked for my crew. I looked for the brave mountaineers [who he had enlisted to help defend the boat]. Where had they hidden, leaving the boat defenseless? They were hanging thick as sardines all over the paddles. I was so disgusted that I was disposed to set the wheels in motion and give them all a ducking, but the Indians had put out the fires and we had no steam.

The Union Army never paid LaBarge for this mission although he visited Washington several times to collect. It was a case of bureaucratic dithering and stalling for no good reason.[22]

Abraham Lincoln died before he could reform Indian Affairs. He had promised reform to the Senate in order to prevent another Indian war.[23] No record could be found of Lincoln's plan. It appears that he did not live long enough to develop one. It was left to Ulysses S. Grant to accomplish this after he was elected president, and he did accomplish some reform.[24] Grant died in poverty of throat cancer in 1885. His book about his reminiscences served to provide for his wife after he died.[25]

John Other Day (Ampaturtokicha) was a Sioux Indian of the Wahpeton band who earned the gratitude of the whites when he saved sixty-two civilians at the Upper Agency. Afterwards he joined Sibley's troops as a scout. He died at Fort Wadsworth, South Dakota, in 1869.[26]

Little Crow was killed by a farmer, Nathan Lamson, not by the army, as Little Crow was picking raspberries on 3 July 1863.[27] Little Crow's son, Wowinpa, was with him when he died.[28] Little Crow's body was thrown into an offal pit in town where it rotted. One of the citizens thought that the face resembled Little Crow. They checked the arms of the body and found that they were disfigured. This confirmed that it was Little Crow. While a young man, Little Crow was wounded by a ball that passed through both forearms. He was taken to Fort Snelling where the surgeon wanted to amputate, but Little Crow refused and his arms were saved. It is difficult to be chief if you have no arms. How would one signal an attack? Little Crow's head was sent to St. Paul. Sibley was outraged and disgusted at the treatment of Little Crow's body and complained to no avail.[29] Five hundred dollars were paid to Nathan Lamson for killing Little Crow.[30] For years, Little Crow's head was displayed at the Minnesota Historical Society and other locations. By the 1970s it was becoming an embarrassment and it was handed over to Little Crow's family, who provided a proper burial. Among those present at the burial was Little Crow's grandson, Jesse Wakeman, who was eighty-seven years of age at that time. Jesse said that the family members decided that Little Crow would be buried by his own people with only his own people on hand. The location of his grave is not known.

George C. Pettie was born in New York in 1828. He moved to Minnesota and was elected to the first Minnesota state legislature from the 15th District in 1857. He served during the 1857–1858 session and his photograph seen in this book is from that session. He enlisted as a private in Company A of the Tenth Minnesota Regiment on 12 August 1862 and served in the Sibley campaign into Dakota Territory in 1863 as well as other campaigns against the Confederacy that followed. On 1 January 1863 he started the diary of his experiences that continued day by day until the end of Sibley's Dakota campaign in the fall of 1863. Pettie's diary stops, but for a little less than a year he tells the reader the experiences of the soldiers in the Tenth Regiment. Each day we see the boredom of camp life in the winter and the terror of combat on the Dakota plains. He was never melodramatic in his presentation but tells us what he saw. Some of this has been included in this book. Some of his recollections are based upon what other soldiers told him and he acknowledges that in his diary. Pettie died of dysentery on 19 January 1865 at Jeffersonville, Clark County, Indiana. Many others died about the same time in Jeffersonville after the Battle of Nashville. Pettie was buried at New Albany National Cemetery in Indiana. Pettie was survived by his wife, Augusta, who died in 1918.

John Pope is remembered by history as the man who lost Second Manassas to General R. E. Lee. Even Pope, in time, came to realize that the Western Indians needed help. He spent army funds, probably illegally, to buy cattle for the Indians, who proved to be very clever at raising them.[31] He continued his career in the army including service in the Apache War. He retired from the army in 1886 and died in an old soldiers home in Sandusky, Ohio, at age 70 on 23 September 1892.[32]

Sterling Price, "Old Pap," lost at the Battles of Pea Ridge and Westport. Rather than surrender at the end of the war he took some of his troops to Mexico hoping to enlist in the service of Maximilian. When this failed, he returned to Missouri where he died in poverty and was buried in St. Louis in 1867.

Alexander Ramsey, the Minnesota governor during the Sioux War, was born near Harrisburg, Pennsylvania, on 8 September 1815. He resigned his Minnesota governorship in July of 1863 and was elected to the U.S. Senate, where he served until 1875. He was secretary of war in the Hayes administration, 1879–1881. He was president of the Minnesota Historical Society, 1849–1863 and 1891–1903.[33] He remained friends with Sibley, his fellow Indian trader from the early years. He died on 22 April 1903. His wife, Anna, died in St. Paul on 29 November 1884.

Gabriel Renville, the Indian chief who assisted the whites during the Sioux War, was born about April 1825. He served as Sibley's chief of scouts in 1864–1865. He was later chief of the Sisseton and Wahpeton bands. He wrote a narrative about the Sioux outbreak and Sibley's expedition in 1865. Renville died in Brown's Valley, Minnesota, on 26 August 1892.[34]

Stephen Riggs was the missionary who escaped with his family from the Upper Agency with the help of friendly Indians. He was born in Steubenville, Ohio, on 23 March 1812. He published a book in 1880 that included his experiences in the Sioux War as well as many articles. Riggs translated the Bible into the Dakota language. He died in Beloit, Wisconsin, on 24 August 1883.[35]

Edwin Curtis Sanders of the Tenth Regiment staff was a Baptist minister who was born in Ashford, New York, in 1827. He fought at the Battle of New Ulm and was wounded before enlisting in G Company of the Tenth Regiment at age 35 on 26 September 1862. He commanded the Tenth Regiment for a short time after the regimental commander was wounded at Nashville and was promoted to major on 15 January 1865. After the war he became pastor of the Le Sueur Baptist Church and was the chaplain of the state senate 1876–1878. He moved to Milwaukee in 1900 and died there on 29 August 1908.[36]

Timothy J. Sheehan, "The Fighting Irishman," who reinforced and took command of Fort Ridgley during the siege, was born in Cork County, Ireland, on 21 December 1835. He was promoted to captain after the siege and was a lieutenant colonel by the end of the war. After the war he was sheriff of Freeborn County, 1871–1883, and Indian agent at White Earth, 1885–1889. He also served as deputy U.S. marshal, 1890–1897.[37] He married Jennie Judge of Albert Lea, Minnesota, in 1866 and they had three sons. She was also from Ireland. He died in St. Paul on 13 July 1913 and is buried in Calvary Cemetery in St. Paul.

Henry Hastings Sibley continued his work to bring peace to the frontier after the Indian campaigns. He left the army in 1866 and returned home. Three of his children had died of illness while he was on the campaigns against the Sioux and his wife died the year after his return. He continued his work on Indian affairs and at treaty-making in what must have been a very lonely life. His purpose was to improve the living conditions of the Sioux. During his career, he was frequently criticized by the press and others for many of his actions. Minnesota citizens even accused him of protecting the Sioux when they should all have been hanged. Reviewing the events of the Indian War, it is hard to find anything he could have done better. He died two weeks short of eighty years of age on 18 February 1891. He was buried in Oakland Cemetery, St. Paul, near many of his soldiers. Sibley's home at Mendota is a historic site today.[38]

Sitting Bull would survive the 1863 campaign to defeat Custer at the Little Big Horn in 1876. He was finally captured and imprisoned. Later released, he joined Buffalo Bill's Wild West Show in 1885 and delighted little children by menacing and making wild gestures during the show. He was not only a great chief, but a great showman, as well. In a sad ending to his life he was again imprisoned and killed by guards in a feeble escape attempt in 1890. He probably summed up this sad chapter in U.S. history when he told his biographer shortly before his death:

> When I was a boy, the Sioux owned the world. The sun rose and set on their land; they sent ten thousand men to battle. Where are the warriors today? Who slew them? Where are our lands? Who owns them? Is it wrong for me to love my own? Is it wicked for me because my skin is red? Because I am Sioux? Because I was born where my father lived? Because I would die for my people and my country? I wish it to be remembered that I was the last man of my tribe to surrender my rifle.

Andrew Jackson Smith, "Whiskey," was one of the oldest generals in the field during the Civil War. He was born in Bucks County, Pennsylvania, on 28 April 1815. He attended the U.S. Military Academy at West Point graduating with the Class of 1838. He ranked thirty-six in a class of forty-five. Smith served in the Mexican War. He rose in rank to command a corps during the Civil War and is best remembered for his defeat of the Confederate Army at Tupelo, Mississippi, which included one of the few defeats of Nathan Bedford Forrest. A. J. Smith was admired by his troops because he shared their hardships. They called themselves A. J.'s Guerrillas. Smith resigned his volunteer commission in 1866 and became colonel of the U.S. 7th Cavalry Regiment. He retired from the military service in April 1869 to become postmaster at St. Louis, Missouri. A. J. died there on 30 January 1897 and is buried in St. Louis.[39]

John Smith enlisted in G Company of the Tenth at age 24 on 15 August 1862 and was discharged as a sergeant on 21 July 1865. His diary was not published until it appeared in *Tales of the Tenth Regiment* by the Joseph R. Brown Heritage Society. Smith's diary follows closely the diary entries of George C. Pettie of A Company of the Tenth.[40]

Standing Buffalo made his escape to Canada after the Battle of Big Mound. He had argued for peace and opposed war all of his life. He was plagued with bad luck the rest of his life. Later, most members of his family died from smallpox and his wife committed suicide (a taboo and rare among Indians) because of the loss of her children. Finally he committed suicide by a hopeless attack on his tormentors after he was accused of cowardice for not joining an attack on another Indian band. He remained a peacemaker until the day he died. He was only forty-two.[41]

Alfred Sully, the son of the painter Thomas Sully, claimed victory when all of the hostiles had been driven west of the Missouri. Neither Sully nor Pope would return east to fight for glory and promotion in the Civil War. Sully was embittered by his assignments to outposts in the West. His campaigns after the war included the Nez Perce Expedition of 1877. He died in Washington state on 27 April 1879 at age fifty-eight. His body was shipped east to be buried in Philadelphia.[42] Many historians consider him to be one of the most capable generals of the Civil War.

George Henry Thomas, "The Rock of Chickamauga," was one of the few Virginians to fight for the North as a general officer. His victory at Nashville destroyed the army of John Bell Hood and is considered to be one of the most decisive battles of the war. He never reconciled with Grant. Perhaps Grant did not trust him because he was a Southerner. He died shortly after the war in San Francisco on 28 March 1870. He was buried in Troy, New York.[43]

John P. Williamson, the missionary who also served as interpreter in 1862, was born at Lac qui Parle, Minnesota, 27 October 1835. He was the son of a missionary and graduated from Marietta College in 1857. He was twenty-eight years old at the time of the Sioux War and his account of the decisive meeting with Little Crow just before the war is found in Chapter 1. Following the defeat of the Sioux, he accompanied them on their long journey to Dakota Territory and later Nebraska. He remained a missionary to the Sioux and at Crow Creek, Dakota Territory, in 1863, when approximately 300 Dakotas died within the first three months. He is credited with saving nearly a thousand Dakotas by persuading the U.S. government to allow them to go on a buffalo hunt when they were starving. He was a writer and possibly his best works are his book on the Dakota language and his Dakota-English Dictionary published in 1902.[44] He died of pneumonia in 1917 at the Yankton Reservation in South Dakota.

James Harrison Wilson, the Union cavalry leader at the Battle of Nashville, survived the war. He resigned as a major general in 1870. He returned to the army in 1898 to fight in the Spanish-American War as a major general of volunteers. Wilson died in Delaware on 23 February 1925. He was the last surviving member of the West Point Class of 1860.[45]

Wowinpa, Little Crow's son, was captured during the Sirocco Campaign. At one point he was sentenced to hang but was later released apparently because of his youth. In later life he got religion and became a Christian. He took the name of Thomas Wakefield.

He is credited with the founding of the Indian Y.M.C.A. He died young in Minnesota in 1876.

Private Asa Hinds of E Company of the Tenth was killed by Rebels near Montgomery, Alabama, on 25 April 1865. He was the last Tenth Regiment soldier to die in combat during the Civil War. Lee's surrender at Appomattox on 7 April 1865 did not end it all. No soldier of any war wants to be the last casualty, but this was Asa Hind's fate: to die nearly three weeks after Lee surrendered. His wife, Augusta, was still living in 1905 in Wisconsin. They appeared to have had one daughter, Rose, born in 1861.

The last victim of the Sioux Indian War was buried in 1919. In June of that year, Edward Gleek cut down an oak tree on his farm near New Ulm, Minnesota. Inside he found a mummified corpse with a journal written by the deceased, Jean La Rue. Additionally, rifle, powder, bullets, and $783.50 were in the tree. La Rue's journal tells what happened. When the troops arrived at New Ulm in 1862 to relieve the town, rifles were fired in celebration. La Rue heard the firing and ran to hide in the hollow oak tree since he thought that it was another Sioux attack. He got stuck in the tree. Apparently it was a good hiding place since his remains was not found until 1919. The final entry in the journal explains what happened: "Can not get out; surely must die. If ever found, send me and all of my money to my mother Suzanne La Rue."[46] Suzanne La Rue could not be located.

The Sioux Indian War in Minnesota was not the end of the Indian wars, but rather the beginning of the wars that plagued the second half of the nineteenth century. Ahead were the Little Big Horn, Wounded Knee and all of the other Indian wars. Unknown to most is the fact that the Indian Wars did not end at Wounded Knee but in 1898 with the Chippewa Uprising at Leech Lake, Minnesota.[47]

Appendices

A. Treaty with the Sioux — Sisseton and Wahpeton Bands, 1851[1]

July 23, 1851. | 10 Stats., 949. | Proclamation, Feb. 24. 1853.

Articles of a treaty made and concluded at Traverse des Sioux, upon the Minnesota River, in the Territory of Minnesota, on the twenty-third day of July, eighteen hundred and fifty-one, between the United States of America, by Luke Lea, Commissioner of Indian Affairs, and Alexander Ramsey, governor and ex-officio superintendent of Indian affairs in said Territory, commissioners duly appointed for that purpose, and See-see-toan and Wah-pay-toan bands of Dakota or Sioux Indians.

ARTICLE 1.

It is stipulated and solemnly agreed that the peace and friendship now so happily existing between the United States and the aforesaid bands of Indians, shall be perpetual.

ARTICLE 2.

The said See-see-toan and Wah-pay-toan bands of Dakota or Sioux Indians, agree to cede, and do hereby cede, sell, and relinquish to the United States, all their lands in the State of Iowa; and, also all their lands in the Territory of Minnesota, lying East of the following line, to wit: Beginning at the junction of the Buffalo River with the Red River of the North; thence along the Western bank of said Red River of the North, to the mouth of the Sioux Wood River; thence along the Western bank of said Sioux Wood River to Lake Traverse; thence, along the Western shore of said lake, to the Southern extremity thereof; thence in a direct line, to the junction of Kampeska Lake with the Tchan-kas-an-data, or Sioux River; thence along the Western bank of said river to its point of intersection with the northern line of the State of Iowa; including all the islands in said rivers and lake.

ARTICLE 3.

[Stricken out.]

Article 4.

In further and full consideration of said cession, the United States agree to pay to said Indians the sum of one million six hundred and sixty-five thousand dollars ($1,665,000,) at the several times, in the manner and for the purposes following, to wit:

1st. To the chiefs of the said bands, to enable them to settle their affairs and comply with their present just engagement; and in consideration of their removing themselves to the country set apart for them as above, which they agree to do within two years, or sooner, if required by the President, without further cost or expense to the United States, and in consideration of their subsisting themselves the first year after their removal, which they agree to do without further cost or expense on the part of the United States, the sum of two hundred and seventy-five thousand dollars, ($275,000): *Provided*, That said sum shall be paid to the chiefs in such manner as they, hereafter, in open council shall request, and as soon after the removal of said Indians to the home set apart for them, as the necessary appropriation therefore shall be made by Congress.

2d. To be laid out under the direction of the President for the establishment of manual-labor schools; the erection of mills and blacksmith shops, opening farms, fencing and breaking land, and for such other beneficial objects as may be deemed most conducive to the prosperity and happiness of said Indians, thirty thousand dollars, ($30,000.) The balance of said sum of one million six hundred and sixty-five thousand dollars, ($1,665,000,) to wit: one million three hundred and sixty thousand dollars ($1,360,000) to remain in trust with the United States, and five per cent interest thereon to be paid, annually, to said Indians for the period of fifty years, commencing the first day of July, eighteen hundred and fifty-two (1852,) which shall be in full payment of said balance, principal and interest, the said payment to be applied under the direction of the President, as follows, to wit:

3d. For a general agricultural improvement and civilization fund, the sum of twelve thousand dollars, ($12,000.) 4th. For educational purposes, the sum of six thousand dollars, ($6,000.) 5th. For the purchase of goods and provisions, the sum of ten thousand dollars, ($10,000.) 6th. For money annuity, the sum of forty thousand dollars, ($40,000.)

Article 5.

The laws of the United States, prohibiting the introduction and sale of spirituous liquors in the Indian country shall be in full force and effect throughout the territory hereby ceded and lying in Minnesota until otherwise directed by Congress or the President of the United States.

Article 6.

Rules and regulations to protect the rights of persons and property among the Indians, parties to this treaty, and adapted to their condition and wants, may be prescribed and enforced in such manner as the President or the Congress of the United States, from time to time, shall direct.

In testimony whereof, the said Commissioners, Luke Lea and Alexander Ramsey, and the undersigned Chiefs and Headmen of the aforesaid See-see-toan and Wah-pay-toan bands of Dakota or Sioux Indians, have hereunto subscribed their names and affixed their seals, in duplicate, at Traverse des Sioux, Territory of Minnesota, this twenty-third day of July, one thousand eight hundred and fifty-one.

L. Lea, [SEAL.]
Alex. Ramsey, [SEAL.]
Een-yang-ma-nee (Running Walker or "the Gun,")
Wee-tchan-h' pee-ee-tay-toan, (the Star face or the "Orphan,")
Ee-tay-wa-keen-yan, ("Limping Devil" or "Thunder Face,")
Eesh-ta-hum-ba, ("Sleepy Eyes,")
Oo-pee-ya-hen-day-a, (Extending his train,)
Hoak-shee-dan-wash-tay, (Good Boy,)
Ee-tay-tcho-ka, (Face in the midst,)
Hay-ha-hen-day-ma-za, (Metal Horn,)
Am-pay-too-sha, (Red Day,)
Eesh-ta-humba-koash-ka, (Sleepy Eyes young,)
A na-wang-ma-nee, (Who goes galloping on,)
Ma-h'pee-wee-tchash-ta, (Cloud man,)
Tan-pa-hee-da, (Sounding Moccasin,)
Eenk-pa, (the upper end,)
Wee-yoa-kee-yay, (Standard,)
Wa-kan-man-nee, (Walking Spirit,)
Ee-tay-sha, (the one that reddens his face,)
Ta-ka-ghay, (Elk maker,)
Wa-ma-ksoon-tay, ("Walnut," or Blunt headed arrow,)
Ma-za-sh'a, (Metal Sounding,)
Ya-shoa-pee, (The wind instrument,)
Noan-pa keen-yan, (Twice Flying,)
Wash-tay-da, (Good, a little,)
Wa-keen-yan-ho-ta, (Grey Thunder,)
Wa-shee-tchoon-ma-za, (Iron French man,)
Ta-pe-ta-tan-ka, (His Big fire,)
Ma-h'pee-ya-h'na-shkan-shkan, (Moving Cloud,)
Wa-na-pay-a, (The pursuer,)
Ee-tcha-shkan-shkan-ma-nee, (Who walks shaking,)
Ta-wa-kan-he-day-ma-za, (His Metal Lightning,)
Ee-tay doo-ta, (Red Face,)
Henok-marpi-yahdi-nape, (Reappearing Cloud,)
Tchan-hedaysh-ka-ho-toan-ma-nee, (the moving sounding Harp)
Ma-zaku-te-ma-ni, (Metal walks shooting,)
A-kee-tchee-ta, (Standing Soldier.)

Signed in presence of Thomas Foster, Secretary. Nathaniel McLean, Indian Agent. Alexander Faribault, Stephen R. Riggs, Interpreters. A. S. H. White; Thos. S. Williamson; W. C. Henderson; A. Jackson; James W. Boal; W. G. Le Duc; Alexis Bailly; H. L. Dousman; Hugh Tyler.

To the Indian names are subjoined marks.

Supplemental Article.

1st. The United States do hereby stipulate to pay the Sioux bands of Indians, parties to this treaty, at the rate of ten cents per acre, for the lands included in the reservation provided for in the third article of the treaty as originally agreed upon in the following words:

ARTICLE 3.

In part consideration of the foregoing cession, the United States do hereby set apart for the future occupancy and home of the Dakota Indians, parties to this treaty, to be held by them as Indian lands are held, all that tract of country on either side of the Minnesota River, from the Western boundary of the lands herein ceded, East, to the Tchay-tam-bay River on the north, and to Yellow Medicine River on the South side, to extend, on each side, a distance of not less than ten miles from the general course of said river; the boundaries of said tract to be marked out by as straight lines as practicable, whenever deemed expedient by the President, and in such manner as he shall direct:" which article has been stricken out of the treaty by the Senate, the said payment to be in lieu of said reservation: the amount when ascertained under instructions from the Department of the Interior, to be added to the trust-fund provided for in the fourth article.

2d. It is further stipulated, that the President be authorized, with the assent of the said band of Indians, parties to this treaty, and as soon after they shall have given their assent to the foregoing *article*, as may be convenient, to cause to be set apart by appropriate landmarks and boundaries, such tracts of country without the limits of the cession made by the first [2d] article of the treaty as may be satisfactory for their future occupancy and home: *Provided*, That the President may, by the consent of these Indians, vary the conditions aforesaid if deemed expedient.

B. Narrative of the Tenth Regiment[1]

In 1890, General J. H. Baker published his narrative of the Tenth. It was brief and is presented here as originally written.

NARRATIVE OF THE TENTH REGIMENT.
BY GEN. J. H. BAKER.

For the purpose of raising the quota of troops to be furnished by the State of Minnesota, under the calls of the president of the United States, made July 2d, for 500,000, and Aug. 4, 1862, for 300,000, six additional regiments of infantry were called for, from the Sixth to the Eleventh inclusive, five regiments being already in the field. By order of the adjutant general of the state (General Order, No. 25, Aug. 12, 1862), Fort Snelling was designated as the general rendezvous of the new regiments. In the midst of the organization of companies for these new regiments the Sioux Indian War unexpectedly broke out (August 18th) on the Western frontier of the state, and threw regular organization into confusion. Some companies, and even squads of men, unassigned and not yet mustered, were ordered to the frontier, thus greatly retarding regimental organization, as was the case with Company I of the Tenth. However, the adjutant general, Oct. 18, 1862, issued an order (General Order, No. 65) assigning and transferring ten several volunteer companies "to compose and constitute the Tenth Regiment, Minnesota Volunteers, and the said captains will take their rank in the order in which they are named, and the said companies be designated as therein indicated, to-wit: Company A, Captain Rufus C. Ambler; Company B, Captain Alonzo J. Edgerton; Company C, Captain Chas. W. Hackett; Company D, Captain W. W. Phelps; Company E, Captain James A. Robson; Company F, Captain George F. White; Company G, Captain Edwin C. Sanders; Company H, Captain M. H. Sullivan; Company I, First Lieut. James H. Gorman; Company K, Captain M. J. O'Connor."

Subsequently, Dec. 1, 1862, this order was modified, substituting John W. Heath as captain of Company E, *vice* James A. Robson, deceased, he having been killed near Belle Plaine by the accidental discharge of a pistol which Lieut. McCarty of Company H was in the act of handing to Captain Robson at the latter's request. The same order (General Order, No. 73) also announced the field and staff officers of the regiment as follows: James H. Baker, colonel, of Blue Earth county; S. P. Jennison, lieutenant colonel, of Goodhue county; Michael Cook, major, of Rice county; J. C. Braden, adjutant, of Houston county; George W. Green, quartermaster, of Steele county; S. B. Sheardown, surgeon, of Winona county; W. W. Clark, first assistant, of Blue Earth county; Alfred M. Burnham, second assistant, of Freeborn county. The recruits, for the greater part, were enlisted from the counties of Freeborn, Dodge, Dakota, Waseca, Steele, Sibley, Le Sueur, Olmsted, Wabasha, Goodhue, Ramsey and Hennepin, and were chiefly drawn from those engaged in agricultural pursuits. The Rev. Ezra R. Lathrop, a clergyman of the Methodist Episcopal Church, was appointed chaplain by the governor March 18, 1863. The rule of promotion was early established, being strictly that of seniority, which was promotions among officers by date of muster into service, and among sergeants by date of warrant.

The first order received for military service was one directed to Col. Baker to prepare his regiment to go to New York, and thence, by steamer, to join Gen. Banks at Turk's Island, near the mouth of the Mississippi, to take part in some contemplated expedition along the Gulf. The Sioux outbreak was followed by the immediate countermanding of this order, and the regiment was directed to report to Gen. H. H. Sibley, commanding against the hostile Sioux. Among the first portion of the Tenth Regiment to engage in the Indian War was a squad of Company I, about eighteen men, under Lieut. M. R. Merrill of Henderson, which voluntarily proceeded to New Ulm to join the company of Capt. Cox August 26th, and reported to Col. Chas. E. Flandrau, commanding in the defense of that place, where they rendered good service. Another squad of the same company, about forty-five men, under Lieut. James H. Gorman, bore a gallant part in the defense of Fort Ridgley and in the battle of Wood Lake. These men, at the time of the Indian outbreak, were on their way to Fort Snelling to enlist in the service of the United States, but patriotically returned with Agent Galbraith to the defense of the imperiled frontier. They served as a body-guard to Gen. Sibley in the campaign of 1862, and were highly complimented by that officer for gallant conduct. They lost one killed and several wounded in the stirring events of the fall of 1862.

A part of Company G of Le Sueur, known as "The Le Sueur Tigers," was also at the defense of New Ulm, August 24th and 25th, under Capt. Sanders. Capt. Sanders himself was wounded in that battle, and four of his men were killed. Company C, Capt. Hackett, was also in the Indian campaign of 1862, prior to regimental organization. By order of Gen. Pope, Company C was mounted, armed with carbines, and ordered to join Gen. Sibley in the field. The company proceeded to the Yellow Medicine Agency, and was employed in guarding the Indian prisoners afterward court martialed. Subsequently Capt. Hackett had charge of all the captured Indians and their families, taking them to the lower agency. Here

Company C was joined by Company F, Capt. White, which had also been mounted, and the two companies were engaged in scouting and burying the dead. After performing many important duties connected with the captured Indians, Capt. Hackett was ordered to Fort Ridgley, and Capt. White to the Winnebago Agency, for the winter. Lieut. Michael Hoy, with a detachment of Company K, also bore a part in the events of 1862. So, also, did Company B, doing duty at the Winnebago Reservation, over-awing that tribe. The Indian campaign for that fall was closed before the complete organization of the regiment, When its organization, however, was completed, in the winter of 1862–63, it was ordered to do guard duty along the frontier. Headquarters for the field and staff were established at Le Sueur, with Company G and part of Company I in garrison. The location of the other companies was as follows: Company A, Captain Ambler, Garden City; Company B, Captain Edgerton, Winnebago Agency; Company C, Captain Hackett, Fort Ridgley; Company D, Captain Phelps, Henderson; Company E, Captain Heath, Henderson; Company F, Captain White, Winnebago Agency; Company H, Captain Sullivan, Swan Lake and Vernon Centre; Company K, Captain O'Connor, Norwegian Lake. Company I was still not mustered by reason of the confusion incident to the Indian campaign during the fall. A part, if not all, of the Renville Rangers held themselves to be state militia, and only enlisted for three months. This difficulty pursued that company till after the arrival of the regiment in St. Louis, when the company organization was completed by the promotion of Private M. J. Severance to be captain, April 4, 1864.

The winter of 1862–63 was spent in doing guard duty along the frontier and building stockades — notably those erected by Company H at Vernon Centre and Company I at New Auburn. A school of instruction was formed at Le Sueur by detail of one commissioned officer and two enlisted men from each company. The detail was changed every thirty days, the first returning to their companies to teach the school of the soldier, while the second was taught and drilled in the school of the company, a third following them for drill in the school of the battalion. This instruction was in charge of Lieut. Col. Jennison, whose study and experience in the Second Minnesota had qualified him for that service. Thus officers and men were gradually and uniformly learning the duties of a soldier's life. The winter passed without a single event to stir the dullness of post life till February, when Col. Baker received orders from Gen. Sibley to take a portion of the regiment and proceed to Mankato to participate in the great Indian execution which was ordered for the 26th of February, 1863 [Baker is wrong here. The execution was scheduled and carried out on 26 December 1862]. The several companies were drawn in and marched by way of Kasota on the 24th, and on the 25th of the month reported to Col. Miller, commanding at Mankato, and in charge of the execution. The force of the Tenth numbered four hundred and forty-two men, being a greater number than was present from any other command. In the arrangement for the execution, Col. Baker, in command of the Tenth, took position in two lines on the North and East sides of the scaffold, a part of the Seventh completing the square. Lieut. Col. Jennison, in command of one company of the Seventh and one of the Tenth, was assigned position in the yard of the prison pending the execution. Capt. White of Company F, having his company temporarily mounted, acted as patrol guard. Surgeons Sheardown and Clark of the Tenth examined the bodies to see that life was extinct. Companies A, B, G, H and K took part in this extraordinary event, while all the field and staff of the regiment were present.

The campaign against the Sioux Indians for the summer of 1863 was under the general direction of Maj. Gen. John Pope, with headquarters at Milwaukee, while the immediate command of the expeditionary forces in the field was entrusted to Gen. H. H. Sibley, in whose command the Tenth Regiment yet remained. In June, 1863, orders were received to join the expeditionary forces at the general rendezvous at Camp Pope, at the mouth of the Red Wood River, about twenty five miles West of Fort Ridgley. The regiment was presently to participate in a regular campaign. Early in June the several companies were withdrawn from their posts and marched to Camp Pope, where the main body of the regiment arrived June 9th, with the exception of Company I, which had been dispatched up the Missouri River with the Winnebago Indians. The company then returned and was stationed at Mananah, Meeker county, and did scout duty on the frontier. The camp had already been established, April 19th, by a detachment of the Sixth Minnesota, which had brought large supplies up the Minnesota River by the steamer Favorite.

The expedition left Camp Pope for the field June 16th. July 4th we arrived at the first crossing of the Sheyenne River, near where Valley City now is, and there awaited the arrival of Lieut. Col. Averill, who, with a cavalry detachment, brought a train of supplies from Fort Abercrombie. Between the crossings of the Sheyenne we saw the first herd of buffalo. The march was exceedingly monotonous, the heat intense, and many sun-strokes occurred in the regiment; grass was scarce and the water in most of the lakes so alkaline as not to be used for drink, or, if so used, was very generally followed with dysenteric results more or less aggravated. We dug many wells by the lakes and sloughs. Every camp was fortified by sod thrown up with shovels. We breakfasted at 3 A.M., and were on the march by sunrise. No event broke the dull uniformity of the days until July 24th, at about 4 P.M., when we struck a large body of Indians at what was called Big Mound, near where Crystal Springs, N. D., now stands. The three infantry regiments alternating in the order of march, brought the Tenth to the front every third day. At Big Mound the Tenth was in the rear. By special detail, Company B, Capt. Edgerton, and later, Companies A, F, C and K, with Lieut. Col. Jennison, participated in that engagement, the remainder of the regiment fortifying and holding the camp upon the lake, which had been placed in command of Col. Baker. The misdelivery of an important order prevented the pursuit by the whole column, the advance all returning to camp so worn and exhausted as to prevent a movement at once, and occasioning the loss of two days. In the action on Sunday, the 26th, at Dead Buffalo Lake, the Tenth Regiment, by its position, did not participate. On Tuesday, July 28th, however, the Tenth being in advance, occurred by far the most important engagement of the expedition. The Indians returned, with every man fit for battle, to resist our further advance. Their purpose was, in one decisive engagement, to settle the contest. The Tenth Regiment being in the front, and by being out and in line some half an hour earlier than ordered, promptly met and repelled the united attack of the largest body of Indians which ever confronted an American army. Nathaniel West, in his "Life and Times of H. H. Sibley," gives a full account of this memorable action. He says (page 312): "The brunt of the conflict was borne by the Tenth Regiment, Col. Baker in front, where the Indian assault was most gallantly met and broken." The number of Indians was estimated at the time, by Joseph R. Brown, chief of scouts, at from 4,000 to 5,000 warriors. The Indians advanced in the dawn of the early morning, in semicircular line, and formed a warlike picture as they confronted the line of battle promptly formed by the Tenth. When, at last, we advanced in battle line, they precipitately broke and fled. It was upon that advance (on the 28th) that the young Teton so miraculously evaded a shower of bullets, and was captured and brought into camp without a mark upon his person. Two days more brought the expedition to the Missouri River. In an expedition into the wilderness and to the Missouri River, under Col. Crooks, to dislodge the Indians and destroy their property, Companies B, F and K of the Tenth, under Lieut. Col. Jennison, participated. It is thought best, as a matter of record, to insert here the official report of Col. Baker, as to the part borne by the Tenth in this celebrated Indian campaign:

REPORT OF COLONEL JAMES H. BAKER. "HEADQUARTERS TENTH REGIMENT. MINNESOTA INFANTRY, "*Camp Williston, Aug 5, 1863.* "Captain R. C. Olin, "*Assistant Adjutant General:*

"I have the honor herewith to submit a report of such part as was borne by my regiment, or any portion of it, in the several actions from July 24th, at Big Mound, to the Missouri River.

"About half-past three o'clock on Friday, the 24th of July, while on the march doing escort duty in the centre, I received information from the general commanding that a large force of Indians was immediately in our front, accompanied by an order, communicated by Lieut. Beever, to prepare my regiment for action, which order was immediately executed. Meantime the train was being corralled on the side of the lake, after which I received orders to form my regiment on the color line indicated for it, immediately in front of the corral and fronting outward from the lake, and to throw up entrenchments along this line, which was speedily done. The action of this day began on my right, more immediately in front of the Seventh (which regiment, being in advance during the day's march, was entitled to the forward position), by the artillery under Captain Jones, when, at 4:30 P.M., I received an order through Captain Olin to deploy a company to support this battery. I immediately deployed Company B, Captain Edgerton, and that company, though fatigued already with an ordinary day's march, continued with the battery (marching for many miles on the double-quick) during the entire pursuit of the enemy for fifteen miles, and throughout the night till sunrise next morning, when they returned from pursuit to the camp, having made during the day and night the almost unparalleled march of quite fifty miles.

"At about five o'clock I received an order through Captain Pope to send Lieut. Col. Jennison with four companies, to be deployed and to follow in the direction of the retreating enemy, as a support for the cavalry and artillery. Lieut. Col. Jennison moved forward with Companies A, F, C and K five miles, more than half of it on the double-quick, and reported his command to the general commanding. Lieut. Col. Jennison was directed to return with his force to camp, and arrived a little after 9 o'clock P.M. At the same time that the first order above alluded to was given, I was directed to assume command of the camp and make the proper dispositions for its defense, which I did by completing all the entrenchments, and organizing and posting such forces as were yet left in camp, not anticipating the return of our forces that night. The action of the 26th of July took place on the side of the camp opposite from my regiment, and consequently we did not participate in it. We were, however, constantly under arms, ready at any moment for orders or an opportunity.

"On Tuesday, the 28th of July, my regiment being in the advance for the day's march, we started out of Camp Ambler at three o'clock in the morning. The general commanding, some of the scouts and a few of the headquarters' wagons had preceded my regiment out of camp, and were ascending the long, sloping hill which gradually rose from Stone Lake. I had just received, directly from the general commanding, orders for the disposition of my regiment during the day's march, when the scouts came from over the hill on a full run, shouting 'They are coming! They are coming!' when immediately a large body of mounted Indians began to make their appearance over the brow of the hill, and directly in the front of my advancing column. I instantly gave the necessary orders for the deployment of the regiment to the right and left, which, with the assistance of Lieut. Col. Jennison, and the great alacrity of commandants of companies, were executed with the utmost rapidity, though a portion of my line was thrown into momentary confusion by the hasty passage through it of the returning scouts and advance ambulance. At this moment an Indian on the brow of the hill shouted, We are too late; they are ready for us!' Another one replied, 'But remember our children and families; we must not let them get them.' Immediately the Indians, all well mounted, filed off to the right and left along the hill in my front with the utmost rapidity. My whole regiment, except one company, was deployed, but the Indians covered my entire front, and soon far outflanked me on both sides, appearing in numbers which seemed almost incredible, and most seriously threatening the train to the right and to the left of my widely extended line. The position of the train was at this moment imminently critical. It had begun to pass out of the corral, around both ends of the small lake, to mass itself in the rear of my regiment in the usual order of march. The other regiments were not yet in position, as the time to take their respective places in the order of march had not yet arrived. Fortunately, however, Captain Jones had early moved out of camp with one section of artillery, and was in the centre of my left wing, and Lieut. Whipple, with another, near the centre of my right, which was acting under Lieut. Col. Jennison.

"Simultaneously with the deployment of the regiment we began a steady advance of the whole line up the hill upon the foe, trusting to the speedy deployment of the other infantry regiments and the cavalry for the protection of the train so threatened on either flank at the ends of the lake. My whole line was advancing splendidly up the hill, directly upon the enemy, the artillery doing fine work, and the musketry beginning to do execution, when I received a peremptory order to halt the entire line, as a further advance would imperil the train. So ardent were both officers and men for the advance that it was with some considerable difficulty that I could affect a halt. Believing fully that the great engagement of the expedition was now begun, and seeing in my front, and reaching far beyond either flank, more than double the number of Indians that had hitherto made their appearance, I took advantage of the halt to make every preparation for a prolonged and determined action. Meantime, long range firing continued throughout the entire line, and frequently the balls of the enemy would reach to and even pass over my men, though it was evident that the range of the Indian guns bore no comparison to ours. About this time I twice received the order to cause the firing to cease, which order I found difficult to execute, owing to the large extent of my line and the intense eagerness of the men.

"I then received orders that, as the train was closed up, I should form my regiment in order of battle, deployed as skirmishers, holding two companies in reserve, and that, thus advancing, our order of march would be resumed. in the face of the enemy. In a few minutes, the disposition being made, all was ready, and in the order of battle indicated we passed the bill and found that the enemy had fled. We saw them but once again for a moment on a distant hill, in great numbers, when they entirely disappeared. My regiment marched in deployed order of battle, in echelon, at the head of the column, for eighteen miles, expecting and ready at any moment to meet the enemy. The number of Indians so suddenly charging upon us was estimated at not less than 1,500 to 2,000. They were well mounted, and moved about with the utmost rapidity, and with their characteristic hideous yells. The artillery, under Captain Jones and Lieut. Whipple, did great execution, as I could well observe, and the fire of my men did effective service, and enabled us to hold the enemy at bay till the train was closed up and the regular positions for its defense made. At least three of the enemy were seen to fall by the fire from my line, three bodies being thrown on ponies and rapidly carried away. The artillery must have killed and wounded a considerable number. Nothing could exceed the eagerness, firmness and gallant bearing of all the officers and men of my command during this unexpected, and by far, numerically, the greatest, effort the Indians had yet made upon the forces of the expedition. In their courage and earnest desire to clear the enemy from the hill by a double-quick charge my officers and men were a unit. Nothing but the imminent peril of the train could induce them to cease the advance they had so gallantly begun.

"On the 30th of July, while at Camp Slaughter, on the Missouri, I received an order to send three companies of my regiment, under Lieut. Col. Jennison, to join an expedition under Col. Crooks, the object of which was to skirmish through the timber and heavy underbrush to the river, and destroy the property of the Indians known to be upon its banks. This most laborious task was assigned to Companies B, F and K and a portion of Company C. A report of their operations will, of course, be given you by the officer commanding the expedition. I desire, captain, to avail myself of this opportunity to express my sincere gratification at the good order, faithful devotion to every duty, most determined perseverance in the long and weary marches, severe guard and trenching labors, and unmurmuring submission to every fatigue which has characterized the officers and men of my regiment during the tedious and arduous marches we have made to the distant shores of the Missouri River. It is with justifiable pride that I here note how nobly they have performed all that has been required at their hands.

"I have the honor to be, captain, very respectfully,
"Your obedient servant,
"J. H. BAKER,
"Colonel of the Tenth Regiment, Minnesota Infantry."
"Capt. R. C. OLIN,
A.A. General, District Minnesota."

We reached the Missouri River July 29th, at about 12 o'clock, having marched from Fort Snelling, a distance of five hundred and eighty-five miles. The precise point on the river was latitude 40° 42,' longitude 100° 35,' near the mouth of Apple Creek, about three miles below where the city of Bismarck now stands. For many reasons we were unable to pursue the rapidly retreating Sioux further than the banks of the Missouri. We had driven the last hostile band out of Minnesota and beyond the Missouri. Long and rapid marches, want of water, days of activity and nights of watching, the almost total absence of forage, and the rapidly diminishing store of provisions, compelled the abandonment of further pursuit. The long and tedious countermarch began on the 20th of August. But little occurred worthy of note on the return march. Sergeant Charles D. Tuthill was shot by a cavalry picket on a dark and stormy night, being mistaken for an Indian. At the crossing of the Sheyenne River the brigade was inspected by Brig. Gen. R. B. Marcy, and the regiment much commended for drill and discipline. Two companies, B and K, were especially complimented in his official report. As Gen. Marcy was inspecting Capt. O'Connor's company, he said to him: "You have a very fine company here, captain. Where were they raised?" "In Ireland, sir," said O'Connor. About 10 o'clock A.M. on the 21st of August we crossed the Wild Rice, and at noon arrived at Fort Abercrombie, the first sign of civilization since the departure early in June. After remaining in camp near the fort for several days we started for home, and at Sauk Centre, September 4th, the Tenth Regiment, with a section of artillery and a battalion of cavalry, under Col. Baker, was detached from the main column, and ordered to march through the Kandiyohi country to Fort Ridgley, and thence to Fort Snelling. Here the regiment was furloughed for a short time. At Camp Pope, June 16th, the day of starting, the expeditionary forces numbered 3,674. The Tenth Regiment, the same day, numbered, present and for duty, 676 men and officers, not counting Company H of the Ninth Regiment, which was attached to the Tenth during the entire campaign. On arriving at the Missouri River the regiment numbered 521 men and officers and 9 of the field and staff. Maj. Cook had been left at Camp Atchison July 18th, near Lake Jessie, with about 300 serviceable men, together with all the invalids and disabled men and animals. With him, also, Surgeon Burnham had been left in charge of all the sick. Surgeon Burnham was subsequently dismissed the service (by Special Order, 475, War Department., A. G. O., Oct. 23, 1863) on the recommendation of Gen. Sibley.

There is no purpose here of offering criticism upon the campaign. If the success was not complete, the hostile Indians were, at least, all driven beyond the Missouri River, and subsequent events showed that their power for mischief was broken. The Tenth Regiment; received its whole quota of praise from the general commanding, both for gallantry and duty faithfully performed throughout the campaign.

GOING SOUTH.

On the 18th of September orders came directing that the Seventh, Ninth and Tenth regiments report, at the earliest practicable day, to the officer commanding the Department of the Missouri, at St. Louis. The furlough having expired October 5th, most of the companies rendezvoused at Fort Snelling, and on the evening of Wednesday, October 7th, on the steamer Northern Light, they left for Dunleith, opposite Dubuque. By the time the boat reached La Crosse all the companies were on board. Disembarking at Dunleith they proceeded by rail to East St. Louis, where they arrived on Monday morning. Crossing the river they were ordered to Camp Jackson, where they remained but a few hours, when the regiment was sent to Benton Barracks, built by Gen. Fremont, three miles from the city. Here, for a fortnight, company and battalion drill consumed the time.

On the 23d of October, 1863, the following order was received:

"HEADQUARTERS OF THE DEPARTMENT OF THE MISSOURI. [*Special Order*, 290.]

"Col. J. H. Baker, Tenth Minnesota Volunteers, is hereby appointed commanding officer of the post of St. Louis. He will at once relieve Col. Livingston, First Nebraska Volunteers, and enter upon the discharge of his office forthwith.

"By command of Major General Schofield.

"O. D. GREEN,

"*Assistant Adjutant General*"

Also, the same date, Col. Baker was ordered to bring his regiment to the city of St. Louis and place it upon garrison and provost duty, relieving the First Nebraska Cavalry and the Tenth Kansas Infantry. Lieut. Col. Jennison assumed command of the regiment, with headquarters at Schofield Barracks. Part of the regiment found quarters at the old Missouri Hotel, where the regimental hospital was also established. The regiment while remaining at the post of St. Louis was engaged in provost duty, guarding military prisons and quartermaster and commissary stores. St. Louis was at that period so large a military post — embracing the prison at Alton, Ill., Gratiot Street Prison, a straggler's camp, an extended and important provost duty, the charge of five forts around the city, with a multitude of lesser detail — that the work of the Tenth, for both men and officers, was constant and exacting. These duties were largely shared by the officers and men of the Seventh Minnesota. Maj. Cook was in charge of the straggler's camp; Capt. Edgerton of the post guard; Capt. O'Connor was district inspecting officer; Adjt. J. C. Braden became post adjutant; Lieut. McConnell became regimental adjutant; Lieut. William McMicken became provost marshal of the city of St. Louis. There was work for every man and officer of the Tenth, and so well did they perform their military duties at St. Louis that they left behind them a good name which is preserved among the old citizens to this day. Order, discipline, good behavior were everywhere maintained, and Minnesota may well feel proud of the record made by all her soldiers in the city of St. Louis. This good conduct affected the military fortunes of the colonel of the regiment, as subsequent developments proved, separating him finally from his command. A year afterward the mayor of the city stated that so marked was the good order maintained by the regiments from Minnesota, that a committee of the city council was specially appointed to go to Washington and see Secretary Stanton., and procure an order for the retention of the Tenth and Seventh Minnesota as a permanent garrison for St. Louis. This request was denied. As the committee were about to leave the secretary's office, the mayor turned and said, "You might at least give us the Minnesota colonel who is now in command." "Yes," said the secretary, "I will do that for you," and then, calling his clerk, issued a War Department order directing Col. Baker to remain in the Department of the Missouri, which order was never revoked, nor was the manner in which it was secured known until after the close of the war. As this terminates Col. Baker's identification with his regiment, it is proper to note that on July 1, 1864, he was placed in command of the subdistrict of St. Louis, which embraced the five counties including and around St. Louis; subsequently he was made provost marshal general of the Department of the Missouri, in which position he remained until the close of the war when he was complimented in orders and made brigadier general by brevet. Adjt. J. O. Braden was assigned to duty with Col. Baker, and so remained until the close of the war. It will be well here to note that during the St. Louis sojourn, there were some changes and matters affecting the regimental history.

Capt. W. W. Phelps of Company D resigned Nov. 3, 1863. Capt. R C. Ambler of Company A was dismissed the service Nov. 10, 1863. Capt. A. J. Edgerton of Company B was discharged to accept promotion Feb., 1864, and the resignation of Capt. C. W. Hackett of Company C was accepted Feb., 1864.

In Consequence of the foregoing, in Company A, First Lieut. L. F. Babcock became captain, Second Lieut. M. L. Strong became first lieutenant, and First Sergt. S. H. Stowers became second lieutenant; in Company B, First Lieut. Wm. McMicken became captain, Second Lieut. Samuel Burwell became first lieutenant, and First Sergt. T. J. Hunt became second lieutenant; in Company C, First Lieut. A. S. Hopson became captain, Second Lieut. John Lathrop became first lieutenant, and First Sergt. W. W. Case became second lieutenant; in Company D, First Lieut. C. L. Davis became captain, Second Lieut. Wm. B. Williams became first lieutenant, and Commissary Sergt. L. S. Meeker became second lieutenant. Second Lieut. O. B. Smith of Company G died at Hickory Street Hospital of typhoid fever, Jan. 8, 1861. He was a most worthy man and an efficient officer. He was succeeded by First Sergt. H. A. McConnell of Company D. Louis Proebsting, hospital steward, was promoted assistant surgeon, April 12, 1864, *vice* Burnham. He subsequently died at Cairo, Oct. 31, 1864. Quartermaster G. W. Green resigned March 23, 1861, and was succeeded by appointment from civil life, at the request of the regiment, of E. N. Leavens of Rice County, a popular and efficient officer. Sergt. Major A. C. Flanders was promoted second lieutenant of Company H, April 21, 1864, in place of McCarthy, resigned. Chas. Eichberg of Company B became sergeant major in place of Flanders, and Warren P. Bissell of Company A succeeded Meeker as commissary sergeant. The principal musicians were G. A. Todd. of Company D and S. S. Goodrich of Company F. A considerable number of recruits were received for the regiment in March. A sufficient number of these were assigned to Company I by Lieut. Col. Jennison to bring that company to the full minimum, and a commission as captain was asked and received, in accordance with the original and continuing wish of the company, for Private Martin J. Severance. On the request of Gen. John B. Sanborn, commanding in southwestern Missouri, First Lieut. E. H. Kennedy of Company F was detailed to duty as aid upon his staff. Lieut. Col. Jennison was appointed provost marshal of North Missouri in March, 1861, at the request of Gen. Clinton B. Fisk, commanding that district. He was relieved within a few weeks to take command of the regiment on its departure from St. Louis.

The winter of 1863–64 was very severe, and some suffering in the regiment ensued. The river at St. Louis being frozen over, booths were erected on the ice. In the month of April, 1864, the men and officers of the regiment took an active interest in the celebrated Mississippi Valley Sanitary Fair, and were conspicuous for good and earnest work. It was at this time, and in this interest, that some of the officers of the regiment ran, during two exhibitions, Robinson's circus, with great success, clearing several thousand dollars for this fair. During the winter a number of officers and privates went before the examining board for officers for colored regiments, and having passed the requisite examination took commissions in that branch of the service. Notable was Captain Edgerton of Company B, who became colonel of a colored regiment and remained in command of the same till some time after the close of the war. Owing to continued ill health, Chaplain Lathrop resigned Oct. 27, 1864.

Early in April rumors came that the Minnesota regiments in Missouri were speedily to be ordered South, and on the 22d of April, 1864, the Tenth Regiment received its orders and left for Columbus, Ky. There they went into camp, occupying the time in company and battalion drill. This was almost the first opportunity which the regiment had enjoyed for such exercises except those that might be used while on the march. No regiment was ever called on for harder drill service than this one, thirty days, and no regiment, their commander affirms, could have responded more willingly. The monotony was broken by a raid to Maysville, Ky., five days, being an attempt to cut off Gen. Forrest on his return from Paducah, but finding he had passed on the regiment returned to Columbus. During this time, April 27th, Companies E and D were sent on detached duty to Island No. 10, remaining there till the regiment was about to leave far Memphis. June 19, 1864, orders came for the regiment to go to Memphis, Tenn. Arriving at that place on the 20th, the city of Memphis became the headquarters of the regiment from June 20th to September 4th of that year, The last of June the regiment was assigned to a place in the Sixteenth Army Corps, left wing, Major General A. J. Smith commanding; in the First Division, Major General Joseph A. Mower commanding; First Brigade, Col. W. L. McMillan of the Ninety-fifth Ohio commanding. In the brigade were the following regiments: Seventy-second Ohio, Lieut. Col. Eaton; Ninety-fifth Ohio, Lieut. Col. Brumbach; One Hundred and Fourteenth Illinois, Capt. Johnson; Ninety-third Indiana, Col. Thomas; Tenth Minnesota, Lieut. Col. Jennison. It remained as here assigned till the close of the war.

BATTLE OF TUPELO.

During their stay in Memphis the regiment participated in several important expeditions, chief of which was the movement ordered by Gen. Sherman for the purpose of attacking Gen. Forrest, then in Mississippi and on his way to cut Sherman's line of communication. On the 11th of July Gen. Smith's forces reached Pontotoc, apparently aiming for Okalona. The cavalry skirmished so heavily with the enemy that the infantry were in part put in line of battle, expecting to meet a considerable force. On the 13th the command changed its course to the East to cut the railroad at Tupelo, and was attacked while on the march, from right and rear, by Forrest, who had about 6,000 Confederates. In a letter dated July 20th, Lieut. Col. Jennison said: "My regiment was in line, placed by Gen. Mower, but did not fire a shot,—except Capt. White's company (F), who were out as skirmishers,—but were shelled by rebel artillery, though owing to their poor practice and uncertainty of my position, it was without effect." Forrest having withdrawn, Gen. Smith's command resumed its march and arrived at Tupelo Hill, about three miles distant, about dark, after a race with Forrest for the position. The regiment bivouacked in line of battle, facing to the north, and confronting Forrest's opposing line of battle. In the night six infantry regiments from Mobile, under command of Gen. D. F. Lee, came and joined Forrest's forces, and Lee, as ranking officer, assumed command. At two o'clock of the morning of the 14th, the Tenth, in obedience to orders, stood at arms until about four o'clock, when they were permitted to breakfast. While so engaged the enemy opened an engagement; the regiment, taking their guns, were marched about ten rods to the front, taking position on the right of the Second Iowa Battery, and through the remainder of that fight they guarded that battery. At 4:30 P.M. the engagement ceased by the withdrawal of the rebel army.

A letter of the regimental commander says: "The Tenth was in reserve, but fired one volley. We were as much exposed as if we were firing. Balls, shells and bullets whistled lively at times. We had one killed and about twelve wounded, among them Maj. Cook; a painful, but not dangerous, flesh wound through the left arm, half way from elbow to shoulder. *** That night Gen. Smith sent me, with my regiment, to hold a certain road in the rear where an attack was expected, and where a rebel success would have been fatal to us." The expected attack was not made on the position held by the Tenth, but to its right, upon the colored troops. It occurred before daylight, and, though very persistent, was unsuccessful. Soon after day Gen. Smith sent for the regiment, and, without returning it to its brigade, himself placed it in position lacing a lively uproar of small arms then arising, where the enemy were evidently renewing the attack. "There!" said the general, with the pleasant manner of one doing a favor, "they may not get through; if they do you can give 'em hell." The rebels were unsuccessful at that point, and the Tenth was soon returned to Gen. Mower's command, while the train moved out for Old Town Creek under the protection of the other division. The letter before quoted continues: "At the same time the rebels renewed their attack and we repulsed them again, the Tenth going in as a reserve again, and getting peppered without a chance to return the fire. After fighting them in our position for an hour or two, until the train was well under way, our forces charged them. They ran like cowards, and we marched away some seven miles." The Tenth Regiment was the last to leave Tupelo Hill, and Gen. Mower remained with it. Just after it had crossed the creek to where the train was already parked, some rebel troops who bad rallied began an attack. It recrossed the creek, deployed, and, with other detachments, drove the troublesome enemy away. The next day the whole command began their return to Memphis, where they arrived the last of July.

On the Tupelo raid Lieut. Col. Jennison received an order from the War Department directing him to detail two officers of the rank of captain to report to the commandant at Fort Snelling, Minn., for recruiting service. Capt. Davis of Company D and Capt. Sullivan of Company H were at the time unfit for duty, although present with the command. Without notifying anyone of the order, except Surgeon Sheardown, in consultation, the commanding officer detailed the captains named, who were thus separated from further service with their regiment. Capt. Sullivan was the ranking captain at the death of Major Cook, but he could not get relieved from detached service and thus lost promotion. At this time Capt. E. H. Kennedy, who, on the resignation of Capt. Heath, had been promoted from Company F to the command of Company E. received from the governor of Missouri authority to raise a regiment of cavalry there, for which leave had been asked while Kennedy was serving in southwestern Missouri. Leave of absence was now sought to enable him to go to his recruiting field, but though urged strenuously by Lieut. Col. Jennison, and favored by Col. McMillan and Gen. Mower, it was refused, and thus Kennedy lost promotion, Other changes in officers were the promotion of Second Lieut. Merrill of Company I to be first lieutenant of Company C, *vice* Lathrop, resigned, and of First Sergt. Eli K. Pickett of Company B to succeed Merrill in Company I. In Company F, Second Lieut. Isaac Hamlin became first lieutenant, *vice* Kennedy, promoted, and was succeeded by First Sergt. James Flannegan of Company K. Chaplain Lathrop had been sent back to Memphis from the Tupelo raid because of ill health, and it is not remembered that he was ever able to rejoin, although his resignation was not immediately accepted.

About this time Gen. Grant ordered Smith to "hang to Forrest." Pursuant to this order, Smith's force, the Tenth Minnesota included, again started in quest of Forrest. At the Tallahatchie River the movement of our command was opposed by three regiments of Forrest's men under Gen. Chalmers. The rebels were speedily driven away. Going into camp at this point, we had an attack from Forrest's forces, which struck the Fifth Minnesota Regiment, and the Tenth was ordered out to their relief and pursued the rebel forces about two miles, to Hurricane Creek, the rebels retreating. Resuming the forward march, we went as far as Oxford, Miss. We found Oxford burning, and it was said to have been done by some of our forces for the burning of Chambersburg, Pa., by the rebels. Hearing that Forrest was in the vicinity of Memphis, we immediately countermarched to that city.

THE RAID AFTER PRICE.

After two days' rest and on the 2d day of September, the First Division (Mower's) of the Sixteenth Army Corps embarked for Devall's Bluff, where it arrived on the evening of the 8th. The next day, passing Brownsville and going into camp, the command there remained several days. After this rest the forces marched directly north, the objective point being Pochahontas, where Price and his command were supposed to be. Near that place, information was received that Price had left that place and captured Pilot Knob and was on his way to St. Louis. The command then turned East and struck the Mississippi River at Cape Girardeau, there taking steamers for St. Louis. There a brief stop was made to procure clothing, and then the regiment, with the brigade battery, upon the steamer War Eagle, proceeded to Jefferson City, Mo., where it arrived October 18th, twenty four hours later than the rest of the brigade, the overloaded boat having driven a snag through her bottom, and the men of the command having had to disembark eight times to march around sand-bars. From Jefferson City to La Mine Bridge by railroad and thence on foot, the regiment with its division marched in pursuit of Price through Sedalia, Lexington and Independence. As the command came nearer the game its movement was more and more of the nature of forced marches. One night, about eleven o'clock, after a long and trying march, word came that Gen. Smith was advised that Gen. Blunt had Price corralled at the Big Blue, and that Smith promised all who would march at 1 o'clock A.M. a chance at Price before noon the next day. Everyone but those whom the surgeon excused set out and made the march, but Gen. Blunt had not been able to hold the enemy until Smith's arrival. From that time the rebels had no rest. An engagement of even half a day with the Union cavalry would bring the pursuing infantry down upon them. Gen. Price thus endeavoring to make his escape around Gen. Smith's infantry, while Smith was hastening to intercept him, Gen. Pleasanton's cavalry were enabled to strike the enemy in flank while in motion, and at one blow they crushed them so completely that the infantry, camping the following night just across the Kansas line, were allowed to set out on their return to St. Louis the next day. Thither the regiment went on foot, through cold and snow, with a practicable railroad upon one side and a navigable river on the other.

The Tenth Regiment saw, on the whole, no harder service than in the raid after Price, and more of the men trace their present disabilities to the exposures of October and November, 1864, than to any other equal period of time. Asst. Surg. Clarke had resigned for disability Sept. 26, 1864, and Asst. Surg. Proebsting died Oct. 31, 1864. For many months Surgeon S. B. Sheardown had been the only medical officer with the regiment. Surgeon Sheardown was eminently skillful both in surgery and medicine; kind-hearted, but not often imposed upon, he performed his duty both to the Government and to the men in his charge thoroughly but unostentatiously. His professional superiors in rank esteemed him highly, and his surviving comrades hold him in affectionate remembrance. Second Lieut. H. A. McConnell, acting adjutant, returning from the Tallahatchie raid unfit for duty, was left at Memphis, and First Lieut. D. Cavanaugh of Company II was detailed as acting adjutant, and so served till his promotion to captain. Lieut. McConnell, being then again fit for duty, and admirably qualified for the position, was reappointed and served to the end of the war in that capacity.

BATTLE OF NASHVILLE.

After the Price pursuit the regiment preceded directly to Nashville, Tenn., having stopped at Benton Barracks, St. Louis, for several days to refit. The regiment arrived at Nashville the morning of November 30th, and marching two and a half miles South went into camp, where they entrenched in line of battle. Desultory firing kept up to the morning of the 15th of December, when the whole line moved out to assault Hood in his works. The details of the memorable fight are so fully set forth in the official report of the officer commanding the regiment after the battle, Capt. Sanders, that his report is here inserted:

"HEADQUARTERS TENTH MINNESOTA INFANTRY, "*Eastport, Miss., Jan. 15,* 1865.

"Brig. Gen. O. MALMROS,
"Adjutant General State of Minnesota,
"GENERAL: I have the honor to report the part taken by the Tenth Minnesota Infantry in the battles of the 15th and 16th before Nashville, Tenn.

"On the morning of the 15th, the regiment, commanded by Lieut. Col. S. P. Jennison, moved from the earthworks near Nashville as centre of the First Brigade First Division, Detachment of the Army of the Tennessee, commanded by Col. W. L. McMillan. It maneuvered until about 2 o'clock P.M., when it took position in front of the left centre of the enemy's lines, and remained in this position a few minutes, when it participated in a successful charge against the enemy, who was strongly entrenched on a commanding eminence, which resulted to him in the loss of four cannon and many prisoners.

"After pausing a few minutes for rest, the regiment, in connection with other regiments of the brigade, moved about a half mile to the right and again charged the enemy, who was surrounded by heavy earthworks upon a high hill, and after a severe struggle had the honor of first planting its colors upon the works and capturing two cannon and over one hundred prisoners.

"It bivouacked for the night upon the ground which was held by the enemy in the morning, On the morning of the 16th it moved about three-fourths of a mile to the left and took position within easy musket range of the enemy's lines, with its left resting on the right of the Second Brigade of Gen. McArthur's division, and its right upon the left of the Ninety-third Indiana of the First Brigade. It remained in this position until about two o'clock, when it moved nearly one hundred rods to the right and formed a line parallel to and in front of the left wing of a division of the Twenty-third Army Corps. It remained. here about forty-five minutes, when, in connection with the Ninety-third Indiana and the One Hundred and Fourteenth Illinois, it charged the salient point in the enemy's lines, and after a severe arid bloody conflict forced him with bayonet from his works, capturing sixteen cannon and 2,000 prisoners, and then joined the pursuit of the scattered and demoralized foe. In all of these sanguinary conflicts the regiment more than realized the expectation of its friends. Every officer and man was at his post and nobly did his duty. Especially did its commander, Lieut. Col. Jennison, display a high order of those qualities requisite in an officer who wins battles over a brave and stubborn foe. His own personal bravery did very much in enabling him to carry, repeatedly, his regiment over the enemy's defenses. In the charge which decided the fate of the day, the last one made, he fell, severely wounded, in front of his command and within a yard of the enemy's works. I should hardly do my duty if I failed to mention Sergeant O'Neil, the color-bearer of the regiment. In all of the charges made, he distinguished himself; and especially so in the last one, in which case he was the first one over the works, and, with one foot upon an enemy. prostrated by his own hands, raised the regimental banner.

"The loss to the regiment in killed and wounded was severe. In the last charges the companies on the left suffered most, being subject to a cross-fire. For the number disabled the loss in killed was unusually great, owing to the near proximity of the combatants. For the same reason the loss of officers was proportionately much larger than that of enlisted men. Many were slightly injured, but not disabled, whose names do not appear among the wounded. In the death of Major Cook and Capt. White the regiment has lost two of its bravest and best officers, and the state two of its most honored and worthy citizens. Nor could their names be associated with braver soldiers or more disinterested patriots than their comrades in death, a catalogue of whom, together with the names of the wounded, I herewith send you.

"I am, general, very respectfully, your obedient servant,

"E. C. SANDERS, "*Captain Commanding Tenth Regiment, Minnesota Infantry.*"

In further explanation of the distinguished part taken by the Tenth in this memorable battle, the following is given: There was a steep hill, over the crown of which the enemy's line extended, and which formed the "key point" to his works in front. Gen. McArthur ordered Col. Macmillan's brigade "to take this hill." The brigade was then moved by the right flank to a position exactly opposite this hill and formed in two lines. The front line consisted of the following regiments, named in their order from right to left: One hundred and Fourteenth Illinois Infantry, Capt. Johnson commanding; Ninety-third Indiana

Infantry, Capt. Hubbard commanding; Tenth Minnesota Infantry, Lieut. Col. Jennison commanding. The assault began at 3:30 P.M. by Coggswell's Independent Battery, and under cover of this fire the brigade advanced. We now quote from Col. Macmillan's report: "Quietly and steadily the brigade moved down one hill and up the other to within a few feet of the enemy's parapet, when we received a volley, which, on our right, went over our heads, but on the left, punished the Tenth Minnesota Infantry severely. Nothing daunted, this gallant regiment, together with the others composing the front line, cleared the enemy's works with a bound. My loss mainly fell on the Tenth Minnesota. Two field officers, six line officers, wounded, and some sixty enlisted men, attest the fiery ordeal through which this regiment passed; and the fact that it reached the rebel works in its front as quickly as the regiments on its right, which were less exposed, is ample evidence of the courage and daring of both officers and men. Lieut. Col. Jennison, the commanding officer, was conspicuous for his high daring, and set a noble example to his officers and men. He fell, severely wounded, on the enemy's works."

Such is the testimony of the commanding officer of the brigade, bearing date "In the field, Dec. 25, 1864," to the courage, efficiency and noble services of the Tenth Minnesota in the battle of Nashville. Gen. Thomas himself' said, Feb. 8, 1865, of the charge of this brigade, that " It was the handsomest feat of arms I ever saw." The highest praise was awarded the Tenth for its gallant charge and distinguished conduct throughout the battle. Here fell Major Cook and Capt. White, two as brave and meritorious soldiers as ever served in the Union army. Major Cook fell, shot through the lungs, and died in the hospital Dec. 27, 1864. Capt. White was shot through the bowels, and died, Dec. 17, 1864, in the hospital. After Lieut. Col. Jennison fell, Capt. Sanders was the ranking officer, He having been temporarily disabled from the effects of a shell, Capt. Severance was in command for a short time, when Capt. Sanders resumed charge till the arrival at Eastport, when Lieut. Col. Jennison, having been able to leave the hospital, rejoined the regiment Feb. 5, 1865. The regiment mustered three hundred and one muskets in this action.

A roster of the men is impracticable. The officers present were as follows: Lieut. Col. Jennison, Maj. Cook, Acting Adjt. Cavanaugh. Surgeon Sheardown, Asst. Surgeons Milligan and Brooks. and Quartermaster Leavens. Of the field and staff: Capts. White, Sanders, Severance and Kennedy; First Lieuts. Burwell, Merrill, Williams, Kittelson. Hamlin, Stewart and Byrnes, and Second Lieuts. Stowers. Hunt, Meeker, Case, Ash. Flannegan, McConnell, Flanders, Pickett and Hoy.

The official returns do not distinguish the casualties of the first day, or the second day before the charge. The rail fence behind which the regiment lay until the movement to the right was within effective rifle range from the stone wall in front of the rebel line, and some casualties occurred there. Dents. Hunt and Hoy and several men were wounded on the skirmish line between the lines. The horses of the acting adjutant and one of the orderlies were shot during this time. When the regiment moved by the flank it was assailed by brisk musketry fire, which struck a few men and killed the horse ridden by Lieut. Col. Jennison. All the officers of the brigade dismounted to make the charge, for which the signal was given by a single bugle in the midst of the battery firing. By Col. McMillan's order no officer spoke word of command, no soldier uttered shout or cheer, in order that some ground might be covered before the enemy knew that the expected movement had begun. The troops had in fact begun the ascent without loss, and the companies of skirmishers in front kept the enemy well down until our men nearly reached a slight crest or ridge in front of the rebel works, and distant there from, where nearest perhaps eight yards, where the left of the regiment received a withering oblique fire from the unassailed enemy beyond their left, which doubly decimated the left division, Companies F and C. On the ridge occurred some few seconds' pause of the more advanced, as the lieutenant colonel had commanded, until the line was closed up, and there a few shots were fired by the assailants, when the men went to and over the works with a rush. Savage fighting there was for a few moments, but the rebels soon chose flight or surrender. As usual with volunteers in their first engagements, wounds that did not disable the soldier or send him to a surgeon were not deemed worthy of mention in the report. Thus, Capt. Kennedy, felled in the charge by the concussion of a rifle-ball so spent that it lodged in his vest, having passed through his coat and overcoat cape, recovered consciousness in a few seconds, started up in a rather dazed way, cried, "Come on, boys!" to men who had already passed him, and never thought of himself as a wounded man. So with Capt. Sanders and numbers of the enlisted men.

Lieut. Col. Jennison wrote to his wife from hospital, December 19th, the following: "We moved out to attack Hood about 9 or 10 A.M. Everything had been in readiness since about six o'clock, but there was such a fog that we could not start. We marched around till afternoon before we were in the right place; then the brigade formed in column of attack, and we were raked with grape and canister while waiting. One man only much injured in the Tenth; I saved my left leg by having a horse that scared at the noise. Col. Thomas, just behind us, was struck and carried off the field. Some cavalry on foot were going to charge the battery. They started for it first, then we went. My colors were first on the parapet. We took four cannon here. My losses were trifling. We had to reform at once and storm a higher hill, which we did. Then we marched off and bivouacked, and the next day commenced to make breastworks — but I have not strength to write about the preliminaries. About 4 P.M. our brigade was ordered to charge and carry a hill which the Twenty-third Corps ought to have carried, but they declined. The Tenth was on the left of the first line, the Ninety-third Indiana on my right; the Seventy-second and Ninety-fifth Ohio in the second line did not extend so as to cover the Tenth Minnesota. The enemy fired at us all the way up; my boys never returned a shot till we were near their works, then they punished a few of them. Just before I reached the parapet I saw a fellow's gun placed across it, and supposed he would look over to aim. I cocked my pistol and leveled it for him. Presently a head appeared where I had expected it, and I fired and I must have scared it. The men were around me, closing up, getting breath, some loading. I called to them to "Go for them clear up to the work, and shoot 'em across it." Yes, Colonel,' they said, and in a second we were there. I fired but once more, and was knocked senseless. With my first consciousness I recognized Col. McMillan's voice demanding a guard detail for *his* prisoners. That let me know which way victory went. Col. Mc. was very kind; he sent four men who wanted to carry me to the ambulance, but I only needed support in walking. *** I am very fortunate. Poor Capt. White was killed; shot through the bowels; died next day. The major was shot through the body; I guess he may recover. Lieuts. Hoy, Hamlin and Case shot in the arm; Lieut. Hunt shot in the face. There were 20 to 25 killed of my brave boys, and 60 to 80 wounded. It was a sad loss, but nothing I could do would have lightened it. The men are all an officer could wish, and I thank God I was permitted to command them in the charge and to live through it.

"Lieut. Col. Jennison was 'knocked senseless,' not by an axe, as the newspapers reported, but by the rifle shot of a Confederate, five or six yards distant, who took aim on seeing Jennison fire the 'once more,' and fired before the revolver could possibly be used on him. He was so hurried, however, that his ball, aimed at the head, lacked less than an inch of missing it altogether.

On December 10th was mustered as assistant surgeon Dr. F. H. Milligan of Wabasha County, appointed from civil life, but who had formerly served in the Third Minnesota Regiment, in place of Proebsting, deceased, and on the 12th of December Dr. C. A. Brooks of Ramsey County was mustered as assistant surgeon, *vice* Clarke, resigned. A commission had been issued two months before to First Lieut. D. Cavanaugh of Company H, as captain, but was missent, and though evidence in abundance of the issue of such commission was presented, the mustering officer required the production of the document. So Cavanaugh served as acting adjutant until Jan. 17, 1865, when he became captain of Company C, *vice* Hopson, resigned. The regimental commander, who did not make the report of the battle, speaks warmly of his ready efficiency as acting adjutant and his cool bravery in action. Upon the death of Captain White, First Lieut. J. M. Gorman of Company I was promoted captain of Company F. The death of Major Cook promoted Captain Sanders to the majority, First Lieut. G. W. Stewart of Company G to be its captain, and Second Lieut. Eli Ash of Company E to be first lieutenant of Company G.

THE CAPTURE OF SPANISH FORT.

After the battle the regiment joined in the pursuit of Hood to the Tennessee River. It then embarked on boats and ascended the river to Eastport, Miss., where they arrived Jan. 7, 1865. At this place the army went into winter quarters. The regiment built log cabins, and remained in camp without any special incident, except short rations, until February 7th, when they embarked for New Orleans, on the way to attack Mobile. They remained in camp, on Gen. Jackson's old battlefield, about ten days, when they embarked for Dauphin Island, where they awaited the concentration of the Thirteenth Corps and the reorganized Sixteenth Army Corps, now consisting of three divisions under the command of Maj. Gen. A. J. Smith, the division containing the Minnesota troops being still the First. After two weeks given to rest, camp duties and collecting and eating the fine oysters of the island waters, the command was transported across Mobile Bay to the mouth of Fish River, about thirty miles South of Spanish Fort, one of the defensive works of Mobile, and about nine miles South of the city. After lauding the regiment marched thence in line of battle to the immediate neighborhood of Spanish Fort, where a regular siege was begun. The regiment participated in throwing up the extensive earthworks which were undertaken, pushing forward approaches and parallels, and in all the events of the siege. Spanish Fort was a very heavy redoubt, and rested on the East shore of the bay of Mobile. This whole work was generally called Spanish Fort, and the main redoubt rested on the site of an old Spanish fort. On the night of the 7th of April, about 5 o'clock P.M., a bombardment was directed against that part consisting of the redoubt proper. The bombardment was heavy and furious, several hundred guns of all caliber taking part. The bombardment was resumed late in the afternoon of the 8th, and was heavier than that of the preceding day, continuing until long after dark. In that same night, after the bombardment, the works were assaulted on that part of the line ear the bombardment was resumed late in the afternoon of the 8th, and was heavier than that of the preceding day, continuing until long after dark. In that same night, after the bombardment, the works were assaulted on that part of the line near Mobile Bay, including the heavy redoubt, when it was found that the rebels had retreated from the works. In the afternoon of the 9th a successful assault was made to the right, at Blakely, and the works were carried, and several thousand rebel prisoners were captured.

The Sixteenth Army Corps, including the Tenth Regiment, then marched to Montgomery, Ala. On the march, near Greenville, the regiment received news at the same time of the surrender of both Lee's and Johnston's armies. While at Montgomery the regiment also learned of the assassination of President Lincoln. In the month of May, the First Brigade, including the Tenth, marched from Montgomery to Meridian, Miss., where the regiment remained inactive till late in July, when the brigade devoted its attention mainly to blackberries and chronic diarrhea.

Promotions in the regiment were now nearly at an end. The companies were all below the minimum and could not have a third officer mustered. Commissions as first lieutenants were obtained, however, for Quartermaster Sergt. Richard Fewer, for meritorious service, and for Color Sergt. Cornelius O' Neil of Company K for gallant and meritorious conduct at the battles of Nashville, Dec. 15 and 16, 1864, and they were assigned to duty in their new grades, the former in Company I, *vice* Gorman, promoted, and the latter in Company A, *vice* Strong, discharged for disability. Corporal George H. Walsh of Company I, for conspicuous good conduct at the last charge on December 16th, was promoted to quartermaster sergeant, *vice* Fewer, promoted, and M. R. Prendergast of Company H, who had been long acting commissary sergeant, was promoted to that position on the discharge of Sergt. Bissell for disability. Lieut. Hoy of Company K was discharged for the disability resulting from his wound, April 13, 1865. Three officers of the line, Capt. Sullivan of Company H and Capt. O'Connor and First Lieut. Byrnes of Company K, were mustered out in the same grade which they held at the muster-in. First Lieut. Charles Kittelson was in command of Company E from January, 1864, until mustered-out. First Lieut. Wm. B. Williams was in continuous command of Company D from July, 1864, until the discharge of the regiment; and Second Lieut. Flanders commanded Company K at the battle of Nashville, where he was wounded, and at the siege of Spanish Fort, where his forage cap was knocked from his head by the fragment of shell which next killed Sergt. Keating, and thereafter to the close of the war. These three lieutenants, neither rash nor timid, neither seeking nor shunning any service, but doing with prompt thoroughness the duty assigned them, were not surpassed in general efficiency by any officers in the regiment. Orders having been received to return to Minnesota for the purpose of being mustered out, the regiment marched to Vicksburg and took steamers to St. Louis, where they remained about three days awaiting transportation home; by steamer thence to St. Paul, where they arrived Aug. 7, 1865. They marched to the capitol, where they were banqueted by the city of St. Paul, The same evening they left for Fort Snelling, where the muster rolls were made out, and finally were formally mustered out Aug. 18, 1865.

C. Tenth Regiment Roster[1]

Roster of Field and Staff Officers of the Tenth Regiment, Minnesota

Names	Age	Mustered In	Mustered Out	Remarks
Colonel				
James H. Baker	33	Nov. 17, '62	Aug 19, '65	Brevet brigadier general, U.S. Volunteers, March 13, '65.
Lieutenant Colonel				
Samuel P. Jennison	32	Sept. 10, '62	Aug.19, '65	Bvt. colonel, U.S.V., Feb 23, '65; Bvt. brig. gen. March 13, '65.

Names	Age	Mustered In	Mustered Out	Remarks
Majors				
Michael Cook	34	Sept. 15, '62		Died Dec 27, '64, of wounds received at Nashville.
Edwin C. Sanders	37	March 1, '65	Aug 19 '65	
Adjutant				
James C. Braden	27	Oct 6, '62	Aug 19 '65	
Quartermasters				
George W. Green	42	Oct. 8, '62		Resigned, March 23, '64.
Eden N. Leavens	38	Apr. 25, '64	Aug. 19, '65	
Surgeon				
Samuel B. Sheardown	36	Oct. 16, '62	Aug. 19, '65	
Assistant Surgeons				
Wm. W. Clark	37	Sept. 10, '62		Resigned Sept. 26, '64.
Alfred H. Burnham	38	Oct. 11, '62		Dismissed Oct. 23, '63
Francis H. Milligan	34	Dec. 10, '64	Aug. 19, '65	
Lewis Proebsting	32	Apr. 12, '64		Hospital steward Oct. 13, '62; died Oct. 31, '64, at Cairo, Ill.
Cyrus A. Brooks	23	Dec. 12, '64	Aug. 19, '65	
Chaplain				
Ezra R. Lathrop		March 10, '63		Resigned Oct. 27. '64.
Sergeant Majors				
Abial C. Flanders	43	Nov. 15, '62		Promoted 2d lieutenant, Company H, April 22, '64.
Charles Eichler	33	Feb. 29, '64	Aug. 19, '65	
Quartermaster Sergeants				
Richard Fewer	40	Aug. 19, '62		Promoted 1st lieutenant, Company I, June 2, '65.
George H. Walsh	18	Nov. 12, '62	Aug. 19, '65	
Commissary Sergeants				
Loren S. Meeker	38	Oct. 13, '62		Promoted 2d lieutenant, Company D, March 30, '64.
Michael R. Pendergast	20	Oct. 21, '62	Aug. 19, '65	
Warren P. Bissell	24	Nov. 14, '62		Discharged per order May 25, '65.
Hospital Steward				
Andrew Black	29	Apr. 12, '64	Aug. 19, '65	
Principal Musicians				
Joseph Culver	36	Aug. 15, '62		Reduced to ranks, Company F July 1, '64.
Geo. A. Todd	26	Oct. 9, '62	Aug 19, '65	
Stephen S. Goodrich	26	Sept. 26, '62	Aug. 19, '65	

Roster of Company A, Tenth Regiment, Minnesota Volunteers

Names	Age	Mustered In	Mustered Out	Remarks
Officers				
Captains				
Rufus C. Ambler	32	Aug. 18, '62		Dismissed Nov. 10, '63.

Names	Age	Mustered In	Mustered Out	Remarks
Officers				
Alonzo J. Edgerton	35	Jan. 22, '62		Transf. from Co. B; colonel, 67th U.S. Colored Inf., Jan. 25, '64.
L. F. Babcock	30	Nov. 11, '63	Aug 19, '65	1st lieutenant, Aug. 18, '62.
First Lieutenants				
M. L. Strong	21	Nov. 11, '63		2d lieutenant, Aug. 10, '62; Discharged for disability, April 4, '64.
Cornelius O'Neil	22	March 31, '65	Aug. 19, '65	Promoted from sergeant, Company K.
Second Lieutenant				
Smith H. Stowers	28	Nov. 11, '63		Promoted from sergeant; discharged per order June '65.
Enlisted Men				
Adams, James H.	21	Aug. 14, '62	May 31, '65	Absent.
Annis, Levi	31	Sept. 6, '62	Aug. 19, '65	Corporal.
Barnes, James	17	Aug. 11, '62		Musician; discharged per order June 17, '65.
Barney, John L.	37	Sept. 6. '62	Aug. 19, '65	Corporal; promoted sergeant.
Barnhard, James	21	Aug. 11. '62	Aug. 19, '65	
Barnhard, William	18	Aug. 11. '62	Aug. 19, '65	
Bartley, John H.	20	Aug. 13, '62	Aug. 19, '65	Promoted corporal.
Berg, Jacob	25	Aug. 11, '62	Aug. 19, '65	
Bissell, Warren P.	24	Nov. 14, '62		Promoted sergeant: transferred to non-com. staff Aug. 1, '64.
Bliss, Calvin G.	24	Aug. 11, '62	Aug. 19, '65	
Bixby, Jacob S.	22	Aug. 11, '62	Aug. 19, '65	
Borchard, Ferdinand	26	Aug. 14, '62	Aug. 28, '65	Absent.
Burns, Alvin	29	Aug. 14, '62	Aug. 19, '65	Promoted corporal.
Burns, Hugh	33	Aug. 12, '62		Died March 20, '65, at Chicago.
Burr, Murdock P.	18	Aug. 11, '62		Discharged for disability Dec. 16 '62.
Carlton, Dexter	43	Aug. 12, '62	Aug. 19, '65	Promoted corporal.
Carpenter, Joseph	18	Aug. 13, '62	Aug. 19, '65	Promoted corporal.
Chambers Frank	26	Aug. 11, '62	Aug. 19, '65	
Curtis, Chas. O.	24	Aug. 11, '62	July 12, '65	Per order.
Curtis, George C.	22	Aug. 11, '62	Aug. 19, '65	
Curtis, Samuel J.	23	Aug. 11 '62	May 17, '65	Per order.
Curtis, Thos. J.	23	Aug. 12, '62	Aug. 19, '65	Promoted corporal.
Davis, John F.	22	Aug. 14, '62		Died Nov. 28, '62, at Garden City, Minn.
Davis, Thomas E.	21	Aug. 11, '62		Died Jan. 30, '65, at Milwaukee, Wisc.
Dopping, Henry	21	Aug. 11, '62		Discharged July 7, '65, while absent.
Drake, Richard M.	21	Aug. 12, '62		Discharged for disability April '64.
Eastman, Alpheus R.	21	Aug. 13, '62		Transferred to Veteran Reserve Corps Jan. 16, '65.
Elliott, Jeremiah	26	Aug. 11, '62	Aug. 19, '65	
Enny, Geo. W.	26	Aug. 11, '62	Aug. 19, '65	
Farrell, John	32	Aug. 11, '62		Transferred to Veteran Reserve Corps April 1, '65.
Flake, Levi	43	Aug. 14, '62	Aug. 19, '65	
Fowler, Francis	18	Aug. 11, '62		Died July 14, '63, at Fort Abercrombie D. T.

Appendix C

Names	Age	Mustered In	Mustered Out	Remarks
Enlisted Men				
Fowler, Lorain	20	Aug. 11, '62		Discharged for disability Dec 10, '63.
Freeman, Samuel M.	28	Aug. 11, '62		Discharged for disability September '64.
Green, Wm.	28	Feb. 11, '64	Aug. 19, '65	Promoted corporal.
Guile, Eben M.	23	Sept. 6, '64	Aug. 19, '65	Corporal.
Hammon, Charles	18	Feb. 15, '63	Aug. 19, '65	
Harty, Wm.	22	Aug. 11, '62	Aug. 19, '65	
Haynes, Asa S.	35	Aug. 12, '62	Aug. 19, '65	Musician.
Hays, Sanford E.		Aug. 14, '62	June 2, '65	Absent.
Heath, John A.	19	Aug. 12, '62		Discharged for disability Nov. 29, '64.
Hess, Jacob W.	32	Aug. 12, '62		Died Feb. 19, '65, at Jeffersonville, Ind.
Houston, Thomas	18	Aug. 13, '62		Died Feb. 10, '63, at Garden City, Minn.
Howe, Samuel	33	March 30, '64	May 10, '65	Per order.
House, Charles S.	33	March 15, '64	May 9, '65	Absent.
Jeffrey, Charles	24	Aug. 11, '62		Discharged in '65; absent.
Johnson, Wm. I.	42	March 31, '64	May 9, '65	Absent.
Jones, Anthony W.	21	Aug. 14, '62	Aug. 19, '65	
Jones, Henry R.	41	Aug. 12, '62	Aug. 19, '65	
Jones, Isaac	21	Feb. 15, '63		Died March 24, '63, at Garden City, Minn.
Kelly, Thomas	22	Sept. 6, '62		Corporal; discharged May '64, for promotion.
Kendig, George	33	Aug. 11, '62	Aug. 19, '65	
Kern, James W.	39	Feb. 29, '64		Discharged for disability Oct. 19, '64.
Kinney, Newcomb	21	Aug. 11, '62	Aug. 19, '65	
Kinney, Stilman M.	23	Aug. 11, '62	May 29, '65	Per order.
Lane, John	31	Aug. 11, '62	Aug. 19, '65	
Martin, Willard E.	25	Sept. 6, '62		Sergeant; discharged per order July 5, '65.
McCrora, John	19	Aug. 11, '62	Aug. 19, '65	
McKinny, Albert	31	Aug. 11, '62		Discharged for promotion.
McNitt, James R.	26	Feb. 27, '64	Aug. 19, '65	
McNitt, Truman E.	20	Aug. 11, '62		Died Sept. 29, '62 at Clinton Falls, Minn.
Melvin, Frank L.	26	March 1, '63	Aug. 19, '65	
Minthorn, Thadeus	41	Sept. 6, '62		Wagoner; discharged for disability C. S. April 9, '64
Miles, Ruhard	33	Aug. 17, '62		Discharged in '65; absent.
Moore, Orlando S.	32	Aug. 14, '62	Aug. 19, '65	
Morris, John	24	Aug. 14, '62	Aug. 19, '65	
Naylor, James	21	Aug. 13, '62	Aug. 19, '65	
Norman, John B.	18	Aug. 12, '62	Aug. 19, '65	
Pascoe, Wm.	18	Feb. 15, '63	Aug. 19, '65	
Pascoe, Henry	21	Jan. 15, '62	Aug. 19, '65	
Pettie, C. B.	27	Aug. 12, '62		Discharged for disability June 13, '65.
Pettie, Geo. C.	34	Aug. 12, '62		Died Jan. 19, '65 at Jeffersonville, Ind.
Pike, Elias G.	20	Aug. 13, '62	June 7, '65	Per order.

Names	Age	Mustered In	Mustered Out	Remarks
Enlisted Men				
Pomeroy, Charles	25	Aug. 12, '62	Aug. 19, '65	
Reece, Isaac	27	Aug. 11, '62		Discharged for disability Nov. 10, '63.
Reed, Andrew W.	30	Aug. 12, '62		Discharged for disability Aug. 5, '64.
Ridout, Andrew J.	32	Sept. 6, '62		Sergeant; discharged per order May 22, '65.
Ring, Eugene P.	21	Sept. 6, '62		Corporal.
Ritchie, Henry	22	Feb. 22, '64	Aug. 19, '65	
Roberts, John L.	18	March 26, '64	June 7, '65	Per order.
Ross, Cornelius F.	25	March 29, '64		Discharged per order May 10, '65.
Russell, Wm. H.	32	Aug. 11, '62	June 17,' 65	Per order.
Sanborn, Benjamin C.	21	Sept. 6, '62		Corporal; discharged in '65; absent.
Scott, Wm.	21	Feb. 15, '63		Discharged for disability March '64.
Shaw, Jotham	33	Aug. 12, '62		Died Jan. 31, '65, at Jeffersonville.
Taylor, Emmons P.	26	Aug. 14, '62		Promoted sergeant; discharged in '65; absent.
Teed, John C.	18	Feb. 11, '64	Aug 19, '65	
Thompson, Arza B.	27	Sept. 6, '62		Sergeant; died Jan. '65, at Nashville.
Thompson, Franklin A.	21	Sept. 6, '62	Aug. 19, '65	Corporal; promoted sergeant.
Thurston, Hubbard N.	29	Sept. 6, '62		Sergeant.
Tuthill, John D.	39	Feb. 25, '64		Died Nov. 11, '65, at Memphis, Tenn.
Vail, Isaac	21	Feb. 15, '62	Aug. 19, '65	
Ware, Marcus	25	Aug. 11, '62		Died Nov. 11, '64, at Memphis, Tenn.
Warfield, John M.	26	Aug. 14, '62	Aug. 19, '65	Promoted corporal.
Webster, Joseph R.	40	Sept. 6, '62		Corporal; killed Dec. 16, '64, at Nashville.
Welch, Melvin H.	26	Aug. 14, '62	Aug. 19, '65	
Wheeler, Walter W.	26	Aug. 14, '62	Aug. 19, '65	
Wilkins, Walter W.	19	Aug. 14, '62	Aug. 19, '65	Promoted corporal.
Winchell, Dempster L.	26	Aug. 11, '62		Discharged for disability Dec. 27, '63.
Yearly, Zeno S.	18	Feb. 15, '63		Died Dec. 8, '64, at Nashville, Tenn.

Roster of Company B, Tenth Regiment, Minnesota Volunteers

Names	Age	Mustered In	Mustered Out	Remarks
Officers				
Captains				
Alonzo J. Edgerton	35	Aug 21, '62		Transferred to Company A, Jan. 22, '64.
Wm. McMicken	34	Jan 22, '64	Aug. 19, '65	1st lieutenant, Nov. 15, '62.
First Lieutenant—				
Samuel Burwell	57	Jan 22, '64	Aug. 19, '65	2d lieutenant, Nov. 15, '62.
Second Lieutenant—				
Thos. J. Hunt	33	Jan. 23, '64	Aug. 19, '65	1st sergeant, Nov. 16, '62.

Appendix C

Names	Age	Mustered In	Mustered Out	Remarks
Enlisted Men				
Anderson, Peter	32	Aug. 15, '62		Died Feb. 15, '65, at Vicksburg.
Andrus, Freeman	27	Aug. 14, '62	Aug. 19, '65	Promoted corporal.
Barker, Silas	41	Aug. 21, '62	Aug. 19, '65	
Barber, John G.	21	Feb. 19, '64	Aug. 19, '65	
Bauman, Wm.	28	Aug. 15, '62	Aug. 19, '65	
Baxter, Leander	21	Aug. 15, '62	July 10, '65	Per order.
Bentley, Edgar	34	Apr. 21, '63	May 30, '65	Per order.
Beymer, James W.	28	Aug. 14, '62	Aug. 19, '65	
Bosley, Wm. M.	18	Aug. 14, '62	Aug. 5, '65	Wounded at Nashville.
Bosworth, S. J.	21	Aug. 14, '62	Aug. 19, '65	
Brown, Charles	23	Aug. 16, '62	Aug. 19, '65	
Bruce, Chas. S.	25	Aug. 14, '62	Aug. 19, '65	Corporal; promoted sergeant.
Burton, Ephraim A.	18	Feb. 26, '64		Transferred to Company I, April 4, '64.
Campbell, Alexander	21	Aug. 21, '62		Died Dec. 27, '64, at Memphis, Tenn.
Barber, John G.	21	Feb. 19, '64	Aug. 19, '65	
Carlough, George	25	Aug. 14, '62		Died at Fort Abercrombie, D.T.
Causdell, John A.	25	Aug. 14, '62		Discharged May 29, '65, for wounds received at Nashville.
Canfield, Charles	18	March 11, '64	July 7, '65	
Clark, Peter	22	Aug. 14, '62	May 24, '65	Per order.
Cook, Eldon T.	20	Feb. 29, '64	Aug. 19, '65	
Conklin, Philip	18	Sept. 6 '64	May 18, '65	Per order.
Cowan, Samuel R.	19	Aug. 14, '62		Died Sept. 11, '64, at Devall's Bluff, Ark.
Crowe, James	23	Dec. 15, '63	Aug. 19, '65	
Crane, Daniel F.	22	Oct. 1, '63	Aug. 19, '65	
Crane, Royal, Jr.	19	Feb. 28, '64		Transferred to Company I, April 4, '64.
Craw, John P.	44	Aug. 15, '62		Discharged for disability, April '63.
Currier, James S.	18	Feb. 26, '64		Transferred to Company I, April 4, '64.
Cutsinger, James	21	Aug. 14, '62	Aug. 19, '65	Promoted corporal.
Daily, Chas. N.	24	Aug. 14, '62	Aug. 19, '65	
Dresbach, Anthony L.	32	Feb. 19, '64		Transferred to Company I, April 4, '64.
Dudley, Oscar L.	19	Feb. 29, '64		Transferred to Company I, April 4, '64.
Durrell, Freman	33	Aug. 14, '62		Discharged for disability, Oct. 30, '64.
Edgerton, Monson G.	33	Aug. 23, '62		Sergeant; 2d lieutenant, 67th U.S. Col. Infantry, March 18, '64.
Eichler, Charles	33	Feb. 29, '64		Promoted quartermaster sergeant.
Ervin, John	26	Feb. 19, '64	Aug. 19, '65	
Farnsworth, Albert	18	Aug. 15, '62	Aug. 19, '65	Promoted corporal.
Fay, Geo. W.	23	Aug. 14, '62	Aug. 19, '65	Promoted corporal, sergeant.
Fellows, Freman W.	27	Aug. 24, '62		Corporal; discharged for disability, April 10, '65.
Flanders, A. C.	43	Aug. 23, '62		Sergeant; transferred for promotion.
Fleener, Christopher H.	29	Aug. 14, '62	Aug. 19, '65	Corporal; promoted sergeant.
Fleener, Henry	33	Aug. 15, '62	Aug. 19, '65	Promoted corporal, sergeant.
Freeman, Anson	28	March 31, '64	Aug. 19, '65	
Fuller, Benjamin	18	Aug. 14, '62	Aug. 19, '65	

Tenth Regiment Roster (Company B)

Names	Age	Mustered In	Mustered Out	Remarks
Enlisted Men				
Garrett, Edward	25	Aug. 14, '62	Aug. 19, '65	Promoted corporal.
Garrison, Frederick	19	Aug. 15, '62	Aug. 19, '65	
Gefts, Josiah	30	Aug. 21, '62		Discharged for disability Jan. 26, '64.
Gere, Samuel A.	30	Aug. 14, '62		Discharged in '65; absent.
Goodman, Stephen O.	18	Feb. 16, '64		Transferred to Company I, April 4, '64.
Gleason, Clark	21	Aug. 23, '62		Sergeant; 2d lieutenant, 68th U.S. Col. Infantry, May 17, '64.
Grems, John	19	Aug. 14, '62		Promoted corporal, sergeant; Discharged per order, June 7, '65.
Groenslitt, James P.	28	Aug. 14, '62		
Gulson, Christopher	22	Aug. 15, '62	Aug. 19, '65	
Hannah, James	39	Aug. 14, '62		Transferred to Veteran Reserve Corps.
Hall, Eclos	28	Feb. 18, '64		Transferred to Company I, April 4, '64.
Hadley, Amos	30	Feb. 18, '64		Transferred to Company I, April 4, '64.
Harter, Phlegmon	19	Aug. 15, '62	Aug. 19, '65	
Heils, Thomas	35	Aug. 14, '62		Transferred to Veteran Reserve Corps, Sept. 30, '64.
Hewitt, Joseph E.	31	Feb. 29, '64	Aug. '65	Absent.
Hoy, Daniel	19	Feb. 24, '64		Transferred to Company I, April 4, '64.
Hurlbut, Clinton E.	18	Feb. 24, '64		Discharged for wounds received in battle of Nashville.
Johnson, Christian	20	Feb. 22, '64		Transferred to Company I, April 4, '64.
Johnson, Isaac	33	Aug. 14, '62		Transferred to Company I, April 11, '64.
Keith, James R.	19	Aug. 15, '62		Transferred to Veteran Reserve Corps, Dec. 16, '63.
Keller, George	18	Feb. 29, '64	Aug. 19, '65	
Keller, Henry	25	Aug. 14, '62	Aug. 19, '65	Promoted corporal.
Keller, Isaac	27	Aug. 15, '62		Transferred to Veteran Reserve Corps, April 1, '65.
Kendall, John V.	23	Aug. 15, '62	Aug. 19, '65	
Kimball, Duram	18	Aug. 14, '62		Absent.
Kinney, James M.	28	Aug. 23, '62		Wagoner; discharged per order July 21, '65.
Kutzer, Wm R.	18	Feb. 19, '64		Transferred to Company I, Apr 4, '64.
Larson, Hans	21	Aug. 15, '62		Discharged in hospital in '65.
Larson, Jacob	28	Aug. 15, '62	Aug. 19, '65	
Larson, Ole	21	Aug. 21, '62	Aug. 19, '65	
Lawrence, Albert	21	Aug. 14, '62	July 11, '65	Absent.
Leavitt, Homer B.	23	Aug. 14, '62	Aug. 19, '65	
Lewis, Christopher	20	Feb. 23, '64		Transferred to Company I, April 4, '64.
Mason, Geo. W.	26	Aug. 14, '62	May 27, '65	
Mastinbrook, John Jr.	22	Aug. 15, '62		Died Nov. 15, '65, at Jefferson Barracks.
Mastinbrook, Wm.	19	March 31, '64	May 31, '65	Absent.

Appendix C

Names	Age	Mustered In	Mustered Out	Remarks
Enlisted Men				
McIntyre, Albert P.	21	Aug. 21, '62	Aug. 19, '65	
McIntyre, Wm. J.	21	Aug. 14, '62	Aug. 19, '65	
Mellinger, Erastus F.	20	Aug. 14, '62	Aug. 1, '65	
Merical, John G.	27	Aug. 14, '62		Corporal; died Dec. 22, '64, of wounds received at Nashville.
Merzer, Wm.	21	Aug. 21, '62	Aug. 1, '65	
Michael, Jacob	27	Aug. 16, '62	Aug. 19, '65	
Miller, Augustus	25	Aug. 21, '62	Aug. 19, '65	Promoted corporal, sergeant.
Miller, Abraham	44	Feb. 15, '64		Transferred to Company I, April 4, '64.
Miner, Amasa T.	33	Aug. 14, '62		Corporal; discharged for disability, March 30, '64.
Moffit, Robert	28	Aug. 14, '62		Corporal; died Feb. 22, '65, at Cairo, Ill.
Montgomery, H. M.	26	Aug. 14, '62	Aug. 19, '65	
Moran, Cornelius	23	Aug. 14, '62		Discharged for disability, Oct. 28, '64.
Morris, Edward	30	Aug. 15, '62		Transferred to Company I, April 4, '64.
Moulton, Oren	29	Feb. 29, '64		Died Jan. 5, '65, at Nashville.
Myers, Felix	40	Aug. 15, '62		Discharged June 11, '65, for wounds received at Nashville.
Newman, Geo. H.	37	Aug. 14, '62		Corporal.
Newman, John H.	18	Sept. 2, '64		Died Jan. 23, '65, at Eastport, Miss.
Neal, George W.	26	Feb. 11, '64	Aug. 19, '65	
Nettleton, John D.	35	Feb. 29, '64		Absent.
Nichols, Alfred	30	Aug. 21, '62	May 31, '65	Per order.
Nunn, Jesse	35	Aug. 14, '62		Corporal; discharged for disability, Dec. 17, '64.
Nye, Reuben	19	Feb. 19, '64		Transferred to Company I, April 4, '64.
Osborne, Wm. H.	24	Aug. 14, '62	Aug. 19, '65	
Palmer, Willis D. L.	16	Aug. 14, '62		Musician; discharged per order, May 31, '65.
Pierce, Richard W.	18	Aug. 14, '62		Discharged for disability, Feb. 9, '65.
Prentiss, Thos. D.	26	Aug. 14, '62	Aug. 19, '65	
Rawlins, Joseph V.	27	Aug. 14, '62		Discharged for disability, Nov. 28, '64.
Reed, Moses	19	Feb. 24, '64		Transferred to Company I, April 4, '64.
Rhinehart, Wm.	18	Sept. 2, '64	Aug. 19, '65	
Rice, Wm.	19	Aug. 15, '62		Died May 17, '64, at Columbus, Ky.
Richardson, Emmett B.	18	Aug. 15, '62	Aug. 19, '65	
Ruthledge, John	23	Aug. 21, '62	Aug. 19, '65	
Scott, Francis M.	21	Feb. 15, '64		Transferred to Company I, April 4, '64.
Scranton, Seth B.	22	Feb. 26, '64		Discharged Jan. 21, '65, for wounds received at Tupelo.
Scranton, S. B.	21	Aug. 21, '62		Discharged for disability, April, '63
Sherman, Daniel W.	25	Aug. 14, '62	July 18, '65	Absent.
Sherwood, Ambrose	18	Aug. 14, '62	Aug. 19, '65	
Staelson, Berent	44	Feb. 22, '64		Transferred to Company I, April 4, '64.

Names	Age	Mustered In	Mustered Out	Remarks
Enlisted Men				
Staples, David H.	29	Feb. 22, '65	Aug. 19, '65	
Stephens, Frederick O.	24	Aug. 14, '62		Discharged per order May 16, '65.
Stevens, M. H.	18	Aug. 14, '62		Discharged per order May 26, '65.
Stevens, Edom H.	24	Feb. 29, '64		Discharged per order Jan. 21, '65.
Stewart, James	24	Aug. 14, '62	Aug. 19, '65	
Thompson, Lafayette F.	38	Aug. 21, '62		Musician; discharged Nov. 5, '63, for promotion.
Thompson, Thomas H.	33	Aug. 15, '62		Died Dec. 14, '64, at Memphis.
Tuthill, Charles D.	30	Aug. 23, '62		Sergeant; dis. March 30, '64, for wounds received in Indian expedition.
Van Allen, Charles	27	Aug. 15, '62		Transferred to Veteran Reserve Corps, Sept. 14, '64.
Waldo, Nathan W.	25	Aug. 14, '62		Discharged for disability, Jan. 21, '64.
Walsh, Orman W.	22	Feb. 24, '64		Transferred to Company I, April 4, '64.
Wedman, Friend W.	35	Aug. 14, '62	Aug. 19, '65	
Wiley, Thos	31	Aug. 14, '62		Transferred to Company I, April 4, '64.
Williams, James L.	19	Feb. 29, '64		Transferred to Company I, April 4, '64.
Wilson, Stephen L.	38	Aug. 21, '62		Died Aug. 16, '64, at Memphis.
Willyard, Henry	34	Aug. 14, '62		Transferred to Company I, April 4, '64.
Woodward, Dorwin E.	25	Aug. 14, '62	Aug. 19, '65	Promoted corporal.
Young, Peter, Jr.	26	Aug. 21, '62	Aug. 19, '65	
Younglove, Charles D.	18	March 30, '63	Aug. 19, '65	Promoted corporal.

Roster of Company C, Tenth Regiment, Minnesota Volunteers

Names	Age	Mustered In	Mustered Out	Remarks
Officers				
Captains				
Chas. W. Hackett	31	Aug. 23, '62		Enrolled Aug. 14, '62; discharged for disability in '64.
Albert S. Hopson	38	Feb. 1, '64		Enrolled Aug. 15, '62; 1st Lt. Aug. 23, '62; discharged for disability, Sept. 26, '64.
Dennis Cavanaugh	26	Sept. 13, '62	Aug. 19, '65	
First Lieutenants				
John Lathrop	29	Feb. 16, '64	March 30, '65	Per order; enrolled Aug. 15, '62; 2d lieutenant Aug. 23, '62.
Micah R. Merrill	33	Aug. 14, '62	Aug. 19, '65	
Second Lieutenant				
Wallace W. Case	22	Feb. 16, '64	Aug. 19, '65 Sept. 2, '62.	Enrolled Aug. 15, '62; 1st sergeant,
Enlisted Men				
Ackley, David	35	Aug. 15, '62	Aug. 19, '65	Wagoner.

Appendix C

Names	Age	Mustered In	Mustered Out	Remarks
Enlisted Men				
Bemis, Hiram	33	Aug. 21, '62		Promoted corporal; discharged for disability, April 11, '62.
Benschoter, Martin W.	32	Sept. 2, '62		Enrolled Aug. 15, '62; Sergeant; dis. for disability, Dec. 3, '63.
Benthall, John M.	29	Aug. 21, '62	Aug. 19, '65	
Burnham, John W.	32	Sept. 2, '62		Enrolled Aug. 15, '62; corporal; promoted sergeant; discharged April 4, '65, for promotion in U.S. Colored Infantry.
Broderick, John	18	March 7, '64		Deserted March 17, '64, at St. Louis.
Buck, Clarence L.	25	Aug. 15, '62	Aug. 19, '65	
Buck, Franklin M.	18	Aug. 15, '62		Absent.
Buck, Deruyter	18	March 31, '64		Died April 9, '65, at Keokuk, Iowa.
Burpee, Silas K.	38	Aug. 15, '62		Straggled from ranks in Arkansas; never heard from since.
Burrows, J. A.				
Burton, John	37	Aug. 15, '62	Aug. 1, '65	Absent.
Byrnes, John	21	Aug. 15, '62	May 29, '65	
Canfield, Wm	21	Aug. 15, '62	Aug. 19, '65	Promoted corporal.
Carroll, Austin D.	22	Sept. 2, '62		Enrolled Aug. 15, '62; corporal; killed Dec. 16, '64, at Nashville.
Case, Elanson H.	22	Aug. 15, '62	Aug. 19, '65	
Chamberlain, Joseph H.	28	Feb. 4, '64	Aug. 19, '65	
Clipperton, Thomas	26	Aug. 15, '62	Aug. 19, '65	
Collier, James M.	32	Sept. 2, '62	Aug. 19, '65	Enrolled Aug. 15, '62; corporal.
Collins, Wm. F.	26	Feb. 29, '64	Aug. 19, '65	
Conner, John	21	Aug. 22, '64		Deserted Nov. 23, '64, at St. Louis.
Crawford, Oliver P.	43	Sept. 2, '62		Enrolled Aug. 15, '62; sergeant; Dis. for disability, Oct. 7, '62.
Cross, Edwin	21	March 31, '64	Apr. 29, '65	Per order.
Cross, David E.	22	Aug. 15, '62	Aug. 19, '65	Promoted corporal and sergeant.
Cross, Thomas J.	23	Aug. 21, '62	Aug. 19, '65	
Davis, Wm. R.	26	Aug. 15, '62		Discharged for disability, May 25, '63.
Davis, Daniel M.	31	Aug. 15, '62		Discharged for disability, April 11,' 63.
Dawley, Chas. G.	21	Sept. 2, '62		Enrolled Aug. 15, '62; corporal; Promoted sergeant; killed at Nashville, Dec. 16, '64.
Day, Edwin A.	21	Aug. 15, '62		Discharged for disability, May 25, '63.
Doeg, Almon H.	21	Aug. 15, '62		Died Dec. 19, '64, of wounds received. at Nashville.
Drew, George W.	19	Aug. 21, '62	Aug. 19, '65	Promoted corporal.
Errickson, Peter	23	Aug. 15, '62	Aug. 19, '65	
Fessenden, Eben	24	Feb. 19, '64		Died February, '65, on hospital steamer *D. A. January.*
Fessenden, Lorenzo N.	26	Feb. 19, '64		Straggled from ranks Sept. '64, in Ark.; not heard from since.
Foley, David	21	Aug. 15, '62		Discharged for disability.
Foster, Chas. D.	18	Aug. 15, '62	Aug. 19, '65	
Foster, James G.	23	Aug. 15, '62		Died March 5, '65, at Memphis.
Foster, Zelotus	21	Aug. 15, '62		Discharged for disability, May 11, '65.

Tenth Regiment Roster (Company C)

Names	Age	Mustered In	Mustered Out	Remarks
Enlisted Men				
Fuller, Irad M.	21	Feb. 28, '63	Aug. 19, '65	
Hancock, Gilbert F.	31	Aug. 15, '62		Died Feb. 28, '65, at Memphis, Tenn.
Harpham, Francis H.	27	Feb. 19, '64		Discharged April 18, '65, of wounds received at Nashville.
Harpham, Henry	35	Feb. 20, '64	Aug. 19, '65	
Hayes, James W.	39	Aug. 15, '62		Promoted corporal and sergeant; Dis. per order, May 19, '65.
Hipple, Henry	25	Sept. 2, '62	Aug. 19, '65	Enrolled Aug. 21, '62; promoted quartermaster.
Holcolm, Oliver H.	29	Sept. 2, '62		Enrolled Aug. 15, '62; serg; dis. for pro., U.S. Colored Infantry.
Jacobson, Benj.	21	Feb. 19, '64	Aug. 19, '65	
Jacobus, James	21	Feb. 16, '64	Aug. 21, '65	Absent; sick.
Johnson, Levi B.	26	Feb. 19, '64	Aug. 21, '65	
Johnson, Lewis	24	Aug. 15, '62		Deserted Dec. 1, '62, at Fort Ridgley.
Juelson, Hans	25	Aug. 15, '62	Aug. 19, '65	
Kelzer, John L.	29	March 1, '64		Died Dec. 31, '64, at White Water, Wisc., on furlough.
Knapp, Francis W.	24	Sept. 2, '62		Corporal; pro. serg; dis. Jan 1, '65, of wounds received at Nashville.
Knowlton, Geo. W.	29	Aug. 16, '62	Aug. 21, '65	
Lawrence, Merritt G.	18	Aug. 16, '62		Died March 26, '63, at Le Sueur, Minn.
Leland, Octavus A.	40	Sept. 2, '62	Aug. 19, '65	Enrolled Aug. 15, '62; musician.
Linstram, Albert	19	Aug. 15, '62	Aug. 21, '65	
Lockey, James W.	21	Aug. 15, '62	Aug. 21, '65	
Mallinson, James W.	18	Aug. 15, '62		Discharged for disability, April 11, '63.
Matterson, Edward H.	19	Aug. 24, '62		Discharged Aug 19, '65; absent.
Matthewson, George	33	Aug. 15, '62		Discharged for disability, Jan. 26, '64.
McKay, Arthur F.	21	Aug. 15, '62	June 5, '65	Per order.
McRay, James H.	33	Feb. 21, '64	Aug. 19, '65	
Miles, Wm. A.	34	Aug. 16, '62		Discharged for disability, March 1, '64.
Moody, Robert	23	Aug. 15, '62		Discharged for disability, Oct. 5, '64.
Mullins, David	21	Feb. 27, '64		Died Feb. 20, '65, on hospital steamer *D. A. January*.
Mullins, Eusebius	19	Aug. 15, '62		Died Jan. 12, '65, at Louisville, Ky., of wounds received at Nashville.
Murphy, John W.	27	Sept. 2, '62		Corporal; killed Dec. 26, '64, at Nashville.
Nelson, Chrest	21	Aug. 15, '62		Killed Dec. 16, '64, at Nashville.
Nelson, John	39	Aug. 21, '62		Discharged for disability.
Nicholson, Demias	25	Aug. 15, '62		Discharged for disability May 28, '65.
Nicholson, Geo. A.	21	Aug. 15, '62	Aug. 19, '65	Promoted corporal.
Nicholson, John	28	March 4, '64		Discharged in hospital in '65.
Olmsted, Royal W.	21	Aug. 15, '62	June 5, '65	Per order.
Orton, Lemuel S.	22	Aug. 22, '62	May 15, '65	Per order.
Osgood, Charles	23	Feb. 20, '64	Aug. 19, '65	

Names	Age	Mustered In	Mustered Out	Remarks
Enlisted Men				
Peck, Josiah A.	28	Aug. 15, '62	Aug. 19, '65	Promoted corporal and sergeant.
Pomeroy, Otis	32	Feb. 4, '64	Aug. 19, '65	
Pope, James R.	23	Aug. 15, '62		Absent.
Pratt, Collins	28	Sept. 2, '62	Aug. 19, '65	Enrolled Aug. 15, '62; musician.
Purvis, William M.	23	Aug. 15, '62	May 12, '65	Per order.
Putnam, Alonzo D.	27	Sept. 2, '62		Enrolled Aug. 21, '62; corporal; dis. for disability, Sept. 30, '63.
Putnam, Geo. C.	30	Aug. 21, '62	May 16, '65	Per order.
Putnam, Nathan A.	37	Sept. 13, '64		Killed Dec. 16, '64, at Nashville.
Robinson, John B.	25	Sept. 2, '62	Aug. 19, '65	Enrolled Aug. 15, '62; sergeant.
Rolph, Robert S.	22	Aug. 21, '62	Aug. 19, '65	Promoted corporal and sergeant.
Rounds, James M.	36	Feb. 8, '64		Absent.
Safford, John L.	26	Aug. 15, '62	Aug. 19, '65	Promoted corporal.
Shilson, Christian	25	Aug. 21, '62	June 24, '65	Per order.
Sleeper, Wm. O.	26	Aug. 15, '62	May 12, '65	Per order.
Smith, Frederick	18	Feb. 23, '64	Aug. 19, '65	
Snyder, Henry	33	Aug. 15, '62		Absent.
Southwick, Henry	24	Aug. 22, '62	Aug. 19, '65	
Starr, Ebenezer L.	23	Aug. 18, '62	Aug. 19, '65	Promoted corporal.
Stewart, Henry	29	Aug. 15, '62	July 17, '65	Absent.
Tenney, Geo. W.	22	Aug. 21, '62		Discharged for disability, 3 Sep, '63.
Thompson, John	19	Aug. 21, '62	Aug. 19, '65	Promoted corporal and sergeant.
Tufft, James K.	19	Aug. 15, '62	Aug. 19, '65	Promoted corporal, Sept. 3, '63.
Tuft, John	44	Aug. 29, '64	Aug. 19, '65	
Warner, Ogden D.	27	Aug. 15, '62	Aug. 19, '65	
Whiting, Horace B.	31	Aug. 21, '62	June 5, '65	Per order.
Wildes, Francis H.	28	Aug. 15, '62		Absent; promoted corporal.
Winter, Daniel	25	Aug. 16, '62		Discharged for disability, April 5, '65.
Winter, John D.	36	Aug. 15, '62	Aug. 19, '65	
Wright, Wm. W.	21	Aug. 21, '62		Died March 1, '63, at Le Sueur, Minn.
Yeoman, Nathaniel	25	Aug. 15, '62		Discharged for disability, June 30, '65.
Young, Daniel	25	Aug. 21, '62		Discharged for disability, Oct. 14, '64.
Young, Salomon	23	Aug. 22, '62		Discharged Sept. 27, '64, for wounds received at Tupelo, Miss.

Roster of Company D, Tenth Regiment, Minnesota Volunteers

Names	Age	Mustered In	Mustered Out	Remarks
Officers				
Captains				
Wm. W. Phelps	36	Sept. 8, '62		Resigned Nov. 3 '63; enlisted as private Aug. 17, '62.
Lewis F. Babcock	30	Nov. 11, '63		Transferred to Company A, March 1, '64.
Charles L. Davis	29	Feb. 16, '64	Aug. 19, '65	2d lieutenant, Aug. 16, '62; 1st lieutenant, Sept. 8, '62.

Names	Age	Mustered In	Mustered Out	Remarks
Officers				
First Lieutenant				
Wm. B. Williams	27	Feb. 16, '64	Aug. 19, '65	2d lieutenant, Sept. 8, '62; Enlisted as private, Aug. 22, '62.
Second Lieutenant				
Loren S. Meeker	38	March 30, '64	Aug. 19, '65	Promoted from commissary sergeant.
Enlisted Men				
Abel, Morgan	26	Aug. 21, '62		Discharged for disability, Feb. 17, '64.
Ammon, Edward	23	Aug. 19, '62	Aug. 19, '65	
Anderson, Halvor	21	Feb. 27, '64	Aug. 19, '65	
Anfinson, Bour	18	Aug. 22, '62	Aug. 19, '65	
Aspen, Henry	21	Aug. 22, '62	July 14, '65	Discharged at Meridian, Miss.
Axsell, Charles	37	Aug. 22, '62		Discharged for disability, May 13, '63.
Banks, John	19	Aug. 21, '62	Aug. 19, '65	Promoted corporal.
Barnes, Walter S.	23	Aug. 21, '62	May 16, '65	At Nashville.
Barnes, Wm. E.	27	Aug. 22, '62		Corporal; discharged.
Beers, Charles W.	43	Aug. 21, '62		Corporal; discharged in '65; absent.
Berg, Ulrick R.	29	Aug. 22, '62		Died Oct. 1, '64, at Memphis.
Blaker, Wm. H.	21	Feb. 27, '64	Aug. 19, '65	
Bonney, Joseph	26	Aug. 21, '62		Died Dec. 23, '62, at Henderson, Minn.
Brown, Henry H.	28	Aug. 20, '62		Corporal; transferred to Veteran Reserve Corps, Sept. 14, '64.
Buck, Deruyter	18	March 31, '64		Transferred to Company C.
Carpenter, Stephen W.	26	Jan. 21, '63	Aug. 19, '65	Musician.
Christopherson, Sever	20	Aug. 22, '62	Aug. 19, '65	
Dayton, Asa H.	28	Aug. 20, '62	Aug. 19, '65	Promoted corporal.
Dolaker, Anfind	27	Aug. 22, '62		Discharged Sept. 14, '63.
Eggleston, Henry K.	24	Aug. 19, '62		Discharged July 14, '65, at Meridian, Miss.
Eggleston, Ira E.	22	Aug. 22, '62	Aug. 19, '65	Wagoner.
Emery, Frederick	18	Aug. 18, '62		Transferred from Company F; Oct. 8, '62.
Erickson, Henry	21	Aug. 22, '62	Aug. 19, '65	
Evenson, Ole	26	Aug. 22, '62	Aug. 19, '65	
Falls, Charles	28	Aug. 22, '62	Aug. 19, '65	
Fessenden, Edwin A.	30	Aug. 22, '62		Died Dec. 23, '62, at Henderson, Minn.
Frederick, Emery	18	Aug. 18, '62		Discharged at Fort Goodhue, Minn. Aug. 7, '63.
Freeman, Oscar H.	27	Aug. 18, '62		Promoted corporal, sergeant.
Gallagher, Owen	45	Aug. 21, '62		Absent.
Gallen, John	22	Feb. 19, '64		Deserted Nov. 23, '64, at St. Louis.
Griffin, Frank	24	March 21, '64		Killed Dec. 16, '64, at Nashville.
Hahn, Wm.	26	Feb. 27, '64	Aug. 19, '65	
Hart, James R.	18	Aug. 22, '62	Aug. 19, '65	
Hasbrouck, Isaac G.	18	Aug. 16, '62	Aug. 19, '65	Promoted corporal.
Herbert, Lemuel	18	Aug. 22, '62	May 20, '65	At Davenport, Iowa.
Hill, Francis D.	32	Aug. 21, '62		Corporal; pro. sergeant; died at Jefferson Barracks, Oct. 18, '64.
Hofer, Jacob	39	Feb. 25, '64		Deserted July 30, '64, at St. Louis.

Appendix C

Names	Age	Mustered In	Mustered Out	Remarks
Enlisted Men				
Horton, Chas. C.	19	Nov. 12, '62	Aug. 19, '65	Promoted corporal.
House, Thos. R.	27	Feb. 17, '64		Absent.
Hus, Ole O.	23	Aug. 22, '62		Died Oct. 18, '64, at Memphis, Tenn.
Ives, Geo. W.	18	Aug. 18, '62		Died Nov. 13, '62, at Fort Snelling, Minn.
Johnson, George	24	Aug. 22, '62	Aug. 19, '65	
Johnson, Nels	18	March 29, '64	May 11, '65	At draft rendezvous, Fort Snelling.
Johnson, John	18	Aug. 31, '64		Died March 13, '65, at Memphis, Tenn.
Johnson, Julius	21	Feb. 27, '64		Transferred to Veteran Reserve Corps, Feb. 21, '65.
Johnson, Peter I.	25	Aug. 21, '62	Aug. 19, '65	Corporal; promoted sergeant.
Kennedy, Thomas				Corporal.
Killoe, Gunder	21	Aug. 22, '62		Deserted Oct. 8, '63, at Fort Snelling.
King, John	44	Aug. 18, '62	Aug. 19, '65	
Klingensmith, Cyrus	32	Aug. 18, '62	July 19, '65	Absent; carried on roll as Smith, Cyrus K.
Knutson, Samuel	35	Aug. 21, '62		Sergeant; discharged.
Larson, Bottol	25	Aug. 21, '62	Aug. 19, '65	
Larson, Ole	21	Aug. 22, '62	Aug. 19, '65	
Larson, Yors	29	Aug. 21, '62		Died Jan. 22, '65, at Jeffersonville, Ind.
Lewiston, Lewis	29	Aug. 22, '62		Corporal; absent.
Little, Thomas J.	18	Aug. 22, '62		Discharged for disability, May 13, '63.
Lumsden, Geo. L.	43	March 8, '64		Killed Dec. 16, '64, at Nashville.
Lusk, Henry	25	Feb. 27, '64		Discharged per order, May 22, '65.
Lysing, John K.	24	Aug. 22, '62	Aug. 19, '65	
McConnell, Henry A.	32	Aug. 17, '62		1st sergeant; discharged March 31, '64, for promotion.
McConnell, Washington J.	45	March 7, '64	Aug. 19, '65	
McCord, E. Kimball	27	Feb. 22, '64	May 24, '65	Per order.
McCord, Theron B.	30	Aug. 18, '62	Aug. 19, '65	Sergeant; reduced to ranks by his consent.
Merrill, John A.	28	Aug. 22, '62	Aug. 19, '65	Promoted corporal, sergeant.
Miller, Charles P.	18	Aug. 22, '62	Aug. 19, '65	Musician.
Miller, John H.	17	Aug. 22, '62	Aug. 19, '65	Musician; promoted corporal.
Mooers, Leonard B.	45	Aug. 21, '62	March 21, '65	At Keokuk, Iowa
Morrison, John	22	March 26, '64		Deserted April 18, '64, at St. Louis, Mo.
Nickels, John	27	Aug. 19, '62	Aug. 19, '65	Promoted corporal.
Nelson, Charles	28	Aug. 21, '62	May 22, '65	Per order.
Nelson, Lars	26	Aug. 18, '62		Discharged at Fort Goodhue, Minn., May 13, '63.
Nelson, Ole	30	Aug. 22, '62		Died Dec. 17, '64 of wounds received at Nashville.
Noble, Charles B.	18	Aug. 21, '62		Absent.
Olson, Edwin	19	Aug. 22, '62	Aug. 19, '65	Promoted corporal.
Olson, Mons	32	Aug. 22, '62	Aug. 19, '65	
Olson, Nels	23	Aug. 31, '64	Aug. 19, '65	
Olson, Olaus	21	Aug. 22, '62	Aug. 19, '65	
Olson, Peter	30	Aug. 22, '62		Discharged at Fort Goodhue, Minn., April 11, '63.

Names	Age	Mustered In	Mustered Out	Remarks
Enlisted Men				
Opdahl, Thorston	21	Aug. 22, '62	Aug. 19, '65	Promoted corporal, sergeant.
Peterson, John	22	Aug. 22, '62		Deserted Oct. 8, '63, at Fort Snelling
Quom, Knudd	18	Aug. 31, '64	Aug. 19, '65	
Reeves, George	18	Aug. 21, '62		Died Dec. 18, '64; wounded at Nashville.
Richards, John	21	Aug. 20, '62		Discharged at Fort Goodhue, Minn., April 11, '63.
Ryan, James	30	Feb. 19, '64		Killed Dec. 16, '64, at Nashville.
Rylan, Cornelius R.	19	Aug. 22, '62	Aug. 19, '65	
Satterly, Nathan	18	Aug. 16, '62	Aug. 19, '65	
Satterly, Simeon P.	44	Aug. 16, '62		Discharged at Fort Goodhue, Minn., Aug. 31, '63.
Scott, Andrew	18	Aug. 31, '64		Died April 2, '65, at Memphis, Tenn.
Shakespeare, George	41	Aug. 18, '62	Aug. 19, '65	Promoted corporal.
Sondreson, Halver	30	Aug. 22, '62	Aug. 19, '65	
Stanky, Martin	30	Aug. 18, '62	May 30, '65	Per order.
Steinerson, Holver	18	Feb. 28, '64		Died Jan. 13, '65, at Chicago, Ill.
Svendson, Torkel	24	Aug. 21, '62	Aug. 19, '65	
Thompson, Wm. R.	21	Aug. 18, '62		Sergeant; discharged per order, May 24, '65.
Thoreson, Ingval	24	Aug. 22, '62	Aug. 19, '65	
Todd, Geo. A.	24	Aug. 22, '62		Corporal; transferred to non-commissioned staff June 20, '63.
Topper, Joseph	25	Aug. 20, '62	Aug. 19, '65	Promoted corporal, sergeant.
Vosburg, Barnet	26	Aug. 18, '62		Discharged at Fort Snelling.
Wallower, David	26	Aug. 19, '62		Absent.
Wallower, Peter	45	Aug. 22, '62		Absent.
Watson, Leander W.	27	Aug. 21, '62	May 29, '65	Per order.
Winter, John	28	Aug. 18, '62		Absent; sergeant; reduced to ranks.
Wightman, David	24	Aug. 22, '62	June 12, '65	Corporal; promoted sergeant.
Wright, Ivy E.	22	Aug. 18, '62		Corporal; discharged at Monroe, Ind., per order April 6, '63.
Yates, Charles M.	22	Aug. 29, '62		Died Feb. 1, '65, at Paducah, Ky.

Roster of Company E, Tenth Regiment, Minnesota Volunteers

Names	Age	Mustered In	Mustered Out	Remarks
Officers				
Captains				
James A. Robson	36	Sept. 8, '62.		Died Nov. 8, '62, from wound received by accd. discharge of pistol.
John W. Heath	40	Nov. 9, '62	Feb. 22, '64	Sept. 8, '62; 1st lieutenant.
Kennedy, Ebenezer H.	29	Feb. 22, '64	Aug. 19, '65	1st lieutenant, Sept. 15, '62.
First Lieutenant				
Charles Kittelson	24	Nov. 9, '62	Aug. 19, '65	2d lieutenant, Sept. 8, '62.
Second Lieutenant				
Eli Ash	33	Nov. 9, '62		1st sergeant, Oct. 13, '62; 1st lieutenant, Company G.

Appendix C

Names	Age	Mustered In	Mustered Out	Remarks
Enlisted Men				
Alshaugh, Christian	35	Sept. 18, '62	Aug. 19, '65	Corporal.
Anderson, Andrew	22	Aug. 13, '62		Died Nov. 3, '62, at Fort Snelling, Minn.
Anderson, Andrew	21	Aug. 18, '62	May 20, '65	Absent.
Anderson, Daniel	20	Aug. 21, '62		Promoted corporal; discharged per order, July 10, '65.
Barden, Gilbert G.	35	Aug. 19, '62		Discharged for disability, Jan. 26, '64.
Bartlett, Henry C.	19	Aug. 14, '62	June 6, '65	
Benson, Stengen	34	Aug. 21, '62		Killed Dec. 16, '64, at Nashville.
Benton, Elisha	20	Jan. 12, '64		Died Feb. 14, '64, at St. Louis, Mo.
Black, Andrew	29	Aug. 13, '62		Pro. hospital steward; trans. to non-com. staff, April 12, '64.
Boven, James	23	Aug. 19, '62	Aug. 15, '65	
Boven, Robert H.	28	Sept. 1, '64	May 13, '65	Per order.
Brownsell, Edwin	21	Aug. 19, '62	Aug. 19, '65	
Burlingame, Henry D.	28	Sept. 18, '62	Aug. 19, '65	Corporal; promoted sergeant.
Bullock, Cyrus E.	36	Aug. 13, '62	June 23, '65	Promoted corporal; absent.
Bullock, Lemuel E.	29	Aug. 21, '62	June 23, '65	Wounded at Nashville; absent.
Campbell, Rodney M.	24	Aug. 14, '62	Aug. 19, '65	
Carpenter, W. G.	23	Aug. 21, '62	Aug. 19, '65	Promoted corporal.
Chamberlain, Fredo	28	Aug. 13, '62		Died Dec. 18, '64, of wounds received at Nashville.
Chandler, Geo. H.	38	Aug. 23, '62		Discharged for disability, Dec. 12, '64.
Christianson, Franz	31	Nov. 20, '62		Died Feb. 16, '65, at Cairo, Ill.
Clark, Samuel	42	Aug. 15, '62		Discharged for disability, Nov. 17, '63.
Cook, James L.	30	Sept. 18, '62	Aug. 19, '65	Sergeant.
Cozzen, Dan. E.	21	Aug. 13, '62	Aug. 19, '65	
Cozzen, Frank	19	March 22, '64	Aug. 19, '65	
Davis, Francis M.	19	Aug. 25, '62	Aug. 19, '65	
Davis, Russell B.	24	Aug. 15, '62		Died Feb. 24, '64, at Le Sueur, Minn.
Deanan, Matthew L.	21	Aug. 21, '62		Died Aug. 22, '63, at Fort Abercrombie, D. T.
Devereaux, Jedediah W.	24	Sept. 18, '62	June 15, '65	Corporal.
Dunning, John G.	42	Sept. 18, '62	Aug. 19, '65	Corporal.
Edson, John	23	Aug. 14, '62		Transferred to Veteran Reserve Corps, March 13, '65.
Erickson, Engebrit	32	Aug. 14, '62	Aug. 19, '65	
Erickson, Tolef	35	Aug. 30, '64	Aug. 19, '65	
Everett, Wm. E.	37	Aug. 19, '62		Discharged for disability, April 11, '65.
Fausty, Patrick				
Ferguson, Ashley	24	Aug. 21, '62	Aug. 19, '65	
Ferguson, Torgus	22	Aug. 22, '62	Aug. 19, '65	
Gates, Geo. W.	18	Aug. 21, '62		Died June 26, '64, at Memphis, Tenn.
Godberg, Lorenzo Dow	32	Aug. 13, '62	Aug. 19, '65	
Golden, Samuel D.	22	March 14, '65	Aug. 19, '65	
Gruby, Augustus	18	Aug. 13, '62	Aug. 19, '65	
Hanson, Martin	30	Aug. 30, '64		Died April 25, '65, at Memphis, Tenn.

Tenth Regiment Roster (Company E)

Names	Age	Mustered In	Mustered Out	Remarks
Enlisted Men				
Hodo, Edward	33	March 28, '64	Aug. 19, '65	
Holmes, John M.	36	Aug. 21, '62		Discharged for disability, Dec. 29, '63.
Hoover, John W.	21	Oct. 4, '62	May 31, '65	Per order.
Huber, Godfrey	18	Aug. 15, '62	Aug. 19, '65	
Hurd, Asa	27	Sept. 18, '62		Wagoner; killed April 25, '65, by rebels, near Montgomery, Ala.
Iverson, Ole	27	Aug. 15, '62		Died Feb. 28, '65, at Prairie du Chien, Wisc.
Iverson, Thomas	19	Aug. 21, '62	Aug. 19, '65	
Johnson, Henry	21	Aug. 22, '62	July 21, '65	Absent.
Johnson, Erick C.	19	Aug. 13, '62	Aug. 19, '65	
Judd, Uriah	25	Aug. 15, '62	June 13, '65	Per order.
Kaiser, John C.	30	Aug. 19, '62	Aug. 19, '65	
Kelley, Rufus	25	Sept. 18, '62	Aug. 19, '65	Corporal; promoted sergeant.
Lair, James	27	Aug. 22, '62		Discharged for disability, April 11, '65.
Lang, Levi	30	Feb. 28, '64		Died March 6, '65, at New Albany, Ind.
Lowe, Wm. H.	29	Sept. 18, '62	July 21, '65	Sergeant; absent.
Lugg, Edward	30	Aug. 30, '64	Aug. 19, '65	
Madson, John	20	Sept. 1, '64	Aug. 19, '65	
Madson, Mads	30	Sept. 1, '64	Aug. 19, '65	
Maixner, Fritz	33	Oct. 4, '62	July 21, '65	Absent.
McMannus, Thomas				
McMeans, David L.	21	Feb. 8, '64		Absent; in confinement for desertion since March '64.
Meeker, Lorin S.	38	Oct. 13, '62		Pro. commissary sergeant; transf. to non-com. staff, Dec. 2, '62.
Mickelson, Christopher	32	Aug. 16, '62		Discharged for disability, Aug. 7, '63.
Middleton, Samuel	44	Feb. 28, '64		Died Feb. 25, '65, at Memphis, Tenn.
Morin, Patrick	21	Aug. 21, '62		Promoted corporal; died Aug. 11, '65, at Fort Snelling, Minn.
Oleson, Peter E.	19	Aug. 13, '62		Musician; discharged for disability, June 20, '65.
Oleson, Ludwig	31	Aug. 18, '62		Deserted Oct. 20, '62.
Osborne, George	29	Sept. 18, '62	July 23, '65	Corporal; absent.
Owen, Elijah W.	42	Aug. 13, '62		Transferred to Veteran Reserve Corps, Dec. 21, '64.
Pace, Israel H.	22	Aug. 21, '62	June 13, '65	Per order.
Park, Benjamin	34	Aug. 15, '62	May 29, '65	Per order.
Parker, Allen	26	Apr. 5, '64		Deserted April 7, '64, at Carondelet, Mo.
Partridge, George H.	31	Sept. 18, '62		Sergeant; died Feb. 3, '65, in hospital at Louisville, Ky.
Perry, Isaac	22	Aug. 22, '62	Aug. 19, '65	
Peterson, Nels	40	Sept. 1, '64	Aug. 19, '65	
Pickett, Eli K.	34	Sept. 18, '62		Sergeant; promoted 2d lieutenant, Company I, June 21, '64.
Peterson, John	23	Aug. 13, '62	Aug. 19, '65	
Peterson, Charles	30	Aug. 21, '62		Discharged for disability, Jan. 20, '65.
Post, Joel M.	27	Feb. 28, '63	Aug. 19, '65	

Names	Age	Mustered In	Mustered Out	Remarks
Enlisted Men				
Prescott, Cyrus S.	32	Aug. 13, '62	Aug. 19, '65	
Proebsting, Lewis	30	Aug. 13, '62		Pro. hospital steward; trans. to non. com. staff, Oct. 23, '62.
Pulford, Joseph	36	Aug. 16, '62	Aug. 24, '65	Absent.
Reynolds, John L.	35	Aug. 13, '62		While absent.
Reynolds, Robert H.	20	Aug. 14, '62	Aug. 19, '65	Promoted corporal.
Rice, Hiram J.	30	Aug. 21, '62		Promoted corporal; discharged for disability, April 11, '65.
Rush, Joel	18	Aug. 15, '62	Aug. 19, '65	
Scoville, John L.	14	Aug. 13, '62	June 29, '65	Musician.
Seeley, James C.	32	Aug. 13, '62		Died Oct. 28, '63, at Fort Abercrombie, D. T.
Shook, Edward	22	March 14, '64		Deserted Nov. 18, '64, at St. Louis, Mo.
Shoyer, Peter P.	43	Aug. 13, '62		While absent.
Sivlie, Harrison	21	Dec. 10, '63	July 25, '65	Per order.
Smith, Henry	23	Aug. 13, '62		Died Jan. 27, '65, at Jeffersonville, Ind.
Smith, James A.	18	Aug. 16, '62		Died Aug. 31, '64, at Memphis of wounds received at Tupelo.
Soper, William	26	March 26, '64		Deserted March 31, '64, at Carondelet, Mo.
Stamp, Daniel	22	Jan. 4, '64		Discharged per order, June 29, '65.
Stearns, Alva S.	19	Sept. 18, '62	Aug. 19, '65	Corporal; promoted sergeant.
Stewart, Jacob	35	Aug. 21, '62		Died April 2, '63, at Le Sueur, Minn.
Tansty, Patrick	43	Aug. 29, '62		Deserted Nov. 18, '64, at St. Louis, Mo.
Thomas, Leander J.	21	Aug. 16, '62	Aug. 19, '65	
Thompson, William	26	Feb. 18, '64		Deserted Feb. 18, '64, at Caroldelet, Mo.
Thornton, John H.	18	Jan. 20, '63	July 27, '65	Absent.
Trigg, Joseph S.	21	Aug. 21, '62	June 2, '65	Absent.
Wamemaker, Samuel	42	Aug. 14, '62		Died Aug. 9, '63.
Ward, Asa	18	Aug. 22. '62	Aug. 19, '65	
Wallace, John	33	March 14, '64		Absent.
Wicks, Lars	43	Sept. 18, '62	Aug. 19, '65	Corporal.
Wilsey, Reuben	25	Aug. 23, '62	Aug. 19, '65	Absent.
Williamson, Henry	19	Dec. 20, '62	June 23, '65	Per order.
Winn, William	21	March 14, '64	Aug. 19, '65	

Roster of Company F, Tenth Regiment, Minnesota Volunteers

Names	Age	Mustered In	Mustered Out	Remarks
Officers				
Captains				
George T. White	27	Sept. 15, '62		Died Dec. 27 '64, of wounds received at Nashville.
James Gorman	23	Feb. 17, '65	Aug. 19, '65	1st lieutenant, Company I, Aug. 14, '62.

Tenth Regiment Roster (Company F)

Names	Age	Mustered In	Mustered Out	Remarks
Officers				
First Lieutenants				
Ebenezer H. Kennedy	29	Sept. 15, '65		Promoted captain, Company E, Feb. 22, '64.
Isaac Hamlin	37	Feb. 22, '64	Aug. 19, '65	2d lieutenant, Sept. 24, '62; wounded at Nashville.
Second Lieutenant				
James Flanigan	21	Feb. 22, '64	Aug. 19, '65	Promoted from sergeant, Company K.
Enlisted Men				
Ayers, Richard	43	Aug. 16, '62		Discharged for disability, May 16, '65.
Ballard, John	29	Feb. 24, '64	May 14, '65	Absent.
Ballou, Henry C.	20	Aug. 15, '62	Aug. 19, '65	Wounded at Tupelo.
Beeth, Robert	37	Aug. 18, '62	Aug. 19, '65	
Bergosen, Neils	29	Aug. 18, '62	Aug. 19, '65	
Birdsell, John A.	23	Aug. 15, '62	Aug. 19, '65	Sergeant; transferred from 46th Illinois.
Blivins, William D.	40	Aug. 18, '62	Feb. 9, '64	Per order.
Blivins, Wm.	21	Apr. 1, '63		Discharged for disability, April 20, '64.
Brown, Francis S.	26	Aug. 15, '62		Sergeant; died Oct. 5, '64, at Fort Snelling.
Brossard, Edward	23	Aug. 14, '62		Promoted corporal; discharged in hospital in '65.
Brown, Chauncey	18	Feb. 24, '64	Aug. 19, '65	
Brisbin. Wm.	19	Aug. 29, '64	Aug. 19, '65	
Brubaker, George E.	24	Aug. 18, '62		Discharged for disability, April 20, '63.
Burch, Roswell	38	Aug. 14, '62	Aug. 19, '65	
Buchan, Andrew	25	Aug. 20, '62		Discharged for disability, April 20, '64.
Canfield, Job A.	38	Aug. 12, '62		Discharged May 18, '65; per order.
Callander, George	19	Feb. 20, '64		Transferred to Company I, April 4, '64.
Chadwick, Charles	23	Aug. 18, '62		Discharged for disability, April 8, '64.
Carrier, Silas D.	26	Aug. 15, '62	Aug. 19, '65	Promoted corporal; died at Fort Snelling, August, '65.
Coddington, Arthur H.	29	Feb. 24, '64		Transferred to Company I, April 4, '64.
Cook, Wm. H.	20	Feb. 10, '64	Aug. 19, '65	
Cooper, Henry	23	Aug. 15, '62		Discharged June 27, '65; sun-struck at Tupelo.
Cooper, Wm. E.	25	Aug. 15, '62		Discharged for disability, April 20, '63.
Corr, Francis H.	18	Feb. 25, '64		Died at Meridian, Minn., while on furlough.
Cox, Joseph D.	20	Aug. 20, '62		Wounded at Oldtown Creek, Miss; dis. while absent in '65.
Culver, Joseph	36	Aug. 15, '62		Musician; discharged for disability, Feb. 16, '65.
Curry, Lorenzo	22	Aug. 16, '62	Aug. 19, '65	Sergeant.
Dreever, George	25	Aug. 18, '62		Transferred to Veteran Reserve Corps, Nov. 29, '63.

Appendix C

Names	Age	Mustered In	Mustered Out	Remarks
Enlisted Men				
Duff, John G.	39	Feb. 22, '64		Transferred to Company I, April 4, '64.
Each, Theodore	34	Aug. 15, '62	Aug. 19, '65	Wounded at Nashville.
Eldridge, Thomas	24	Aug. 18, '62		Absent.
Emery, Frederick	18	Aug. 18, '62		Transferred to Company D, Oct. 8, '62.
Ferguson, Jesse J.	37	Aug. 20, '62		Killed Dec. 16, '64, at Nashville.
Fengle, Michael	18	Aug. 20, '63	Aug. 19, '65	
Fleming, Chandler K.	19	Jan. 3, '64		Killed Dec. 16, '64, at Nashville.
Forrester, Charles H.	27	Aug. 12, '62	May 18, '65	Per order; corporal; sun-struck at Tupelo.
Fish, Samuel J.	21	Feb. 26, '64		Transferred to Company I, April 4, '64.
Francis, Marshall A.	20	Aug. 14, '62		Corporal; discharged for disability, Jan. 6, '65.
Gallagher, James	26	Aug. 16, '62		Died Oct. 26, '64, at Jefferson City, Mo.
Glanville, Amos E.	23	Aug. 15, '64	Aug. 19, '65	Corporal; promoted sergeant.
Gleason, Samuel	41	Aug. 18, '62	Aug. 19, '65	
Glendening, James	14	Aug. 14, '62	Aug. 29, '65	Absent.
Goodrich, Stephen S.	28	Aug. 16, '62		Musician; transferred to Veteran Reserve Corps, Nov. 20, '63.
Graves, George	18	Aug. 15, '62	May 18, '65	Per order.
Gregory, Alfred D.	21	Aug. 18, '62		Discharged for disability, April 1, '65.
Green, Francis	32	Jan. 26, '64	May 30, '65	Per order.
Grover, Charles	32	Aug. 18, '62	May 26, '65	Per order.
Grover, Silas	20	Aug. 18, '62		Died May 30, '64, at Columbus, Ky.
Hacker, Theodore	18	Aug. 15, '62		Killed Dec. 16, '64, at Nashville.
Haines, Caleb	18	Feb. 24, '64	Aug. 19, '65	Promoted corporal.
Hanson, Hans	33	Feb. 24, '64		Transferred to Company I, April 4, '64.
Hanson, Knute	37	Aug. 16, '62	June 9, '65	Per order.
Harrison, Alexander	26	Feb. 26, '64	Aug. 19, '65	Wounded at Nashville.
Hatsaul, Christian	29	Aug. 18, '62	Aug. 29, '65	
Healy, Franklin	24	Aug. 15, '62	Aug. 19, '65	Promoted corporal.
Herring, Daniel	30	Feb. 28, '63		Discharged per order June 13, '65.
Herring, Lewis	26	Aug. 15, '62		Died May 9, '65, at Willett's Point, New York Harbor.
Hill, James B.	40	Feb. 26, '64	Aug. 19, '65	
Howe, John	20	Aug. 15, '62	Aug. 19, '65	
Ives, Geo. W.	18	Aug. 18, '62		Transferred to Company D, Oct. 8, '62.
Johnson, Charles W.	28	Aug. 18, '62	May 16, '65	Per order.
Johnson, James	21	Aug. 14, '62		Discharged for disability, Dec. 30, '63.
Johnson, Ole	40	Feb. 26, '64		Transferred to Company I, April 4, '64.
Jones, Hiram A.	24	Aug. 16, '62		Transferred to Veteran Reserve Corps, Nov. 20, '63.
Jones, Thomas	18	Feb. 10, '64		Discharged for disability, July 22, '64; wound at Columbus, Ky.
Kaine, Rodger	44	Feb. 24, '64		Died Jan. 29, '65, at Louisville, Ky.
Kennedy, John	18	Feb. 26, '64	Aug. 19, '65	

Tenth Regiment Roster (Company F)

Names	Age	Mustered In	Mustered Out	Remarks
Enlisted Men				
King, John	44	Aug. 18, '62		Transferred to Company D, Oct. 8, '62.
Kreiger, August	26	Aug. 18, '62	May 22, '65	Drowned in Mississippi River.
Lafayette, Louis A.	30	Aug. 14, '62		Discharged for disability, Dec. 10, '63
Larson, George	28	Aug. 20, '62	Aug. 19, '65	
Leahman, Charles	21	Aug. 8, '63	Aug. 19, '65	
Lee, George Washington	23	Aug. 15, '62	Aug. 19, '65	
Leonard, Levi A.	34	Aug. 14, '62	July 8, '65	Absent.
Lincoln, Francis	18	Aug. 29, '63		Died April 7, '65, at Mound City, Ill.
Lincoln, Willard H.	19	Aug. 16, '62		Discharged for disability, May 16, '63.
Lyng, Isaac	41	Sept. 3, '63		Died March 10, '65, at Dauphin Island.
Mack, Dauphin	26	Feb. 28, '63		Transferred to Company I, April 4, '64.
Martin, Preston	44	Feb. 24, '63		Transferred to Company I, April 4, '64.
McCabe, William	18	Feb. 26, '63	Aug. 19, '65	
McCabe, John	19	Feb. 24, '63	Aug. 19, '65	
McDaniels, David	31	Aug. 18, '62	Aug. 19, '65	Corporal.
Miner, Charles	18	Aug. 20, '62	Aug. 19, '65	Promoted corporal.
Morgan, Milton M.	32	Aug. 11, '62		Transferred to Veteran Reserve Corps, Dec. 14, '64.
Mosher, Hiram A.	27	Aug. 18, '62		3d orderly serg; discharged for Disability, April 7, '65; wound at Nashville.
Nariconge, Andrew J.	31	Aug. 15, '62	Aug. 19, '65	
Newkirk, Jacob	34	Aug. 14, '62		Died April 26, '65, at Baton Rouge, La.
Nock, George	43	Aug. 29, '63	Aug. 19, '65	Served in Mexican War.
Norcott, George W.	20	Aug. 18, '62	Aug. 19, '65	
Northrup, Geo. C.	26	Aug. 18, '62	July 12, '65	
Northrup, John B.	25	Aug. 18, '62	Aug. 19, '65	
Now, Andrew	20	Aug. 15, '62	Aug. 19, '65	
Olebaugh, Charles	37	Aug. 11, '62		Transferred to Veteran Reserve Corps, March 11, '65.
Oleson, Hans	18	Aug. 15, '62		Killed Dec. 16, '64, at Nashville.
Oleson, Ole	27	Feb. 28, '63		Transferred to Company I, April 4, '64.
Pickett, John I.	30	Aug. 16, '62		Died March 11, '65, at Memphis.
Preston, George R.	44	Feb. 26, '63	May 30, '65	Per order.
Preston, Samuel	35	Aug. 18, '62	Aug. 19, '65	
Quiggle, Robert	21	March 31, '63	March 19, '65	
Reynolds, Charles B.	37	Feb. 10, '63		Transferred to Company I, April 19, '65.
Rice, John S.	33	Aug. 16, '62		Discharged for disability, Oct. 19, '64.
Riggles, Daniel	33	Aug. 18, '62		Transferred to Veteran Reserve Corps, Nov. 20, '63
Robbins, Myron A.	26	Aug. 16, '62	Aug. 19, '65	Promoted corporal.
Roberts, Carlton W.	32	Aug. 19, '62	Aug. 19, '65	Corporal; promoted sergeant.

Names	Age	Mustered In	Mustered Out	Remarks
Enlisted Men				
Ruff, Henry	21	Aug. 20, '62		Died Aug. 7, '64, at Memphis, Tenn.
Satterly, Nathan	18	Aug. 16, '62		Transferred to Company D, Oct. 8, '62.
Satterly, Simeon P.	44	Aug. 16, '62		Transferred to Company D, Oct. 8, '62.
Shaw, Andrew I	28	Aug. 15, '62		Corporal; discharged per order Jan. 9, '65.
Sherwood, Donald A.	38	Aug. 15, '62		Discharged for disability, July 21, '65.
Shumway, Geo. T.	21	Aug. 15, '62		Absent.
Simpson, Alexander	26	Aug. 15, '62		Discharged for disability, Oct. 25, '63.
Smith, Alvin	30	Aug. 15, '62		Died March 16, '65, at Memphis, Tenn.
Snider, David	21	Aug. 15, '62	Aug. 19, '65	Corporal; sun-struck at Tupelo; wounded at Nashville.
Snider, Jacob	19	Feb. 10, '63	Aug. 19, '65	
Soaper, Leonard	19	Feb. 10, '63	Aug. 19, '65	
Stanky, Martin	30	Aug. 18, '62		Transferred to Company D, Oct. 8, '62.
Stewart, Jesse I.	39	Aug. 12, '62		1st sergeant; discharged for disability, Aug. 3, '64.
Storer, Martin V. B.	21	Aug. 15, '62		Discharged for disab., Sept. 3, '63; wound at Winnebago Agency.
Swan. Benjamin	43	Aug. 20, '62	Aug. 19, '65	
Taylor, Wm. W.	27	Aug. 27, '62		Transferred to Veteran Reserve Corps, March 1, '65.
Vogle, Michael	18	Aug. 20, '62	Aug. 19, '65	
Vosburg, Barney	26	Aug. 18, '62		Transferred to Company D, Oct. 2, '62.
Warner, Lafayette	38	Feb. 24, '63		Discharged for disability, March 1, '65.
Wait, Simeon	41	Aug. 15, '62		Discharged for disability, Nov. 3, '63.
Wheeler, John A.	25	Aug. 14, '62		1st lieutenant, 66th U.S. Colored Infantry, Feb. 21, '64.
Whitman, James R.	26	Aug. 14, '62	Aug. 19, '65	Wagoner.
Wilsey, Americus R.	27	Aug. 27, '62	Aug. 19, '65	
Winkleman, Joseph	24	Aug. 20, '62	Aug. 19, '65	
Wood, Parvenues J.D.	28	Aug. 28, '62	May 10, '65	Per order.
Woodbury, Geo. H.	24	Aug. 12, '62	Aug. 19, '65	Promoted corporal, sergeant; wounded at Nashville.
Wooden, Wm.	21	Aug. 15, '62	Aug. 19, '65	
Yarigan, Henry	21	Aug. 16, '62	Aug. 19, '65	

Roster of Company G, Tenth Regiment, Minnesota Volunteers

Names	Age	Mustered In	Mustered Out	Remarks
Officers				
Captains				
Edwin C. Sanders	35	Sept. 26, '62		Promoted major, Jan. 15 '65.
George W. Stewart	39	Feb. 17, '65	Aug. 19, '65	1st lieutenant, Oct. 28, '62.

Tenth Regiment Roster (Company G)

Names	Age	Mustered In	Mustered Out	Remarks
Officers				
First Lieutenant				
Eli Ash	33	Nov. 9, '62	Aug. 17, '65	2d lieutenant, Nov. 9, '62.
Second Lieutenants				
Oliver B. Smith	34	Sept. 26, '62		Died Jan 4, '64, at St. Louis, Mo.
Henry A. McConnell	32	Aug. 17, '62	Aug. 19, '65	Promoted from sergeant, Company D.
Enlisted Men				
Abbott, John D.	33	Sept. 16, '62		Discharged in '65; absent.
Almich, Frederick	33	Sept. 19, '62	Aug. 19, '65	
Assenmaker, Henry	32	Sept. 28, '62	Aug. 19, '65	Corporal; promoted sergeant; wounded at Spanish Fort.
Ayer, A.				
Baker, Criss	22	Sept. 28, '62	Aug. 19, '65	Corporal; promoted sergeant.
Bateman, Perry S.	34	Sept. 28, '62	Aug. 19, '65	Wagoner.
Beach, Joseph	28	Sept. 28, '62		Musician; discharged for disability, May 13, '63.
Bigelow, William H.	18	Sept. 16, '62	Aug. 19, '65	
Brenlochr, John	41	Sept. 17, '62		Discharged Aug. 29, '65; absent.
Buffington, Samuel	38	Sept. 15, '62	Absent.	
Canfield, Levi	28	Sept. 18, '62	Aug. 19, '65	
Canfield, Wellington	21	Sept. 15, '62	Aug. 19, '65	
Coffee, John	18	Sept. 15, '62	Aug. 19, '65	
Coggswell, Norman		Jan. 13, '63		Absent.
Copperts, John	21	Sept. 15, '62		Killed Dec. 16, '64, at Nashville.
Cori, Flori	18	Sept. 15, '62		Died at New Orleans, La., May 10, '65, of wounds received at Spanish Ft.
Cosby, Eli	18	Sept. 15, '62	Aug. 19, '65	
Crosby, Atwood	25	Sept. 19, '62	Aug. 19, '65	Promoted corporal.
Crosby, Lemuel	18	Sept. 15, '62	Aug. 19, '65	
Davis, John H.		March 1, '63	Aug. 19, '65	
Davis, Thomas R.	15	Sept. 28, '62		Musician; discharged per order May 4, '65.
De Laughter, John H.		Feb. 29, '64		Absent.
De Lavergue, Hiram	45	Sept. 16, '62	May 16, '65	Per order.
Dietz, August	35	Sept. 15, '62	May 17, '65	Per order.
Dobbin, Hugh	18	Sept. 15, '62		Drowned May 30, '63, at Usher's Landing, Missouri River.
Doescher, August		Feb. 8, '64	June 5, '65	Per order.
Doherty, James	26	Sept. 28, '62	Aug. 19, '65	Corporal; promoted sergeant.
Doherty, Patrick		March 31, '64	May 11, '65	Per order.
Doherty, Samuel	24	Sept. 15, '62	Aug. 19, '65	
Dohl, Abraham	41	Sept. 28, '62	Aug. 19, '65	Corporal.
Donahue, Owen	21	Aug. 20, '62		Drowned April 23, '64, in Mississippi River; fell overboard.
Dugnan, Caeser	41	Sept. 15, '62		Discharged for disability, Aug. 29, '63.
Eames, Charles E.	18	Sept. 18, '62	Aug. 19, '65	
Erkle, Frederick	23	Sept. 15, '62	Aug. 19, '65	Promoted corporal.
Faddis, John M.	35	Sept. 16, '62	Aug. 19, '65	
Fogler, John	40	Oct. 28, '62	Aug. 19, '65	
Fowler, Thomas	19	March 1, '64		Died Feb. 22,' 65, at Cairo, Ill.
Francis, Irelan M.	34	Sept. 15, '62		1st sergeant; discharged for disability, April 30, '64.

Names	Age	Mustered In	Mustered Out	Remarks
Enlisted Men				
Frederick, Frank	22	Sept. 16, '62		Died Feb. 19, '63, at Kelso, Minn.
Freeman, John	21	Sept. 16, '62		Died Feb. 15, '65, at Louisville, Ky.
Gibbs, Wm. H.	18	Sept. 15, '62	Aug. 19, '65	
Gibbs, Charles M.	18	Feb. 9, '64	Aug. 19, '65	
Giegerick, Ferdinand	41	Sept. 16, '62	Aug. 19, '65	
Hammond, Geo. W.	37	Sept. 17, '62		Died Dec. 2, '64, at Jefferson City, Mo.
Haney, Amos C.	19	Sept. 28, '62		Corporal; killed Nov. 12, '64; accidentally shot.
Harris, James	37	Sept. 16, '62	May 16, '65	Per order.
Hochstatter, John	18	Feb. 22, '63	Aug. 19, '65	
Hurd, Michael		Aug. 22, '62		Court-martialed and drummed out of service, Jan. 10, '63.
Hynson, Mathew M.	38	Sept. 15, '62	Aug. 19, '65	
Iten, Mike	22	Dec. 14, '62		Died Jan. 18, '65, at Jeffersonville, Ind.
Iten, Jacob	32	Dec. 15, '62		Died Feb. 15, '65, at Memphis, Tenn.
Killer, Phillip K.	27	Sept. 28, '62	Aug. 19, '65.	Corporal.
King, James	35		Aug. 13, '62	Drummed out of service, Jan. 10, '63, by sentence of ct-martial.
King, Thomas	18	Aug. 13, '62		Killed July 14, '64, at Tupelo, Miss.
Kinsey, Henry	29	Sept. 28, '62		Sergeant; discharged June 30, '65.
Klinkhemmer, Peter	18	Sept. 15, '62	Aug. 19, '65	
Kroska, Fernon	23	Sept. 15, '62	Aug. 19, '65	
Kulp, Benjamin	18	Feb. 8, '64		Discharged for disability, Aug. 6, '64.
Laabs, William	29	Sept. 15, '62	July 14, '65	Promoted corporal; absent.
Linnen, James	41	Sept. 16, '62		Discharged in hospital Aug. 15, '65.
Linnett, John	31	Sept. 15, '62	July 14, '65	Absent.
Lipke, John	42	Sept. 15, '62		Discharged for disability, Dec. 4, '63.
Lumpp, Henry A.	23	Sept. 15, '62	Aug. 19, '65	Promoted corporal.
Magdens, Louis	38	Sept. 15, '62	Aug. 19, '65	
McConkey, James A.	17	Feb. 12, '64	Aug. 19, '65	
Miles, Cammel S.	18	Sept. 14, '62	Aug. 19, '65	
Murphy, Dennis	21	Sept. 16, '62	Aug. 19, '65	
Nagle, Charles	27	Sept. 15, '62		Discharged for disability, May 13, '63.
Nagle, Frederick	39	Sept. 15, '62	Aug. 19, '65	Promoted corporal and sergeant.
Nettleton, Edward F	32	Sept. 16, '62	Aug. 19, '65	
Norton, George	28	Apr. 15, '64	May 29, '65	Per order.
Oleson, Ole	18	Sept. 14, '62		Died July 23, '64, at Mound City, Ill.
Peck, Alphonso R.	18	Sept. 16, '62	Aug. 19, '65	
Randall, Boyd	26	Sept. 15, '62		Discharged for disability, May 13, '63.
Randall, James	24	Sept. 15, '62		Died at Jefferson Barracks, Mo.
Randall, William	18	Sept. 16, '62		Absent; discharged July 26, '65
Randolph, Stephen A.	20	Aug. 15, '62	Aug. 19, '65	Promoted corporal.
Reed, Joseph	28	Aug. 15, '62		Promoted corporal; died June 28, '63, at Le Sueur, Minn.
Reider, Peter		Sept. 18, '62	Aug. 19, '65	
Robbins, Henry	26	Aug. 8, '62		Died Sept. 27, '64, at Memphis, Tenn.
Rost, John				Wounded at Spanish Fort.

Names	Age	Mustered In	Mustered Out	Remarks
Enlisted Men				
Ruggles, John	19	Aug. 15, '62	Aug. 19, '65	
Ryker, Jared S.	41	Feb. 9, '64	Aug. 19, '65	
Sack, Charles	24	Feb. 24, '64	Aug. '65	Absent.
Sagle, Charles	19	Aug. 15, '62	Aug. 19, '65	Promoted corporal.
Sauter, Peter	36	Aug. 15, '65		Absent; discharged May 11, '65.
Schwartz, Frederick	32	Aug. 15, '62		Transferred to Veteran Reserve Corps, April 1, '65.
Seal, John E.	24	Aug. 15, '62		
Smith, George, Jr.	23	Aug. 15, '62		Discharged for disability, Sept. 28, '64.
Smith, James	28	Aug. 16, '62	Aug. 19, '65	
Smith, John	24	Sept. 28, '62		Sergeant; discharged July 21, '65.
Smith, Peter	21	Aug. 16, '62	Aug. 19, '65	
Smith, William	26	Aug. 16, '62		Promoted corporal; wound at Nashville; dis. June 20, '65; absent.
Sparr, Louis	23	Aug. 15, '62	Aug. 19, '65	
Stemple, Bernard	23	Feb. 19, '64		Deserted Oct. 23, '64, at Lexington, Mo.
Stone, Simon	21	Sept. 28, '62	Aug. 19, '65	Corporal.
Storbeck, F.A.	31	Aug. 17, '62	Aug. 19, '65	Promoted corporal.
Sunderman, Harmon	18	Aug. 18, '62	Aug. 19, '65	
Thomas, Andrew W.	18	Aug. 16, '62	Aug. 19, '65	
Tobias, Matthew	33	Aug. 15, '62	Aug. 19, '65	
Vasterling, Henry	22	Sept. 28, '62		Corporal; killed Dec. 16, '64, in battle of Nashville.
Wagner, George	19	Aug. 15, '62	Aug. 19, '65	
Waterson, E. H.				Wounded at Spanish Fort.
Willwording, Nickolas	18	Aug. 15, '62		Deserted Feb. 18, '63, at Kelso, Minn.
Wise, Samuel J.	43	Sept. 28, '62		Sergeant; discharged per order, June 30, '65.
Zelt, Adam	35	Sept. 28, '62		Sergeant; discharged for disability, July 14, '65.

Roster of Company H, Tenth Regiment, Minnesota Volunteers

Names	Age	Mustered In	Mustered Out	Remarks
Officers				
Captains				
Michael H. Sullivan	35	Sept. 13, '62	Aug. 19, '65	
First Lieutenant				
Dennis Cavanaugh	26	Sept. 13, '62		Captain, Company C, Sept. 26, '64.
Second Lieutenants				
Dennis McCarthy	26	Sept. 13, '62		Discharged per order, April 21, '64.
Abiel C. Flanders	43	Nov. 15, '62	Aug. 19, '65	
Enlisted Men				
Bohan, John	17	Jan. 15, '62		Discharged per order, June 13, '65.
Bowen, Charles C.	20	Aug. 16, '62	Aug. 19, '65	
Bradley, James	19	Feb. 26, '64		Died April 8, '64, at St. Louis, Mo.

Appendix C

Names	Age	Mustered In	Mustered Out	Remarks
Enlisted Men				
Buckley, John	19	Aug. 16, '62	Aug. 19, '65	
Byrne, Christopher	28	Sept. 13, '62	Aug. 19, '65	Sergeant.
Byrne, Patrick	25	Aug. 20, '62		Sergeant; died Dec. 8, '63, at Louisville, Ky.
Caldwell, Alex. G.	18	Jan. 5, '64		Deserted March 15, '64, at New Orleans, La.
Callaghan, John	29	Aug. 21, '62	Aug. 19, '65	
Carroll, James	21	Aug. 14, '62		Deserted June 21, '64, at Memphis, Tenn.
Chase, Wesley	18	Aug. 22, '62		Died Jan. 14, '63, at St. Peter, Minn.
Christianson, Fred	26	Aug. 15, '62		Deserted Oct. 29, '62, at Fort Snelling.
Collins, John	18	Aug. 16, '62	Aug. 19, '65	
Condon, Patrick	23	Aug. 24, '62	Aug. 19, '65	
Conaghty, Thos. P.	26	Aug. 22, '62		Discharged per order, July 10, '65.
Conlin, Patrick	18	Aug. 21, '62	Aug. 19, '65	
Consadine, James J.	21	Sept. 13, '62		Corporal; deserted April 21, '64, at St. Louis, Mo.
Conway, James	20	Sept. 13, '62		Corporal; deserted Oct. 7, '63, at Fort Snelling.
Conniff, Thomas	28	March 5, '64	Aug. 19, '65	
Conner, Lawrence	18	Feb. 26, '62		Died April 7, '64, at St. Louis, Mo.
Costello, Bartholomew	18	Aug. 15, '62	Aug. 19, '65	
Cramsie, Edward A.	26	Aug. 13, '62	Aug. 19, '65	
Crawford, Hugh	30	Aug. 14, '62		Deserted November, '63, at St. Louis, Mo.
Cronin, Patrick	40	Oct. 21, '62		Discharged per order, July 1, '65.
Cudmore, Patrick	33	Aug. 16, '62		Discharged May 16, '65.
Dardis, Christopher	21	Aug. 29, '62	Aug. 19, '65	
Devereaux, Andrew	24	Sept. 13, '62	Aug. 19, '65	Sergeant.
Dibble, Hiram J.	35	Aug. 14, '62		Discharged per order, June 26, '65.
Dixon, John	18	Feb. 1, '64	Aug. 19, '65	
Doney, Xavier	21	Aug. 29, '62		Discharged per order, Jan. 15, '64.
Dreger, Sylvester	38	Aug. 29, '62		In prison at Alton, Ill., on discharge of regiment.
Elliott, Wm.	45	Aug. 14, '62		Deserted Oct. 30, '62 at Fort Snelling.
Finerty, Michael	18	Aug. 22, '62		Discharged per order, June 9, '65.
Fox, Edward	21	Aug. 16, '62	Aug. 19, '65	
Foy, Michael	18	Feb. 8, '64		Transferred to Veteran Reserve Corps, Jan. 4, '65.
Fraybold, Joseph A.	18	March 19, '64		Discharged per order, May 11, '65.
Gorman, Henry	21	Jan. 15, '64		Deserted Feb. 6, '64 at St. Louis.
Gregg, Dennis	19	Feb. 8, '64		Deserted March 15, '65, at New Orleans, La.
Hanley, Michael	28	Aug. 16, '62	Aug. 19, '65	
Harper, Arthur A.	29	Aug. 14, '62		Discharged per order, May 18, '65.
Harris, Patrick	30	Aug. 16, '62	Aug. 19, '65	
Henry, Michael W.	19	Aug. 19, '62	Aug. 19, '65	
Henry, Miles	18	Sept. 13, '62		Musician; died May 25, '65, at New Orleans, La.
Hetherington, Thomas	29	March 5, '64	Aug. 19, '65	
Hunt, Robert	22	Sept. 13, '62	Aug. 20, '65	Corporal.
Idoux, Nickolas	40	Aug. 15, '62		Discharged for disability, Aug. 5, '64.

Tenth Regiment Roster (Company H)

Names	Age	Mustered In	Mustered Out	Remarks
Enlisted Men				
Irvine, Clover G.	19	Sept. 13, '62		Musician; discharged July 10, '65.
Jeffers, Michael	32	Sept. 13, '62	Aug. 19, '65	1st sergeant.
Jordan, Anthony	18	Feb. 26, '64	Aug. 19, '65	
Keating, James	32	Aug. 20, '62	Aug. 19, '65	
Keating, Patrick	24	Sept. 18, '62		Serg.; mort. wound at Spanish Fort; died April 19, '65, at New Orleans, La.
Kelly, John	19	Aug. 21, '62	Aug. 19, '65	
Kennedy, Thomas	23	Sept. 13, '62		Corporal; transf. to 15th Regt., Vet. Res. Corps, July 20, '64.
Kilroy, Martin	18	Aug. 16, '62	Aug. 19, '65	
La Clare, Elzero	22	Aug. 16, '62		
La Duke, Antoine	21	Oct. 8, '62	Aug. 19, '65	
Leo, John	22	Aug. 16, '62		Discharged per order, July 19, '65.
Lightcap, Geo. W.	28	Sept. 13, '62	Aug. 19, '65	Corporal.
Logue, Hamilton	22	Aug. 21, '62	Aug. 19, '65	Promoted corporal.
McManus, Thomas	35	Aug. 16, '62		Deserted April 23, '64, at St. Louis, Mo.
McLaughlin, James	21	Aug. 16, '62	Aug. 19, '65	
McBride, James	22	Sept. 18, '62		Deserted Feb. 20, '64, at St. Louis, Mo.
McAndrew, Patrick	40	Aug. 22, '62	Aug. 19, '65	Promoted corporal.
McCarthy, Florence	18	March 19, '64		Discharged per order, May 11, '65.
McEntyre, Daniel	43	Aug. 30, '64		
McGrath, Patrick	35	Feb. 8, '64	Aug. 19, '65	
McKenna, Patrick		Aug. 20, '62	Aug. 19, '65	
McNallan, Walter		Aug. 22, '62	Aug. 19, '65	Promoted corporal.
McNeal, Hugh		Aug. 17, '62		Died March 12, '65, at New Albany, Ind.
McNulty, Patrick	27	Aug. 22, '62		Died Jan. 26, '63, at Crystal Lake, Minn.
Meagher, Thomas	25	Jan. 20, '64		Discharged for disability, Oct. 26, '64
Mulgrew, John		Aug. 16, '62		Discharged per order, July 25, '65.
Murphy, Thomas	23	Sept. 13, '62		Wagoner; deserted Oct. 7, '63, at Fort Snelling.
Nagle, Michael	32	March 30, '64	Aug. 19, '65	
Noon, Martin		Aug. 22, '62	Aug. 19, '65	
O'Brien, Daniel		Sept. 29, '62	Aug. 19, '65	Promoted corporal.
O'Brien, James	18	Sept. 13, '62		Sergeant; wounded at Nashville; discharged July 6, '65.
O'Brien, John		Sept. 29, '62	Aug. 19, '65	
O'Brien, Patrick		Sept. 18, '62	Aug. 19, '65	
Olson, Amon		Aug. 21, '62		Died Jan. 21, '65, at Nashville.
O'Maley, Thomas		Aug. 22, '62		Discharged for disability, June 13, '64.
O'Neal, James	26	Sept. 13, '62		Corporal; deserted Feb. 6, '64, at St. Louis, Mo.
Peat, Eneas S.		Aug. 12, '62		Transferred to 15th Regiment, Vet. Res. Corps, Dec. 21, '64.
Perkins, James		Aug. 15, '62	Aug. 19, '65	
Powers, Thomas		Aug. 22, '62		Died Dec. 8, '63, at Fort Snelling.
Prenderegast, Michael R.		Aug. 14, '62		Transferred to non-commissioned staff, May 25, '65.
Quenett, Prudent		Aug. 21, '62		Deserted Oct. 7, '63, at Fort Snelling.

Names	Age	Mustered In	Mustered Out	Remarks
Enlisted Men				
Radabaugh, Samuel	37	Feb. 20, '64		Never joined company; no record of discharge.
Roach, Michael		Aug. 16, '62	Aug. 19, '65	
Robbeault, Peter		Aug. 18, '62		Discharged for disability, March 9, '65.
Robegea, John		Aug. 14, '62	Aug. 19, '65	
Ryan, Thomas		Sept. 23, '62		Discharged per order, July 19, '65.
Smith, John	25	Feb. 1, '64		Deserted Nov. 25, '64, at St. Louis, Mo.
Smith, Patrick J.		Aug. 13, '62		Discharged for disability by wound, April 19, '65.
Stokes, John	26	Jan. 15, '64	Aug. 19, '65	
Sullivan, Edward		Aug. 21, '62	Aug. 19, '65	Promoted corporal.
Sullivan, Jeremiah	21	Sept. 13, '62	Aug. 19, '65	Corporal and sergeant.
Tierney, David		Aug. 21, '62	Aug. 19, '65	
Tope, Jacob		Aug. 21, '62	Aug. 19, '65	
Wall, John	22	Sept. 13, '62	Aug. 19, '65	Corporal.
Whalen, John		Aug. 21, '62		Died Oct. 21, '64, at Memphis, Tenn.

Roster of Company I, Tenth Regiment, Minnesota Volunteers

Names	Age	Mustered In	Mustered Out	Remarks
Officers				
Captains				
Martin J. Severance	37	Apr. 4, '64	Aug. 19, '65	Private, Company I, Aug. 14, 62.
First Lieutenants				
James Gorman	24	Aug. 14, '62		Promoted captain, Company F, March 12, '65.
Richard Fewer	40	June 2, '65	Aug. 19, '65	Promoted from non-commissioned staff.
Second Lieutenants				
Michael R. Merrill	33	Aug. 14, '62		Promoted 1st lieutenant, Company C, March 30, '64.
Eli K. Pickett	34	Sept. 18, '62	Aug. 19, '65	Promoted from sergeant, Company E
Enlisted Men				
Alexander, Phillips	26	Aug. 14, '62	Aug. 19, '65	
Allen, Geo. F.	19	March 8, '64	Aug. 19, '65	
Bacon, Peter	36	Aug. 22, '62	Aug. 19, '65	
Baker, Robert	26	Aug. 14, '62		Killed Aug. 20, '62, in battle with Indians.
Beardsley, Orsey	24	Aug. 14, '62	Aug. 19, '65	Promoted corporal.
Beatty, Benj. B.	24	Oct. 8, '62	Aug. 19, '65	Promoted corporal.
Beatty, Samuel B.	22	Aug. 14, '64	Aug. 19, '65	
Beatty, Wm. S.	32	Dec. 20, '62	Aug. 19, '62	Sergeant.
Bergen, Andrew V.	31	Nov. 10, '62		Discharged for disability, Dec. 10, '62.
Bergen, Christopher	18	Feb. 20, '64	Aug. 19, '65	Musician.
Blair, David P.	28	Aug. 14, '62	Aug. 19, '65	

Tenth Regiment Roster (Company I)

Names	Age	Mustered In	Mustered Out	Remarks
Enlisted Men				
Blasing, Ludwig H.	22	Aug. 20, '62	Aug. 19, '65	
Boomhover, David	18	Aug. 14, '62		Died July 18, '64, at Memphis, Tenn.
Boyer, Peter	21	Aug. 14, '62		Killed Sept. 2, '62, in Battle of Birch Coolie, Minn.
Brown, Nathaniel R.	35	Aug. 16, '62		Deserted Sept. 28, '63, at Henderson, Minn.
Bullis, David	32	Aug. 16, '62		Deserted April 28, '63, at Le Sueur, Minn.
Burnell, Samuel	23	Aug. 14, '62		Discharged per order, June 29, '65.
Burton, Ephraim A.	18	Feb. 26, '64	Aug. 19, '65	
Callender, George	19	Feb. 20, '64	Aug. 19, '65	
Campbell, Jeremiah	26	Aug. 14, '62		Discharged for disability, Sept. 2, '64.
Campbell, John	38	Aug. 14, '62		Died Feb. 19, '65, at Cairo, Ill.
Clark, James	21	Aug. 15, '62		Died in Minnesota in '65.
Coddington, Arthur H.	29	Feb. 24, '64	Aug. 19, '65	
Conrad, John	18	March 3, '63	Aug. 19, '65	Promoted corporal.
Crane, Royal, Jr.	19	Feb. 29, '64		Absent on detached service; discharged June 26, '65.
Currier, James S.	18	Feb. 26, '64	Aug. 19, '65	
Delaney, James	40	Aug. 14, '62	Aug. 19, '65	
Doolin, John	18	Nov. 5, '62		Died in Minnesota in '65.
Doolin, Thomas	44	Oct. 22, '62		Discharged for disability, Feb. 23, '64.
Dowd, Albah	18	March 8, '64	Sept. '65	Absent.
Downs, Francis	18	Feb. 29, '64	Aug. '65	Absent.
Dresbach, Anthony L.	32	Feb. 19, '64	Aug. 19, '65	
Dudley, Oscar L.	19	Feb. 29, '64		Discharged per order, May 26, '65.
Duff, John G.	39	Feb. 22, '64		Died Dec. 29, '65, at Nashville, Tenn., from wounds.
Fadden, Abram	28	Aug. 20, '62		Deserted Aug. 6, '63, at Henderson, Minn.
Fadden, Charles	19	Aug. 14, '62	Aug. 19, '65	Promoted corporal.
Fadden, George	27	Aug. 16, '62	Aug. 19, '65	
Fadden, James	21	Aug. 14, '62	Aug. 19, '65	Promoted corporal and sergeant.
Fish, Samuel, Jr.	21	Jan. 26, '64		Deserted Feb. 26, '65, at New Orleans, La.
Frankenfield, Amos	17	Dec. 20, '62		Corporal; discharged July 10, '65; Absent.
Goodman, Stephen O.	18	Feb. 16, '64	Aug. 19, '65	
Gordon, Austin B.	18	Feb. 8, '64	Aug. 19, '65	
Gorman, John	18	Nov. 12, '62		Discharged for disability, May 13, '63.
Green, Benjamin	36	March 29, '64		Deserted April 24, '64, at St. Louis, Mo.
Hadley, Amos	30	Feb. 18, '64		Died July 1, '65, at Chicago, Ill.
Hall, Ecles	28	Feb. 15, '64	Aug. 19, '65	Promoted corporal.
Hanson, Hans	33	Feb. 24, '64	Aug. 19, '65	
Hoxie, Nerie T.	32	Feb. 24, '64	Aug. 19, '65	
Hoy, Daniel	19	Feb. 24, '64		Discharged July 20, '65; absent.
Hyland, James F.	23	Feb. 26, '64		Died March 20, '65, at Memphis, Tenn.
Johnson, Christian	20	Feb. 22, '64	Aug. 19, '65	

Appendix C

Names	Age	Mustered In	Mustered Out	Remarks
Enlisted Men				
Johnson, Isaac	33	Aug. 14, '62		Transferred from Company B, April 11, '64; missing Sept. 25, '64, at Pocahontas, Ark.
Johnson, Ole	40	Feb. 26, '64	Aug. 19, '65	
Kutzler, Wm. R.	18	Feb. 19, '64		Promoted corporal; discharged July 27, '65; absent.
Lewis, Christopher	20	Feb. 23, '64	Aug. 19, '65	
Mack, Dauphin	26	Feb. 28, '64		Absent; discharged August, '65.
Mandigo, Sylvester M.	26	Nov. 12, '62	Aug. 19, '65	Corporal; promoted sergeant.
Manuel, Ferdinand	18	Aug. 14, '62	Aug. 19, '65	
Martin, Preston	44	Feb. 24, '63		Absent; discharged August, '65.
McCuen, John A.	18	Aug. 14, '62	Aug. 19, '65	
McCuen, Wm. H.	44	Aug. 14, '62	Aug. 19, '65	Absent.
Miller, Abraham	44	Feb. 15, '64		Absent; discharged July 16, '65.
Mitchell, Charles	42	Aug. 14, '62		Discharged for disability, May 1, '64.
Morris, Edward	30	Aug. 15, '62		Transferred from Co. B, April 4, '64; dis. per order, May 9, '64.
Nye, Reuben	19	Feb. 19, '64	Aug. 19, '65	
Oleson, Ole	27	Feb. 28, '64	Aug. 19, '65	
Ott, Dominick	20	Dec. 20, '62		Corporal; discharged May 29, '65, at New Orleans.
Paul, Ernest	30	Aug. 16, '62		
Peck, John W.	27	Sept. 1, '62		1st sergeant; 1st lieutenant, 68th U.S. Colored Inf., Feb. 28, '64.
Pitner, Charles	28	March 23, '64		Deserted April 24, '64, at St. Louis, Mo.
Quinn, Thomas F.	22	Feb. 29, '64	Aug. 19, '65	
Reynolds, Charles B.	37	Feb. 10, '63	Aug. 19, '65	
Reynolds, Geo. J.	44	Nov. 12, '62		Wagoner; died July 9, '64, at Memphis, Tenn.
Reynolds, Wm. W.	15	Jan. 20, '63		Discharged for disability, Nov. 9, '64.
Reed, Geo. W.	38	Nov. 12, '62	Aug. 19, '65	Sergeant.
Reed, Moses	19	Feb. 24, '64	Aug. 19, '65	
Richardson, James	28	Aug. 21, '62		Promoted corporal; discharged July 18, '65; absent.
Salisbury, Russell	34	Aug. 14, '62	Aug. 19, '65	
Scott, Francis M.	21	Feb. 15, '64	Aug. 19, '65	
Spencer, Washington	26	Aug. 14, '62		Deserted June 28, '63, at Shakopee, Minn.
Stacy, Marshall	18	June 17, '64		Discharged Oct. 22, '64, at Jefferson Barracks, Mo.
Staelson, Berent	44	Feb. 22, '64		Discharged per order, May 31, '65.
Tennant, James D.	20	Aug. 14, '62		Died April 22, '63, at Le Sueur, Minn.
Vanossa, Joseph	28	Aug. 14, '62		Killed Aug. 22, '62, at Fort Ridgley, Minn.
Van Woert, Wm. I	25	March 25, '64		Discharged for disability, Feb. 14, '65.
Walo, Joseph A.	21	March 7, '64	Aug. 19, '65	
Walsh, George H.	18	Nov. 12, '62		Corp; pro. serg., q. serg.; transf. to non-com. staff, July 1, '65.
Walsh, Orman W.	22	Feb. 24, '64	Aug. 19, '65	
Walsh, Thomas	38	Aug. 14, '62	Aug. 19, '65	Promoted sergeant.
Wenige, Fred J.	34	March 8, '64		Discharged Nov. 9, '65; absent.

Names	Age	Mustered In	Mustered Out	Remarks
Enlisted Men				
Wheatly, Harrison J.	27	Aug. 14, '62	Aug. 19, '65	
Whitford, Wm.	38	Aug. 14, '62	Aug. 19, '65	
Williams, James D.	19	Feb. 29, '64	Aug. 19, '65	
Wiley, Thomas	31	Aug. 14, '62	Aug. 19, '65	Transferred from Company B, April 4, '64.
Willyard, Henry	34	Aug. 14, '62	Aug. 19, '65	Transferred from Company B, April 4, '64.
Woodward, George	18	Jan. 10, '63	Aug. 18, '65	

Roster of Company K, Tenth Regiment, Minnesota Volunteers

Names	Age	Mustered In	Mustered Out	Remarks
Officers				
Captains				
Michael J. O'Connor	29	Sept. 27, '62	Aug. 19, '65	
First Lieutenant				
Wm. Burns	37	Sept. 6, '62	Aug. 19, '65	
Second Lieutenant				
Michael Hoy	30	Sept. 6, '62		Wounded at Nashville Dec. 16, '64; Discharged April 13, '65.
Enlisted Men				
Bracken, Daniel	23	Sept. 4, '62		Corporal; killed Dec. 16, '64, in battle of Nashville.
Broderick, Wm.	26	Aug. 15, '62		Discharged for disability, July 26, '64.
Brezett, Alfred	21	Aug. 23, '63	Aug. 19, '65	
Burke, Patrick	27	Aug. 22, '62		Killed Nov. 21, '64, at St. Louis, by provost guard.
Candron, Andrew	33	Aug. 15, '62	Aug. 19, '65	Promoted corporal.
Cannon, Patrick	37	Feb. 24, '64	Aug. 19, '65	
Carney, Patrick	27	Aug. 15, '62	Aug. 19, '65	
Clifford, Thomas	35	Aug. 15, '62	Aug. 19, '65	
Cobb, Joseph F.	40	Aug. 22, '62		Discharged per order, May 18, '65.
Conlin, James	23	Aug. 19, '62		Deserted Sept. 8, '63, at Fort Snelling.
Connelly, Christopher	30	Oct. 14, '62	Aug. 19, '65	Musician.
Connelly, James	22	Aug. 22, '62	Aug. 19, '65	
Connelly, Michael T.	27	Aug. 26, '62	Aug. 19, '65	Promoted corporal.
Costello, John	20	Aug. 13, '62		Transferred to Veteran Reserve Corps, Nov. 18, '63.
Coyle, James	40	Aug. 25, '62		Discharged for disability, April 3, '63
Cox, Hugh A.	28	Aug. 14, '62	Aug. 19, '65	
Daly, Timothy	19	Aug. 18, '62	Aug. 19, '65	
Daly, William	27	Aug. 20, '62	Aug. 19, '65	
Desjarlgh, David	25	Sept. 1, '62		Discharged per order, Aug. 31, '64.
Dixon, Michael	27	Aug. 22, '62		Discharged Aug. 16, '65; absent.
Dunn, William	27	Sept. 4, '62	Aug. 19, '65	Sergeant.
Duffy, James	23	Nov. 1, '62	Aug. 19, '65	

Appendix C

Names	Age	Mustered In	Mustered Out	Remarks
Enlisted Men				
Eustis, Patrick	25	Aug. 13, '62		Deserted May 12, '63, at Le Sueur, Minn.
Fewer, Richard	40	Aug. 19, '62		Transferred to non-commissioned staff, Dec. 27, '62.
Flanigan, James	27	Oct. 16, '62		1st sergeant; promoted to Company F, April 21, '64.
Flood, Mathew	34	Oct. 16, '62	Aug. 19, '65	Sergeant; reduced to ranks, Feb. 12, '63.
Gafney, Thomas	35	Aug. 15, '62	Aug. 19, '65	
Gannia, Joseph	39	Sept. 1, '62		Discharged per order, March 30, '65.
Gallegher, John	21	Aug. 22, '62	Aug. 19, '65	
Gleeson, Patrick	21	Aug. 14, '62	Aug. 19, '65	Promoted corporal.
Gleeson, John	21	Jan. 27, '64	Aug. 19, '65	
Grace, William	30	Aug. 14, '62		Deserted April 25, '63, at Le Sueur, Minn.
Hannon, Peter	21	Aug. 23, '62		Deserted Sept. 7, '63, at Fort Snelling.
Hays, Cornelius	35	Aug. 15, '62		Deserted May 10, '63, at Le Sueur, Minn.
Hays, James	33	Aug. 15, '62	Aug. 19, '65	
Hawkins, Thomas	27	Aug. 20, '62		Deserted Sept. 7, '63, at Fort Ridgley.
Hennesy, Kerr	21	Aug. 18, '62		Deserted Nov. 10, '64; arrested; claimed to be a minor; case tested by civil court and discharged.
Herrons, Benjamin	48	Aug. 22, '62	Aug. 19, '65	
Higgins, John	32	Feb. 12, '64		Discharged in '65; absent.
Horan, Thomas	21	Aug. 13, '62	Aug. 19, '65	
Hoy, William	27	Aug. 22, '62		Deserted Nov. 12, '62, at St. Peter, Minn.
Keating, Robert	18	Jan. 24, '64		Deserted; arr'st'd and imprs'd., March 20, '64; not heard from since.
Kennedy, Patrick	27	Aug. 14, '62		Discharged for disability in '65.
Kernan, Peter	21	Aug. 22, '62		Deserted Sept. 7, '63, at Fort Snelling; killed by provost guard while being arrested.
Keegan, Owen	27	Sept. 4, '62	Aug. 19, '65	Sergeant.
Killila, John	30	Aug. 22, '62	Aug. 19, '65	
Lilas, Patrick	35	Jan. 28, '64		Deserted March 25, '64, at St. Louis, Mo.
Lysight, John	19	Feb. 12, '64	Aug. 19, '65	
Lytle, Alexander	18	Feb. 11, '64		Discharged for disability, Nov. 19, '64.
Manning, James	30	Aug. 13, '62		Discharged per order, Feb. 13, '65.
Maloney, Patrick	18	Aug. 19, '62		Died Aug. 10, '65, at St. Paul.
Martin, Edward	30	Aug. 14, '62	Aug. 19, '65	
McCann, Hugh	26	Aug. 15, '62		Deserted Feb. 10, '63, at Le Sueur, Minn.
McCarron, Thomas	30	Sept. 4, '62	Aug. 19, '65	Corporal; promoted sergeant.
McCloud, Patrick	18	Oct. 8, '62	Aug. 19, '65	Musician.
McCool, Wm.	21	Aug. 22, '62	Aug. 19, '65	
McCoy, James	21	Sept. 3, '62		Discharged by order, June 10, '65.
McCue, Robert	35	Aug. 19, '62		Discharged for disability, Jan. 4, '64.

Names	Age	Mustered In	Mustered Out	Remarks
Enlisted Men				
McDonough, Thomas	21	Sept. 3, '62		Discharged Aug. 19, '65; absent.
McGran, John	21	Aug. 22, '62		Died Sept. 27, '63, at Fort Ridgley.
McGrann, Owen	25	Oct. 16, '62	Aug. 19, '65	Corporal; reduced to ranks, Jan. 16, '63.
McGruth, Michael	42	Sept. 2, '64	Aug. 19, '65	
McKeon, James	21	Aug. 22, '62	Aug. 19, '65	
McMonnamon, Michael	32	Aug. 16, '64		Killed Dec. 16, '64, at Nashville.
Mohan, Michael	45	Aug. 22, '62		Died March 6, '63, at St. Anthony, Minn.
Molan, Daniel	18	Aug. 22, '62	Aug. 19, '65	
Monaham, James	21	Aug. 22, '62		Deserted Nov. 10, '62, at St. Peter, Minn.
Moore, Michael	29	Aug. 20, '62		Discharged per order, March 5, '64.
Moran, Edward	42	Aug. 25, '62		Deserted May 20, '63, at Le Sueur, Minn.
Murphy, Daniel	35	Aug. 22, '62		Discharged per order, June 5, '65.
Nash, James	21	Aug. 16, '62		Wounded at Nashville; discharged in '65; absent.
Nary, Edward	18	Aug. 13, '62	Aug. 19, '65	
O'Brien, Francis B.	18	March 22, '64	Aug. 19, '65	
O'Bryan, Wm.	26	Aug. 22, '62	Aug. 19, '65	
O'Connor, Patrick	22	Aug. 22, '62		Deserted June 21, '64, at Memphis.
O'Gorman, James Joseph	19	Aug. 13, '62		Discharged July 10, '65, at St. Paul.
O'Gorman, Michael	18	Aug. 18, '62		Discharged per order, March 14, '64.
O'Gorman, Wm.	18	Aug. 14, '62		Discharged per order, July 10, '65.
O'Hara, Thomas	23	Oct. 16, '62	Aug. 19, '65	Corporal.
O'Neil, Cornelius	22	Oct. 16, '62		Sergeant; discharged July 11, '65, for promotion.
Page, Daniel	32	Aug. 20, '62	Aug. 19, '65	
Quinlin, Patrick	42	Aug. 31, '64	Aug. 19, '65	
Quinn, Patrick	29	Aug. 22, '62		Deserted Sept. 7, '63, at Fort Snelling.
Ready, John	25	Aug. 15, '62	Aug. 19, '65	
Reardon, Wm.	20	Jan. 26, '64	Aug. 19, '65	
Riley, James	21	Aug. 23, '62	Aug. 19, '65	
Roche, Luke	22	Aug. 14, '62		Died in Minnesota while on sick furlough.
Ronan, Patrick	21	Aug. 21, '62		Promoted corporal.
Sauce, Alexander	21	Aug. 22, '62	Aug. 19, '65	
Seberry, John	21	Sept. 3, '62	Aug. 19, '65	
Seibert, Edward	40	Aug. 11, '62	Aug. 19, '65	
Sexton, Daniel	30	Oct. 16, '62		Wagoner; transferred to Veteran Reserve Corps, Nov. 18, '63.
Shea, Daniel	25	Dec. 26, '63	Aug. 19, '65	
Shaw, David	23	Sept. 4, '62	Aug. 19, '65	Corporal.
Sheehan, Patrick	30	Aug. 21, '62	Aug. 19, '65	
Sheehan, Wm.	18	Aug. 21, '62	Aug. 19, '65	
Sheehey, Dennis	23	Sept. 4, '62		Captured Jan. 10, '65; corporal; discharged July 25, '65; absent.
Sheridan, John	26	Aug. 15, '62	Aug. 19, '65	Promoted sergeant.
Smith, Michael	25	Jan. 28, '64		Deserted Nov. 21, '64, at St. Louis.
Stewart, George	32	Oct. 13, '62	Aug. 19, '65	Corporal.
Summers, Michael	26	Aug. 27, '62		Discharged per order March 10, '64.

Names	Age	Mustered In	Mustered Out	Remarks
Enlisted Men				
Sullivan, Patrick	21	Aug. 14, '62	Aug. 19, '65	
Sullivan, John	21	Dec. 4, '63		Captured Jan. 10, '65; discharged July 26, '65
Swift, Dion	25	Aug. 20, '62	Aug. 19, '65	Promoted corporal.
Ward, Peter	44	Aug. 16, '62	Aug. 19, '65	
Welsh, Andrew	24	Aug. 16, '62	Aug. 19, '65	Corporal; promoted sergeant.
White, Patrick	18	Aug. 14, '62	Aug. 19, '65	
Wood, Timothy	29	Aug. 16, '62	Aug. 19, '65	

D. The Casualties[1]

Roster of Tenth Regiment, Minnesota

In 1890 General Baker published a detailed account of all Tenth Regiment soldiers killed or wounded during the Civil War. These rosters are provided in Appendix C. Eleven hundred and forty-six soldiers fought in the Tenth. Unfortunately, General Baker's records had many errors and are incomplete. This appendix provides details of the Tenth Regiment casualties. Three out of four soldiers who died in the Tenth were from disease or misadventure. Misadventure covers a variety of causes such as accidents, drowning or brawls, which were popular among the soldiers then and now. Drownings occurred while crossing rivers or in a few cases, the soldier fell off of a steamboat. There was no time for swim lessons on the frontier. Disease is a broad category. Many died from pneumonia, dysentery, or from drinking bad water as both Sibley and Baker mentioned. There were many other diseases that are trivial today, but often fatal during the Civil War. Those who fought in the East had a slight edge in terms of medical treatment and care. In Dakota Territory a soldier who became ill could rely on an overly busy surgeon, himself and his buddies. There were no friendly homes for recovery, just hundreds of miles of endless prairie. The number of desertions in the West were fewer than the East and were often a deadly fate. A soldier who straggled (fell behind the column) on the prairie would be dealt with by the Sioux. At the end of the war, those that straggled in the South would be killed by unreformed rebels. The point is that in the East, a deserter could find his way home, but in the West it often meant death. The muster rolls simply say absent, deserted, or "straggled from ranks and was never heard from again." Simply stated, thousands of soldiers in the West went to war and were never heard from, again: a sad fate.

Killed in Action or Died of Wounds

Names	Age	Mustered In	Remarks
Baker, Robert	26	Aug. 14, '62	Killed Aug. 20, '62, in battle with Indians.
Benson, Stengen	34	Aug. 21, '62	Killed Dec. 16, '64, at Nashville.

The Casualties (Killed or Died of Wounds)

Names	Age	Mustered In	Remarks
Boyer, Peter	21	Aug. 14, '62	Killed Sept. 2, '62, in Battle of Birch Coolie, Minn.
Bracken, Daniel	23	Sept. 4, '62	Corporal; killed Dec. 16, '64, in Battle of Nashville.
Carroll, Austin D.	22	Sept. 2, '62	Enrolled Aug. 15, '62; corporal; killed Dec. 16, '64, at Nashville.
Chamberlain, Fredo	28	Aug. 13, '62	Died Dec. 18, '64, of wounds received at Nashville.
Cook, Michael	34	Sept. 15, '62	Died Dec 27, '64, of wounds received at Nashville.
Copperts, John	21	Sept. 15, '62	Killed Dec. 16, '64, at Nashville.
Cori, Flori	18	Sept. 15, '62	Died at New Orleans, La., May 10, '65, of wounds received at Spanish Ft.
Dawley, Chas. G.	21	Sept. 2, '62	Enrolled Aug. 15, '62; corporal; promoted sergeant; killed at Nashville Dec. 16, '64.
Doeg, Almon H.	21	Aug. 15, '62	Died Dec. 19, '64, of wounds received at Nashville.
Duff, John G.	39	Feb. 22, '64	Died Dec. 29, '65, at Nashville, Tenn., from wounds.
Ferguson, Jesse J.	37	Aug. 20, '62	Killed Dec. 16, '64, at Nashville.
Fleming, Chandler K.	19	Jan. 3, '64	Killed Dec. 16, '64, at Nashville.
Griffin, Frank	24	March 21, '64	Killed Dec. 16, '64, at Nashville.
Hacker, Theodore	18	Aug. 15, '62	Killed Dec. 16, '64, at Nashville.
Hurd Asa	27	Sept. 18, '62	Wagoner; killed April 25, '65, by rebels, near Montgomery, Ala.
Keating, Patrick	24	Sept. 13, '62	Serg.; mort. wound at Spanish Fort; died April 19, '65, at New Orleans, La.
King, Thomas	18	Aug. 13, '62	Killed July 14, '64, at Tupelo, Miss.
Lumsden, Geo. L.	43	March 8, '64	Killed Dec. 16, '64, at Nashville.
McMonnamon, Michael	32	Aug. 16, '64	Killed Dec. 16, '64, at Nashville.
Merical, John G.	27	Aug. 14, '62	Corporal; died Dec. 22, '64, of wounds received at Nashville.
Mullins, David	21	Feb. 27, '64	Died Feb. 20, '65, on hospital steamer *D. A. January*.
Mullins, Eusebius	19	Aug. 15, '62	Died Jan. 12, '65, at Louisville, Ky., of wounds received at Nashville.
Murphy, John W.	27	Sept. 2, '62	Corporal; killed Dec. 26, '64, at Nashville.
Nelson, Chrest	21	Aug. 15, '62	Killed Dec. 16, '64 at Nashville.
Nelson, Ole	30	Aug. 22, '62	Died Dec. 17, '64, of wounds received at Nashville.
Oleson, Hans	18	Aug. 15, '62	Killed Dec. 16, '64, at Nashville.
Putnam, Nathan A.	37	Sept. 13, '64	Killed Dec. 16, '64, at Nashville.
Reeves, George	18	Aug. 21, '62	Died Dec. 18, '64; wounded at Nashville.
Ryan, James	30	Feb. 19, '64	Killed Dec. 16, '64, at Nashville.
Smith, James A.	18	Aug. 16, '62	Died Aug. 31, '64, at Memphis of wounds received at Tupelo.
Vanossa, Joseph	28	Aug. 14, '62	Killed Aug. 22, '62, at Fort Ridgley, Minn.
Vasterling, Henry	22	Sept. 28, '62	Corporal; killed Dec. 16, '64, in Battle of Nashville.
Ware, Marcus	25	Aug. 11, '62	Died Nov. 11, '64, at Memphis, Tenn. Wounded at Tupelo.
Webster, Joseph R.	40	Sept. 6, '62	Corporal; killed Dec. 16, '64, at Nashville.
White, George T.	27	Sept. 15, '62	Died Dec. 27 '64, of wounds received at Nashville.

Total Killed: 37

Wounded in Action

Some understanding of the treatment of the wounded is found in the reminiscences of Thomas Jefferson Hunt of the Tenth Regiment, who was wounded in the second day of the Battle of Nashville. His recollections are included below.

> I have been asked to express the feelings of the soldiers in battle and the sensations of one when wounded.
>
> These questions can have many and varied answers and all be true. They are as varied as the men exercised.
>
> The zealous recruit is anxious to get into a battle and is bold even to rashness; a few casualties by his side generally correct his rashness. Another class are pale with fear, but the general expression of countenance is that of sober determination; closed lips and set teeth bear silent witness that the gravity of the situation is felt. The veteran goes to the field fully aware of his danger but with resolute purpose. After the first fire is exchanged, fear subsides, but lying idle, exposed to the enemy's balls is most exacting. A small number skulk or try to evade their duties; they are the exceptions — the cowards. The old soldier avoids unnecessary exposure and seeks all proper protection but when ranks are broken by shot or shell, he closes to the colors, while the same disturbance will scatter the untried.
>
> The sensations of the wounded open another varied field of inquiry. The first sensations of the wounded are not severe in proportion to the danger from the wound received. A gun shot in the extremities usually gives much more pain than those more severe in other parts of the body. Some have told me that the most terrible wounds give only a sting, others that a great disposition to sleep came over them in an instant, another that numbness attacked the part injured.
>
> The after effects of wounds are as varied as the injuries; some suffer for years. For myself it is in dreams that again I see the carnage of battle. I hear the roar of cannon, the whiz of the minnieball, the bursting of shell, and feel again the shock of the wounded. I shut my eyes in vain to obscure the flash of a volley fired full in my face. All this panorama comes to me now after nearly forty years. It did not until after war had ended, but like Banquo's ghost, it will not down.
>
> One soldier in a charge was struck on the wrist by a ball which nearly severed his hand; he grabbed it with the other hand and kept in line for a time, then, realizing his condition, he stopped and yelled to his comrades, "Go on; I'll come when I get it done up."
>
> Another, being one of eleven who were either killed or wounded by a single shell, arose and asked, "Boys, what makes it so dark?," not knowing what had taken place.
>
> Another cried and made a great noise at the loss of a small toe. Still another had to be ordered to the rear when one arm was disabled. Again one stood guard over a prisoner whose one hand was useless.
>
> Among numbers gathered around the surgeons at the rear of the fighting line, waiting their turns, rarely would a groan or a murmur be heard. On one occasion the last words of a wounded and expiring man, awaiting his turn were, "I am mighty easy now."[2]

Concerning his own wound on the second day of Nashville, Hunt tells us:

> Something struck me on the right jaw, which I thought was a cannon ball or a shell, and I supposed that my entire jaw was gone, but putting my hand to my face, I found I was mistaken. That I was pleased goes without saying. Putting my fingers in my mouth, I found a tooth from my upper jaw on my tongue and judging from the hole in my cheek I concluded that the bullet had gone out of my mouth, which also greatly pleased me. The wound bled freely and I needed a surgeon. I encouraged a soldier near me, who complained of a wound in his foot, to crawl to the rear with me. He found his wound so slight that he returned, and before night received a mortal wound.

I found the field surgeon in the rear and many a wounded man around him, waiting his turn. I sat down to await my turn, but soon grew faint and fell over. All pain was now gone. I heard the surgeon say, "Give that man some whiskey," and someone raised my head, put a cup to my lips and urged, "Drink." I took two swallows and soon I could see, then arose and did not lie down until late that night in the hospital. The surgeon put into the wound what I now know was powdered copperas, which measurably stopped the hemorrhage. Then I went with others from our line to a large house farther back, where many surgeons were dressing wounds and amputating limbs. The first surgeon I met shook his head and directed me to our regimental surgeon. He was more than busy and directed me to an operating table saying, "Get on there." At this I shook my head and pointed to my cheek. He put his fingers in the hole and said that he felt a ball, which I did not believe at first, but he was right, for he took two teeth and fragments of my jaw from under my tongue, which had been driven there by the ball. A lotion and bandages were applied and I was turned loose. I drank some milk and went around to see the wounded, one of whom had died since coming with me from the field.

We were soon conveyed to a hospital in Nashville. Another lieutenant of our regiment who was wounded in the right arm was with me. He agreed to talk for me and I to write for him. We were put into one room and during the night I awoke, to find him walking the floor. Seeing me awake he turned and said, "Hunt, as badly as my wound aches, I would not have it well and be again where I was when I received it, for $5,000. I have sometimes thought that bullet saved my life if it did come near taking it, for it gave me two months to recruit."

I stayed in the hospital a week, then journeyed to Louisville, where I spent two weeks in a like institution. From there I met a brother in Olney, Ill. My wound healed in my cheek but not my mouth. I learned to talk slowly and hated to hear my own voice and think others did also. The last fragment of bone was taken from my mouth the following August, after which it fully healed. I am in a measure tongue-tied so I can make some sounds with difficulty and others not at all, and stammer and fall with the first words when I read, and always soon tire when so doing.[3]

The list of the wounded follows.

Names	Age	Mustered In	Mustered Out	Remarks
Ayer, A				Wounded at Spanish Fort.
Ballou, Henry C.	20	Aug. 15, '62	Aug. 19, '65	Wounded at Tupelo.
Banks, John	19	Aug. 21, '62	Aug. 19, '65	Promoted corporal. Wounded at Tupelo.
Barnes, Walter S.	23	Aug. 21, '62	May 16, '65	Wounded at Nashville.
Bosley, Wm. M.	18	Aug. 14, '62	Aug. 5, '65	Wounded at Nashville.
Brossard, Edward	23	Aug. 14, '62		Promoted corporal; discharged in hospital in '65. Wounded at Nashville.
Bullock, Lemuel E.	29	Aug. 21, '62	June 23, '65	Wounded at Nashville; absent.
Bruce, Chas. S.	25	Aug. 14, '62	Aug. 19, '65	Corporal; promoted sergeant. Wounded at Tupelo.
Cannon, Patrick	37	Feb. 24, '64	Aug. 19, '65	Wounded at Nashville.
Carlton, Dexter	43	Aug. 12, '62	Aug. 19, '65	Promoted corporal. Wounded at Tupelo
Case, Elanson H.	22	Aug. 15, '62	Aug. 19, '65	Wounded at Nashville.
Case, Wallace W.	22	Feb. 16, '64	Aug. 19, '65	Enrolled Aug. 15, '62; 1st sergeant, Sept. 2, '62. Wounded at Nashville.
Causdell, John A.	25	Aug. 14, '62		Discharged May 29, '65, for wounds received at Nashville.
Condon, Patrick	23	Aug. 24, '62	Aug. 19, '65	Wounded at Spanish Fort.
Connelly, Michael T.	27	Aug. 26, '62	Aug. 19, '65	Promoted corporal. Wounded at Nashville.

Names	Age	Mustered In	Mustered Out	Remarks
Cox, Joseph D.	20	Aug. 20, '62		Wounded at Oldtown Creek, Miss; dis. while absent in '65.
Crosby, Atwood	25	Sept. 19, '62	Aug. 19, '65	Promoted corporal. Wounded at Tupelo.
Davis, Francis M.	19	Aug. 25, '62	Aug. 19, '65	Wounded at Nashville.
Each, Theodore	34	Aug. 15, '62	Aug. 19, '65	Wounded at Nashville.
Eastman, Alpheus R.	21	Aug. 13, '62		Transferred to Veteran Reserve Corps, Jan. 16, '65. Wounded at Tupelo.
Eichler, Charles	33	Feb. 29, '64	Aug. 19, '65	Wounded at Nashville.
Flanders, Abiel C.	43	Apr. 22, '62	Aug. 19, '65	Wounded at Nashville.
Flood, Mathew	34	Oct. 16, '62	Aug. 19, '65	Sergeant; reduced to ranks Feb. 12, '63; wounded at Nashville.
Hoy, Michael	30	Sept. 6, '62		Wounded at Nashville, Dec. 16, '64; discharged April 13, '65.
Hamlin, Isaac	37	Feb. 22, '64	Aug. 19, '65	2d lieutenant, Sept. 24, '62; wounded at Nashville.
Harpham, Francis H.	27	Feb. 19, '64		Discharged April 18, '65, of wounds received at Nashville.
Harrison, Alexander	26	Feb. 26, '64	Aug. 19, '65	Wounded at Nashville.
Hasbrouck, Isaac G.	18	Aug. 16, '62	Aug. 19, '65	Promoted corporal. Wounded at Nashville.
Hunt, Robert	22	Sept. 13, '62	Aug. 20, '65	Corporal. Wounded at Nashville.
Hunt, Thomas J.	33	Jan. 23, '64	Aug. 19, '65	1st sergeant, Nov. 16, '62. Wounded at Nashville.
Hurlbut, Clinton E.	18	Feb. 24, '64		Discharged for wounds received in Battle of Nashville.
Jennison, Samuel P.	32	Sept. 10, '62	Aug. 19, '65	Bvt. colonel U.S.V., Feb 23, '65; Bvt. brig. gen., March 13, '65; wounded at Nashville.
Keller, Isaac	27	Aug. 15, '62		Transferred to Veteran Reserve Corps, April 1, '65. Wounded at Tupelo.
Kelley, Rufus	25	Sept. 18, '62	Aug. 19, '65	Corporal; promoted sergeant. Wounded at Nashville.
Kinsey, Henry	29	Sept. 28, '62		Sergeant; discharged June 30, '65. Wounded at Nashville.
Knapp, Francis W.	24	Sept. 2, '62		Corporal; pro. serg; dis. Jan 1, '65, of wounds received at Nashville.
La Clare, Elzero	22	Aug. 16, '62		Wounded at Nashville.
Leo, John	22	Aug. 16, '62		Discharged per order July 19, '65; wounded at Spanish Fort.
Lockey, James W.	21	Aug. 15, '62	Aug. 21, '65	Wounded at Tupelo.
Maixner, Fritz	33	Oct. 4, '62	July 21, '65	Absent. Wounded at Nashville.
Matterson, Edward H.	19	Aug. 24, '62		Discharged Aug. 19, '65; absent. Wounded at Nashville.
McCoy, James	21	Sept. 3, '62		Discharged by order June 10, '65. Wounded at Nashville.
Morris, John	24	Aug. 14, '62	Aug. 19, '65	Wounded at Nashville.
Mosher, Hiram A.	27	Aug. 18, '62		3d orderly serg; discharged for disability, April 7, '65; wound at Nashville.
Murphy, Daniel	35	Aug. 22, '62		Discharged per order, June 5, '65. Wounded at Spanish Fort.
Myers, Felix	40	Aug. 15, '62		Discharged June 11, '65, for wounds received at Nashville.

The Casualties (Wounded; Died of Disease or Accident)

Names	Age	Mustered In	Mustered Out	Remarks
Nary, Edward	18	Aug. 13, '62	Aug. 19, '65	Wounded at Nashville.
Nash, James	21	Aug. 16, '62		Wounded at Nashville; discharged in '65; absent.
O'Brien, James	18	Sept. 13, '62		Sergeant; wounded at Nashville; discharged July 6, '65.
Olson, Olaus	21	Aug. 22, '62	Aug. 19, '65	Wounded at Nashville.
Pace, Israel H.	22	Aug. 21, '62	June 13, '65	Per order. Wounded at Nashville.
Pike, Elias G.	20	Aug. 13, '62	June 7, '65	Per order. Wounded at Tupelo.
Prentiss, Thos. D.	26	Aug. 14, '62	Aug. 19, '65	Wounded at Nashville.
Ronan, Patrick	21	Aug. 21, '62	Aug. 19, '65	Promoted corporal. Wounded at Nashville.
Rost, John				Wounded at Spanish Well.
Ruthledge, John	23	Aug. 21, '62	Aug. 19, '65	Wounded at Tupelo.
Scranton, Seth B.	22	Feb. 26, '64		Discharged Jan. 21, '65, of wounds received at Tupelo.
Seibert, Edward	40	Aug. 11, '62	Aug. 19, '65	Wounded at Nashville.
Smith, Patrick J.		Aug. 13, '62		Discharged for disability by wound, April 19, '65.
Smith, William	26	Aug. 16, '62		Promoted corporal; wound at Nashville; dis. June 20, '65; absent.
Snider, David	21	Aug. 15, '62		Corporal; sun-struck at Tupelo; wounded at Nashville.
Stewart, George	32	Oct. 13, '62	Aug. 19, '65	Corporal. Wounded at Tupelo.
Stewart, James	24	Aug. 14, '62	Aug. 19, '65	Wounded at Nashville.
Tobias, Matthew	33	Aug. 15, '62	Aug. 19, '65	Wounded at Tupelo.
Tuthill, Charles D.	30	Aug. 23, '62		Sergeant; dis. March 30, '64, for wounds received in Indian expedition.
Walsh, Thomas	38	Aug. 14, '62	Aug. 19, '65	Promoted sergeant. Wounded at Nashville.
Waterson, E. H.				Wounded at Spanish Fort.
Wightman, David	24	Aug. 22, '62	June 12, '65	Corporal; promoted sergeant. Wounded at Nashville.
Williams, James D.	19	Feb. 29, '64	Aug. 19, '65	Wounded at Tupelo.
Woodbury, Geo. H.	24	Aug. 12, '62	Aug. 19, '65	Promoted corporal, sergeant; Wounded at Nashville.
Wooden, Wm.	21	Aug. 15, '62	Aug. 19, '65	Wounded at Nashville.
Woodward, George	18	Jan. 10, '63	Aug. 18, '65	Wounded at Nashville.
Young, Salomon	23	Aug. 22, '62		Discharged Sept. 27, '64, for wounds received at Tupelo, Miss.

Total Wounded: 73

Died of Disease, Misadventure, or Accident

Names	Age	Mustered In	Remarks
Anderson, Andrew	22	Aug. 13, '62	Died Nov. 3, '62, at Fort Snelling, Minn.
Anderson, Peter	32	Aug. 15, '62	Died Feb. 15, '65, at Vicksburg.
Benton, Elisha	20	Jan. 12, '64	Died Feb. 14, '64, at St. Louis, Mo.
Berg, Ulrick R.	29	Aug. 22, '62	Died Oct. 1, '64, at Memphis.
Bonney, Joseph	26	Aug. 21, '62	Died Dec. 23, '62, at Henderson, Minn.

Appendix D

Names	Age	Mustered In	Remarks
Boomhover, David	18	Aug. 14, '62	Died July 18, '64, at Memphis, Tenn.
Bradley, James	19	Feb. 26, '64	Died April 8, '64, at St. Louis, Mo.
Buck, Deruyter	18	March 31, '64	Died April 9, '65, at Keokuk, Iowa.
Burke, Patrick	27	Aug. 22, '62	Killed Nov. 21, '64, at St. Louis, by provost guard.
Burns, Hugh	33	Aug. 12, '62	Died March 20, '65, at Chicago.
Byrne, Patrick	25	Aug. 20, '62	Sergeant; died Dec. 8, '63, at Louisville, Ky.
Campbell, Alexander	21	Aug. 21, '62	Died Dec. 27, '64, at Memphis, Tenn.
Campbell, John	38	Aug. 14, '62	Died Feb. 19, '65, at Cairo, Ill.
Carlough, George	25	Aug. 14, '62	Died at Fort Abercrombie, D.T.
Carrier, Silas D.	26	Aug. 15, '62	Promoted corporal; died at Fort Snelling, August, '65.
Chase, Wesley	18	Aug. 22, '62	Died Jan. 14, '63, at St. Peter, Minn.
Christianson, Franz	31	Nov. 20, '62	Died Feb. 16, '65, at Cairo, Ill.
Clark, James	21	Aug. 15, '62	Died in Minnesota in '65.
Conner, Lawrence	18	Feb. 26, '62	Died April 7, '64, at St. Louis, Mo.
Corr, Francis H.	18	Feb. 25, '64	Died at Meridian, Minn., while on furlough.
Cowan, Samuel R.	19	Aug. 14, '62	Died Sept. 11, '64, at Devall's Bluff, Ark.
Davis, John F.	22	Aug. 14, '62	Died Nov. 28, '62, at Garden City, Minn.
Davis, Thomas E.	21	Aug. 11, '62	Died Jan. 30, '65, at Milwaukee, Wisc.
Davis, Russell B.	24	Aug. 15, '62	Died Feb. 24, '64, at Le Sueur, Minn.
Deanan, Matthew L.	21	Aug. 21, '62	Died Aug. 22, '63, at Fort Abercrombie, D. T.
Dobbin, Hugh	18	Sept. 15, '62	Drowned May 30, '63, at Usher's Landing, Missouri River.
Donahue, Owen	21	Aug. 20, '62	Drowned April 23, '64, in Mississippi River; fell overboard.
Doolin, John	18	Nov. 5, '62	Died in Minnesota in '65.
Fessenden, Eben	24	Feb. 19, '64	Died February, '65, on hospital steamer *D. A. January*.
Fessenden, Edwin A.	30	Aug. 22, '62	Died Dec. 23, '62, at Henderson, Minn.
Foster, James G.	23	Aug. 15, '62	Died March 5, '65, at Memphis.
Fowler, Francis	18	Aug. 11, '62	Died July 14, '63, at FortAbercrombie, D. T.
Fowler, Thomas	19	March 1, '64	Died Feb. 22,' 65, at Cairo, Ill.
Freeman, John	21	Sept. 16, '62	Died Feb. 15, '65, at Louisville, Ky.
Frederick, Frank	22	Sept. 16, '62	Died Feb. 19, '63, at Kelso, Minn.
Gallagher, James	26	Aug. 16, '62	Died Oct. 26, '64, at Jefferson City, Mo.
Gates, Geo. W.	18	Aug. 21, '62	Died June 26, '64, at Memphis, Tenn.
Grover, Silas	20	Aug. 18, '62	Died May 30, '64, at Columbus, Ky.
Hammond, Geo. W.	37	Sept. 17, '62	Died Dec. 2, '64, at Jefferson City, Mo.
Hancock, Gilbert F.	31	Aug. 15, '62	Died Feb. 28, '65, at Memphis, Tenn.
Haney, Amos C.	19	Sept. 28, '62	Corporal; killed Nov. 12, '64; accidentally shot.
Hanson, Martin	30	Aug. 30, '64	Died April 25, '65, at Memphis, Tenn.
Henry, Miles	18	Sept. 13, '62	Musician; died May 25, '65, at New Orleans, La.
Herring, Lewis	26	Aug. 15, '62	Died May 9, '65, at Willett's Point, New York Harbor.
Hess, Jacob W.	32	Aug. 12, '62	Died Feb. 19, '65, at Jeffersonville, Ind.
Hill, Francis D.	32	Aug. 21, '62	Corporal; pro. sergeant; died at Jefferson Barracks, Oct. 18, '64.
Hodley, Amos	30	Feb. 24, '64	Died July 1, '65, at Chicago, Ill.
Houston, Thomas	18	Aug. 13, '62	Died Feb. 10, '63, at Garden City, Minn.
Hus, Ole O.	23	Aug. 22, '62	Died Oct. 18, '64, at Memphis, Tenn.
Hyland, James F.	23	Feb. 26, '64	Died March 20, '65, at Memphis, Tenn.
Iten, Jacob	32	Dec. 15, '62	Died Feb. 15, '65, at Memphis, Tenn.

The Casualties (Died of Disease or Accident)

Names	Age	Mustered In	Remarks
Iten, Mike	22	Dec. 14, '62	Died Jan. 18, '65, at Jeffersonville, Ind.
Ives, Geo. W.	18	Aug. 18, '62	Died Nov. 13, '62, at Fort Snelling, Minn.
Iverson, Ole	27	Aug. 15, '62	Died Feb. 28, '65, at Prairie du Chien, Wisc.
Johnson, John	18	Aug. 31, '64	Died March 13, '65, at Memphis, Tenn.
Jones, Isaac	21	Feb. 15, '63	Died March 24, '63, at Garden City, Minn.
Kaine, Rodger	44	Feb. 24, '64	Died Jan. 29, '65, at Louisville, Ky.
Keizer, John L.	29	March 1, '64	Died Dec. 31, '64, at White Water, Wisc., on furlough.
Kernan, Peter	21	Aug. 22, '62	Deserted Sept. 7, '63, at Fort Snelling; killed by provost guard while being arrested.
Kreiger, August	26	Aug. 18, '62	Drowned in Mississippi River.
Lang, Levi	30	Feb. 28, '64	Died March 6, '65, at New Albany, Ind.
Larson, Yors	29	Aug. 21, '62	Died Jan. 22, '65, at Jeffersonville, Ind.
Lawrence, Merritt G.	18	Aug. 16, '62	Died March 26, '63, at Le Sueur, Minn.
Lincoln, Francis	18	Aug. 29, '63	Died April 7, '65, at Mound City, Ill.
Lyng, Isaac	41	Sept. 3, '63	Died March 10, '65, at Dauphin Island.
Maloney, Patrick	18	Aug. 19, '62	Died Aug. 10, '65, at St. Paul.
Mastinbrook, John, Jr.	22	Aug. 15, '62	Died Nov. 15, '65, at Jefferson Barracks.
Matterson, Edward H.	19	Aug. 24, '62	Died at New Orleans.
McGran, John	21	Aug. 22, '62	Died Sept. 27, '63, at Fort Ridgley.
McNeal, Hugh		Aug. 17, '62	Died March 12, '65, at New Albany, Ind.
McNitt, Truman E.	20	Aug. 11, '62	Died Sept. 29, '62, at Clinton Falls, Minn.
McNulty, Patrick	27	Aug. 22, '62	Died Jan. 26, '63, at Crystal Lake, Minn.
Middleton, Samuel	44	Feb. 28, '64	Died Feb. 25, '65, at Memphis.
Moffit, Robert	28	Aug. 14, '62	Corporal; died Feb. 22, '65, at Cairo, Ill.
Mohan, Michael	45	Aug. 22, '62	Died March 6, '63, at St. Anthony, Minn.
Morin, Patrick	21	Aug. 21, '62	Promoted corporal; died Aug. 11, '65, at Fort Snelling, Minn.
Newkirk, Jacob	34	Aug. 14, '62	Died April 26, '65, at Baton Rouge, La.
Newman, John H.	18	Sept. 2, '64	Died Jan. 23, '65, at Eastport, Miss.
Moulton, Oren	29	Feb. 29, '64	Died Jan. 5, '65, at Nashville.
Olson, Amon		Aug. 21, '62	Died Jan. 21, '65, at Nashville.
Oleson, Ole	18	Sept. 14, '62	Died July 23, '64, at Mound City, Ill.
Partridge, George H.	31	Sept. 18, '62	Sergeant; died Feb. 3, '65, in hospital at Louisville, Ky.
Pickett, John I.	30	Aug. 16, '62	Died March 11, '65, at Memphis.
Pettie, Geo. C.	34	Aug. 12, '62	Died Jan. 19, '65, at Jeffersonville, Ind.
Powers, Thomas		Aug. 22, '62	Died Dec. 8, '63, at Fort Snelling.
Proebsting, Lewis	32	Apr. 12, '64	Hospital steward, Oct. 13, '62; died Oct 31, '64, at Cairo, Ill.
Randall, James	24	Sept. 15, '62	Died at Jefferson Barracks, Mo.
Reed, Joseph	28	Aug. 15, '62	Promoted corporal; died June 28, '63, at Le Sueur, Minn.
Reynolds, Geo. J.	44	Nov. 12, '62	Wagoner; died July 9, '64, at Memphis, Tenn.
Rice, Wm.	19	Aug. 15, '62	Died May 17, '64, at Columbus, Ky
Robbins, Henry	26	Aug. 8, '62	Died Sept. 27, '64, at Memphis, Tenn.
Robson, James A.	36	Sept. 8, '62.	Died Nov. 8, '62, from wound received by accd. discharge of pistol.
Roche, Luke	22	Aug. 14, '62	Died in Minnesota while on sick furlough.
Ruff, Henry	21	Aug. 20, '62	Died Aug. 7, '64, at Memphis, Tenn.
Scott, Andrew	18	Aug. 31, '64	Died April 2, '65, at Memphis, Tenn.
Seeley, James C.	32	Aug. 13, '62	Died Oct. 28, '63, at Fort Abercrombie, D. T.
Shaw, Jotham	33	Aug. 12, '62	Died Jan. 31, '65, at Jeffersonville, Ind.
Smith, Alvin	30	Aug. 15, '62	Died March 16, '65, at Memphis, Tenn.
Smith, Henry	23	Aug. 13, '62	Died Jan. 27, '65, at Jeffersonville, Ind.

Names	Age	Mustered In	Remarks
Smith, Oliver B.	34	Sept. 26, '62	Died Jan 4, '64, at St. Louis, Mo.
Steinerson, Holver	18	Feb. 28, '64	Died Jan. 13, '65, at Chicago, Ill.
Stewart, Jacob	35	Aug. 21, '62	Died April 2, '63, at Le Sueur, Minn.
Tennant, James D.	20	Aug. 14, '62	Died April 22, '63, at Le Sueur, Minn.
Thompson, Arza B.	27	Sept. 6, '62	Sergeant; died Jan. '65, at Nashville.
Thompson, Thomas H.	33	Aug. 15, '62	Died Dec. 14, '64, at Memphis.
Tuthill, John D.	39	Feb. 25, '64	Died Nov. 11, '65, at Memphis, Tenn.
Wamemaker, Samuel	42	Aug. 14, '62	Died Aug. 9, '63.
Whalen, John		Aug. 21, '62	Died Oct. 21, '64, at Memphis, Tenn.
Wilson, Stephen L.	38	Aug. 21, '62	Died Aug. 16, '64, at Memphis.
Wright, Wm. W.	21	Aug. 21, '62	Died March 1, '63, at Le Sueur, Minn.
Yates, Charles M.	22	Aug. 29, '62	Died Feb. 1, '65, at Paducah, Ky.
Yearly, Zeno S.	18	Feb. 15, '63	Died Dec. 8, '64, at Nashville, Tenn.

Total Died of Disease or Accident: 112

Discharged for Disability

Names	Age	Mustered In	Remarks
Abel, Morgan	26	Aug. 21, '62	Discharged for disability, Feb. 17, '64.
Axsell, Charles	37	Aug. 22, '62	Discharged for disability, May 13, '63.
Ayers, Richard	43	Aug. 16, '62	Discharged for disability, May 16,' 65
Barden, Gilbert G.	35	Aug. 19, '62	Discharged for disability, Jan. 26, '64
Beach, Joseph	28	Sept. 28, '62	Musician; discharged for disability, May 13, '63.
Bemis, Hiram	33	Aug. 21, '62	Promoted corporal; discharged for disability, April 11, '62.
Benschoter, Martin W.	32	Sept. 2, '62	Enrolled Aug. 15, '62; Sergeant; dis. for disability, Dec. 3, '63.
Bergen, Andrew V.	31	Nov. 10, '62	Discharged for disability, Dec. 10, '62.
Blivins, Wm.	21	Apr. 1, '63	Discharged for disability, April 20, '64.
Broderick, Wm.	26	Aug. 15, '62	Discharged for disability, July 26, '64.
Brubaker, George E.	24	Aug. 18, '62	Discharged for disability, April 20, '63.
Buchan, Andrew	25	Aug. 20, '62	Discharged for disability, April 20, '64.
Burr, Murdock P.	18	Aug. 11, '62	Discharged for disability, Dec. 16 '62
Campbell, Jeremiah	26	Aug. 14, '62	Discharged for disability, Sept. 2, '64
Chadwick, Charles	23	Aug. 18, '62	Discharged for disability, April 8, '64.
Chandler, Geo. H.	38	Aug. 23, '62	Discharged for disability, Dec. 12, '64.
Clark, Samuel	42	Aug. 15, '62	Discharged for disability, Nov. 17, '63.
Cooper, Wm. E.	25	Aug. 15, '62	Discharged for disability, April 20, '63.
Coyle, James	40	Aug. 25, '62	Discharged for disability, April 3, '63
Craw, John P.	44	Aug. 15, '62	Discharged for disability, April, '63.
Crawford, Oliver P.	43	Sept. 2, '62	Enrolled Aug. 15, '62; sergeant; dis. for disability, Oct. 7, '62.
Culver, Joseph	36	Aug. 15, '62	Musician; discharged for disability, Feb. 16, '65.
Davis, Daniel M.	31	Aug. 15, '62	Discharged for disability, April 11,' 63.
Davis, Wm. R.	26	Aug. 15, '62	Discharged for disability, May 25, '63.
Day, Edwin A.	21	Aug. 15, '62	Discharged for disability, May 25, '63.
Dempster, L.	26	Aug. 11, '62	Discharged for disability, Dec. 27, '63.
Doolin, Thomas	44	Oct. 22, '62	Discharged for disability, Feb 23, '64.
Drake, Richard M.	21	Aug. 12, '62	Discharged for disability, April '64.
Dugnan, Caeser	41	Sept. 15, '62	Discharged for disability, Aug. 29, '63.
Durrell, Freman	33	Aug. 14, '62	Discharged for disability, Oct. 30, '64.

The Casualties (Discharged for Disability) 173

Names	Age	Mustered In	Remarks
Everett, Wm. E.	37	Aug. 19, '62	Discharged for disability, April 11, '65.
Fellows, Freman W.	27	Aug. 24, '62	Corporal; discharged for disability, April 10, '65
Foley, David	21	Aug. 15, '62	Discharged for disability.
Foster, Zelatus	21	Aug. 15, '62	Discharged for disability, May 11, '65.
Fowler, Lorain	20	Aug. 11, '62	Discharged for disability, Dec 10, '63
Freeman, Samuel M.	28	Aug. 11, '62	Discharged for disability, Sep. '64.
Francis, Marshall A.	20	Aug. 14, '62	Corporal; discharged for disability, Jan. 6, '65.
Francis, Irelan M.	34	Sept. 15, '62	1st sergeant; discharged for disability, April 30, '64.
Gere, Samuel A.	30	Aug. 14, '62	Discharged in '65; absent.
Gorman, John	18	Nov. 12, '62	Discharged for disability, May 13, '63.
Gregory, Alfred D.	21	Aug. 18, '62	Discharged for disability, April 1, '65.
Gefts, Josiah	30	Aug. 21, '62	Discharged for disability, Jan. 26, '64.
Hackett, Chas. W.	31	Aug. 23, '62	Enrolled Aug. 14, '62; discharged for disability in '64.
Heath, John A.	19	Aug. 12, '62	Discharged for disability, Nov 29, '64.
Hopson, Albert S.	38	Feb. 1, '64	Enrolled Aug. 15, '62; 1st lt., Aug. 23, '62; discharged for disability, Aug. 5, '64.
Holmes, John M.	36	Aug. 21, '62	Discharged for disability, Dec. 29, '63.
Idoux, Nickolas	40	Aug. 15, '62	Discharged for disability, Sept. 26, '64.
Johnson, James	21	Aug. 14, '62	Discharged for disability, Dec. 30, '63.
Kennedy, Patrick	27	Aug. 14, '62	Discharged for disability in '65.
Kern, James W.	39	Feb. 29, '64	Discharged for disability, Oct. 19, '64
Klophenstine, Gilghen	35	Aug. 14, '62	Discharged for disability, Jan. 21, '64.
Kulp, Benjamin	18	Feb. 8, '64	Discharged for disability, Aug. 6, '64.
Lafayette, Louis A.	30	Aug. 14, '62	Discharged for disability, Dec. 10, '63.
Lair, James	27	Aug. 22, '62	Discharged for disability, April 11, '65.
Lincoln, Willard H.	19	Aug. 16, '62	Discharged for disability, May 16, '63.
Lipke, John	42	Sept. 15, '62	Discharged for disability, Dec. 4, '63.
Little, Thomas J.	18	Aug. 22, '62	Discharged for disability, May 13, '63.
Lytle, Alexander	18	Feb. 11, '64	Discharged for disability, Nov. 19, '64.
Mallinson, John W.	18	Aug. 15, '62	Discharged for disability, Apr. 11, '63.
Matthewson, George	33	Aug. 15, '62	Discharged for disability, Jan. 26, '64
McCue, Robert	35	Aug. 19, '62	Discharged for disability, Jan. 4, '64.
Meagher, Thomas	25	Jan. 20, '64	Discharged for disability, Oct. 26, '64
Mickelson, Christopher	32	Aug. 16, '62	Discharged for disability, Aug. 7, '63.
Miles, Wm. A.	34	Aug. 16, '62	Discharged for disability, March 1, '64.
Miner, Amasa T.	33	Aug. 14, '62	Corporal; discharged for disability, March 30, '64
Minthorn, Thaddeus	41	Sept. 6, '62	Wagoner; discharged for disability, C. S. April 9, '64
Mitchell, Charles	42	Aug. 14, '62	Discharged for disability, May 1, '64.
Moody, Robert	23	Aug. 15, '62	Discharged for disability, Oct. 5, '64
Moran, Cornelius	23	Aug. 14, '62	Discharged for disability, Oct. 28, '64.
Mosher, Hiram A.	27	Aug. 18, '62	3d orderly serg; discharged for disability, April 7, '65; wound at Nashville.
Nagle, Charles	27	Sept. 15, '62	Discharged for disability, May 13, '63.
Nelson, John	39	Aug. 21, '62	Discharged for disability.
Nicholson, Demias	25	Aug. 15, '62	Discharged for disability, May 28, '65.
Nunn, Jesse	35	Aug. 14, '62	Corporal; discharged for disability, Dec. 17, '64.
Oleson, Peter E.	19	Aug. 13, '62	Musician; discharged for disability, June 20, '65.
O'Maley, Thomas		Aug. 23, '62	Discharged for disability, June 13, '64.
Peterson, Charles	30	Aug. 21, '62	Discharged for disability, Jan. 20, '65.
Pettie, C. B.	27	Aug. 12, '62	Discharged for disability, June 13, '65.
Pierce, Richard W.	18	Aug. 14, '62	Discharged for disability, Feb. 9, '65.

Names	Age	Mustered In	Remarks
Putnam, Alonzo D.	27	Sept. 2, '62	Enrolled Aug. 21, '62; corporal; dis. for disability, Sept. 30, '63.
Randall, Boyd	26	Sept. 15, '62	Discharged for disability, May 13, '63.
Rawlins, Joseph V.	27	Aug. 14, '62	Discharged for disability, Nov. 28, '64.
Reece, Isaac	27	Aug. 11, '62	Discharged for disability, Nov. 10,' 63
Reed, Andrew W.	30	Aug. 12, '62	Discharged for disability, Aug. 5, '64.
Rice, Hiram J.	30	Aug. 21, '62	Promoted corporal; discharged for disability, April 11, '65.
Rice, John S.	33	Aug. 16, '62	Discharged for disability, Oct. 19, '64.
Reynolds, Wm. W.	15	Jan. 20, '63	Discharged for disability, Nov. 9, '64.
Robbeault, Peter		Aug. 18, '62	Discharged for disability, March 9, '65.
Sherwood, Donald	38	Aug. 15, '62	Discharged for disability, A.July 21, '65.
Scott, Wm.	21	Feb. 15, '63	Discharged for disability, March '64.
Scranton, S. B.	21	Aug. 21, '62	Discharged for disability, April '63.
Simpson, Alexander	26	Aug. 15, '62	Discharged for disability, Oct. 25, '63.
Smith, George, Jr.	23	Aug. 15, '62	Discharged for disability, Sept. 28, '64.
Stewart, Jesse I.	39	Aug. 12, '62	1st sergeant; discharged for disability, Aug. 3, '64.
Storer, Martin V. B.	21	Aug. 15, '62	Discharged for disab., Sept. 3, '63; wound at Winnebago Agency
Strong, M. L.	21	Nov. 11, '63	2d lieutenant, Aug. 10, '62; discharged for disability, April 4, '64.
Tenney, Geo. W.	22	Aug. 21, '62	Discharged for disability, 3 Sep, '63.
Van Woert, Wm. I.	25	March 25, '64	Discharged for disability, Feb. 14, '65.
Waldo, Nathan W.	25	Aug. 14, '62	Discharged for disability, Jan. 21, '64.
Wait, Simeon	41	Aug. 15, '62	Discharged for disability, Nov. 3, '63.
Warner, Lafayette	38	Feb. 24, '63	Discharged for disability, March 1, '65.
Winter, Daniel	25	Aug. 16, '62	Discharged for disability, April 5, '65.
Yeoman, Nathaniel	25	Aug. 15, '62	Discharged for disability, June 30, '65.
Young, Daniel	25	Aug. 21, '62	Discharged for disability, Oct. 14, '64.
Zelt, Adam	35	Sept. 28, '62	Sergeant; discharged for disability, July 14, '65.

Total Discharged for Disability: 106

The Deserters

There were relatively few deserters from the Tenth Regiment and they are listed below. There are several reasons for this. Soldiers knew that it was very unwise to desert in Indian territory where they would be killed by the Sioux or in rebel-land in Mississippi immediately after the war when they could be killed by unrepentant rebels. There were several notes in records that said that a soldier straggled from ranks and was not heard from again. The meaning of that is clear: the soldier was probably killed by rebels. In the East, the situation was different. For example, a soldier could desert after the Battle of Manassas and find his way home without worry of being killed or being arrested along the way (unless he did something stupid, like attract attention). There were no mass desertions in the West because the records indicate that soldiers deserted at different times. Only Killoe and Peterson (seen below) deserted at the same time. This was 8 October 1863 at Fort Snelling. At that time, these two soldiers had just completed the summer campaign in Dakota Territory and they were now facing a typical uncomfortable cold winter at Fort Snelling when their comfortable homes were not far away. They left with the knowledge that the provost marshal would probably not be sending anyone to arrest them on the frontier in a cold Minnesota winter. Most of the desertions were from E and I Company which would indicate that desertion was contagious, but on a small scale. The ethic aspect enters the situation. Many of these soldiers had escaped the potato famine in Ireland and did not have a high regard for authority. When things were not to their liking, they left. There is no indication of cowardice since none deserted before or during a battle. There are dozens of records that simply say absent. Most of these occurred months after the Civil War was over. Apparently many of the soldiers did not see the point in continuing in the army months after the war was over, so they simply went home to their families. Also, they were smart enough to realize that they would not be pursued and executed for desertion months after the war had ended. The list below includes those court-martialed and drummed out of the Tenth Regiment which may or not have been for the offense of desertion. The record does not indicate all offenses.

Names	*Age*	*Mustered In*	*Remarks*
Brown, Nathaniel R.	35	Aug. 16, '62	Deserted Sept. 28, '63, at Henderson, Minn.
Bullis, David	32	Aug. 16, '62	Deserted April 28, '63, at Le Sueur, Minn.
Caldwell, Alex. G.	18	Jan. 5, '64	Deserted March 15, '64, at New Orleans, La.
Carroll, James	21	Aug. 14, '62	Deserted June 21, '64, at Memphis, Tenn.
Christianson, Fred	26	Aug. 15, '62	Deserted Oct. 29, '62, at Fort Snelling
Conway, James	20	Sept. 13, '62	Corporal; deserted Oct. 7, '63, at Fort Snelling.
Conner, John	21	Aug. 22, '64	Deserted Nov. 23, '64, at St. Louis.
Crawford, Hugh	30	Aug. 14, '62	Deserted November '63, at St. Louis, Mo.
Elliott, Wm.	45	Aug 14, '62	Deserted Oct. 30, '62 at Fort Snelling.
Gallen, John	22	Feb. 19, '64	Deserted Nov. 23, '64, at St. Louis.
Gorman, Henry	21	Jan. 15, '64	Deserted Feb. 6, '64, at St. Louis.
Gregg, Dennis	19	Feb. 8, '64	Deserted March 15, '65, at New Orleans, La
Hofer, Jacob	39	Feb. 25, '64	Deserted July 30, '64, at St. Louis.
Killoe, Gunder	21	Aug. 22, '62	Deserted Oct. 8, '63, at Fort Snelling.
Johnson, Lewis	24	Aug. 15, '62	Deserted Dec. 1, '62, at Fort Ridgley
McManus, Thomas	35	Aug. 16, '62	Deserted April 23, '64, at St. Louis, Mo.
McBride, James	22	Sept. 18, '62	Deserted Feb. 20, '64, at St. Louis, Mo.
McMeans, David L.	21	Feb. 8, '64	Absent; in confinement for desertion since March '64.
Oleson, Ludwig	31	Aug. 18, '62	Deserted Oct. 20, '62.
Parker, Allen	26	Apr. 5, '64	Deserted April 7, '64, at Carondelet, Mo.
Peterson, John	22	Aug. 22, '62	Deserted Oct. 8, '63, at Fort Snelling.
Quenett, Prudent		Aug. 21, '62	Deserted Oct. 7, '63, at Fort Snelling.
Shook, Edward	22	March 14, '64	Deserted Nov. 18, '64, at St. Louis, Mo.
Soper, William	26	March 26, '64	Deserted March 31, '64, at Carondelet, Mo.
Stemple, Bernard	23	Feb. 19, '64	Deserted Oct. 23, '64, at Lexington, Mo.
Tansty, Patrick	43	Aug. 29, '62	Deserted Nov. 18, '64, at St. Louis, Mo.
Thompson, William	26	Feb. 18, '64	Deserted Feb. 18, '64, at Caroldelet, Mo.
Willwording, Nickolas	18	Aug. 15, '62	Deserted Feb. 18, '63, at Kelso, Minn.

Total Deserters: 28

Veteran Reserve Corps

During the Civil War, soldiers who were wounded could be assigned to the Veteran Reserve Corps or Invalid Corps as it was at first called to perform light duty. General Orders defined the corps.

War Department General Orders No. 105, issued by the Adjutant General's Office on April 28, 1863, authorized the creation of the Veteran Reserve Corps (VRC) originally called the Invalid Corps. The Corps consisted of companies and battalions made up of

- officers and enlisted men unfit for active field service because of wounds or disease contracted in the line of duty, but still capable of performing garrison duty
- officers and enlisted men in service and on the Army rolls otherwise absent from duty and in hospitals, in convalescent camps, or otherwise under the control of medical officials, but capable of serving as cooks, clerks, orderlies, and guards at hospitals and other public buildings
- officers and enlisted men honorably discharged because of wounds or disease and who wanted to reenter the service.[4]

The Invalid Corps was renamed the Veteran Reserve Corps because confusion with the damaged goods stamp I.C. (inspected-condemned) affected volunteer morale.

This was an individual decision. For example, Sergeant Major Eicher who lost an arm at Nashville continued to serve until the end of his three year enlistment (August 1865). He could have entered the Veteran Reserve Corps after he was wounded. The system was not perfect and some cases of the assignment to the Veteran Reserve Corps cannot be explained. More numerous were the discharges for disability which could have been anything from a fever, dysentery, recurring infection or the aftermath of a battle wound. Below is a list of Tenth Regiment soldiers who were discharged to the Veteran Reserve Corps. This list is related to the wounded list above, but sometimes it is difficult to reconcile the records of the Tenth. Of all of the Tenth soldiers transferred to the Veteran Reserve Corps, only two were a result of battle wounds. The others were from disease or other disabilities not identified in the records.

Names	*Age*	*Mustered In*	*Remarks*
Brown, Henry H.	28	Aug. 20, '62	Corporal; transferred to Veteran Reserve Corps Sept. 14, '64.
Costello, John	20	Aug. 13, '62	Transferred to Veteran Reserve Corps Nov. 18, '63.
Dreever, George	25	Aug. 18, '62	Transferred to Veteran Reserve Corps Nov. 29, '63.
Eastman, Alpheus R.	21	Aug. 13, '62	Transferred to Veteran Reserve Corps Jan. 16, '65. Slight wound in the arm at Tupelo.
Farrell, John	32	Aug. 11, '62	Transferred to Veteran Reserve Corps April 1, '65.
Foy, Michael	18	Feb. 8, '64	Transferred to Veteran Reserve Corps Jan. 4, '65.
Hannah, James	39	Aug. 14, '62	Transferred to Veteran Reserve Corps.
Heils, Thomas	35	Aug. 14, '62	Transferred to Veteran Reserve Corps, Sept. 30, '64.
Johnson, Julius	21	Feb. 27, '64	Transferred to Veteran Reserve Corps Feb. 21, '65.
Keith, James R.	19	Aug. 15, '62	Transferred to Veteran Reserve Corps Dec. 16, '63.
Keller, Isaac	27	Aug. 15, '62	Transferred to Veteran Reserve Corps April 1, '65. Wounded at Tupelo in the head, slight.
Morgan, Milton M.	32	Aug. 11, '62	Transferred to Veteran Reserve Corps Dec. 14, '64.
Owen, Elijah W.	42	Aug. 13, '62	Transferred to Veteran Reserve Corps Dec. 21, '64.
Olebaugh, Charles	37	Aug. 11, '62	Transferred to Veteran Reserve Corps March 11, '65.

Names	Age	Mustered In	Remarks
Peat, Eneas S.		Aug. 12, '62	Transferred to 15th Regiment, Vet. Res. Corps, Dec. 21, '64.
Riggles, Daniel	33	Aug. 18, '62	Transferred to Veteran Reserve Corps Nov. 20, '63
Schwartz, Frederick	32	Aug. 15, '62	Transferred to Veteran Reserve Corps April 1, '65.
Taylor, Wm. W.	27	Aug. 27, '62	Transferred to Veteran Reserve Corps March 1, '65.

Total Transferred: 18

Total losses from all causes were 374 or over one-third of the Tenth Regiment's strength of 1,115.

E. Eating on the March

Lieutenant Thomas Jefferson Hunt of the Tenth Regiment describes how soldiers ate on the march.

Few know how our soldiers fared and were fed while on the long marches during the war, and perhaps it will improve the appetite of some to be informed. Where it could be done, one pound of fresh beef each evening, immediately after being slaughtered, was issued to each man; or rather as many pounds to each company as men in it. Sometimes the company boiled the beef entire for all the men, but usually it was divided into as many parts as there were messes and then subdivided into smaller amounts to the soldiers. The cooking was the rub. One could fry his in a tin plate, another would hold his on a sharpened stick in the flames and others would put it on the coals.

Bacon was sometimes issued instead of beef and was three-fourths of a pound per day. What was not eaten for supper and breakfast was usually put in the haversack for lunch. While on the tramps the bacon was usually fried. Hard bread ration was twelve ounces daily, sugar and coffee—two ounces of the former and a less amount of the latter to each, every three days, at night. Each soldier had a small bag to carry these articles in, which helped to fill his haversack. While in the South each soldier carried his pint tin cup, and empty fruit can with a wire handle. This can was his coffee pot, and if he was an expert, he would boil a pint of water by holding his coffeepot of water on a stick over a fire and have it boiled and steeped in three minutes. These were his rations day in and day out except when they ran out and then the country was raided and everything that a hungry mortal could swallow was appropriated.

I may here be affirmed that it was proved beyond dispute that the soldier could endure more on hard bread, bacon and coffee than on any other rations that could then be secured. The man that would deny the soldier his coffee and sugar would be held to be his mortal foe. No substitute has been found for it. Those who are injured by it can complain of the quantity they use, not the quality.

Beans were rarely carried on the march, but they beat all the vegetables catalogued for sustenance. A vegetarian would be a poor soldier in a severe march. His bed was the ground, a few green leaves scraped from a bush or limb made his mattress and in a measure defended him from the dampness of the ground. His rubber blanket suspended on an incline under which he lay was his shelter. He carried his tin plate, surplus hard bread, meat, sugar, and coffee in his haversack. His canteen and rubber blanket, or sometimes a piece of muslin three and a half feet square supplied with buttons and buttonholes to match, took the place of his rubber blanket. These with his gun, cartridge box and fifty rounds of ammunition, weighing in the aggregate thirty pounds, were a load no weakling could endure and march as our corps did over twenty-five miles a day for many consecutive days.

> When rations failed came the tug of war; then cattle, sheep, hogs, poultry — everything edible was taken that could be found on the line of march, and mounted foragers on both sides for four or five miles ranged the country for supplies. I was one of three who in a destitute region in Mississippi carried a pumpkin fifteen miles, which alone made the supper and breakfast for four. It tasted better than nothing, even without salt. It was found that men of medium weight stood the march better than the large or heavy ones.[1]

In Missouri Hunt described what happened when food ran out:

> Our rations ran entirely out and sometimes beeves [beef] and corn were not found. Sweet potatoes were at times our only edibles. Corn was too ripe to roast and we grated the corn on improvised graters for the succeeding day, which with beef we killed when we could find it, was our sustenance.[2]

F. The Tribes

There is always difficulty understanding which Native American nations fought against the Tenth Regiment during the wars of 1862–1863. Below is a summary of the Minnesota Indian tribes. The focus is on the Eastern Sioux who fought in the 1862 war. This is a very brief attempt to capture a small amount of the rich history of Native Americans in Minnesota. Like most histories of the Sioux, this is written from the outside point of view, that is by a person who is not a Native American. An insider's view has many more advantages, but the problem is that history of this period had to be extracted from white records since the written records of the Native Americans are sadly lacking.

In 1859, there were nearly twenty thousand Indians in Minnesota. These were the Sioux, Ojibway or Chippewa and the Winnebago.[1] The Chippewa and Winnebago are not addressed in any detail in this book because they did not join the war against the white man which is the subject of this book. The Chippewa and Winnebago were traditional enemies of the Sioux[2] and were a source of scouts for General Sibley and others.[3] The Tenth Minnesota reports mention the stationing of troops with the Winnebago to intimidate them and prevent them from joining Little Crow's war.

The terms Dakota and Sioux are used interchangeably in many writings but they do not mean the same thing. Dakota has the meaning of friends while Sioux has the meaning of snake, a term given to them by their enemies, the Chippewa.[4] The term Sioux was widely used during the conflict and has been used throughout this book. The term Dakota is preferred by members of this nation and has the meaning alliance of friends. This nation is bound together by a common language, the Dakota. The Eastern Sioux tribes in Minnesota were Sissetons, Wahpetons, Wahpekutes and Little Crow's Mdewkanton tribe.[5] These tribes were also called the Santee Sioux. They are at times referred to as the Woodland Sioux because of their home. Further west in Dakota Territory and beyond, the other Sioux tribes were the Yanktons, Yanktonais, and the Tetons that accounted for more than half the Sioux population.[6] These are sometimes called the Plains Sioux. In his 1863 campaign in Dakota Territory, General Sibley mentions these last three tribes as those that he fought against. The Teton chiefs included Sitting Bull and Gall. Occasionally, one sees the term Santee Sioux used during the Civil War. This is another name for the Eastern Sioux.[7] Not all of the Sioux tribes fought against the whites during the Indian war in Minnesota and Dakota

Territory. We see the Sissetons under Chief Standing Buffalo trying to make peace with the whites and nearly all of the Sioux at the Yellow Medicine Agency refusing to join Little Crow in his war. Folwell in his excellent four volume history of Minnesota broke down each of the tribes into bands identified by their leader. He identified twenty-nine bands for the four tribes of the Eastern Sioux. Of these the leaders of the Mdewakanton tribe are of interest because they led the fight against the whites: Little Crow, Big Eagle, Shakopee, The Jug, Rattling Moccasin, Red Middle Voice, Mankato, Traveling Hail, Wacouta, and Wabasha.[8] These are white names applied to Indian leaders and are not their Indian names. For example, Little Crow was known as Thaoyata Duta which translates to His Red Nation. We see the names of these leaders in the military reports and letters of the whites engaged in fighting the war. A review of the maps of Minnesota today show many of these names as town or street names. These were not used to honor the Indian warrior who fought against the whites but to use a name shared by earlier history or such geographic features as rivers. As an example, Shakopee, Minnesota, is located on the site of Shakopee's encampment. Shakopee meant the six because an ancestor of Shakopee, the chief in 1862, had sextuplet boys and so Chief Shakopee was known to whites as Little Six. Anyone interested in playing blackjack or other indoor sports can visit the Little Six Casino twenty-five minutes south of the Twin Cities and it is open 24–7. Casinos and other gaming establishments are the cash cows for many Native Americans today.[9]

The casino windfall for Native Americans started in the 1970s near Leech Lake, Minnesota, when a Chippewa couple filed suit to avoid a tax bill maintaining that they could not be taxed because they resided on Indian reservation lands. The case went to the Supreme Court, which agreed. The states did not have the authority to tax Indians on Indian reservations. Furthermore, the states did not have the authority to *regulate* Indian activities on Indian reservations. This set the stage for happy times by Indians on Indian reservations which gave birth to the casinos that we see today. A part of this is the theory that the tribal nations are "domestic dependent nations" and hence not subject to state laws. We see this in the Sioux War of 1862 when Little Crow representing a sovereign nation declared war on the United States. Also, Justice Brennan and others had hoped that the revenue produced by gaming would improve life on the reservations and this was achieved as Meyer points out in his book on the Santee Sioux.[10]

Whites and Half Breeds

Whites and the Sioux frequently intermarried and the offspring were called half breeds or mixed bloods. Some became very influential among the Sioux, such as Joseph Renville, who had more influence with the Sioux than any other man.[11] Many mixed bloods became interpreters and thus provided good service to both races. During the Sioux War some assisted whites in escaping and on the other hand, a few were convicted of war crimes and were among those hanged in December 1862.

Agriculture and Hunting

Before the whites flooded into Sioux lands an early traveler described the delicate ecosystem of the Sioux. Men and boys hunted while the women harvested a variety of foodstuffs. These included rice, corn, sugar maples, berries, nuts and roots.[12] These were nomads who moved frequently and did not plant and harvest crops. That came later with the efforts of missionaries to civilize the Sioux.

Language

The Reverend Stephen R. Riggs spent many years with the Sioux and attempted to learn and translate their unwritten language. He writes, "It was of course to be phonetic, as nearly as possible. The English alphabet was used as far as it could be. These were the principles that guided and controlled the writing of Dakota."[13] The product of this work was, among other things, a Dakota-English Dictionary.

Garments and Footwear

Sioux women wore coat, skirt, leggings, moccasins and a blanket.[14] Men wore heavy blankets and buffalo skins in the winter. In summer shirts made of cotton were used. Leggings were nearly as long as their legs made of buckskin or cloth and in cold weather, both could be worn. Breech-cloth was made of blue woolen cloth.[15]

Dwellings

Houses in summer were bark supported by poles. Tepees were made of eight dressed buffalo skins sewed in a conical shape twelve feet in height and ten to twelve feet in diameter at the base. When warmed by a good fire in winter, they were fairly comfortable.[16]

Weapons

Bow and arrows were common and effective in hunting buffalo, but the Sioux preferred smooth-bore muskets, making shot from bars of lead for general use. The only weapons used exclusively for war were spears and war-clubs. War-clubs were made from a flat piece of wood, often hickory two and one half feet long and an inch thick.[17]

Government

Government was democratic. Decisions were reached in council where a majority vote decided the issue. The Dakotas had no permanent officers except the chief and chief soldier who had no powers beyond those granted by the majority.[18]

After the Dust Settled

While Sibley was campaigning in Dakota Territory fighting the Sioux, in 1863–1865, action was in progress to deport the Sioux from Minnesota. Hundreds of Sioux had already fled Minnesota to Dakota Territory after the Battle of Wood Lake. It was surprising that the Winnebago who had not participated in the 1862 war were included in the roundup. This was because the Winnebago had displaced whites in Blue Earth County, Minnesota, when they were driven from Wisconsin in 1855. The whites in Blue Earth County, Minnesota, saw the Sioux War as an opportunity to get rid of the Winnebago, which is exactly what happened.[19] As a consequence, a massive deportation of Sioux and Winnebago occurred after Sibley's victory at Wood Lake.

Indian Census of 1890

Twenty-seven years after the deportations of 1863, the Indian Census of 1890 in Minnesota shows a significant Native American population: 10,096. These are all Chippewa. No Sioux or Winnebago are included. The census states: "The Sioux and Winnebago Indians were removed to Dakota.... The Chippewa, being the principal Indians, remained in Minnesota and are the only Indians in the state."[20] This is not true. Lincoln pardoned Big Eagle who returned to Minnesota and died there in 1916. Sibley kept 137 Sioux in Minnesota to act as scouts after the deportation of early 1863.[21] After the Civil War, the Department of the Interior collected information on what was called the Scattered Sioux in Minnesota. The count at that time was 374.[22] Undoubtedly other Sioux and Winnebago drifted back to Minnesota and blended into the general population and were not counted as Indians in the Census. To complicate matters, some of the Sioux drifted back and forth over the Minnesota-Dakota border. The exact number of Sioux in Minnesota by 1900 cannot be determined, but the population continued to grow during the twentieth century at locations such as Birch Coulee and Prairie Island.

G. The Trials

> *I then directed ... a classification of all who were proven to have participated in massacres as distinguished from participation in battles [italics are from the Congressional Record]. This class numbered forty, and included the two convicted of female violation. One of the number is strongly recommended by the commission which tried them for commutation to ten years' imprisonment. I have ordered the other thirty-nine to be executed.*[1]
>
> —A. Lincoln

After a series of battles between Sibley's forces and Little Crow's, the Sioux were decisively defeated at the Battle of Wood Lake on 18 September not far from Fort Ridgley. While Little Crow was withdrawing from Wood Lake, the anti-war element among the Sioux gained the upper hand at the Sioux camp and took control of the hostages that the Sioux had collected during their rampages in the Minnesota Valley. This element was prepared to defend the hostages by force against Little Crow.[2] When Sibley arrived at the Indian camp on 26 September, he found nothing but friendly Sioux who were happy to release the hostages since most of the Sioux who had committed capital crimes had fled. It was hard to find a hostile since all, including other tribes, were expressing their anger with Little Crow. The hostages were released and Sibley renamed the camp Camp Release. "Sibley announced that the Sioux should consider themselves prisoners of war until he could discover and hang the guilty ones among them."[3] Sibley wanted an unconditional surrender by Little Crow and he sent him a message to that effect. There would be no formal surrender by Little Crow. He fled west with many of his followers. By November, more than 2,000 of the Sioux had surrendered to Sibley near Fort Ridgley.

A military tribunal was convened to try those Sioux suspected of war crimes. The entire process of the military tribunal was flawed from start to finish. Years later Sibley would admit that the trials were drumhead justice, meaning that they were an unfair, biased or hastily conducted judicial proceeding that ended in a harsh punishment.[4] The drumhead term originated from military justice quickly administered on bivouac using a drum as the judge's bench for the trial.[5] A military commission was convened near Fort Ridgley by General Sibley to try the Sioux for crimes allegedly committed during the uprising. Military commissions had been in use in the United States since the Mexican War. In the case of the Minnesota Sioux Indian trials, martial law, a precondition for a military commission, was not in effect.[6] This meant that the trials were illegal.[7] The members of the commission were all involved in the fighting and could not be viewed as impartial judges. Furthermore, Sibley acted as convening authority and accuser, and he approved the sentences, a violation of U.S. Article of War 65.[8] In defense of Sibley, it was difficult if not impossible to find any officer on the frontier who was a disinterested party, not engaged in the war. While this created an unsatisfactory atmosphere for the administration of justice, the exigencies of the situation required prompt action and some legal requirements could not be accommodated.

Sibley promised the Sioux when they surrendered that only those guilty of killing civilians would be punished.[9] He did this to encourage other Sioux who had escaped to also surrender. The problem was that once convened, because of public pressure, the commission expanded the trials to include any Sioux who had fired on federal troops or had otherwise participated in the war. Since the Sioux were considered to be a sovereign nation by treaty with the U.S. government, they could not be tried for exercising their rights as belligerents.[10] Instead, they should have been held as prisoners of war with rights associated with that status.[11]

Members of the commission were Colonel Crooks, Lieutenant Colonel Marshall, Captain Grant, Captain Bayley, and Lieutenant Olin. The commission recorder was Lieutenant Isaac Heard. These officers were selected by Sibley from Minnesota regiments fighting in the Indian war. They tried a total of 392 Sioux.[12] Of this number, there were death sentences for 303 and the others were found not guilty/acquitted or were convicted with imprisonment. President Lincoln would review the trial records and approve the death sentences for thirty-nine of the Sioux (the rest were imprisoned, both those found not guilty as well as those convicted). The trials were conducted over a six-week period, from 28 September through 9 November 1862. As many as thirty to forty trials were conducted on some days with a record of forty-two in one day during the period of the trials, 28 September through 9 November 1862. The problem was that the citizens of Minnesota were outraged by the Sioux atrocities. Some lynchings of the Sioux had occurred and more were likely. It was entirely possible that troops might have to fire on citizens to protect the Sioux prisoners. The view at that time was that it was necessary to proceed with all speed in conducting the trials and calm the frontier through the convictions of more than a few Sioux. After attacks on the Sioux prisoners by citizens in New Ulm that left fifteen injured soldier guards, two

Sioux dead and others wounded, Sibley made the following comment in a letter to his wife, Sarah, indicating the outrage of the citizenry: "The Dutch she devils! [referring to the ladies of New Ulm]—They are as fierce as tigresses."[13]

The trial records show that the charges were read and that Antoine Frenier was the interpreter during the trials.[14] The Reverend Riggs, a missionary with the Sioux, was asked to interview the prisoners before the trials to determine which were implicated. Riggs in effect acted as a grand jury for the court.[15] Riggs was clearly unhappy with this role but complied.[16]

> As Riggs explained it, "instead of taking individuals for trial, against whom some specific charge could be brought, the plan was adopted to subject all the grown men, with a few exceptions, to the investigation of the commission, trusting that the innocent could make their innocence appear." Thus, all Indians were considered guilty by the military commission until proven innocent, and that proof had to be presented by the accused.[17]

This sub-rosa agreement among the members of the commission in order to speed things along is not evident in the trial records and was a major flaw in the proceedings. Guilty until proven innocent may be doctrine in some countries, but not in the United States. The sentences were announced in court. Defense comments by the accused were heard by the commission, but no defense counsel was present to represent the defendants.

Firing on Federal troops was a common charge that was not relevant since the Sioux had belligerent status and a right to make war. For those charged with capital crimes the commission recorder, Isaac Heard, states, "No one was sentenced to death for mere robbery.... It was required that it should be proven by the testimony of witnesses, unless the prisoner admitted the fact, that he had fired in the battles, or bought ammunition, or acted as a commissary in supplying provisions to the combatants, or committed some separate murder."[18] Heard unwittingly condemned the entire process with this remark. As seen earlier, engaging in battle as a member of a sovereign nation is the right of a belligerent. The reason for this unusual process was that the commission was under pressure to convict as many Sioux as possible, as quickly as possible, in order to calm the unrest on the frontier. It is evident that if Little Crow or a defense counsel had been present at the trials, they could have done an excellent job in counseling Sioux defendants. Little Crow understood the legal process. He carefully declared war on the U.S. and the chiefs voted on it. This was to insure that all would understand that the Sioux were belligerents and were to be treated as prisoners of war. The Sioux on trial did not understand this point and the members of the commission apparently did not care. Comments by the Sioux before they were executed reveal that they still did not understand this point (see Appendix I).

There were other problems with the trials. When rarely called, the testimony of eyewitnesses to murders may have been unreliable given cultural differences and the stress that the witnesses were under when the murders occurred. As an example, the wife of Howard Baker, who was one of the few survivors of the Acton murders, stated at the Acton inquest that six Sioux were involved and identified them as all middle-aged.[19] All other accounts identify the number as four and Big Eagle, who knew the four men and later named them, described them as "young fellows."[20] In spite of all of the problems with the trials as described, above, a review of trial records and survivor statements indicate that for those accused of capital crimes against civilians, sufficient evidence existed to prove the charges. Those that were hanged had many witness statements in the record, some dubious, some not. The trial records of the rest of the Sioux, for the most part, had none. No witnesses were called if the defendant admitted guilt.

After signing off on the death penalty for 303 Sioux in November, Sibley was hesitant to hang 303 human beings on his own authority although many were demanding that he immediately hang them all. Also, Sibley had an immense sense of justice as had been seen before and after this incident. What followed was a classic example of buck-passing. Those screaming for immediate justice included the press, settlers, and General John Pope. Pope blundered badly, by demanding that all Sioux (guilty or not) be summarily executed. He was not disciplined for his outrageous remarks that did nothing but further inflame the frontier. Sibley cabled Governor Alexander Ramsey asking for approval to proceed with the hangings. Hanging was the method of execution used when commanders had an experienced hangman available as well as planking and rope for a scaffold. When armies were on the move, execution was by musketry.[21] Ramsey cabled back saying it was now a military matter and Sibley should ask his chain of command for approval. Sibley cabled General John Pope, his superior, asking for approval to hang the Indians. Pope cabled back that it was beyond his authority and he passed the buck to his superior in Washington, General Henry Halleck, the Army general in chief. Halleck cabled back saying that it was beyond his authority and he passed the request to Lincoln. The Law of 24 December 1861 gave divisional commanders the final determination in appeals of death sentences, but under the 17 July 1862 amendment, the president was to review every death sentence.[22]

In this manner, Lincoln became involved in the case and requested trial records from Pope who merely telegraphed the list of names of the condemned. Lincoln asked again for the trial records (all 2,000 pages) and these were forwarded to Lincoln by General Pope on 15 November. A very unusual event occurred at this time. The cost of telegraphing a list of 303 names was $400 and this appeared in the press. When Congress found out about the bill, the senators were outraged at the cost and demanded that Pope pay out of pocket for the telegraph bill. Pope was miffed over this whole affair and refused to use the telegraph subsequent to this event preferring mail instead. This did not help the flow of information from White House to Pope. The time taken from conviction until Lincoln had the records was fast given the transportation available at that time. It took less than two weeks.

Lincoln was performing a delicate balancing act. Congressional elections were due in November 1862 and Lincoln was in danger of losing his Republican majority (he did not).[23] Lincoln was working on the Emancipation Proclamation, possibly the most important document of his presidency. There was concern that Britain and France would recognize the Confederacy. Some thought that the manner in which Lincoln dealt with these trials could influence recognition of the Confederacy, but most disagree. Great Britain would be the last nation to have qualms over treatment of the natives given their record in India and elsewhere. In any event, the signing of the Emancipation Proclamation on 1 January 1863 ended Southern hopes for recognition.

The war was not going well. While Lee had been stopped at Antietam (the bloodiest day in U.S. military history), General George McClellan failed to pursue Lee and Lincoln fired McClellan (for the last time). In Lincoln's words, McClellan had a bad case of the "slows." With the issue of Lee in Maryland unresolved, Lincoln was searching for a new general. He would select Ambrose Burnside, who presided over the greatest Union defeat of the Civil War in December at Fredericksburg. Lincoln took time out from what he was doing to direct his attention to the Sioux Indian trials. The problem was that a misstep in any one of the above crucial areas could spill over into others. It is not surprising that when Lincoln finally decided the Indian affair, his message to the Senate was very lengthy and left no room for misinterpretation.[24] He included in his reply the charges against each condemned Sioux, his rationale for commuting the other sentences and the mail and cables that he had received from Minnesota. A little background on Lincoln is relevant: in the past, when handed capital cases for his approval, he would first look to find any judicial error. If he found any, he was delighted and he would disapprove the death penalty and return the soldier to duty or commute the sentence.[25] At last, the Sioux had found someone who would give them a fair hearing. Carl Sandburg, Lincoln's biographer, states that Lincoln personally reviewed each case before making a decision. This is not true in the case of the Sioux. Lincoln asked the Department of Justice to assign two attorneys to the executive to review all cases and provide recommendations to him. Justice assigned two attorneys, George C. Whiting and Francis H. Ruggles, to the cases.[26] Lincoln did not have the time to personally review 303 trial records given all of his other activities identified above. Lincoln may well have provided his philosophy on capital cases to these two attorneys, but we have no record of that.

The environment at this time was one of intense pressure for a quick decision. Western senators were receiving irate letters from their constituents, and Lincoln was getting his share of similar mail which he included in his reply to the Senate.[27] Review of some of these indicate that people were upset with Lincoln for not approving all sentences instantly. At this time, Bishop Whipple from Minnesota, who was a prominent cleric (Lincoln always insured that he spoke with people of prominence who came to see him), visited Lincoln in an effort to gain his intervention on behalf of the Sioux. He explained the abuses by the whites (the illegal conduct of the traders and others) that had led to the Sioux uprising. As Whipple finished, Lincoln looked up and said: "Bishop, a man thought that monkeys could pick cotton better than Negroes could because they were quicker and their fingers were smaller. He turned a lot of them into his field, but found that it took two overseers to watch one monkey. It takes more than one honest man to watch one Indian Agent."[28]

Lincoln took as much time as he thought he could before announcing his decision to Sibley in a letter dated 6 December 1862 that identified those Sioux who would hang.[29] The others received prison sentences of ten years. The hangings were carried out in Mankato, Minnesota, on 26 December 1862, six days after Lincoln signed the Emancipation Proclamation. In a very typical Lincoln comment at the end of his letter to General Sibley,[30] he made it clear that the prisoners should receive humane treatment. Lincoln was a veteran of the Black Hawk War, so he knew how far emotion could drive settlers to punish Indians.[31] Unfortunately, the prisoners did not receive humane treatment. Nearly half were dead from starvation or disease by the time President Johnson pardoned the Sioux in 1866. In one case, Sarah Wakefield, a settler in Minnesota, wrote to Lincoln explaining that the Indian named Chaska had saved her life and she was assured by the army that Chaska was safe and would not be harmed. It was bad luck for Chaska because his name was similar to that of a condemned Sioux, Chaskay-don (prisoner number 121), and they marched Chaska to the gallows by mistake.[32] Lincoln provided condolences to Mrs. Wakefield. There was speculation on the frontier that Sarah Wakefield's relationship with Chaska was a bit closer than she might wish to admit and that she was mentally unbalanced and making a big deal over a small problem (from the settlers' point of view). Chaska's relationship with Sarah Wakefield may have caused the mistaken hanging of Chaska.

Lincoln provided his reply to Congress on the Indian war in his message dated 11 December 1862.[33] In his lengthy, handwritten reply that was printed in the Congressional

Record, Lincoln summarized the crimes of the Sioux, the list of the condemned, the comments of the settlers and the heart of the whole affair that was not addressed by the military commission: Lincoln was clear in stating that the Sioux engaged in battles should not be executed while those guilty of massacres should be hanged. What Lincoln may not have known was that he was dealing with a fraction of those who had committed capital crimes. Most of those guilty of murder had fled to the Dakota Territory when Sibley approached the Indian camp.[34]

Problems occurred: a review of Lincoln's letter to the Senate reveals contradictions. On the second page he made it clear to the Senate, as seen above, that the Sioux who participated in battle should be treated as prisoners of war, but he sentenced them to ten years' in prison, which appears to have violated General Order Number 100 that dealt with treatment of POWs.[35] On page 8 of his letter to the Senate (Senate printed version),[36] he deals with White Dog (prisoner number 35), who sprang the trap on Captain Marsh's command at Redwood Ferry that killed Captain Marsh and most of his command. No one had seen White Dog participate in any massacre or rape, but he would hang.[37] In his report to the Senate, Lincoln listed the crimes of all thirty-eight and said, "White Dog was the leader of the party that attacked Captain Marsh's company, and was the man who detained Captain Marsh in conversation until the Indians crossed the river and surrounded the command, and then gave them the signal to fire."[38]

White Dog continued to claim that he had been trying to warn Marsh of the ambush (see Appendix I. Among the condemned Sioux, White Dog was senior, since he was a chief in Wabash's camp. His skill as a soldier had caused the death of Captain Marsh and most of his command. To add to White Dog's problems (after his imprisonment) was the fact that he reportedly had been quite a lady's man among both Indian and white women.[39] This reputation did not endear him to the white male settler population in Minnesota. Everything seemed to be against White Dog's survival. He was also a leader of the mission movement to cause Sioux warriors to start farming instead of the nomadic hunting that they had traditionally enjoyed. The Sioux resented his work and when he turned on the settlers and joined the war, the settlers were further outraged at his betrayal. In Lincoln's handwritten letter to General Sibley, he carefully spelled, phonetically, the Sioux name for each prisoner and identified the prisoner number. This was to make sure that no prisoner was hanged by mistake (see Appendix H). In only one case did Lincoln add the white man's name for the prisoner in his letter to Sibley: the case was White Dog.[40] This difference has not been explained, but it may be that Lincoln wanted to make it clear to all that White Dog would hang. Perhaps Lincoln did not want to handle another wave of outrage if White Dog's sentence was commuted. There is no record of any adverse congressional reaction to Lincoln's 11 December letter. It appears that everyone in Washington wanted this issue behind them. This was the end of a sad affair in Washington. The night before he was hanged, White Dog's statement was recorded by a reporter:

> Shoon-ka-ska (White Dog) says that when the outbreak took place, he ran away, and did not get any of the stolen property. At the ferry, he talked with Quinn. First, called to them to come over, but when he saw that the Indians were in ambush, he beckoned to Capt. Marsh to stay back. He says that his position and conduct at the ferry were misunderstood and misrepresented; that he wanted peace, and did not command the Indians to fire on Capt. Marsh's men; that another man could be put to death for that. He complains bitterly that he did not have a chance to tell the things as they were; that he could not have an opportunity of rebutting the false testimony against him. (His further testimony is unreadable.)[41]

The Harper's sketch of the trials: The boy glared at the prisoners as he accused them.

After Lincoln's review, a very curious document found its way into the trial records. It can best be described as a census of prisoners at Mankato and is dated 12 January 1863.⁴² The document was an effort to account for the 392 Sioux originally tried. Names of those prisoners who had already been executed were, of course, missing. The list included the forty-nine found not guilty or who were acquitted. Why these forty-nine Sioux were still in custody is unexplained. Two theories are protective custody because the possibility of a lynching was real, or more likely, a concern that if released, these Sioux would join forces with the others who were still engaged in killing white civilians. One page of the census is missing, but it can be reconstituted by going through the trial records. The missing page would have included the name of prisoner 121, Chaskay-don. This page would have been an embarrassment to the government, because Chaskay-don was supposed to be dead. Chaska, Sarah Wakefield's rescuer, was hanged by mistake, and Chaskay-don, who murdered a pregnant white woman, was still very much alive. There is no record to show that Chaskay-don was ever punished. The census also lists the names of the Sioux who had died in captivity as of 31 December 1862: less than a month after imprisonment, the death list was already growing. If corrections previously noted are made, the list can be reconciled and accounts for the 392 Sioux originally tried. By the time the surviving prisoners were released, nearly half of those originally imprisoned had died of disease or starvation. A sketch in *Harper's Weekly* carried a story quoted, below.

> Quite an incident occurred while I [this may have been Adrian John Ebell who was writing for *Harper's* at this time] was there. A boy who had escaped after seeing the murder and outrage of his mother and sisters was brought in to look at the prisoners, and, if possible, identify them. One of the friendly Indians, who had distinguished himself by his bravery and humanity, accompanied the party to act as interpreter. When we entered the log-house that served for a prison the captives were mostly crouched on the floor, but one of them arose and confronted us with a defiant scowl. Another, supporting himself on his arm, surveyed the party with a look like a tiger about to spring. The boy advanced boldly, and pointed him out without hesitancy. Subsequent investigation showed that this wretch had murdered eleven persons. The boy's eyes flashed as he told the sickening tale of his mother's murder, and the spectators could scarce refrain from killing the wretch on the spot. He never relaxed his sullen glare, and seemed perfectly indifferent when told of his identification by the interpreter. The entire country steams with slaughter, and there is scarce a family in the large district that was the scene of the outbreak that has not lost a member; and many are entirely cut off, and nothing left to indicate their fate but their devastated homes and the chance admissions of the prisoners.[43]

H. Lincoln's Report to Congress[1]

37th CONGRESS SENATE Ex. Doc. 3d Session No. 7

MESSAGE

of the

PRESIDENT OF THE UNITED STATES

In Answer to

A resolution of the Senate of the 15th instant in relation to the Indian barbarities in Minnesota

DECEMBER 11, 1862 — Read, referred to the Committee on Indian Affairs, and ordered to be printed.

To the Senate of the United States:

In compliance with your resolution of December 5, 1862, requesting the President "to furnish the Senate with all information in his possession touching the late Indian barbarities in the State of Minnesota, and also the evidence in his possession upon which some of the principal actors and headmen were tried and condemned to death," I have the honor to state that on receipt of said resolution I transmitted the same to the Secretary of the Interior, accompanied by a note a copy of which is herewith enclosed, marked A, and in response to which I received through that Department a letter of the Commissioner of Indian Affairs, a copy of which is herewith enclosed, marked B.

I further state that on the 8th day of November last I received a long telegraphic dispatch from Major-General Pope, at St. Paul, Minn., simply announcing the names of the persons sentenced to be hanged. I immediately telegraphed to have transcripts of the records in all the cases forwarded to me, which transcripts, however, did not reach me until two or three days before the present meeting of Congress. Meantime I received, through telegraphic dispatches and otherwise, appeals in behalf of the condemned, appeals for their execution, and expressions of opinion as to proper policy in regard to them and to the Indians generally in that vicinity, none of which, as I understand, falls within the scope of your inquiry. After the arrival of the transcripts of records, but before I had sufficient opportunity to examine them, I received a joint letter from one of the Senators and two of the Representatives from Minnesota, which contains some statements of fact not found in the records of the trials, and for which reason I herewith transmit a copy, marked C. I also, for the same reason, enclose a printed memorial of the citizens of St. Paul addressed to me and forwarded with the letter aforesaid.

Anxious to not act with so much clemency as to encourage another outbreak on the one hand, nor with so much severity as to be real cruelty on the other, I caused a careful examination of the records of trials to be made, in view of first ordering the execution of such as had been proved guilty of violating females. Contrary to my expectations, only two of this class were found. I then directed a further examination, and a classification of all who were proven to have participated in *massacres*, as distinguished from participation in *battles*. This class numbered forty, and included the two convicted of female violation. One of the number is strongly recommended by the commission which tried them for commutation to ten years' imprisonment. I have ordered the other thirty-nine to be executed on Friday, the 19th instant. The order was dispatched from here on Monday, the 8th instant, by a messenger to General Sibley, and a copy of which order is herewith transmitted, marked D.

An abstract of the evidence as to the forty is herewith enclosed, marked E.

To avoid the immense amount of copying, I lay before the Senate the original transcripts of the records of trials as received by me. This is as full and complete a response to the resolution as it is in my power to make.

ABRAHAM LINCOLN.
DECEMBER 11, 1862

A.

Executive Mansion,
Washington, December 5, 1862.

Sir: Please have the Commissioner of Indian Affairs make out and send me as complete an answer to the enclosed resolution of the Senate as the means for so doing can be found in his office.

Yours, very truly,
A. LINCOLN.
The Hon. Secretary of the Interior.

B.

Department of the Interior,
Office of Indian Affairs, December 8, 1862.

Sir: Your note of this date, accompanied with letter of the President of December 5, 1862, and a copy of the resolution of the Senate of same date, has been received.

In compliance with the request therein contained, I have the honor to state that this office is possessed of no information concerning the matter inquired of other than that contained in my late official report, and the documents accompanying the same, all of which has been reported to you and is now before the country.

Herewith I return the papers enclosed to me.

Very respectfully, your obedient servant,
WM. P. DOLE,
Commissioner.

Hon. C. B. Smith,
Secretary of the Interior.

C.

To the President of the United States:

Sir: We have learned, incidentally, that you intend to pardon or reprieve a large majority of the Indians in Minnesota who have been formally condemned for their participation in the brutal massacres of our people in the months of August and September last.

If this be your purpose, as representatives from that State, we beg leave most respectfully to protest against it; and we do so for the following reasons:

These Indians were condemned, most of them, upon the testimony of women whom they had carried into captivity, after having murdered their fathers, husbands, and brothers, and who were treated by these Indians with a brutality never known in this country, nor equaled in the practices of the most barbarous nations.

There were nearly ninety female captives. They were the wives and daughters of our neighbors and friends.

They were intelligent and virtuous women; some of them were wives and mothers, others were young and interesting girls. These savages, to whom you purpose to extend your executive clemency, when the whole country was quiet, and the farmers were busily engaged in gathering their crops, arose with fearful violence, and, travelling from one farmhouse to another, indiscriminately murdered all the men, boys, and little children they came to; and although they sometimes spared the lives of the mothers and daughters, they did so only to take them into a captivity which was *infinitely worse than death.*

Mr. President, let us relate to you some facts with which we fear you have not heretofore been made acquainted. These Indians, whom (as we understand) you propose to pardon and set free, have murdered in cold blood nearly or quite one thousand of our people, ravaged our frontier for a distance of more than a hundred and fifty miles North and South, burned the houses of the settlers, and driven from their homes more than ten thousand of our people. They seized and carried into captivity nearly one hundred women and young girls, and in nearly every instance treated them with the most fiendish brutality. To show you, sire, the enormity of these outrages, we beg leave to state a few facts, which are well known to our people, but delicacy forbids that we should mention the names of the parties to whom we refer.

In one instance some ten or twelve of these Indians visited the house of a worthy farmer, who, at the time, was engaged with his sons in stacking wheat. They stealthily approached the fence where this honest farmer was at work, and, seizing their opportunity, shot the father and his two sons at the stack. They then went to the house, killed two little children in the presence of their mother, who was quite ill of consumption, and then they took the sick mother and a beautiful little daughter, thirteen years of age, into captivity.

But this is not all, nor is it the most appalling feature of this awful tragedy. Its horror is yet to be revealed. After removing these unhappy prisoners to a lodge which was some miles away, these fiends incarnate, placing a guard over the body of the weary and exhausted mother, took her little girl outside of the lodge, removed all her clothes, and fastened her upon her back on the ground. They then commenced their work of brutality upon the body of this young girl. One by one they violated her person, unmoved by her cries and unchecked by the evident signs of her approaching dissolution. This work was continued until her Heavenly Father relieved her from suffering. They left her dead upon the ground. This outrage was committed within a few feet of a *sick and dying mother*.

There is another instance of a girl eighteen years of age. We knew her well before and at the time of her capture. She was as refined and beautiful a girl as we had in the State. None had more or better friends; no one was more worthy of them than she. She was taken captive by these Indians. She was taken, her arms were tied behind her, she was made fast to the ground, and ravished by some eight or ten of these convicts before the cords were unloosed from her limbs. This girl fortunately lived to testify against the wretches who had thus violated her.

Without being more specific we will state that all or nearly all the women who were captured were violated in this way. Again: there was a little boy brought to St. Paul, who father and mother had been murdered, whose life was spared, as a witness of the horrid nature of this massacre. His right eye was cut completely out; it had fallen from its socket and perished on his cheek. His two little sisters, aged, respectively, six and four years, were also saved, but in an awfully mutilated condition; their tender arms mangled with the savages' knives, and otherwise fearfully wounded, and left on the ground for dead.

Mr. President, there was no justification or pretext, even, for these brutalities. We state what we know when we say that the Sioux agent, Major Galbraith, has labored faithfully and efficiently for the welfare of these Indians. The government, as you know, has built a house and opened a farm for every one of these Indians who would reside upon and cultivate it. Missionaries, as our worthy Bishop can testify, have labored zealously among them for their spiritual welfare. There has been paid to them yearly the interest upon two millions of dollars. Farming implements have been purchased, and farmers have been employed by the government to improve and cultivate their lands.

These Indians are called by some prisoners of war. There was no war about it. It was wholesale robbery, *rape, murder*. These Indians were not at war with their murdered victims.

The people of Minnesota, Mr. President, have stood firm by you and by your administration; they have given both you and it their cordial support; *they* have *not* violated the *law*; they have borne these sufferings with a patience such as but few people ever exhibited under such extreme trial. These Indians are now at their mercy; but our people have not risen up to slaughter them, because they believed that their President would deal with them justly.

We are told, Mr. President, that a committee from Pennsylvania, whose families are living happily in their pleasant homes in that State, have called upon you and petitioned you to pardon these Indians. We have a high respect for the religious sentiments of your petitioners, but we submit that it is in bad taste; indeed that it is entirely unbecoming them to interfere in matters with which they are so little acquainted, and which relate to the security of our own people.

We *protest against the pardon* of these Indians, because, if it is done, the Indians will become more insolent and cruel than they ever were before, believing, as they certainly will believe, that their great father at Washington either justified their acts or is afraid to punish them for their crimes.

We *protest against it* because, if the President does not permit these executions to take place under the forms of law, the outraged people of Minnesota will dispose of these wretches without law. These two peoples cannot live together. We do not wish to see mob law inaugurated in Minnesota, as it certainly will be, if you force the people to it.

We tremble at the approach of such a condition of things in our State.

You can give us peace, or you can give us lawless violence. We pray you, sir, in view of all that we have suffered, and of the danger which still awaits us, *let the law be executed; let justice be done our people.*

With high respect, we are, sir, your obedient servants,
M. S. WILKINSON.
CYRUS ALDRICH.
WM. WINDOM.

MEMORIAL.

To the President of the United States:

We, the citizens of St. Paul, in the State of Minnesota, respectfully represent that we have heard with fear and alarm, through the public newspapers, report of an intention on the part of the United States government to dismiss without punishment the Sioux warriors captured by our soldiers; and further, to allow the several tribes of Indians lately located upon reservations within this State to remain upon the reservations.

Against any such policy we respectfully, but firmly, protest. The history of this continent presents no event that can compare with the late Sioux outbreak in wanton, unprovoked, and fiendish cruelty. All that we have read of Indian warfare in the early history of this country is tame in contrast with the atrocities of this late massacre. Without warning, in cold blood, beginning with the murder of their best friends, the whole body of the annuity Sioux commenced a deliberate scheme to exterminate every white person upon the land once occupied by them, and by them long since sold to the United States. On carrying out this bloody scheme they have spared neither age nor sex, only reserving for the gratification of their brutal lusts the few white women whom the rifle, the tomahawk, and the scalping knife spared. Nor did their fiendish barbarities cease with death, as the mutilated corpses of their victims, disemboweled, cut limb from limb, or chopped into fragments, will testify. These cruelties, too, were in many cases preceded by a pretence of friendship; and in many instances the victims of these more than murders were shot down in cold blood as soon as their backs were turned, after a cordial shaking of the hand and loud professions of friendship on the part of the murderers.

We ask that the same judgment should be passed and executed upon these deliberate murderers, these ravishers, these mutilators of their murdered victims, that would be passed upon white men guilty of the same offence. The blood of hundreds of our murdered fellow-citizens cries from the ground for vengeance. "Vengeance is mine, I will repay saith the Lord," and the authorities of the United States are, we believe, the chosen instruments to execute that vengeance. Let them not neglect their plain duty.

Nor do we ask alone for vengeance. We demand security for the future. There can be no safety for us or for our families, unless an example shall be made of those who have committed these horrible murders and barbarities we have related. Let it be understood that these Indians can commit such crimes and be pardoned upon surrendering themselves, and there is henceforth a torch for every white man's dwelling, and a knife for every white man's heart upon our frontier.

Nor will even the most rigorous punishment give perfect security against these Indians so long as any of them are left among or in the vicinity of our border settlements. The Indian's nature can no more be trusted than the wolf's. Tame him, cultivate him, strive to Christianize him as you will, and the sight of blood will in an instant call out the savage, wolfish, devilish instincts of the race. It is notorious that among the earliest and most murderous of the Sioux, in perpetrating their late massacre, were many of the "civilized Indians," so called, with their hair cut short, wearing white men's clothes, and dwelling in brick houses built for them by the government.

These facts are well known to our border settlers, and appreciated by them as they cannot be by those who live in the midst of populous communities, far away from the savage foe. These facts have made the question simply whether the Indians or the white race shall possess Minnesota. What immigrant will bring his family to a land where the savages are in such close proximity that he is liable any day to be shot by an ambushed foe in his own door-yard, or on his return home from his day's labor to find his family outraged and murdered.

Minnesota is the best farming State in the Union, by its natural advantages of soil, climate and position. It is capable of sustaining a purely agricultural population of millions, and in addition possesses great facilities for manufacturing.

Shall we who have made our homes here under the promised protection of the national government, who have paid that government the required price for the land on which we have made our homes, be driven into exile by the savages from whom government bought the soil of almost the whole State, and against whom that government is bound to protect us?

We respectfully ask, we demand, that the captive Indians now in the hands of our military forces, proved before a military commission to be guilty of murder, and even worse crimes, shall receive the punishment due those crimes. This, too, not merely as a matter of vengeance, but as much more a matter of security for our border settlers.

We hope that men whose friends and relations have been foully murdered by these Indian devils will not be compelled to take vengeance into their own hands, as they assuredly will if government shall fail in its duty in the matter.

D.

Executive Mansion,
Washington, December 6, 1862.

Ordered, That of the Indians and half-breeds sentenced to be hanged by the military commission composed of Colonel Crooks, Lieutenant Colonel Marshall, Captain Grant, Captain Bayley, and Lieutenant Olin, and lately sitting in Minnesota, you cause to be executed, on Friday, the nineteenth day of December instant, the following named, to wit:

Te-he-hdo-ne-cha	No. 2 by the record.
Ta-zoo, alias Plan-doo-ta	No. 4 by the record.
Wy-a-teh-to-wah	No. 5 by the record.
Hin-han-shoon-ko-yag	No. 6 by the record.
Muz-za-bom-a-du	No. 10 by the record.
Wah-pay-du-ta	No. 11 by the record.

Wa-he-hud	No. 12 by the record.
Sua-ma-ni	No. 14 by the record.
Ta-te-mi-ma	No. 15 by the record.
Rda-in-yan-kua	No. 19 by the record.
Do-wan-sa	No. 22 by the record.
Ha-pan	No. 24 by the record.
Shoon-ka-ska (White Dog)	No. 35 by the record.
Toon-kan-e-chah-tah-mane	No. 67 by the record.
E-tay-hoo-tay	No. 68 by the record.
Am-da-cha	No. 69 by the record.
Hay-pee-don, or Wamne-omne-ho-ta	No. 70 by the record.
Mahpe-o-ke-na-ji	No. 96 by the record.
Henry Milord, a half-breed	No. 115 by the record.
Chaskay-don, or Chaskay-etah	No. 121 by the record.
Baptist Campbell, a half-breed	No. 138 by the record.
Tah-ta-kay-gay	No. 155 by the record.
Ha-pink-pa	No. 170 by the record.
Hypolite Ange, a half-breed	No. 175 by the record.
Na-pay-shue	No. 178 by the record.
Wa-kan-tan-ka	No. 210 by the record.
Toon-kan-ka-yag-e-na-jin	No. 225 by the record.
Ma-kat-e-na-jin	No. 254 by the record.
Pa-zee-koo-tay-ma-ne	No. 264 by the record.
Ta-ta-hde-don	No. 279 by the record.
Wa-she-choon, or Toon-can-shkan-mene-hay	No. 318 by the record.
A-e-cha-ga	No. 327 by the record.
Ha-tan-in-koo	No. 333 by the record.
Chay-ton-hoon-ka	No. 342 by the record.
Chan-ka-hda	No. 359 by the record.
Hda-hin-hday	No. 373 by the record.
O-ya-tay-a-koo	No. 377 by the record.
May-hoo-way-wa	No. 382 by the record.
Wa-kin-yan-na	No. 383 by the record.

The other condemned prisoners you will hold, subject to further orders, taking care that they neither escape nor are subjected to any unlawful violence.

ABRAHAM LINCOLN,
President of the United States.

Brigadier General H. H. Sibley,
St. Paul, Minnesota.

E.

Sir: Having, by your directions, examined the records of the convictions of Sioux Indians by the military commission ordered by Brigadier General Sibley, we submit the following list of those who were convicted of rape and murder, viz:

No. 1. O-TA-KLA, alias GODFREY, a negro. — engaged extensively in the massacres, and, though sentenced to be hung, recommended to have his punishment commuted to imprisonment for ten years, because of the valuable testimony and information he furnished the commission.

No. 2. TE-HE-HDO-NE-CHA. — Engaged in the massacres; took a white woman prisoner, and *ravished* her.

No. 4. TAZOO, alias PLAN-DOO-TA. — Convicted of participating in the murder of Mr. Patville, and of ravishing a young girl.

No. 5. WY-A-TAH-TO-WAH. — Confesses to have participated in the murder of Mr. Francis Patville, and to have been engaged in three battles.

No. 6. HIN-HAN-SHOON-KO-YAG-MA-NE. — Convicted of the murder of Alexander Hunter, and of having taken and had Mrs. Hunter a prisoner until she was rescued from him by another Indian.

No. 10. MUZ-ZA-BOM-A-DU. — Convicted of the murder of an old man and two children.

No. 11. WAH-PA-DU-TA. — Confesses that he was engaged in the massacres, and that he shot a white man.

No. 12. WA-HE-HUD. — Convicted of participating in the battles, and of murder.

No. 14. SUA-MA-NI. — Convicted of the murder of two persons.

No. 15. TA-TE-MI-MA. — Convicted of murder, and of the capture of women and children.

No. 19. RDA-IN-YAN-KUA. — Took a prominent part in all the battles, including the attack on New Ulm, leading and urging the Indians forward, and opposing the giving up of the captives when it was proposed by others.

No. 22. DO-WAN-SA. — Convicted of the murder of a white woman, and of the design to *ravish* her daughter, who was wounded by him and killed by another Indian before he had carried his design into execution.

No. 24. HA-PAN. — Confessed that he was in all the battles and at the murder of Mr. Patville, and that he aided in taking a white woman (Miss Williams) prisoner.

No. 35. SHOON-KA-SHA. (White Dog.) — Was the leader of the party that attacked Captain Marsh's company, and was the man who detained Captain Marsh in conversation until the Indians crossed the river and surrounded the command, and then gave them the signal to fire.

No. 67. TOON-KAN-CHAH-TAY-MANE. — Said in presence of witness that he shot a man in an ox-wagon, and was in several battles.

No. 68. E-TAY-HOO-TAY. — Told witness that he killed Divoll and seven white persons across the river; that the second day after crossing the river he killed a man and a woman.

No. 69. OM-DA-CHA. — Took witness; David Farribault, prisoner, who says he shot two persons at his house.

No. 70 HAY-PEE-DON, or WAMNE-OMNE-HO-TA. — Cut Mrs. Thieler with a hatchet after she had been shot by another Indian, and fired many shots at the fort.

No. 96. MAHPE-O-KE-NA-JI. — Convicted of the murder of Antoine Young, and of participating in the murder of another man, four women, and eleven children.

No. 115. HENRY MILORD, a half-breed. — Convicted of participating in the murder of a white man and woman. — (See cases 138 and 175.)

No. 121. CHASKAY-DON, or CHASKAY-ETAY. — Convicted of shooting and cutting open a woman who was with child.

No. 138. BAPTISTE CAMPBELL, a half-breed.—Confessed that he was one of the party who murdered a man and woman, and that he shot first.—(See cases 115 and 175.)

No. 155 TAY-TA-KA-GAY.—Convicted of murdering or of participating in the murder of Amos W. Huggins.

No. 170. HA-PINK-PA.—Convicted of the murder of Garvie.

No. 175. HYPOLITE ANGE, a half-breed.—Confesses that he was one of the party that murdered a white man, and that he fired at him.—(See cases 115 and 138.)

No. 178. NA-PA-SHUE.—Convicted of participating in a massacre, and boasted that he had killed nineteen persons.

No. 210. WA-KAN-TAN-KA.—Convicted of the murder of a white man not named.

No. 225. TOON-KAN-KA-YAG-E-NA-JIN.—Convicted of participating in the murder of a white man at the Big Woods.

No. 254. MA-KAT-E-NA-JIN.—Convicted of participating in the massacres near New Ulm, and of encouraging the young men to do so.

No. 264. PA-ZE-KOO-TAY-MA-NE.—Convicted of participating in the murder of a party of eight white men.

No. 279. TA-TAY-HDE-DON.—Convicted of participating in the massacre at Beaver creek, and of taking captive a white woman.

No. 318. WA-SHE-CHOON, OR TOON-KAN-SHKAN-SHKAN-MENE-HAY.—Convicted of participating in the murder of LaButt's son.

No. 327. A-E-CHA-GA.—Convicted of participating in the murder of an old man and two girls.

No. 333. HA-TAN-IN-KOO.—Convicted of participating in the murder of a man at Green lake; admits that he struck him with an axe after he had been shot by others of the party.

No. 342. CHAY-TON-HOON-KA.—Proved to have been one of a party that committed the massacres at Beaver creek.

No. 359. CHAN-KA-HDA.—Is proven to have been of the party, and present when Patville was killed, and to have saved Mary Anderson (who had been wounded) from being killed, and to have taken her prisoner.

No. 373. HDA-HIN-HDAY.—Convicted of the murder of Mrs. Adam's child, and others. Was one of the party that brought Mrs. Adams in.

No. 377. O-YA-TAY-A-KOO.—Convicted of participating in the murder of Patville.

No. 382. MA-HOO-WAY-WA.—Convicted of participating in the massacre at "Travellers' Home," and of murdering a man on the road near there.

No. 383. WA-KIN-YAN-NA.—Convicted of participating in the murder, near the "Travellers' Home," of an old man, two young girls, and two boys.

To facilitate your reference to these particular cases we have withdrawn the papers from the records of the commission and submit them herewith.

With great respect, your obedient servants,
GEORGE C. WHITING.
FRANCIS H. RUGGLES.
Executive Mansion, *December 5, 1862.*

I. The Executions

The largest mass execution ever conducted in the United States was a matter of great interest to the citizens of Minnesota who had suffered greatly at the hands of the Sioux. This account of the executions was compiled by correspondents on the scene and published two days later by a newspaper in St. Paul. It provides a fascinating description of the bureaucratic aspects of the execution as well as the last words of each of the condemned the night before they were to be hanged. Most of the accused still claimed that they were innocent. One of the condemned was pardoned by Lincoln at the last minute — hence the number of last minute statements is thirty-nine, not the thirty-eight that were actually executed. There was a great concern that even at this late date, a lynching attempt could be launched by irate citizens. For this reason, hundreds of troops including the Tenth Regiment were deployed around the scene of the executions to maintain order. The account of the reporters follows. The astounding thing is that the tone and nature of the comments by the reporters in 1862 are the exactly the same as seen by the public in the 21st century. Only the media has changed. Read on.

The Execution of the Sioux Murderers[1]

> 38 Savages Expiate their Crimes on the Scaffold
> Proceedings before the day of execution
> The Military Orders of Col. Miller
> Statements and Confessions of the Condemned
> Baptismal and other religious ceremonies
> Preparations for Death

The Execution

From our own reporter.
Mankato, Friday Evening, Dec 26.

We arrived at Mankato early this morning. All along the Valley we found great excitement existing in reference to the execution of the convicted Sioux murderers, who were sentenced to expiate their awful crimes upon the gallows to-day. Every community in the whole Western part of the State had its representative on the ground this morning, and from the nearer ones, there were hundreds present. We saw none of the indications of mere idle curiosity, which commonly stimulate the gathering of crowds to witness an execution; but, in the place of that, there was a desire to be present, from a sense of duty, to witness the death of a portion of a horde of savage fiends who had desolated a whole frontier, and to give countenance by their presence, to the justice of the sentence of the Military Court which condemned them, and of the confirmatory sentence of the President.

Before narrating the incidents of the day, we have thought it might be interesting to give a description of the preceding events, covering the preparations made, the official orders promulgated, and the statements and confessions of the condemned, that the whole account of this most remarkable event in the history of our State, might be presented in consecutive order. And with reference to these, we beg to acknowledge our obligations to the editor of the Mankato Record, for his courtesy in furnishing us proof-sheets of the documents given, thus saving us the trouble of transcribing them, and enabling us to place this narrative before our readers in full and at an early date.

Beginning with the present week, we find the first order to be on
Prohibiting The Sale of Liquor to Indians
On Monday afternoon the following order was read on the dress parade:

GENERAL ORDER NO. 18

HEADQUARTERS INDIAN POST,
Mankato, Dec 22d, 1862

All persons residing in Mankato and the adjoining territory, for the distance of ten miles from these headquarters, are hereby notified to sell or give no intoxicating liquors of any description, including wine and beer, to the enlisted men of the United States forces in this valley or vicinity, unless it be upon an order from, or approved by the Colonel commanding.

Any violation of this order will be followed by the immediate seizure and destruction of all the liquors of the offender, and by such other punishment as the nature of the case may demand.

A vigilant patrol will be organized to visit suspected places, wagons, rooms, booths, etc., and to carry these orders into execution.

J. K. ARNOLD,
Adjutant 7th Regt. Min. Vols.
Post Adjutant.

APPOINTMENT OF MARSHALS.

On Monday evening the following order was issued and read on dress parade, announcing Marshals to aid in preserving order on the day of execution.

GENERAL ORDERS NO. 17

HEADQUARTERS INDIAN POST,
Mankato, Dec 22d, 1862

Col. Benjamin F. Smith, of Mankato; Major W. H. Dike, of Faribault; Hon. Henry A. Swift and H. W. Lamberton, Esq., of St. Peter; Edwin Bradley, Mr. E. H. Dike, of Mankato; and Reuben Butters of Kasota, together with such other good citizens as they may select, are hereby requested to act at this place on Friday, 26th inst., as Mounted Citizen Marshals, Col. B. F. Smith as Chief and the others as assistants.

The Colonel Commanding respectfully recommends that they assemble at Mankato the present evening and adopt such wholesome measures as may contribute to the preservation of good order, and strict propriety during the said 26th instant.

By order of the Col. Commanding,
J.K. ARNOLD, Post Adjutant.

Citizens Petition for Martial Law.

For the better preservation of order on the day of execution, citizens of Mankato, on Tuesday last, addressed the following note to Colonel Miller, requesting him to declare martial law in the town and vicinity.

Mankato, December 22, 1862

Stephen Miller, Col. 7th Reg't Minn. Vols.

Sir: There is every probability that at the execution of a portion of the Sioux Indians, on the 26th instant, now in your charge, there will be a large collection of people at this place, and in view of the excited state of the country occasioned by the outrages perpetrated by these Indians, it is apprehended that some disturbance may possibly occur on the occasion. Desirous to see law and order maintained, of prohibiting the sale of all intoxicating liquor for three days, including the day before and the day after the execution, at the town and within a circle of five miles thereof. This, we presume, cannot be done without the declaration of martial law, and if this suggestion meets your views, we will be happy to see you do so; and will use our influence to aid you in preserving the peace of the community and in maintaining the supremacy of the law. In making this suggestion we have no desire to intermeddle with your duties as a military officer, or to dictate to you what course you shall take on that occasion; our principal object being to inform you that in case you should take the same view of the matter that we do, that you may rely on our sustaining you in that course.

The above letter was signed by a large number of citizens of Mankato, including, we believe, nearly or quite all the dealers in intoxicating liquors in the town.

Martial Law Declared.

On Wednesday evening the following order in accordance with the above request, was issued by Col. Miller.

Headquarters Indian Post,
Mankato, Dec. 24, 1862

GENERAL ORDER NO. 21.

The Colonel Commanding publishes the following Rules to govern all who may be concerned: and for the preservation of the public peace, declares Martial Law, over all the territory within a circle of ten miles of these Headquarters.

It is apprehended by both civil and military authorities, as well as by many of the prominent citizens and business men, that the use of intoxicating liquors, about the time of the approaching Indian execution may result in a serious riot or breach of the peace; and the unrestrained distribution of such beverages to enlisted men is always subversive of good order and military discipline.

The good of the service, the honor of the State, and the protection of all concerned, imperatively requires that, for a specified period, the sale, gift, or use, of all intoxicating drinks, including wines, beer, and malt liquors, be entirely suspended.

From this necessity, and for the said purposes, martial law is hereby declared in and about all territory, buildings, tents, booths, camps, quarters, and other places within the aforesaid limits, to take effect at three o'clock on Thursday morning, the 25th inst.

Accordingly, the sale, tender, gift or other use of all intoxicating liquors as above named, by soldiers, sojourners, or citizens, is entirely prohibited until Saturday evening, the 27th instant, at eleven o'clock.

The said prohibition to continue as to sales or gifts of all intoxicating liquors as before described, to enlisted men in the service of the Unites States — except upon special written orders or permission from these headquarters — until officially revoked by the commandant of this post.

For the purpose of giving full scope and effect to this order, a special patrol will visit all suspected camps, tents, booths, rooms, wagons and other places, and seize and destroy all liquors, so tendered, given, sold, or used, and break the vessels containing the same, and report this circumstances, with the name of the offender, to these headquarters.

This order will be read at the head of every company of the United States forces serving or coming within said limits.

STEPHEN MILLER.
Colonel 7th Regiment Minn. Vols.,
Commanding Post.

Official:
J. K. ARNOLD
Adjutant 7th Regiment Minnesota Volunteers,
   Post Adjutant.

Reading of the Death Warrant

On Monday last the thirty-nine Indians sentenced by the President were selected out and confined in an apartment separate and distinct from the other Indians.

About half-past two o'clock, Col. Miller, accompanied by his staff officers, ministers, and a few others, visited them in their cell for the purpose of reading to them the President's approval of their sentence, and the order for their execution. The Rev. Mr. Riggs acted as interpreter and through him Col. Miller addressed the prisoners in substance as follows:

The commanding officer at this place has called to speak to you upon a very serious subject this afternoon. Your Great Father at Washington, after carefully reading what the witnesses have testified in your several trials, has come to the conclusion that you have each been guilty of wantonly and wickedly murdering his white children; and for this reason he has directed that you each be hanged by the neck until you are dead, on next Friday; and that order will be carried into effect on that day at ten o'clock in the forenoon.

Good ministers — both Catholic and Protestant — are here, from amongst whom each of you can select your spiritual adviser, who will be permitted to commune with you constantly during the four days that you are yet to live.

The Colonel then instructed Adjutant Arnold to read to them in English the letter of President Lincoln, which in substance orders that thirty-nine prisoners, whose names are given, shall be executed at the time above stated. The Rev. Mr. Riggs then read the letter in the Dakota language.

The Colonel further instructed Mr. Riggs to tell them that they have sinned so against their fellow-men that there is no hope of clemency except in the mercy of God, through the merits of the Blessed Redeemer, and that he earnestly exhorted them to apply to that as their only remaining source of consolation.

The occasion was one of much solemnity to the persons, though but very little emotion was manifested by the Indians. A half-breed, named Milford, seemed much depressed in spirits. All listened attentively, and at the conclusion of each sentence, indulged their usual grunt or signal of approval. At the reading of that portion of the warrant condemning them to be hanged by the necks, the response was quite feeble, and was given by only two or three. Several Indians smoked their pipes composedly during the reading, and one was observed in particular who, when the time of execution was designated, quietly knocked the ashes from his pipe and filled it afresh with his favorite kinno-kinnick; while another was slowly rubbing a pipe-full of the same article in his hands, preparatory to a good smoke.

The Indians were evidently prepared for the visit and the announcement of their sentence—one or two having overheard soldiers talking about it when they were removed to a separate apartment.

At the conclusion of the ceremony, Col. Miller instructed Major Brown to tell the Indians that each would be privileged to designate the minister of his choice, that a record of the same would be made, and the minister so selected would have free intercourse with him.

The Colonel and spectators then withdrew, leaving the ministers in consultation with the prisoners.

The Indians under sentence were confined in a back room on the first floor of Leech's stone building, chained in pairs, and closely and strongly guarded.

NAMES OF THE CONDEMNED.

The following are the Indian names of the condemned Indians, also the meaning of each, as translated by Ref. S. R. Riggs:

Dakota.	English.
Te-he-do-ne-cha	One who forbids his house.
Ptan-doo-ta, or Ta-joo	Red Otter
Wy-a-tah-ta-wa	His People
Hin-hau-hoon-ka-yag-ma-ne	One who walks clothed with an Owl's Tail
Ma-za-boon-doo	Iron Blower
Wan-pa-doo-ta	Red Leaf
Wa-he-kna	Don't know the meaning
Rwa-ma-ne	Tinkling Walker
Ta-tay-me-ma	Round Wind
Rda-in-yan-ka	Rattling Runner
Do-wan-sa	The Singer
Ha-pan	Second child if a son
Shoon-ka-sha	White Dog
Toon-kan-e-chah-tay-ma-ne	One who walks by his grandfather
E-tay-doo-tay	Red Face
Am-da-cha	Broken to Pieces
Hay-pe-dan	The Third Child, if a son
Mah-pe-o-ke-ne-jin	Who stands on the cloud
Henry Milord	a half-breed
Chas-ka-dan	The First Born, if a son
Baptiste Campbell	a half-breed
Ta-tay-ka-gay	Wind Maker
Ha-pin-kpa	The tip of the horn
Hypolite Ange	a half-breed
Na,pay-shin	One who does not flee
Wa-kan-tan-ka	Great Spirit
Toon-kan-ko-yag-e-na-jin	One who stands Clothed with his Grandfather
Ma-ka-ta-e-ne-jin	One who stands on the earth
Pa-za-koo-tay-wa-nee	One who walks prepared to shoot
To-tay-hde-dan	Wind comes home

Dakota.	English.
Wa-she-choon	Frenchman
A-e-che-ga	To grow Upon
Ho-tan-in-koo	Voice that Appears Coming
Chao-tan-hoon-ka	The parent Hawk
Chan-ka-had	Near the Wood
Hda-hin-hday	To make a rattling noise suddenly
O-ya-tay-a-koo	The coming People
Ma-hoo-way-wa	He comes for me
Wa-kin-yan-na	Little Thunder

CONFESSIONS AND PROTESTATIONS OF THE CONDEMNED.

The following is a synopsis of the conversations held with the condemned prisoners, by the Rev. S. R. Riggs, and written out by him for publication, as an authentic record of their dying confessions and protestations:

Te-he-do-ne-cha (One who forbids his House) says he was asleep when the outbreak took place at the Lower Agency. He was not present at the breaking open of the stores, but afterwards went over the Minnesota and took some women captives. The men who were killed there, he says, were killed by other Indians, whom he named.

Ptan-doo-ta, alias Ta-joo (Red Otter) says he had very sore eyes at the time of the outbreak, and was at that time down opposite Fort Ridgley. He was with the party that killed Patwell and others. Maza-bom-do killed Patwell. He himself took Miss Williams captive. Says he would have violated the women, but they resisted. He thinks he did a good deed in saving the women alive.

Wy-a-tah-ta-wa, (His People) says he was at the attack on Capt. Marsh's company, and also at New Ulm. He and another Indian shot a man at the same time. He does not know whether he or the Indian killed the white man. He was wounded in following up another white man. He was at the battle of Birch Coolie, where he fired his gun four times. He fired twice at Wood Lake.

Hin-han-shoon-ko-yag-ma-ne (One who walks clothed in an Owl's Tail) says he is charged with killing white people, and so condemned. He does not know certainly that he killed anyone. He was in all the battles. That is all he has to say.

Ma-za-hom-doo (Iron Blower) says he was down on the Big Cottonwood when the outbreak took place; that he came that day into New Ulm and purchased various articles, and then started home. He met the Indians coming down. Saw some men in wagons shot, but does not know who killed them. He was present at the killing of Patwell and others, but denies having done it himself. He thinks he did well by Mattie Williams and Mary Swan, in keeping them from being killed. They now live and he has to die, which he thinks not quite (fair?)

Wah-pa-doo-ta (Red Leaf) is an old man. He says he was mowing when he heard of this outbreak. He saw some men after they were killed about the Agency, but did not kill anyone there. He started down to the Fort, and went on to the New Ulm settlement. There he shot at a man through a window, but does not think he killed him. He was himself wounded at New Ulm.

Wa-he-hua, (do not know what this name means,) says he did not kill anyone. If he had believed he had killed a white man he would have fled with Little Crow. The witnesses lied on him.

Sna-ma-ne (Tinkling Walker) says he was condemned on the testimony of two German boys. They say he killed two persons. The boys told lies, he was not at that place at all.

Ta-tay-me-ma, (Round Wind) is a brother-in-law of the former well known Mr. Joseph Renville. He was the public camp crier of Little Crow, before and during the outbreak. After the battle of Wood Lake, he came over to the opposition, and was the crier at Camp Release, when the captives were delivered up. He was condemned on the testimony of two German boys, who said they saw him kill their mother. The old man denies the charge — says he was not across the river at the time, and that he was unjustly condemned. He is the only one of the thirty-nine who has been at all in the habit of attending Protestant worship. On last Sabbath he requested Dr. Williamson to baptize him, professing repentance and faith in Jesus Christ; which was done on Monday, before he knew that he was among those to be hung at this time. May God have mercy on his soul.

Rda-in-yan-ka, (Rattling Runner) says he did not know of the uprising on Monday, the 18th of August, until they had killed a number of men. He then went out and met Little Crow, and tried to stop the murders, but could not. The next day his son was brought home wounded from Fort Ridgley. He forbade the delivery of the white captives to Paul when he commanded them, and he supposes that he is to be hung for that.

Do-wan-sa (The Singer) says he was one of six who were down in the Swan Lake neighborhood. He knows that they killed two men and two women, but this was done by the rest of the party, and not by himself.

Ha-pin (Second Child, if a son) says he was not in the massacres of New Ulm nor the Agency. He was with the company who killed Patwell and his companions. He took one of the women. O-ya-tay-ta-wa killed Patwell.

Shoon-ka-ska (White Dog) says that when the outbreak took place, he ran away, and did not get any of the stolen property. At the ferry, he talked with Quinn. First, called to them to come over, but when he saw that the Indians were in ambush, he beckoned to Capt. Marsh to stay back. He says that his position and conduct at the ferry were misunderstood and misrepresented; that he wanted peace, and did not command the Indians to fire on Capt. Marsh's men; that another man could be put to death for that. He complains bitterly that he did not have a chance to tell the things as they were; that he could not have an opportunity of rebutting the false testimony against him. (His further testimony is unreadable).

Toon-kan-e-chah-tay-ma-ne (One who walks by his grandfather) says he took nothing from the stores except a blanket. He was at Fort Ridgley, but killed nobody. He is charged with killing white persons, but he did not. They were killed by another man.

E-tay-doo-tay (Red-Face) says he was woke up on Monday, the 18th of August, and went with others to the stores, but did not kill anyone.

Am-da-cha (Broken to Pieces) says he was doctoring a girl when he learned about the outbreak at the Lower Agency. He went with others and brought some things from Mr. Forbes' store. He fired his gun only twice, but thinks he did not kill anyone.

Hay-pe-dan (The Third Child, if a son) says he was not at the stores until all was over there. He was with Wabasha, and with him opposed the outbreak. He was afterwards driven into it by being called a coward. He went across the Minnesota River and took two horses, and afterwards captured a woman and two children. He tried to keep a white man from being killed, but could not. He was at the ferry when Marsh's men were killed, but had only a bow and arrows there. He was in three battles and shot six times, but does not know that he killed anyone.

Mah-pe-o-ke-na-jin (Who Stands on the Clouds) Cut nose — says that when Little Crow proposed to kill the traders, he went along. He says he is charged with having killed a carpenter; but he did not do it. He fired off his gun in one of the stores. His nephew was killed at Fort Ridgley. He was out at Hutchinson when his son was killed. Little Crow took them out. He was hungry and went over the river to kill an ox, when there he saved Mr. Brown's family.

Henry Milord, a half-breed. Henry says he went over the Minnesota River with Baptiste Campbell and others. They were forced to go by Little Crow. He fired his gun at a woman, but does not think that he killed her. Several others fired at her also. He did not see her afterwards. Henry Milord was raised by Gen. Sibley. He is a smart, active, intelligent young man; and as such, would be likely to be drawn into the Dakota rebellion. Indeed it was next to impossible for young men, whether half-breeds or full bloods, to keep out of it. They are to be pitied as well as blamed.

Chas-kay-dan (The First Born, if a son) says he went to the stores in the morning of Monday. There he saw Little Crow taking away goods. He then went up to Red Wood, with a relation of his. They were there told that a white man was coming on the road. They went out to meet him; but the first who came along was a half-breed. They let him pass. Then came along Mr. Gleason and Mrs. Wakefield. His friend shot Mr. Gleason, and attempted to fire on him, but his gun did not go off. He saved Mrs. Wakefield and the children; and now he dies while she lives.

Baptiste Campbell is the son of Scott Campbell, who was for many years United States Interpreter at Fort Snelling. He thinks they ought to have had a new trial. Says he did not speak advisedly when before the military commission. He went over the Minnesota River with four others. They were sent over by Little Crow, and told to get all the cattle they could and kill every white man — if they did not the Soldiers' Lodge would take care of them. They went over to a farm between Beaver Creek and Birch Coolie, where they found a lot of cattle which they attempted to drive. The cattle, however, ran away, and then their attention was called to the owner. Campbell fired off his gun first, but did not hit the man. He says his statement before the commission was misunderstood. He said he was a good shot, and if he had fired on the man he would have killed him. He fired over him intentionally. He fired because he felt compelled to do so by command of Little Crow. Campbell says that Little Crow compelled him and his brother Joseph to go out to Hutchinson. They tried to get away at the time of the attack on Captain Strout's company, but were prevented. They were forced to go to the battle of Hutchinson. Little Crow told them that if they did not kill white men they would be killed; but he did not shoot any men there.

Ta-ta-Ra-gay (Wind Maker) is quite a young man, grandson of Sacred Walker, who took care of Mrs. Josephine Higgins and her children in their captivity. He was one of those who killed Amos W. Huggins, at Lac-qui-Parle. The other two, who are probably the most guilty, have escaped. He says he was at Red Iron's village when he heard of the outbreak. Another Indian urged him to go up with him and kill Mr. Huggins. He refused at first, but afterwards went. His comrade shot Mr. H. and killed him. He then (unreadable). He refused at first, but afterwards went. His comrade shot Mr. H. and killed him. He then fired off his gun, but held it up.

Hay-pin-kpa (The Tip of the Horn) is condemned because he boasted of having shot Stewart B. Garvie with an arrow. As it is not known that Mr. Garvie was shot with an arrow, but with buck-shot, it is probably true, as he said before the Commission, that he lied about it. This is not the first time a man has been killed for lying. He now says that they determined to send off all the white people from Yellow Medicine without killing any. Mr. Garvie refused to go. He did not shoot him. He dies without being guilty of the charge, and he trusts in the Great Spirit to save him in the other world.

Hypolite Auge is a half-breed. He says he had been a clerk in one of the stores for a year previous to the outbreak. He was sent down the Minnesota River with Baptiste Campbell and others by Little Crow. He shot the white man, but not until after he had been killed by others.

Na-pay-shne (One who does not Flee) says that at the time of the outbreak he was quite lame; that he was not engaged in any of the massacres. He was not engaged in any of the battles, but was forced with others to come down to the Yellow Medicine before the battle of Wood Lake. He dies for no fault of his.

Wa-kan-tan-ka (Great Spirit) says he was not present at the commencement of the outbreak. He was along with the company which came down towards New Ulm. He saw the men in two wagons killed, but he did not kill anyone. He says one witness before the Commission testified that he killed one of those men, but the witness lied on him.

Toon-kan-ko-yag-e-na-jin, (One who Stands clothed with his Grandfather,) says that he was in the battle of Birch Coolie. He was also in the battle at Hutchinson, but does not know that he killed anyone.

Ma-ka-ta — e-na-jin, (One who Stands on the Earth), is an old man. He says he has not used a gun for years. He was down at New-Ulm, but did not kill anyone. He had two sons killed. He wants to have the truth told.

Pa-za-koo-tay-ma-ne, (One who walks Prepared to shoot,) says that he was out in a war party against the Chippewa when the outbreak took place. When he came back the massacres were over. He did not kill anyone. He says that his statement before the Commission was misunderstood. When he was asked whether he was on a war party and fired his gun, he replied, "Yes," but it was against the Chippewa's, and not the whites.

Ta-tay-hde-dan, (Wind Comes Home,) says that the men of Rice Creek were the authors of the outbreak. He tried to keep them from killing white people, but only succeeded partially.

Wa-she-choon, (Frenchman), says he did not know anything about killing white people. He is to die for no crime. He was very much affected.

A-e-cha-ga, (To Grow Upon,) is charged with participating in the murder of an old man and two girls. He made neither confession nor denial.

Ho-tan-in-koo, (Voice that appears coming) says he did not have a gun. He was at the Big Woods, and struck a man with his hatchet after he had been shot by another man. He did not abuse any white woman.

Khay-tan-hoon-ka, (The Parent Hawk,) says he did not kill anyone. He was down at Fort Ridgeley. He was also over at Beaver Creek and took horses from there, but did not kill the man.

Chan-ka-had (Near the Wood,) says he took Mary Anderson captive after she had been shot by another man. He thinks it rather hard that he is to be hung for another's crime.

Hda-hin-hday. (To make a Rattling Noise Suddenly) says that he was up north at the time of the outbreak and did not come down until after the killing of the whites was past. He was at the battle of Wood Lake. He says he is charged with having killed two children, but the charge is false.

O-ya-tay-a-kee, (The Coming People,) says he was with the company who killed

Patwell and others. He is charged with striking him with his hatchet after he was shot. This charge he denies.

Ma-hoo-way-ma, (He comes for me,) says he was out in one of the raids towards the Big Woods. He did not kill anybody, but he struck a woman who had been killed before. He was himself wounded.

Wa-kin-yan-wa, (Little Thunder,) says that he is charged with having murdered one of Coursall's children, but the child is still living. He has seen the child since he was before the Military Commission. He has done nothing worthy of death. And now, guilty and not guilty, may God have mercy upon these thirty-nine poor human creatures; and if it be possible save them in the other world, through Jesus Christ His Son. Amen. In making these statements, confessions and denials, they were generally calm; but a few individuals were quite excited. They were immediately checked by others, and told that they were all dead men, and there was no reason why they should not all tell the truth. Many of them have indicated letters to their friends in which they say that they are very dear to them, but will see them no more. They exhort them not to cry or change their dress for them. Some of them say they expect to go and dwell with the Good Spirit and express the hope that their friends will all join them. On Tuesday evening they extemporized a dance, with a wild Indian song. It was feared that this was only a cover for something else which might be attempted, and their chains were thereafter fastened to the floor. It seems, however, rather probable that they were only singing their death-song. Their friends from the other prison have been in to bid them farewell, and they are now ready to die. S. R. R.

LETTER FROM ONE OF THE CONDEMNED INDIANS

The following is a copy of a letter from one of the condemned prisoners to his chief and father-in-law, Wabasha. It was taken down in the exact language dictated by the prisoner:

"Wabasha: You have deceived me. You told me that if we followed the advice of General Sibley, and give ourselves up to the whites, all would be well — no innocent man would be injured. I have not killed, wounded, or injured a white man, or any white persons. I have not participated in the plunder of their property; and yet to-day, I am set apart for execution and must die in a few days, while men who are guilty will remain in prison. My wife is your daughter, my children are your grandchildren. I leave them all in your care and under your protection. Do not let them suffer, and when my children are grown up, let them know that their father died because he followed the advice of his chief, and without having the blood of a white man to answer for to the Great Spirit. My wife and children are dear to me. Let them not grieve for me. Let them remember that the brave should be prepared to meet death; and I will do so as becomes a Dacotah."

Your Son-in-Law,
RDA-IN-YAN-KNA.

The above Indian was convicted of participating in the murders and robberies at the Upper Agency; and the sworn testimony at Washington differs materially from his confession as given above.

THE LAST INTERVIEWS OF
THE CONDEMNED WITH THEIR FRIENDS.

Wednesday, the 24th, was set apart for the interviews between the condemned and such of their relatives and friends as were confined in the main prison; for the purpose of exchanging adieus, and for the delivery of such messages to absent relatives as each one might desire to send. Major Brown was present during these interviews, and describes them as very sad and affecting. The following is taken from his account furnished to the Mankato Record:

Each Indian had some word to send his parents or family. When speaking of their wives and children almost everyone was affected to tears. Good counsel was sent to the children. They were in many cases exhorted to an adoption of Christianity and the life of good feeling toward the whites. Most of them spoke confidently of their hopes of salvation. They had been constantly attended by the Rev. Dr. Williamson, the Rev. Van Ravoux and the Rev. S. R. Riggs, whose efforts in bringing these poor criminals to a knowledge of the merits of the Blessed Redeemer, had been eminently successful. These gentlemen are all conversant with the Dakota language and could converse and plead with the Indians in their own language.

There is a ruling passion with Indians, and Ta-zoo could not refrain from its enjoyment even in this sad hour. Ta-ti-mi-ma was sending word to his relatives not to mourn his loss. He said he was old; and could not hope to live long under any circumstances, and his execution would not shorten his days a great deal, and dying as he did innocent of any white man's blood, he hoped would give him a better chance to be saved; therefore he hoped his friends would consider his death but as a removal from this to a better world. I have every hope, said he, of going direct to the abode of the Great Spirit, where I shall always be happy. This last remark reached the ears of Ta-zoo, who was also speaking to his friends, and he elaborated upon it in this wise: "Yes, tell our friends that we are being removed from this world over the same path they must shortly travel. We go first, but many of our friends may follow us in a very short time. I expect to go direct to the abode of the Great Spirit, and to be happy when I get there; but we are told that the road is long and the distance great, therefore, as I am slow in all my movements, it will probably take me a long time to reach the end of the journey, and I should not be surprised if some of the young, active men we will leave behind us will pass me on the road before I reach the place of my destination."

In shaking hands with Red Iron and Akipa, Ta-zoo said: "Friends, last summer you were opposed to us. You were living in continual apprehension of an attack from those who were determined to exterminate the whites. Yourselves and families were subjected to many taunts, insults, and threats. Still you stood firm in your friendship for the whites, and continually counseled the Indians to abandon their raids against the whites. Your course was condemned at the time, but now we see your wisdom. You were right when you said the whites could not be exterminated, and the attempt indicated folly. Then you and your families were prisoners, and the lives of all in constant danger. To-day you are here at liberty, assisting in feeding and guarding us, and thirty-nine men will die in two days because they did not follow your example and advice."

Several of the prisoners were completely overcome during the leave taking, and were compelled to abandon conversation. Others again (and Tazoo was one) affected to disregard the dangers of their position, and laughed and joked apparently as unconcerned as if they were sitting around a camp fire in perfect freedom.

INTERVIEWS OF WOMEN WITH THE CONDEMNED.

On Thursday, the 25th, the women employed as cooks for the prisoners, all of whom had relations among the condemned, were admitted to the prison. This interview was less sad but was still interesting. Locks of hair, blankets, coats, and almost every other article in the possession of the prisoners were given in trust for some relative or friend who had been forgotten or overlooked during the interview of the day previous. At this interview far less feeling was displayed than at the interview of Wednesday. The idea of allowing women to witness their weakness is repugnant to an Indian, and will account for this. The messages sent were principally advice to their friends to bear themselves with fortitude and refrain from great mourning. The confidence of many in their salvation was again reiterated.

BAPTISM OF PRISONERS.

On Thursday evening the ordinance of baptism was solemnized by the Catholic priests present, and received by a considerable number of the condemned. Some of them entered into the ceremony with an apparently earnest feeling, and an intelligent sense of the solemn character. All seemed resigned to their fate, and depressed in spirits. Most of those not participating in the ceremony sat motionless, and more like statues than living men.

FRIDAY, EXECUTION DAY — AN INTERVIEW WITH THE PRISONERS.

On Friday morning, we accompanied the Rev. Father Ravoux to the prison of the condemned. The whole number were sitting and lying about, in pairs, and disposed as comfortably as their chained condition would permit. There was very little conversation kept up among them, though occasionally one would mutter a few words to another in unintelligible jargon. As a crowd they sat and lay there, smoking their pipes as unconcernedly as if they were engaged in council over some unimportant matter of tribal concern. Absolutely impassive, smoking and rarely muttering, as if their lease of life was eternal, and not bounded by three or four short hours.

The Reverend Father spoke to them of their condition and fate, and in such terms as the devoted priest only can speak. He tried to infuse them with courage — bade them to hold out bravely sand be strong, and to show no sign of fear. While Father Ravoux was speaking to them, old Tazoo broke out in a death-wail, in which one after another joined, until the prison room was filled with a wild, unearthly plaint, which was neither of despair nor grief, but rather a paroxysm of savage passion, most impressive to witness and startling to hear, even by those who understood the language of the music only. During the lulls of their death-song, they would resume their pipes, and with the exception of an occasional mutter, or the rattling of their chains, they sat motionless and impassive; until one among the elder would break out in the wild wail, when all would join again in the solemn preparation for death.

Following this, the Rev. Dr. Williamson addressed them in their native tongue; after which they broke out again in their song of death. This last was thrilling beyond expression. The trembling voices, the forms shaking with passionate emotion, the half uttered words through set teeth, all made up a scene which no one who saw can ever forget.

The influence of the wild music of their death-song upon them was almost magical. Their whole manner changed after they had closed their singing, and an air of cheerful unconcern marked all of them. It seemed as if during their passionate wailing, they had passed in spirit through the valley of the shadow of death, and already had their eyes fixed on the pleasant hunting grounds beyond.

As their friends came about them, they bade them cheerful farewells, and in some cases there would be peals of laughter, as they were wished pleasant journeys to the spirit-land.

They bestowed their pipes upon their favorites, and so far as they had, gave keepsake trinkets to all. Major Brown said there was as much of laughter and fun as if they were going to a feast.

While we were there, the chains were cut from them, and their hands bound behind them. White-Day, begged to be left free, without tying, and it seemed mortification to all when they were bound. One, right in front of us, with a smiling face, which nothing seemed to change, trembled all over, even while he smiled, as the irons were struck from him, and his arms were pinioned. The half-breeds were most visibly affected while these preparations for the gallows were in progress.

They had evidently taken great pains to make themselves presentable for their last appearance on the stage of life. Most of them had little pocket mirrors, and before they were bound, employed themselves in putting on the finishing touches of paint, and arranging their hair according to the Indian mode. All had religious emblems, mostly crosses, of fine gilt or steel, and these were displayed with all the prominence of an exquisite or a religious. Many were painted in war style, with bands, and beads, and feather, and were decked as gaily as for a festival.

None were admitted within the prison besides the priests, the reporters, and the officers and men of the provost guard. They expressed a desire to shake hands with the reporters who were to write about how they looked and acted, and with the artist who was to picture their appearance. So we had to go through the ordeal of shaking hands with the thirty-nine. The hands of most were of the natural warmth, while those of others were cold as ice. Nearly all, on shaking hands, would point their fingers to the sky, and say as plainly as they could, "Me going up!" White Day told us it was Little Crow who got them into the scrape, and now they had to die for it. One said to us there was a Great Spirit above who would take him home, and that he should die happy. Thus the time passed during the tying of hands, and striking off the manacles.

At a little after nine o'clock, the Reverend Father Ravoux entered the prison again, to perform the closing religious exercises. The guard fell back as he came in, the Indians ranging themselves around the room. The Father addressed the condemned at some length, and appeared much affected. He kneeled on the floor in their midst, and prayed with them, all following and uniting with him in an audible voice. They appeared like a different race of beings while going through these religious exercises. Their voices were low and humble, and every exhibition of Indian bravado was banished.

THE HOUR CALLED

While Father Ravoux was speaking to the Indians, and repeating, for the hundredth time, his urgent request that they must think to the last of the Great Spirit before whom they were about to appear, Provost Marshal Redfield entered and whispered a word in the ear of the good priest, who immediately said a word or two in French to Henry Milord, a half-breed who repeated it in Dacotah to the Indians, who were all lying down around the prison. In a moment, every Indian stood erect, and as the Provost Marshal opened the door, they fell in behind him with the greatest alacrity. Indeed, a notice of release, pardon, or reprieve could not have induced them to leave the cell with more apparent willingness, than this call to death. We followed on behind them, and as those at the head of the procession came out of the basement, at the opposite side of the gallows, and directly in front, we heard a sort of a death-wail sounded, which was immediately caught up by all the condemned, and was chanted in unison until the scaffold was reached. At the foot of the steps there was no delay. Capt. Redfield mounted the drop, at the head, and the Indians crowded after him, as if it were a race to see which would get up first. They actually crowded on each other's heels, and as they got to the top, each took his position, without any assistance from those who were detailed for that purpose. They still kept up a mournful wail, and occasionally there would be a piercing scream.

The ropes were soon arranged around their necks, not the least resistance being offered. One or two, feeling the noose uncomfortably tight, attempted to loosen it, and, although their hands were tied, they partially succeeded. The movement, however, was noticed by the assistants, and the cords re-arranged. The white caps, which had been placed on the top of their heads, were now drawn down over their faces, shutting out forever the light of day from their eyes. Then ensued a scene that can hardly be described, and which can never be forgotten. All joined in shouting and singing, as it appeared to those who were ignorant of the language. The tones seemed somewhat discordant, and yet there was harmony in it. Save the moment of cutting the rope, it was the most thrilling moment of the awful scene. And it was not their voices alone. Their bodies swayed to and fro, and their every limb seemed to be keeping time. The drop trembled and shook as if all were dancing. The most touching scene on the drop was their attempts to grasp each other's hands, fettered as they were. They were very close to each other, and many succeeded. Three or four in a row were hand in hand, and all hands swaying up and down with the rise and fall of their voices. One old man reached out each side, but could not grasp a hand. His struggles were piteous, and affected many beholders.

We were informed by those who understand the language, that their singing and shouting was only to sustain each other — that there was nothing defiant in their last moments, and that no "death song," strictly speaking was chanted on the gallows. Each one shouted his own name, and called on the name of his friend, saying in substance, "I'm here! I'm here!"

THE EXECUTION.

Captain Burt hastily scanned all the arrangements for the execution, and motioned to Major Brown, the signal officer, that all was ready. There was one tap of the drum, almost drowned by the voices of the Indians — another, and the stays of the drop were knocked away, the rope cut, and with a crash, down came the drop. One rope broke, but not until the neck of the victim was dislocated, whose body came down on the drop with a heavy thud, and a crash of the boards. There was no struggling by any of the Indians for the space of half a minute — the only movements were the natural vibrations occasioned by the fall.

In the meantime, a new rope was placed around the neck of the one who fell, and, it having been thrown over the beam, he was soon hanging with the others. After the lapse of a minute, several drew up their legs once or twice, and there was some movement of the arms. One Indian, at the expiration of ten minutes, breathed, but the rope was better adjusted, and life was soon extinct. It is unnecessary to speak of the awful sight of thirty-eight human beings suspended in the air. Imagination will readily supply what we refrain from describing.

REMOVING THE BODIES.

After the bodies had hung for about half an hour, the physicians of the several regiments present examined the bodies and reported that life was extinct. Soon after several United States mule teams appeared, when the bodies were taken down and dumped into the wagons without much ceremony, and were carried down to the sand bar in front of the city, and were all buried in the same hole. The half-breeds were buried in one corner of the hole, so that they can be disinterred by their friends.

MILITARY.

The military force for the day was disposed as follows: Col. Wilkin of the 9th regiment, took command of all the troops of the 6th and 9th regiments, and formed them in line of battle at 8½ o'clock, in front of the scaffold, and river front.

Col. Baker, in command of the 10th regiment took up a position on the north side of the scaffold.

Lieut. Col. Marshall, with four companies of the 7th regiment, occupied the South side of the scaffold.

Lieut. Col. Jennison, with one company of the 10th and one of the 7th regiment, occupied the prison yard until the drop fell, when he was relieved by Major Bradley with two companies of the 10th and one company of the 9th.

Companies C, I and K, of the 7th, formed a reserve in front of the prison.

Major Buell, with three companies of cavalry, formed outside of the other forces, under orders of the Colonel Commanding.

Capt. White's mounted company acted as patrol guard.

Lieut. Kennedy's detachment of Capt. White's company were detailed to act as special messengers.

Each commandant of Infantry formed a strong line of sentinels in front of his troops, according to the directions of the Colonel Commanding.

The whole military part of the programme was carried out in the best style. There was no confusion, and every detachment knew its appointed place, and stuck to it. We have never before seen a finer military display in the State. Many detachments came from a long distance, and had a hard tramp of it, and also were not very comfortably quartered in Mankato. Much credit is due to Col. Miller, as well as to all others field officers, for the excellence of their arrangements for the execution, and the good order which everywhere prevailed.

Everything was conducted in the most orderly and quiet manner. As the drop fell the citizens could not repress a shout of exultation, in which the soldiers joined. A boy soldier, who stood beside us, had his mother, and brothers and sisters killed; his face was pale and quivering, but he gave a shout of righteous exultation when the drop fell. The people, who had gathered in great crowds, and who had maintained a degree of order that had not been anticipated, quietly dispersed as the wagons bore the bodies of the murderers off to burial. Few, we take it, who witnessed the awful scene, will voluntarily look upon its like again.

Chapter Notes

Introduction

1. *St. Paul Pioneer*, 20 August 1865, 2.
2. The president bestows the Medal of Honor in the name of Congress.
3. General Nelson Miles, a veteran of the Civil and Indian Wars and himself a Medal of Honor winner was asked in 1916 to lead a panel reviewing Medal of Honor awards and rescind those awards that were not warranted. Miles rescinded 911 awards, but not his own medal. Included in those rescinded were all 864 members of the 27th Maine and the award to William F. Cody. It seems that "Buffalo Bill" was a civilian scout during the Indian Wars and therefore not entitled to the award. Teddy Roosevelt was recommended for the Medal of Honor for his charge at San Juan Hill during the Spanish-American War, but the award was denied. By then, awards had been tightened up to make sure that only the most deserving received the award. The awards for Thomas Gere and John Schofield, mentioned later, survived Miles' review and they died in possession of their Medals of Honor. Others who did not survive the review were asked to return their medals, but by then most were dead and their medals were not returned.
4. The General Sibley who fought for the South was a graduate of the West Point Class of 1838. After the war he moved to Egypt where he devoted his skills to supporting that government and became a brigadier general in the Egyptian army.
5. Gary Clayton Anderson, *Through Dakota Eyes* (St. Paul: Minnesota Historical Society Press, 1988), 23.
6. Mark Diedrich, *Dakota Oratory* (Rochester, MN: Coyote Books, 1989), 46–47.
7. Gary Clayton Anderson, *Little Crow: Spokesman for the Sioux* (St Paul: Minnesota Historical Society Press, 1986), 130.
8. Years later, the author's grandmother and great-grandmother would recall trading with the Indians and helping them when they needed help. It was a way of life on the frontier. If you wanted to survive, you needed to cooperate with everyone including your white neighbors and Native Americans. There was no federal or state safety net to rescue you in hard times.
9. Alvin M. Josephy, Jr., *The Civil War in the American West* (New York: Knopf, 1991), 133.
10. Steven E. Woodworth, *Jefferson Davis and His Generals: The Failure of Confederate Command in the West* (Lawrence: University Press of Kansas, 1990), 18–19.
11. *Ibid.*
12. After Woolson's death, it was thought that some Confederate veterans had outlived him, but this could not be proved. Confused memories of those Confederates who claimed to be veterans and records lost during the Civil War led researchers to conclude that those who died after Woolson were not soldiers in the Confederate Army.
13. Charles E. Flandrau, *The History of Minnesota and Tales of the Frontier* (St. Paul: Porter, 1900), 134–135.
14. Jerome Big Eagle, "A Sioux Story of the War," in Collections *of the Minnesota Historical Society* 6, 386. Chief Big Eagle's narrative was recorded in June 1894 and was published by Robert Holcombe in the *St. Paul Pioneer Press* on July 1, 1894. Holcombe indicated that Big Eagle was frank and unreserved in his testimony. He was sixty-seven years old at that time. Big Eagle's testimony has been reprinted several times since by authors and the Minnesota Historical Society. The page numbers given here are from the Minnesota Historical Society Collection's reprint of the testimony.
15. Micheal Clodfelter, *The Dakota War: The United States Army Versus the Sioux, 1862–1865* (Jefferson, NC: McFarland, 1998), 39.
16. William Watts Folwell, *A History of Minnesota*, vol. 2 (St. Paul: Minnesota Historical Society, 1924), 292.
17. *St. Paul Pioneer*, April 6, 1864.
18. Thomas Jefferson Hunt, *Observations of T. J. Hunt in the Civil War: A Narrative of the Military Life of T. J. Hunt in the Sioux Indian and Civil Wars of 1862–1865*. [Undated], 34.

Chapter 1

1. Diedrich, *Dakota Oratory*, 67.
2. The annuity would arrive at Fort Ridgley the day after the war started. It was too late.
3. The money was due in early July. There were two reasons for the tardy arrival of funds. Congress was late in appropriating the funds (a war was on) and once appropriated a controversy developed as to the form: should it be paper money or gold coinage which had been used in the past. Gold was decided and shipped.
4. Folwell, *A History of Minnesota*, vol. 2, 265
5. Stephen R. Riggs, *Mary and I: Forty Years with the Sioux* (Chicago: Holmes, 1880), 148.

6. Minnesota Board of Commissioners, *Minnesota in the Civil and Indian Wars,* vol. 1, 245.
7. Folwell, *A History of Minnesota,* vol. 2, 232.
8. Both Alexander Ramsey, the governor of Minnesota, and General Sibley had been Indian traders and had profited greatly from these shenanigans.
9. Minnesota Board of Commissioners, *Minnesota in the Civil and Indian Wars,* vol. 1, 246–247.
10. Winifred W. Barton, *John P. Williamson: A Brother to the Sioux* (New York: Revell, 1919), 18.
11. *Ibid.* There has been some debate since then as to when Myrick made this comment, but most historians agree that this triggered the war. All that was needed was an incident to start the conflict, and that quickly arrived.
12. *Ibid.,* 19.
13. Anderson, *Little Crow: Spokesman for the Sioux,* 128.
14. Duane Schultz, *Over the Earth I Come: The Great Sioux Uprising of 1862* (New York: Thomas Dunne Books, 1992), 29.
15. Minnesota Board of Commissioners, *Minnesota in the Civil and Indian Wars,* 1861–1865, vol. 1, 455.
16. Folwell, *A History of Minnesota,* vol. 2, 168.
17. *Ibid.,* 105.
18. Minnesota Board of Commissioners, *Minnesota in the Civil and Indian Wars,* 1861–1865, vol. 1, 455.
19. Diedrich, *Dakota Oratory,* 67.
20. Actually, Little Crow was no longer their chief and had been replaced, but the Sioux continued to look upon him as their leader as subsequent events would demonstrate.
21. Big Eagle, "A Sioux Story of the War," in *Collections of the Minnesota Historical Society* 6, 388–389.
22. A. C. Smith, "The Sioux Uprising in Meeker County," in *A Random Historical Sketch of Meeker County,* 1877, 11–12.
23. Diedrich, *Dakota Oratory,* 67.
24. Big Eagle, "A Sioux Story of the War," in *Collections of the Minnesota Historical Society* 6, 387.
25. Diedrich, *Dakota Oratory,* 67.
26. Big Eagle, "A Sioux Story of the War," in *Collections of the Minnesota Historical Society* 6, 389.
27. Diedrich, *Dakota Oratory,* 66.
28. *Ibid.,* 67.
29. Flandrau. *The History of Minnesota and Tales of the Frontier,* 142.
30. Kenneth Carley, *The Dakota War of 1862* (St. Paul: Minnesota Historical Society Press, 1961), 12. Lynd had abandoned his first Sioux wife for another, and it has been theorized that his killing was not random: the relatives of his first wife wanted him dead.
31. Anderson, *Little Crow: Spokesman for the Sioux,* 135–136.
32. Flandrau, *The History of Minnesota and Tales of the Frontier,* 142.
33. Carley, *The Dakota War of 1862,* 26.
34. *Ibid.*
35. *Pioneer and Democrat,* 20 August 1862, 1.
36. Carley, *The Dakota War of 1862,* 26.
37. Minnesota Board of Commissioners, *Minnesota in the Civil and Indian Wars,* 1861–1865, vol. 1, 250.
38. Anderson, *Little Crow: Spokesman for the Sioux,* 139.
39. Diedrich, *Dakota Oratory,* 69.
40. Folwell, *A History of Minnesota,* vol. 2, 126
41. Anderson, *Little Crow: Spokesman for the Sioux,* 144.
42. Gabriel Renville, *A Sioux Narrative of the Outbreak in 1862, and of Sibley's Expedition in 1863* (14 December 1903), 3–4.
43. Folwell, *A History of Minnesota,* vol. 2, 117.
44. *Ibid.,* 118.
45. C. M. Oehler, *The Great Sioux Uprising* (New York: Oxford University Press, 1997), 45.
46. *Ibid.,* 67.
47. Charles S. Bryant and Abel B. Murch, *A History of the Great Massacre by the Sioux Indians, in Minnesota: Including the Personal Narratives of the Many Who Escaped* (Cincinnati: Rickey and Carroll, 1864), 120.
48. Charles Alexander McMurry, *Pioneer History Stories of the Mississippi Valley* (Bloomington: Public-School, 1894), 82–83.
49. Diedrich, *Dakota Oratory,* 70.
50. Renville, *A Sioux Narrative of the Outbreak in 1862, and of Sibley's Expedition in 1863,* 3–4.
51. Riggs, *Mary and I: Forty Years with the Sioux,* 148.
52. *Ibid.,* 155.
53. Ebell was born in Ceylon in 1840 and was a student at Yale before he traveled to Chicago where he taught music and gave magic-lantern shows (today, we call this a slide show: a light source and mirror used to project through an image onto a screen). While in Chicago he decided to go north to Minnesota with his assistant, Edwin R. Lawton, to photograph Indians in August 1862. He arrived in August and took photographs before going to the Upper Agency, where he had hoped to photograph the payment of annuities. He made a number of photographs there before the Sioux War broke out. He joined the missionary column as they escaped and he made this photograph at a rest stop. It may be the best photograph of the Sioux War.
54. Marion P Satterlee, *Outbreak and Massacre by Dakota Indians in Minnesota in 1862* (Bowie: Heritage Books, 2001), 2.
55. Riggs, *Mary and I: Forty Years with the Sioux,* 159–163.
56. *Pioneer and Democrat,* 22 August 1862, 1.
57. Nathaniel West, *The Ancestry, Life, and Times of Hon. Henry Hastings Sibley, L.L.D* (St. Paul: Pioneer Press, 1889), 257.
58. Rhonda R. Gilman, *Henry Hastings Sibley: Divided Heart* (St. Paul: Minnesota Historical Society, 2004), 168.
59. *Ibid.,* 184.
60. *Pioneer and Democrat,* 22 August 1862, 1.
61. Big Eagle, "A Sioux Story of the War," in *Collections of the Minnesota Historical Society* 6, 392.
62. Anderson, *Little Crow: Spokesman for the Sioux,* 144.
63. Folwell, *A History of Minnesota,* vol. 2, 130.
64. *Ibid.*
65. *Pioneer and Democrat,* 6 September 1862.
66. Folwell, *A History of Minnesota,* vol. 2, 131.
67. Big Eagle, "A Sioux Story of the War," in *Collections of the Minnesota Historical Society* 6, 392–393.

68. Jones would later be promoted to captain commanding the 3rd Battery of Light Artillery that would play a major role in Sibley's campaign the following year.

69. Folwell, *A History of Minnesota*, vol. 2, 132.

70. *Ibid.*, 133.

71. Big Eagle, "A Sioux Story of the War," in *Collections of the Minnesota Historical Society* 6, 393.

72. Folwell, *A History of Minnesota*, vol. 2, 361.

73. Jacob Nix, *The Sioux Uprising in Minnesota, 1862: Jacob Nix's Eyewitness History* (Indianapolis: Indiana German-American Society, 1994), 88.

74. L. A. Fritsche, *Memories of the Battle of New Ulm* (Westminster, MD: Heritage Books, 2007), 81–82

75. *Ibid.*

76. Schultz, *Over the Earth I Come: The Great Sioux Uprising of 1862*, 153.

77. Minnesota Board of Commissioners, *Minnesota in the Civil and Indian Wars, 1861–1865*, vol. 1, 732.

78. Carley, *The Dakota War of 1862*, 36–37.

79. *Ibid.*, 37.

80. Folwell, *A History of Minnesota*, vol. 2, 374.

81. Minnesota Board of Commissioners, *Minnesota in the Civil and Indian Wars, 1861–1865*, vol. 1, 770.

82. *Ibid.*, 455–456.

83. *Ibid.*, 732.

84. Dee Brown, *Bury My Heart at Wounded Knee* (New York: Holt, Rhinehart & Winston, 1970), 51.

85. Fritsche, *Memories of the Battle of New Ulm*, 58.

86. Hunt, *Observations of T. J. Hunt in the Civil War: A Narrative of the Military Life of T. J. Hunt in the Sioux Indian and Civil Wars of 1862–1865*, 3.

87. Anderson, *Through Dakota Eyes*, 14.

88. Gilman, *Henry Hastings Sibley: Divided Heart*, 173.

89. *Ibid.*, 174.

90. *Ibid.*

91. Isaac V.D. Heard, *History of the Sioux War and Massacres of 1862 and 1863* (New York: Harper & Brothers, 1864), 119.

92. Gilman, *Henry Hastings Sibley: Divided Heart*, 176.

93. *Ibid.*

94. Schultz, *Over the Earth I Come: The Great Sioux Uprising of 1862*, 178–179.

95. Carl Sandburg, *Abraham Lincoln The War Years*, vol. 1 (New York: Harcourt, Brace, 1939), 537.

96. *Ibid.*

97. *Ibid.*, 533.

98. Sarah F. Wakefield, *Six Weeks in the Sioux Tepees* (Minneapolis: Atlas, 1863), 42.

99. *Ibid.*, 42–43.

100. Anderson, *Little Crow: Spokesman for the Sioux*, 153.

101. A. P. Connolly, *A Thrilling Narrative of the Minnesota Massacre and Sioux War of 1862–63: Graphic Accounts of the Siege of Fort Ridgley, Battles of Birch Coolie, Wood Lake, Big Mound, Stoney Lake, Dead Buffalo Lake and Missouri River* (Chicago: Connolly, 1896), 110.

102. Big Eagle, "A Sioux Story of the War," in *Collections of the Minnesota Historical Society* 6, 393–394.

103. Connolly, *A Thrilling Narrative of the Minnesota Massacre and Sioux War of 1862–63: Graphic Accounts of the Siege of Fort Ridgley, Battles of Birch Coolie, Wood Lake, Big Mound, Stoney Lake, Dead Buffalo Lake and Missouri River*, 112–113.

104. Big Eagle, "A Sioux Story of the War," in *Collections of the Minnesota Historical Society* 6, 395.

105. Connolly, *A Thrilling Narrative of the Minnesota Massacre and Sioux War of 1862–63: Graphic Accounts of the Siege of Fort Ridgley, Battles of Birch Coolie, Wood Lake, Big Mound, Stoney Lake, Dead Buffalo Lake and Missouri River*, 112–116.

106. Big Eagle, "A Sioux Story of the War," in *Collections of the Minnesota Historical Society* 6, 394.

107. Gilman, *Henry Hastings Sibley, Divided Heart*, 178.

108. *Ibid.*

109. Minnesota Board of Commissioners, *Minnesota in the Civil and Indian Wars*, 485.

110. Big Eagle, "A Sioux Story of the War," in *Collections of the Minnesota Historical Society* 6, 396–397.

111. Connolly, *A Thrilling Narrative of the Minnesota Massacre and Sioux War of 1862–63: Graphic Accounts of the Siege of Fort Ridgley, Battles of Birch Coolie, Wood Lake, Big Mound, Stoney Lake, Dead Buffalo Lake and Missouri River*, 126.

112. Gilman, *Henry Hastings Sibley: Divided Heart*, 179.

113. Connolly, *A Thrilling Narrative of the Minnesota Massacre and Sioux War of 1862–63: Graphic Accounts of the Siege of Fort Ridgley, Battles of Birch Coolie, Wood Lake, Big Mound, Stoney Lake, Dead Buffalo Lake and Missouri River*, 125.

114. Diedrich, *Dakota Oratory*, 71.

115. Gilman, *Henry Hastings Sibley: Divided Heart*, 177.

116. Association of Graduates, United States Military Academy, *The Register of Graduates and Former Cadets of the United States Military, 2010* (West Point: Association of Graduates, 2010), 4–38.

117. Clodfelter, *The Dakota War: The United States Army Versus the Sioux, 1862–1865*, 55.

118. *Farmer's Minneapolis Tribune*, 11 October 1862, 1.

119. Minnesota Board of Commissioners, *Minnesota in the Civil and Indian Wars, 1861–1865*, vol. 1, 416–417.

120. *Farmer's Minneapolis Tribune*, 11 October 1862, 1

121. Folwell, *A History of Minnesota*, vol. 2, 160–161.

122. Minnesota Board of Commissioners, *Minnesota in the Civil and Indian Wars, 1861–1865*, vol. 1, 441–442.

123. James R. Hart, "Historical Reminiscences of Service in the Dakota and Minnesota," in *Dakota Conflict of 1862 Manuscripts Collections* (microfilm edition, roll 2, Minnesota Historical Society), 2.

124. *Ibid.*, 744–745.

125. *Ibid.*, 256–257.

126. *Ibid.*, 746.

127. Hart, "Historical Reminiscences of Service in the Dakota and Minnesota," in *Dakota Conflict of 1862 Manuscripts Collections*, 2.

128. Minnesota Board of Commissioners, *Minnesota in the Civil and Indian Wars*, 1861–1865, vol. 1, 257.
129. Diedrich, *Dakota Oratory*, 78.
130. Clodfelter, *The Dakota War: The United States Army Versus the Sioux, 1862–1865*, 55
131. *Ibid.*
132. Minnesota Board of Commissioners, *Minnesota in the Civil and Indian Wars*, 1861–1865, vol. 1, 149.
133. *Ibid.*,151.
134. Andrea R. Foroughi, *Go If You Think It Your Duty* (St. Paul: Minnesota Historical Society, 2008), 107.
135. Big Eagle, "A Sioux Story of the War," in *Collections of the Minnesota Historical Society* 6, 397–398.
136. *Ibid.*, 398–399.
137. Clodfelter, *The Dakota War, The United States Army Versus the Sioux, 1862–1865*, 56–57.
138. Foroughi, *Go If You Think It Your Duty*, 120–122.
139. Big Eagle, "A Sioux Story of the War," in *Collections of the Minnesota Historical Society* 6, 399.
140. *Ibid.*
141. Folwell, *A History of Minnesota*, vol. 2, 243.
142. George C. Pettie, "Diary of George C. Pettie, Co. A, 10th Reg." Steele County, Minnesota, 1863, 2.
143. *Ibid.*, 4.
144. *Ibid.*, 5.
45. Hunt, *Observations of T. J. Hunt in the Civil War: A Narrative of the Military Life of T. J. Hunt in the Sioux Indian and Civil Wars of 1862–1865*, 3.
146. Foroughi, *Go If You Think It Your Duty*, 135.
147. Amos B. Watson, *Reminiscences of the Sioux Outbreak*, 6.
148. *Ibid.* Doctors needed cadavers for research and the Sioux were kind enough to provide an abundant supply. Dr. William Worrall Mayo, who with his sons founded the Mayo Clinic at Rochester, Minnesota, is said to have gotten the body of He Who Stands in Clouds.
149. Hank H. Cox, *Lincoln and the Sioux Uprising of 1862* (Nashville: Cumberland House, 2005), 149.

Chapter 2

1. Folwell, *A History of Minnesota*, vol. 2, 255.
2. Cox, *Lincoln and the Sioux Uprising of 1862* (Nashville: Cumberland House, 2005), 195.
3. Oehler, *The Great Sioux Uprising*, 234.
4. Cox, *Lincoln and the Sioux Uprising of 1862*, 195.
5. Carley, *The Dakota War of 1862*, 76.
6. Folwell, *A History of Minnesota*, vol. 2, 258.
7. *Ibid.*
8. This came from a meeting Sheridan had with tribes in 1869. Sheridan later denied that he said anything like that, but others claim that it came out during the meeting.
9. Folwell, *A History of Minnesota*, vol. 2, 257.
10. Schultz, *Over the Earth I Come: The Great Sioux Uprising of 1862*, 280.
11. *Ibid.*
12. Folwell, *A History of Minnesota*, vol. 2, 256.
13. Joseph R. Brown Heritage Society, *Tales of the Tenth Regiment 1862–1863*, 16–18.
14. Carley, *The Dakota War of 1862*, 80.
15. Oehler, *The Great Sioux Uprising*, 228–29.
16. Robert Huhn Jones, *The Civil War in the Northwest: Nebraska, Wisconsin, Iowa, Minnesota and the Dakotas* (Norman: University of Oklahoma Press, 1960), 74.
17. Richard N. Ellis, *General Pope and U.S. Indian Policy* (Albuquerque: University of New Mexico Press, 1970), 27.
18. *Ibid.*
19. U.S. War Department, *The War of Rebellion: A Compilation of the Official Records of the Union and Confederate Armies*, Ser. 1, Vol. 22, Pt. 2 (Washington, DC: Government Printing Office, 1880–1901), Sibley's letter to Acting Assistant Adjutant-General J.F. Meline, 907–908.
20. Kenneth Carley, *The Dakota War of 1862* (St. Paul: Minnesota Historical Society Press, 1961), 88.
21. *St. Paul Pioneer*, 6 April 1864.
22. Josephy, *The Civil War in the American West*, 132.
23. Nathaniel West, *The Ancestry, Life, and Times of Hon. Henry Hastings Sibley, L.L.D* (St. Paul: Pioneer Press, 1889), 304.
24. Hunt, *Observations of T. J. Hunt in the Civil War: A Narrative of the Military Life of T. J. Hunt in the Sioux Indian and Civil Wars of 1862–1865*, 5.
25. Bryant and Murch, *A History of the Great Massacre by the Sioux Indians, in Minnesota: Including the Personal Narratives of the Many Who Escaped*, 494.
26. Minnesota Board of Commissioners, *Minnesota in the Civil and Indian Wars*, 1861–1865, vol. 1, 523.
27. Sitting Bull's participation is uncertain. Some historians state that he was there. Others indicate that he is thought to have been in the battles.
28. Paul N. Beck, *Inkpaduta Dakota Leader* (Norman: University of Oklahoma Press, 2008), 120.
29. *Ibid.*
30. Pension record of Ira Eggleston, 1893.
31. West, *The Ancestry, Life, and Times of Hon. Henry Hastings Sibley, L.L.D.*, 307.
32. Connolly, *A Thrilling Narrative of the Minnesota Massacre and Sioux War of 1862–63: Graphic Accounts of the Siege of Fort Ridgley, Battles of Birch Coolie, Wood Lake, Big Mound, Stoney Lake, Dead Buffalo Lake and Missouri River*, 205.
33. *Ibid.*, 209–210.
34. Pettie, "Diary of George C. Pettie, Co. A, 10th Reg.," 7.
35. Folwell, *A History of Minnesota*, vol. 2, 267–268
36. James R. Hart, "Historical Reminiscences of Service in the Dakota and Minnesota," 1.
37. Gilman, *Henry Hastings Sibley: Divided Heart*, 179.
38. Ellis, *General Pope and U.S. Indian Policy*, 2.
39. Langdon Sully, *No Tears for the General: The Life of Alfred Sully, 1821–1879* (Palo Alto, CA: American West, 1974), 168.
40. *Minnesota in the Civil and Indian Wars*, 1861–1865, vol. 1, 455.
41. Kurt D. Bergemann, *Brackett's Battalion: Minnesota Cavalry in the Civil War and Dakota War* (St. Paul: Minnesota Historical Society, 2004), 99.

42. Clodfelter, *The Dakota War: The United States Army Versus the Sioux, 1862–1865*, 84.
43. Minnesota Board of Commissioners, *Minnesota in the Civil and Indian Wars*, 1861–1865, vol. 1, 457.
44. Pettie, "Diary of George C. Pettie, Co. A, 10th Reg.," 9.
45. U.S. War Department, *The War of Rebellion: A Compilation of the Official Records of the Union and Confederate Armies*, Ser. 1, Vol. 22, Pt. 2, Sibley's letter to Acting Assistant Adjutant-General J.F. Meline, 907–908.
46. Pettie, "Diary of George C. Pettie, Co. A, 10th Reg.," 12.
47. Anderson, *Though Dakota Eyes*, 284.
48. Clodfelter, *The Dakota War: The United States Army Versus the Sioux, 1862–1865*, 95.
49. Anderson, *Though Dakota Eyes*, 284.
50. Hunt, *Observations of T. J. Hunt in the Civil War: A Narrative of the Military Life of T. J. Hunt in the Sioux Indian and Civil Wars of 1862–1865*, 6–7.
51. *Ibid.*
52. U.S. War Department, *The War of Rebellion: A Compilation of the Official Records of the Union and Confederate Armies*, Ser. 1, Vol. 22, Pt. 1, 354.
53. Pettie, "Diary of George C. Pettie, Co. A, 10th Reg.," 13–14.
54. West, *The Ancestry, Life, and Times of Hon. Henry Hastings Sibley, L.L.D*, 309.
55. Minnesota Commandery L. L, *Glimpses of the Nation's Struggle. Volume II* (Wilmington: Broadfoot Publishing, 1992), 197–198.
56. *Ibid.*, 188–189.
57. Captain John W. Burnham, "Sibley's Expedition of 1863," (*The Record [Fargo], June 1896*), 2–5.
58. Diedrich, *Dakota Oratory*, 85.
59. Pettie, "Diary of George C. Pettie, Co. A, 10th Reg.," 14.
60. Clodfelter, *The Dakota War: The United States Army Versus the Sioux, 1862–1865*, 104.
61. Pettie, "Diary of George C. Pettie, Co. A, 10th Reg.," 14.
62. Hiram Martin Chittenden, *History of Early Steamboat Navigation on the Missouri River, Life and Adventures of Joseph La Barge*, vol. 2 (New York: Harper, 1903), 443.
63. John E. Sunder, *The Fur Trade on the Upper Missouri, 1840–1865* (Norman: University of Oklahoma Press, 1993), 246.
64. Chittenden, *History of Early Steamboat Navigation on the Missouri River, Life and Adventures of Joseph La Barge*, vol. 2, 300.
65. Clodfelter, *The Dakota War: The United States Army Versus the Sioux*, 1862–1865, 77.
66. *Ibid.*
67. Sunder, *The Fur Trade on the Upper Missouri, 1840–1865*, 247.
68. Clodfelter, *The Dakota War: The United States Army Versus the Sioux, 1862–1865*, 78.
69. Minnesota Board of Commissioners, *Minnesota in the Civil and Indian Wars*, 1861–1865, vol. 1, 460.
70. Clodfelter, *The Dakota War: The United States Army Versus the Sioux, 1862–1865*, 105.
71. Minnesota Board of Commissioners, *Minnesota in the Civil and Indian Wars*, 1861–1865, vol. 1, 459.
72. *Ibid.*
73. *Ibid.*, 459–460.
74. Pettie, "Diary of George C. Pettie, Co. A, 10th Reg.," 14–15.
75. Minnesota Board of Commissioners, *Minnesota in the Civil and Indian Wars*, 1861–1865, vol. 1, 354.
76. Minnesota Board of Commissioners, *Minnesota in the Civil and Indian Wars*, 1861–1865, vol. 2, *Official Reports and Correspondence* (St. Paul, MN: Pioneer Press, 1899), 301.
77. *Ibid.*
78. Gilman, *Henry Hastings Sibley: Divided Heart*, 199.
79. Burnham, "Sibley's Expedition of 1863," 2–5.
80. Anderson, *Through Dakota Eyes*, 270.
81. Robert W. Larson, *Gall: Lakota War Chief* (Norman: University of Oklahoma Press, 2007), 43.
82. Clodfelter, *The Dakota War: The United States Army Versus the Sioux, 1862–1865*, 116.
83. U.S. War Department, *The War of Rebellion: A Compilation of the Official Records of the Union and Confederate Armies*, Ser. 1, Vol. 22, Pt. 1, 357.
84. Hart, "Historical Reminiscences of Service in the Dakota and Minnesota," in *Dakota Conflict of 1862 Manuscripts Collections*, 6.
85. *Ibid.*
86. Gilman, *Henry Hastings Sibley: Divided Heart*, 200.
87. Pettie, "Diary of George C. Pettie, Co. A, 10th Reg.," 18.
88. *Ibid.*
89. *Ibid.*
90. Ellis, *General Pope and U.S. Indian Policy*, 22.
91. Chittenden, *History of Early Steamboat Navigation on the Missouri River, Life and Adventures of Joseph La Barge*, vol. 1, 94–95.
92. Clement A. Lounsberry, *Early History of North Dakota: Essential Outlines of American History* (Washington, DC: Liberty Press, 1919), 292.
93. Sully, *No Tears for the General: The Life of Alfred Sully, 1821–1879*, 169.
94. Clodfelter, *The Dakota War: The United States Army Versus the Sioux, 1862–1865*, 113.
95. Spencer, "The Letters of Milton Spencer," 133.
96. Sully, *No Tears for the General: The Life of Alfred Sully, 1821–1879*, 178.
97. Clodfelter, *The Dakota War: The United States Army Versus the Sioux, 1862–1865*, 137–138.
98. Lounsberry, *Early History of North Dakota: Essential Outlines of American History*, 295.
99. *Ibid.*
100. Folwell, *A History of Minnesota*, vol. 2, 280.
101. *Ibid.*, 279.
102. Robert G. Athearn, *Forts of the Upper Missouri* (Englewood Cliffs: Prentice-Hall, 1967), 114.
103. Hart, "Historical Reminiscences of Service in the Dakota and Minnesota," in *Dakota Conflict of 1862 Manuscripts Collections*, 6–7.
104. Ellis, *General Pope and U.S. Indian Policy*, 28–29.
105. Pettie, "Diary of George C. Pettie, Co. A, 10th Reg.," 26.

106. Folwell, *A History of Minnesota*, vol. 2, 277.
107. Minnesota Board of Commissioners, *Minnesota in the Civil and Indian Wars, 1861–1865*, vol. 1, 461.
108. Clodfelter, *The Dakota War: The United States Army Versus the Sioux, 1862–1865*, 150.
109. *Ibid.*
110. Athearn, *Forts of the Upper Missouri*, 115.

Chapter 3

1. U.S. War Department. *The War of Rebellion: A Compilation of the Official Records of the Union and Confederate Armies Official Records*, Ser. 1, Vol. 39, Pt. 2, p. 142.
2. Minnesota Board of Commissioners, *Minnesota in the Civil and Indian Wars, 1861–1865*, vol. 1, 461.
3. *Ibid.*, 462–463.
4. Hunt, *Observations of T. J. Hunt in the Civil War: A Narrative of the Military Life of T. J. Hunt in the Sioux Indian and Civil Wars of 1862–1865*, 9–10.
5. Woodworth, *Jefferson Davis and His Generals: The Failure of Confederate Command in the West*, 254–255. Jefferson Davis, the president of the Confederacy, also elected to be the commander in chief. As such he failed because he did not have the time to deal with the problems in the West, was not able to enforce discipline on insubordinate generals, and found that he could not fire old, incompetent generals who were his friends. Most important, he was always in poor health and hesitated to take action on problems.
6. The *Hunley* was recovered and brought to shore in 2000. It is currently being restored in Charleston, South Carolina. The remains of the crew were recovered and buried after nearly 150 years in the deep.
7. Minnesota Board of Commissioners, *Minnesota in the Civil and Indian Wars, 1861–1865*, vol. 1, 463.
8. Association of Graduates, United States Military Academy, *The Register of Graduates and Former Cadets of the United States Military*, 2010, 4–24.
9. Stanley F Horn. *The Decisive Battle of Nashville* (Knoxville: University of Tennessee Press, 1978), 170–171.
10. U.S. War Department. *The War of Rebellion: A Compilation of the Official Records of the Union and Confederate Armies Official Records*, Ser. 1, Vol. 39, Pt. 2, p. 123.
11. Carley. *Minnesota in the Civil War*, 110.
12. Hunt, *Observations of T. J. Hunt in the Civil War: A Narrative of the Military Life of T. J. Hunt in the Sioux Indian and Civil Wars of 1862–1865*, 12.
13. *Ibid.*
14. *Ibid.*, 11.
15. *Ibid.*, 13–14.
16. Minnesota Board of Commissioners, *Minnesota in the Civil and Indian Wars, 1861–1865*, vol. 1, 463–464.
17. U.S. War Department. *The War of Rebellion: A Compilation of the Official Records of the Union and Confederate Armies Official Records*, Ser. 1, Vol. 39, Pt. 1, p.252.
18. Minnesota Board of Commissioners, *Minnesota in the Civil and Indian Wars, 1861–1865*, vol. 1, 464.
19. Hunt, *Observations of T. J. Hunt in the Civil War: A Narrative of the Military Life of T. J. Hunt in the Sioux Indian and Civil Wars of 1862–1865*, 15.
20. John Allan Wyeth, *That Devil Forrest: The Life of General Nathan Bedford Forrest* (Baton Rouge: Louisiana State University Press, 1989), 398.
21. *Ibid.*
22. *Ibid.*, 399.
23. *Ibid.* Exact wording of this phase is not clear, but Forrest said something like this.
24. *Ibid.*
25. *Ibid.*, 398.
26. Albert Castel, *General Sterling Price and the Civil War in the West* (Baton Rouge: Louisiana State University Press, 1996), 208.
27. Hunt, *Observations of T. J. Hunt in the Civil War: A Narrative of the Military Life of T. J. Hunt in the Sioux Indian and Civil Wars of 1862–1865*, 15.
28. Minnesota Board of Commissioners, *Minnesota in the Civil and Indian Wars, 1861–1865*, vol. 1, 465.
29. Hunt, *Observations of T. J. Hunt in the Civil War: A Narrative of the Military Life of T. J. Hunt in the Sioux Indian and Civil Wars of 1862–1865*, 18.
30. Castel, *General Sterling Price and the Civil War in the West*, 13.
31. *Ibid.*, 16.
32. *Ibid.*, 81.
33. *Ibid.*, 66.
34. Josephy, *The Civil War in the American West*, 377.
35. Castel, *General Sterling Price and the Civil War in the West*, 201.
36. *Ibid.*, 202, 206.
37. Josephy, *The Civil War in the American West*, 378.
38. Castel, *General Sterling Price and the Civil War in the West*, 204.
39. Josephy, *The Civil War in the American West*, 378
40. Castel, *General Sterling Price and the Civil War in the West*, 200. Price told Kirby Smith that Federal forces in Missouri consisted mainly of unreliable militia.
41. *Ibid.*, 209.
42. Hunt, *Observations of T. J. Hunt in the Civil War: A Narrative of the Military Life of T. J. Hunt in the Sioux Indian and Civil Wars of 1862–1865*, 16.
43. Castel, *General Sterling Price and the Civil War in the West*, 218–219.
44. The commander was General Curtis, but Blunt made up the bulk of Curtis' command and is generally referred to in this fight as commanding.
45. It took over twenty years before Frank and Jesse James received justice. The James gang met its demise during the Northfield, Minnesota, bank raid in 1876. Some members of the gang were killed, while Frank and Jesse would escape. Later, Frank would be imprisoned and Jesse would be killed. The Younger boys were captured and imprisoned in Stillwater, Minnesota. Cole Younger would become a hero when he saved people during a fire at the prison and would later be released.
46. Minnesota Board of Commissioners, *Minnesota in the Civil and Indian Wars, 1861–1865*, vol. 1, 465.

47. Hunt, *Observations of T. J. Hunt in the Civil War: A Narrative of the Military Life of T. J. Hunt in the Sioux Indian and Civil Wars of 1862–1865*, 19.
48. *St. Paul Pioneer*, 26 November 1864, 2.
49. Lincoln carried Missouri by a vote of 72,000 over McClellan's 31,000.
50. Hunt, *Observations of T. J. Hunt in the Civil War: A Narrative of the Military Life of T. J. Hunt in the Sioux Indian and Civil Wars of 1862–1865*, 19–20.

Chapter 4

1. Sung to the tune of "The Yellow Rose of Texas."
2. The name is disputed. Some say it is based upon a remark by Jefferson Davis that Hood had a lion's heart and a wooden head. Hood's troops called him "Old Pegleg" because he rode with a cork leg replacing the one that had been amputated.
3. Richard M. McMurry, *John Bell Hood and the War for Southern Independence* (Lincoln: University of Nebraska Press, 1982), 67.
4. Woodworth, *Jefferson Davis and His Generals: The Failure of Confederate Command in the West*, 292.
5. Donald Stroker, *The Grand Design Strategy and the U.S. Civil War* (New York: Oxford University Press, 2010), 378–383.
6. McMurry, *John Bell Hood and the War for Southern Independence*, 162–166.
7. U.S. War Department, *The War of Rebellion: A Compilation of the Official Records of the Union and Confederate Armies, Official Records*, Ser. 1, Vol. 38, Pt. 3, 622–24.
8. McMurry, *John Bell Hood and the War for Southern Independence*, 177.
9. Association of Graduates, United States Military Academy, *The Register of Graduates and Former Cadets of the United States Military*, 2010, 4–25.
10. Woodworth, *Decision in the Heartland: The Civil War in the West*, 131.
11. McMurry, *John Bell Hood and the War for Southern Independence*, 174.
12. *Ibid.*, 175.
13. It was Cleburne who had urged Jefferson Davis and Robert E. Lee to enlist African Americans in the Confederate Army in return for their freedom. It would be only weeks before the collapse of the Confederacy that Cleburne's advice was heeded. By then, it was too late and Cleburne was dead.
14. General Thomas Jordan and J. P. Pryor, *The Campaigns of Lieut.-Gen N. B. Forrest and of Forrest's Cavalry* (Dayton, OH: Morningside Bookshop, 1977), 627–28.
15. McMurry, *John Bell Hood and the War for Southern Independence*, 176.
16. Horn, *The Decisive Battle of Nashville*, 167–74.
17. *Ibid.*, 22–23.
18. Hunt, *Observations of T. J. Hunt in the Civil War: A Narrative of the Military Life of T. J. Hunt in the Sioux Indian and Civil Wars of 1862–1865*, 20.
19. Jack Hurst, *Nathan Bedford Forrest. A Biography* (New York: Vintage Books, 1994), 238.
20. Benson Bobrick, *The Battle of Nashville* (New York: Knopf, 2010), 96.
21. Lincoln had actually test fired the Spencer early in the war and endorsed its use.
22. Bobrick, *The Battle of Nashville*, 95.
23. Hunt, *Observations of T. J. Hunt in the Civil War: A Narrative of the Military Life of T. J. Hunt in the Sioux Indian and Civil Wars of 1862–1865*, 21.
24. *Ibid.*, 20.
25. U.S. War Department, *The War of Rebellion: A Compilation of the Official Records of the Union and Confederate Armies*, Ser. 1, Vol. 45, Pt. 1, 132–133.
26. Horn, *The Decisive Battle of Nashville*, 95–6.
27. Hunt, *Observations of T. J. Hunt in the Civil War: A Narrative of the Military Life of T. J. Hunt in the Sioux Indian and Civil Wars of 1862–1865*, 21.
28. Horn, *The Decisive Battle of Nashville*, 97.
29. U.S. War Department, *The War of Rebellion: A Compilation of the Official Records of the Union and Confederate Armies*, Ser. 1, Vol. 45, Pt. 2, 194–5, 210.
30. *Ibid.*, 194–195.
31. *Ibid.*, 210.
32. Hunt, *Observations of T. J. Hunt in the Civil War: A Narrative of the Military Life of T. J. Hunt in the Sioux Indian and Civil Wars of 1862–1865*, 23.
33. Horn, *The Decisive Battle of Nashville*, 136–138.
34. *Ibid.*, 126.
35. *Ibid.*, 128–129.
36. Hunt, *Observations of T. J. Hunt in the Civil War: A Narrative of the Military Life of T. J. Hunt in the Sioux Indian and Civil Wars of 1862–1865*, 24.
37. Horn, *The Decisive Battle of Nashville*, 140–141.
38. Hunt, *Observations of T. J. Hunt in the Civil War: A Narrative of the Military Life of T. J. Hunt in the Sioux Indian and Civil Wars of 1862–1865*, 26.
39. Bobrick, *The Battle of Nashville*, 100–101.
40. Horn, *The Decisive Battle of Nashville*, 152–153.
41. Hunt, *Observations of T. J. Hunt in the Civil War: A Narrative of the Military Life of T. J. Hunt in the Sioux Indian and Civil Wars of 1862–1865*, 27.
42. Horn, *The Decisive Battle of Nashville*, 163.

Chapter 5

1. Robert E. Lee, *HQ Northern Virginia, General Order No. 9*, 10 April 1865, 1.
2. There would be other skirmishes, such as Palmetto Ranch in Texas, and the surrender of other Confederate forces such as Kirby Smith's, but the war was over, at last. It had been a long journey to get there.
3. Minnesota Board of Commissioners, *Minnesota in the Civil and Indian Wars, 1861–1865*, vol. 1, 470.
4. Stroker, *The Grand Design Strategy and the U.S. Civil War*, 388.
5. *Ibid.*, 389.
6. *Ibid.*, 398.
7. After the war, Canby would be assassinated by Captain Jack of the Modoc tribe while he was trying to negotiate a peace with the Indians. Captain Jack was later captured and hanged.
8. Hunt, *Observations of T. J. Hunt in the Civil War: A Narrative of the Military Life of T. J. Hunt in the Sioux Indian and Civil Wars of 1862–1865*, 29.

9. *Ibid.*
10. *Ibid.*, 32.
11. *Ibid.*, 32–33.
12. *Ibid.*, 33.
13. *Ibid.*, 33–34.
14. *St. Paul Pioneer*, 20 August 1865, 2.
15. In old photos, it is almost impossible to distinguish the Medal of Honor from the GAR membership badge. Perhaps the veterans wanted it that way. Many of the veterans show a medal. To check whether or not it is the Medal of Honor, go to http://www. history. army.mil/moh.html.gov.

Epilogue

1. Minnesota Historical Society, *Collections of the Minnesota Historical Society*, vol. 14, *Minnesota Biographies, 1655–1912* (St. Paul: Minnesota Historical Society, 1912), 29.
2. Cox, *Lincoln and the Sioux Uprising of 1862*, 197.
3. This was a weak excuse. More likely, the people in Minnesota were still trying to enact revenge. The note on the back of the order was typical of Lincoln. He would often write notes on the back of correspondence to his cabinet or others.
4. Big Eagle, "A Sioux Story of the War," in *Collections of the Minnesota Historical Society* 6, 399.
5. *Collections of the Minnesota Historical Society*, vol. 14, *Minnesota Biographies, 1655–1912*, 68.
6. *Ibid.*, 84.
7. *Ibid.*, 94.
8. *Ibid.*, 134.
9. *Ibid.*, 136.
10. Folwell, *A History of Minnesota*, vol. 2, 168.
11. *Collections of the Minnesota Historical Society*, vol. 14, *Minnesota Biographies, 1655–1912*, 200.
12. *Ibid.*, 226.
13. Larson, *Gall: Lakota War Chief*, 56.
14. *Collections of the Minnesota Historical Society*, vol. 14, *Minnesota Biographies, 1655–1912*, 251–252.
15. Minnesota Board of Commissioners, *Minnesota in the Civil and Indian Wars, 1861–1865*, vol. 1, 478.
16. Association of Graduates, United States Military Academy, *The Register of Graduates and Former Cadets of the United States Military, 2010*, 4–77.
17. *Collections of the Minnesota Historical Society*, vol. 14, *Minnesota Biographies, 1655–1912*, 356.
18. Beck, *Inkpaduta: Dakota Leader*, 140.
19. *Ibid.*, 74.
20. *Collections of the Minnesota Historical Society*, vol. 14, *Minnesota Biographies, 1655–1912*, 371.
21. *Ibid.*, 385.
22. Sunder, *The Fur Trade on the Upper Missouri, 1840–1865*, 258.
23. Cox, *Lincoln and the Sioux Uprising of 1862*, 197.
24. William S. McFeely, *Grant* (New York: Norton, 1981), 307–308.
25. *Ibid.*, 496–497.
26. *Collections of the Minnesota Historical Society*, vol. 14, *Minnesota Biographies, 1655–1912*, 571.
27. Some authors, for example, Dee Brown (a librarian), viewed Little Crow as the victim in this war who did nothing wrong. To refute that, a few of many examples: he ordered the murder of all whites at the Lower Agency and he was wearing the garment of a recently murdered settler when he died in the raspberry patch, shot by a young white settler.
28. Wowinapa was sentenced to be hanged but the sentence was commuted. He became a Christian and took the name Thomas Wakeman. He was the founder of the YMCA among the Indians.
29. Schultz, *Over the Earth I Come: The Great Sioux Uprising of 1862*, 274.
30. Anderson, *Little Crow: Spokesman for the Sioux*, 178.
31. Cox, *Lincoln and the Sioux Uprising of 1862*, 198.
32. Association of Graduates, United States Military Academy, *The Register of Graduates and Former Cadets of the United States Military, 2010*, 4–27.
33. *Collections of the Minnesota Historical Society*, vol. 14, *Minnesota Biographies, 1655–1912*, 624.
34. *Ibid.*, 634.
35. *Ibid.*, 643.
36. *Ibid.*, 668.
37. *Ibid.*, 696–697.
38. *Ibid.*, 702–703.
39. Association of Graduates, United States Military Academy, *The Register of Graduates and Former Cadets of the United States Military, 2010*, 4–24.
40. Joseph R. Brown Heritage Society, *Tales of the Tenth Regiment 1862–1863* (printed by the Historical Society of Henderson, Minnesota).
41. Diedrich, *Dakota Oratory*, 97.
42. Association of Graduates, United States Military Academy, *The Register of Graduates and Former Cadets of the United States Military, 2010*, 4–26.
43. *Ibid.*, 4–25.
44. *Collections of the Minnesota Historical Society*, vol. 14, *Minnesota Biographies, 1655–1912*, 863.
45. Association of Graduates, United States Military Academy, *The Register of Graduates and Former Cadets of the United States Military, 2010*, 4–42.
46. Cox, *Lincoln and the Sioux Uprising of 1862*, 199.
47. Jerome A. Greene, *Indian War Veterans, Memories of Army Life and Campaigns in the West, 1864–1898* (New York: Savas Beatie, 2007), 220–227.

Appendix A

1. "Treaty of Traverse de Sioux." *Indian Affairs Laws and Treaties* http://digital.library.okstate.edu/KAPPLER/Vol2/treaties/sio0588.htm, 1904. Accessed 9/13/2008: 1–3.

Appendix B

1. Minnesota Board of Commissioners, *Minnesota in the Civil and Indian Wars, 1861–1865*, vol. 1, 455–471.

Appendix C

1. Minnesota Board of Commissioners, *Minnesota in the Civil and Indian Wars, 1861–1865*, vol. 1, 472–487. Some may ask why there is no Company J listed in the Tenth Regiment's roster. The answer is that there was

no Company J in the Tenth or any other regiment. The "why" may be of interest. Some say it goes back to the American Revolution when a British regiment (Company J), fled in terror before the Patriots' guns. The facts are less interesting. It appears that in the 18th and 19th century, the handwritten "I" was very similar to the hand written "J." So much so that the two letters could be confused. This was a problem when people are trying to account for and pay the troops as well as other actions. As a consequence, the use of Company J as a unit designation was discontinued. This roster corrects errors and adds people omitted from the original 1890 roster that was published with the regimental narrative seen in Appendix B.

Appendix D

1. *Minnesota Board of Commissioners, Minnesota in the Civil and Indian Wars, 1861–1865*, vol. 1.
2. Hunt, *Observations of T. J. Hunt in the Civil War: A Narrative of the Military Life of T. J. Hunt in the Sioux Indian and Civil Wars of 1862–1865*, 39–40.
3. *Ibid.*, 24–27
4. U.S. Department of War. *General Order Number 105* (Washington, DC: Government Printing Office, 28 April 1863).

Appendix E

1. Hunt, *Observations of T. J. Hunt in the Civil War: A Narrative of the Military Life of T. J. Hunt in the Sioux Indian and Civil Wars of 1862–1865*, 16–17.
2. *Ibid.*, 5.

Appendix F

1. Henry Benjamin Whipple, *Lights and Shadows of a Long Episcopate: Being Reminiscences of the Right Reverend Henry Benjamin Whipple, Bishop of Minnesota* (New York: Macmillan, 1899), 33.
2. Bryant and Murch, *A History of the Great Massacre by the Sioux Indians, in Minnesota: Including the Personal Narratives of the Many Who Escaped*, 14.
3. Clodfelter, *The Dakota War: The United States Army Versus the Sioux, 1862–1865*, 15.
4. Carley, *The Dakota War of 1862*, 1.
5. Anderson, *Little Crow: Spokesman for the Sioux*, 6.
6. Roy W. Meyer, *History of the Santee Sioux. United States Indian Policy on Trial* (Lincoln: University of Nebraska Press, 1993), vii.
7. Theodore P. Savas, *Journal of the Indian Wars*, Vol. 1, No. 3 (Mason City: Savas, 2000), 86.
8. Folwell, *A History of Minnesota*, vol. 2, 226.
9. Meyer, *History of the Santee Sioux: United States Indian Policy on Trial*, 388.
10. Ibid., 389.
11. Samuel W. Pond, *Dakota Life in the Upper Midwest* (St. Paul: Minnesota Historical Society Press, 1986), 17.
12. Gary Clayton Anderson, *Kinsmen of Another Kind* (St. Paul: Minnesota Historical Society, 1984), 3.
13. Riggs, *Mary and I: Forty Years with the Sioux*, 36.
14. Pond, *Dakota Life in the Upper Midwest*, 31.
15. *Ibid.*, 34–35.
16. *Ibid.*, 38–39.
17. *Ibid.*, 41.
18. *Ibid.*, 67.
19. Schultz, *Over the Earth I Came: The Great Sioux Uprising of 1862*, 280.
20. *U.S. Indian Census of 1890*, 337.
21. Meyer, *History of the Santee Sioux: United States Indian Policy on Trial*, 259.
22. *Ibid.*, 264.

Appendix G

1. Lincoln, *In Answer to a Resolution of the Resolution of the Senate. Message of the President of the United States*, 2.
2. Folwell, *A History of Minnesota*, vol. 2, 183.
3. Brown, *Bury My Heart at Wounded Knee: An Indian History of the American West*, 58.
4. Gilman, *Henry Hastings Sibley: Divided Heart*, 185.
5. Robert I. Alotta, *Civil War Justice: Union Army Executions Under Lincoln* (Shippensburg, PA: White Mane, 1989), 15.
6. Martial law was declared after the trials had ended.
7. Carol Chomsky, "The United States Dakota War Trials: A Study in Military Injustice," *Stanford Law Review* 43 (1990): 13–98, 64.
8. Ibid., 56.
9. Anderson, *Kinsmen of Another Kind*, 275–76.
10. Chomsky, "The United States Dakota War Trials: A Study in Military Injustice," *Stanford Law Review*, 72.
11. This brings up an interesting dilemma: if the Sioux, members of a sovereign nation, could be tried and executed for firing on federal troops, then surely the same could be done to Confederate soldiers, who were not considered to be members of a sovereign nation by the Union. This prospect would have delighted some radicals in Congress who wanted Confederates from Jeff Davis on down to be executed.
12. Many of these were mixed bloods (also called "half-breeds" or "cut hairs" as they were referred to by the Sioux), but the term "Sioux" is applied to all.
13. Gilman, *Henry Hastings Sibley: Divided Heart*, 187.
14. Heard, *History of the Sioux War and Massacres of 1862 and 1863*, 252.
15. *Ibid.*, 251.
16. Cox, *Lincoln and the Sioux Uprising of 1862*, 154.
17. Schultz, *Over the Earth I Come: The Great Sioux Uprising of 1862*, 247.
18. Heard, *History of the Sioux War and Massacres of 1862 and 1863*, 269.
19. A.C. Smith, "The Sioux Uprising in Meeker County." In *A Random Historical Sketch of Meeker County* (1877), 11.
20. These four did not surrender to Sibley but escaped to the Dakota Territory. They were not heard of

again although Big Eagle claimed that one was still alive in 1894.

21. Alotta, *Civil War Justice: Union Army Executions Under Lincoln*, 37.

22. *Ibid.*, 4.

23. Lincoln went on to win Minnesota in the 1864 presidential election, but Alexander Ramsey would later tell him that he would have won by a greater margin if he had hanged more Indians. Lincoln replied that he would not hang a man for votes.

24. Lincoln, *In Answer to a Resolution of the Senate, Message of the President of the United States*.

25. Cox, *Lincoln and the Sioux Uprising of 1862*, 184.

26. Lincoln, *In Answer to a Resolution of the Senate, Message of the President of the United States*, 7–9.

27. *Ibid.*, 2–6.

28. Whipple, *Lights and Shadows of a Long Episcopate: Reminiscences and Recollections of the Right Reverend Henry Whipple, Bishop of Minnesota*, 136–37. It should be noted that both Sibley and Ramsey were Indian traders early in their careers and profited immensely from the Treaty of Traverse de Sioux. Therefore, a large measure of blame for this disaster falls on the two key government participants in Minnesota.

29. Lincoln, *Order, Letter to General H. H. Sibley, December 6, 1862*, 1–4. Lincoln approved the death sentences of 39, but Sibley asked that one sentence be commuted (Ta-te-mi-ma, Prisoner number 15). Lincoln agreed.

30. *Ibid.*, 4.

31. Cox, Lincoln and the Sioux Uprising of 1862, 165.

32. *Ibid.*, 199. Joe Brown, who knew nearly all of the Sioux that were involved, was called in to select the Sioux on the president's list. As far as is known, Chaska was Joe's only mistake.

33. Lincoln, *In Answer to a Resolution of the Senate, Message of the President of the United States*.

34. Schultz, *Over the Earth I Come: The Great Sioux Uprising of 1862*, 249.

35. This is a stretch since General Order 100 (called the Lieber Code) was under review but it was not approved until 24 April 1863. Lincoln knew about it. He was a friend of Franz Lieber and he had asked Lieber to review and establish a code of war. The point is that based upon Article 75 and Article 76 of the Lieber Code, the imprisoned should have been released at that time, not 1866 when nearly half were dead.

36. Lincoln, *In Answer to a Resolution of the Senate. Message of the President of the United States*, 8.

37. Cox, *Lincoln and the Sioux Uprising of 1862*, 190.

38. Lincoln, *In Answer to a Resolution of the Senate. Message of the President of the United States*, 8.

39. Cox, *Lincoln and the Sioux Uprising of 1862*, 68.

40. Lincoln, *Order, Letter to General H. H. Sibley*, Washington, DC, December 6, 1862, 2.

41. *St. Paul Pioneer*, "The Execution of the Sioux Murderers," December 28, 1862, 1–3. The point is that at his death, White Dog still did not understand: as a soldier he was entitled to fight the troops and should be treated as a prisoner of war. It did not matter. He would hang regardless of what he said.

42. U.S. Army, Military Commission, *Sioux War Trials, 1862*; Trial Transcripts; File 1423, Minnesota Historical Society, St. Paul, Minnesota.

43. *Harper's Weekly*, 20 December 1862.

Appendix H

1. Abraham Lincoln, *In Answer to a Resolution of the Senate. Message of the President of the United States*, Washington, DC: U.S. Senate, 1862, 1–11.

Appendix I

1. *The St. Paul Pioneer*, "The Execution of the Sioux Murderers," 28 December 1862, 1–2.

Bibliography

Primary Sources

BOOKS

Athearn, Robert G. *Soldier in the West: The Civil War Letters of Alfred Lacey Hough*. Philadelphia: University of Pennsylvania Press, 1957.

Blegen, Theodore C. *Lincoln's Secretary Goes West: Two Reports by John G. Nicolay*. La Crosse, WI: Sumac Press, 1965.

Flandrau, Charles E. *The History of Minnesota and Tales of the Frontier*. St. Paul: Porter, 1900.

Fritsche, L. A. *Memories of the Battle of New Ulm*. Westminster, MD: Heritage Books, 2007.

Hart, James R. "Historical Reminiscences of Service in the Dakota and Minnesota." In *Dakota Conflict of 1862 Manuscripts Collections,* microfilm edition, roll 2. St. Paul: Minnesota Historical Society.

Heard, Isaac V.D. *History of the Sioux War and Massacres of 1862 and 1863*. New York: Harper & Brothers, 1864.

Nix, Jacob. *The Sioux Uprising in Minnesota, 1862: Jacob Nix's Eyewitness History*. Indianapolis: Indiana German-American Society, 1994.

Pond, Samuel W. *Dakota Life in the Upper Midwest*. St. Paul: Minnesota Historical Society Press, 1986.

Reynolds, Thomas C. *General Sterling Price and the Confederacy*. St. Louis: University of Missouri Press, 2009.

Riggs, Stephen R. *Mary and I: Forty Years with the Sioux*. Chicago: W. G. Holmes, 1880.

Smith, Hampton, ed. *Brother of Mine: The Civil War Letters of Thomas and William Christie*. St. Paul: Minnesota Historical Society Press, 2010.

Wakefield, Sarah F. *Six Weeks in the Sioux Tepees*. Minneapolis: Atlas, 1863.

Whipple, Henry Benjamin. *Lights and Shadows of a Long Episcopate: Being Reminiscences of the Right Reverend Henry Benjamin Whipple, Bishop of Minnesota*. New York: Macmillan, 1899.

ARTICLES

Big Eagle, Jerome. "A Sioux Story of the War," In *Collections of the Minnesota Historical Society* 6, St. Paul, Minnesota Historical Society, 1894, 382–400.

Continental Monthly, "The Causes of the Minnesota Massacre," August 1864.

Daniels, Dr. Asa W. "Boyhood Reminiscences of Life Among the Dakotas and the Massacre in 1862." In *Collections of the Minnesota Historical Society* 15. St. Paul: Minnesota Historical Society, 1910.

Farmer's Minneapolis Tribune, "Milton Stubb's Account of the Indian War," 11 October 1862.

Humphrey, John Ames. "Reminiscences of the Little Crow Uprising." In *Collections of the Minnesota Historical Society* 15. St. Paul: Minnesota Historical Society, 1910.

St. Paul Pioneer, "The Execution of the Sioux Murderers," December 28, 1862.

Pioneer and Democrat, "Serious Outbreak of the Sioux Indians, Several Persons Murdered," St. Paul, August 22, 1862.

PUBLIC DOCUMENTS

Lee, Robert E. *HQ Northern Virginia, General Order No. 9*, April 10, 1865.

Lincoln, Abraham. *Order. Letter to General H. H. Sibley*, December 6, 1862, Washington, DC: U.S. Government Printing Office, 1862.

_____. *In Answer to a Resolution of the Senate: Message of the President of the United States*. Washington, DC: U.S. Senate, 1862.

"Treaty of Traverse de Sioux." *Indian Affairs Laws and Treaties http://digital.library.okstate.edu/KAPPLER/Vol2/treaties/sio0588.htm*, 1904. Accessed September 13, 2008: 1–3.

U.S. War Department. *The War of Rebellion: A Compilation of the Official Records of the Union and Confederate Armies*. Series 1, Vols. 13, 22, 34, 41, 48. Washington, DC: Government Printing Office, 1880–1901.

_____. *General Officers. List and Short Record of General Officers Appointed from Minnesota, and Other Minnesota Officers who were Brevetted as General Officers*. Washington, DC: Government Printing Office, 1890.

_____. *General Order Number 105*. Washington, DC: Government Printing Office, 28 April 1863.

U.S. Senate. *Indian Barbarities in Minnesota.* Washington, DC: Government Printing Office, 1862.
Report on Population of the United States, Eleventh Census: 1890. Washington, DC: U.S. Government Printing Office, 1895.

UNPUBLISHED SOURCES

Joseph R. Brown Heritage Society. *Tales of the Tenth Regiment, 1862–1863.* Henderson, MN: Historical Society of Henderson, Minnesota. 1994.
Hart, James R. "Historical Reminiscences of Service in the Dakotas and Minnesota," in Dakota Conflict of 1862 Minnesota Historical Society Manuscripts Collections, microfilm edition, roll 2, Minnesota Historical Society.
Hunt, Thomas Jefferson. *Observations of T. J. Hunt in the Civil War: A Narrative of the Military Life of T. J. Hunt in the Sioux Indian and Civil Wars of 1862–1865.* St. Paul: Minnesota Historical Society Collections. N.d.
Pettie, George C. "Diary of George C. Pettie, Co. A, 10th Reg." Steele County, MN, 1863. St. Paul: Minnesota Historical Society Collections.

Secondary Sources

BOOKS

Alotta, Robert I. *Civil War Justice: Union Army Executions Under Lincoln.* Shippensburg, PA: White Mane, 1989.
Ambrose, Stephen E. *Crazy Horse and Custer.* New York: Random House, 1996.
Anderson, Gary Clayton. *Little Crow: Spokesman for the Sioux.* St Paul: Minnesota Historical Society Press, 1986.
_____. *Through Dakota Eyes.* St. Paul: Minnesota Historical Society Press, 1988.
_____. *Kinsman of Another Kind.* St. Paul: Minnesota Historical Society Press, 1984.
Association of Graduates, United States Military Academy. *The Register of Graduates and Former Cadets of the United States Military, 2010.* West Point: Association of Graduates, 2010.
Athearn, Robert G. *Forts of the Upper Missouri.* Englewood Cliffs, NJ: Prentice-Hall, 1967.
Barton, Winifred W. *John P. Williamson: A Brother to the Sioux.* New York: Revell, 1919.
Beck, Paul N. *Inkpaduta: Dakota Leader.* Norman: University of Oklahoma Press, 2008.
Bennett, Charles W. *Historical Sketches of the Ninth Michigan Infantry.* Coldwater, MI: Daily Courier Printers, 1913.
Bergemann, Kurt D. *Brackett's Battalion. Minnesota Cavalry in the Civil War and Dakota War.* St. Paul: Minnesota Historical Society, 2004.
Bessler, John D. *Legacy of Violence: Lynch Mobs and Executions in Minnesota.* Minneapolis: University of Minnesota Press, 2003.
Bird, Roy. *Civil War and the Indian Wars.* Gretna, LA: Pelican, 2007.
Bobrick, Benson. *The Battle of Nashville.* New York: Knopf, 2010.
Brown, Dee. *Bury My Heart at Wounded Knee.* New York: Holt, Rinehart & Winston, 1970.
Bryant, Charles S., and Abel B. Murch. *A History of the Great Massacre by the Sioux Indians, in Minnesota: Including the Personal Narratives of the Many who Escaped.* Cincinnati: Rickey and Carroll, 1864.
_____. *History of the Minnesota Valley.* Minneapolis: NorthStar, 1882.
Carley, Kenneth. *Minnesota in the Civil War: An Illustrated History.* St. Paul: Minnesota Historical Society Press, 2000.
_____. *Minnesota in the Civil War.* Minneapolis: Ross & Haines, 1961.
_____. *The Dakota War of 1862.* St. Paul: Minnesota Historical Society Press, 1961.
Castel, Albert. *General Sterling Price and the Civil War in the West.* Baton Rouge: Louisiana State University Press, 1996.
Chittenden, Hiram Martin. *History of Early Steamboat Navigation on the Missouri River: Life and Adventures of Joseph La Barge*, vols. 1 and 2. New York: Harper, 1903.
Clinton, Catherine, and Nina Silber. *Divided Houses: Gender and the Civil War.* New York: Oxford Press, 1992.
Clodfelter, Micheal. *The Dakota War: The United States Army Versus the Sioux, 1862–1865.* Jefferson, NC: McFarland, 1998.
Committee on the 30th National Encampment, G.A.R. *Souvenir and Official Program of the 30th National Encampment of the Grand Army of the Republic.* St. Paul: Pioneer Press, 1896.
Connolly, A.P. (Alonzo P.) *A Thrilling Narrative of the Minnesota Massacre and Sioux War of 1862–63: Graphic Accounts of the Siege of Fort Ridgley, Battles of Birch Coolie, Wood Lake, Big Mound, Stoney Lake, Dead Buffalo Lake and Missouri River.* Chicago: Connolly, 1896.
Cox, Hank H. *Lincoln and the Sioux Uprising of 1862.* Nashville: Cumberland House, 2005.
Davis, William C. *The Image of War: 1861–1865*, vols. 1–6. New York: Doubleday, 1983.
Derounian-Stodola, Kathryn Zabelle. *The War in Words. Reading the Dakota Conflict through Captivity Literature.* Lincoln: University of Nebraska Press, 2009.
Diedrich, Mark. *Dakota Oratory.* Rochester, MN: Coyote Books, 1989.
Ellis, Richard N. *General Pope and U.S. Indian Policy.* Albuquerque: University of New Mexico Press, 1970.

Folwell, William Watts. *A History of Minnesota*, vol. 2. St. Paul: Minnesota Historical Society, 1924.

Foroughi, Andrea R. *Go If You Think It Your Duty*. St. Paul: Minnesota Historical Society, 2008.

Gilman, Rhoda R. *Henry Hastings Sibley: Divided Heart*. St. Paul: Minnesota Historical Society Press, 2004.

_____. *Northern Lights: The Story of Minnesota's Past*. St. Paul: Minnesota Historical Society, 1989.

Greene, Jerome A. *Indian War Veterans: Memories of Army Life and Campaigns in the West, 1864–1898*. New York: Savas Beatie, 2007.

Hafendorfer, Kenneth A. *Nathan Bedford Forrest: A Distant Storm—The Murfreesboro Raid, July 13, 1862*. Louisville: KH Press, 1997.

Horn, Stanley F. *The Decisive Battle of Nashville*. Knoxville: University of Tennessee Press, 1978.

Hurst, Jack. *Nathan Bedford Forrest: A Biography*. New York: Vintage Books, 1994.

Johnson, Frederick L. *Goodhue County, Minnesota: A Narrative History*. Red Wing, MN: Goodhue County Historical Society Press, 2000.

Johnson, W. Fletcher. *Life of Sitting Bull and History of the Indian War 1890–'91*. Philadelphia: Edgewood, 1891.

Jones, Robert Huhn. The *Civil War in the Northwest: Nebraska, Wisconsin, Iowa, Minnesota and the Dakotas*. Norman: University of Oklahoma Press, 1960.

Jordan, General Thomas, and J. P. Pryor. *The Campaigns of Lieut.-Gen N. B. Forrest and of Forrest's Cavalry*. Dayton, OH: Morningside Bookshop, 1977.

Josephy, Alvin M., Jr. *The Civil War in the American West*. New York: Knopf, 1991.

Keenan, Jerry. *The Great Sioux Uprising: Rebellion on the Plains, August–September 1862*. Cambridge, MA: De Capo Press, 2003.

LaPoint, Ernie. *Sitting Bull: His Life and Legacy*. Salt Lake City: Smith, 2009.

Lass, William E. *Minnesota: A History*. New York: Norton, 1983.

Larson, Robert W. *Gall: Lakota War Chief*. Norman: University of Oklahoma Press, 2007.

Lombard, C. W. *History of the Third Infantry Regiment, Minnesota Volunteers*. Faribault, MN: Lombard, 1869.

Lounsberry, Colonel Clement A. *Early History of North Dakota: Essential Outlines of American History*. Washington, DC: Liberty Press, 1919.

McConkey, Harriet E. Bishop. *Dakota War Whoop*. Chicago: Lakeside Press, 1965.

McDonough, James Lee. *Chattanooga: Death Grip on the Confederacy*. Knoxville: University of Tennessee Press, 1984.

McFeely, William S. *Grant*. New York: Norton, 1981.

McMurry, Charles Alexander. *Pioneer History Stories of the Mississippi Valley*. Bloomington, IL: Public-School, 1894.

McMurry, Richard M. *John Bell Hood and the War for Southern Independence*. Lincoln: University of Nebraska Press, 1982.

Meyer, Roy W. *History of the Santee Sioux: United States Indian Policy on Trial*. Lincoln: University of Nebraska Press, 1993.

Minnesota Board of Commissioners. *Minnesota in the Civil and Indian Wars*, vol. 1. St. Paul: Pioneer Press, 1891.

_____. *Minnesota in the Civil and Indian War*, vol. 2. St. Paul: Pioneer Press, 1899.

Minnesota Commandery L. L. *Glimpses of the Nation's Struggle*, vols. 1–6. Wilmington, NC: Broadfoot, 1992.

Minnesota Historical Society. *Collections of the Minnesota Historical Society*, vol. 14, *Minnesota Biographies, 1655–1912*. St. Paul: Minnesota Historical Society, 1912.

Michno, Gregory, and Susan Michno. *A Fate Worse Than Death: Indian Captivities in the West, 1830–1885*. Caldwell, ID: Caxton Press, 2007.

Moe, Richard. *The Last Full Measure*. New York: Holt, 1993.

Monaghan, Jay. *Civil War on the Western Border, 1854–1865*. Boston: Little, Brown, 1955.

Monjeau, Corinne L. *The Dakota Indian Internment at Fort Snelling, 1862–1864*. St. Paul: Prairie Smoke Press, 2006.

Oehler, C. M. *The Great Sioux Uprising*. New York: Oxford University Press, 1997.

Oneroad, Amos E., and Alanson B. Skinner. *Being Dakota*. St. Paul: Minnesota Historical Society Press, 2003.

Powers, Thomas. *The Killing of Crazy Horse*. New York: Knopf, 2010.

Richardson, Heather Cox. *Wounded Knee: Party Politics and the Road to an American Massacre*. New York: Basic Books, 2010.

Raban, Jonathan. *Mark Twain: Life on the Mississippi*. New York: Literary Classics of the United States, 1991

Sandburg, Carl. *Abraham Lincoln: The War Years*, vols. 1–4. New York: Harcourt, Brace, 1939.

Sateren, Shelley Swanson. *A Civil War Drummer Boy: The Diary of William Bircher, 1861–1865*. Mankato, MN: Blue Earth Books, 2000.

Satterlee, Marion P. *Outbreak and Massacre by Dakota Indians in Minnesota in 1862*. Bowie, MD: Heritage Books, 2001.

Savas, Theodore P. *Journal of the Indian Wars*, vol. 1, no. 3. Mason City, IA: Savas, 2000.

Schultz, Duane. *Over the Earth I Come: The Great Sioux Uprising of 1862*. New York: Thomas Dunne Books, 1992.

Shea, William L., and Earl J. Hess. *Pea Ridge Civil*

War Campaign in the West. Chapel Hill: University of North Carolina Press, 1992.
Sherman, Josepha. *Indian Tribes of North America*. New York: New Line Books, 2006.
Shields, Joseph W. *From Flintlock to M1*. New York: Coward-McCann, 1954.
Streeter, James, Jr. *The Civil War—The Struggle for Tennessee: Tupelo to Stones River*. Alexandria, VA: Time-Life Books, 1985.
Stroker, Donald. *The Grand Design Strategy and the U.S. Civil War*. New York: Oxford University Press, 2010.
Sully, Langdon. *No Tears for the General: The Life of Alfred Sully, 1821–1879*. Palo Alto, CA: American West, 1974.
Sunder, John E. *The Fur Trade on the Upper Missouri, 1840–1865*. Norman: University of Oklahoma Press, 1993.
Symonds, Craig L. *A Battlefield Atlas of the American Civil War*. London, UK: Ian Allan, 1985.
Twain, Mark. *The Autobiography of Mark Twain*. New York: HarperCollins, 1966.
_____. *The Autobiography of Mark Twain*, vol. 1. Berkeley: University of California Press, 2010.
Utley, Robert M. *Sitting Bull: The Life and Times of an American Patriot*. New York: Holt, 1993.
Viola, Herman J., ed. *Indian Nations of North America*. Washington, DC: National Geographic Society, 2010.
Wakefield, John F. *The Battle of Nashville, 1864*. Florence, AL: Honors Press, 2001.
Ward, Geoffrey C. *Mark Twain: An Illustrated Biography*. New York: Knopf, 2001.
West, Nathaniel. *The Ancestry, Life, and Times of Hon. Henry Hastings Sibley, L.L.D*. St. Paul: Pioneer Press, 1889.
Wiley, Bell Irvin. *The Life of Johnny Reb, the Common Soldier of the Confederacy*. Baton Rouge: Louisiana State University Press, 1943.
_____. *The Life of Billy Yank, the Common Soldier of the Union*. Baton Rouge: Louisiana State University Press, 1952.
Wills, Brian Steel. *The Confederacy's Greatest Cavalryman: Nathan Bedford Forrest*. Lawrence: University Press of Kansas, 1992.
Woodworth, Steven E. *Decision in the Heartland: The Civil War in the West*. Westport, CT: Praeger, 2008.
_____. *Jefferson Davis and His Generals The Failure of Confederate Command in the West*. Lawrence: University of Kansas Press, 1990.
Wyeth, John Allan. *That Devil Forrest: The Life of General Nathan Bedford Forrest*. Baton Rouge: Louisiana State University Press, 1989.

ARTICLES

Beck, Paul N. "'One Day Was Much Like Another.' Union Soldiers on the Dakota Expeditions 1863–1864." In *Military History of the West* 30, no. 1 (Spring 2000).
Blakely, C. H. "A Defense of Colonel Lester." *St. Paul Press*, August 14, 1862.
Burnham, Captain John W. "Sibley's Expedition of 1863," *The Record* (Fargo, ND), June 1896, 2–5.
Carley, Kenneth. "As Red Men Viewed It: Three Indian Accounts of the Uprising." In *Minnesota History*, September 1962.
Chomsky, Carol. "The United States Dakota War Trials: A Study in Military Injustice." *Stanford Law Review* 43 (1990): 13–98.
Fitzharris, Joseph C. "Our Disgraceful Surrender: The Third Minnesota Infantry's Disintegration and Reconstruction in 1862–1863," *Military History of the West* 30, no. 1 (Spring 2000).
Lass, William E. "The Removal from Minnesota of the Sioux and Winnebago Indians," *Minnesota History*, December 1963.
Millikan, William. "The Great Treasure of the Fort Snelling Prison Camp," *Minnesota History*. 62, no. 1 (Spring 2010).
St. Paul Pioneer. "The Execution of the Sioux Murderers," December 28, 1862: 1–3.
Trenerry, Walter N. "Lester's Surrender at Murfreesboro," *Minnesota History* 39, no. 5 (Spring 1965).
Woolworth, Alan R. "Adrian J. Ebell, Photographer and Journalist of the Dakota War of 1862," *Minnesota Historical Society Collections*, Summer 1994.
Zdon, Al. "Colvill of Minnesota," *Minnesota History* 61, no. 6 (Summer 2009).

ONLINE DATABASES

Ancestry. http://www.ancestry.com.
National Park Service. *Civil War Soldiers and Sailors System*. http://www.civilwar.nps.gov/cwss/
U.S. Army. http://www.history.army.mil/moh.html.gov

UNPUBLISHED SOURCES

Allanson, George Gray. *Biographical Data on Joseph R. Brown*. Minnesota Historical Society Collections, 1933.
Smith, A. C. "The Sioux Uprising in Meeker County." In *A Random Historical Sketch of Meeker County*. Minnesota Historical Society Collections, 1877.

Index

Acton 16, 18, 24, 37, 38, 39, 49, 53, 106, 183
Anaconda Plan 8, 77
Anderson, "Bloody Bill" 85
annuity 7, 11, 12, 14, 16, 19, 22, 66, 67, 106, 112, 192, 213
Appomattox 86, 97, 98, 100, 110
Atlanta 77, 78, 79, 81, 87, 88, 105

Baker, Col. James Heaton 2, 14, 15, 61, 63, 64, 67, 68, 75, 76, 77, 82, 98, 101, 102, 103, 131, 164, 211; in Narrative 114–130
Battle of Big Mound 61, 62, 63, 64, 69, 109, 215, 216, 224
Battle of Dead Buffalo Lake 10, 65, 66, 68, 117, 215, 216, 224
Battle of Pea Ridge 82, 107, 225
Battle of Stony Lake 67, 68, 69
Battle of Westport 85, 107, 226
Battle of Whitestone Hill 73
Beauregard, Gen. P.G.T. 87, 88
Benton Barracks 41, 76, 77, 86, 121, 126
Big Eagle, Jerome 7, 9, 81, 103, 179, 181, 183, 213, 214, 215, 216, 220, 222, 223; in Indian war 16–45
Big Woods 16, 60, 196, 205, 206
Birch Coulee 33, 34, 36, 37, 38, 39, 60, 103, 159, 165, 181, 202, 204, 205, 215, 216, 224
Bowler, James Madison 41, 43, 47, 103
Brackett's Battalion 60, 216, 224
Brown, Maj. Joseph R. "Old Joe" 33, 34, 35, 103, 109, 117, 201, 207, 209, 210, 216, 220, 222, 224, 226
Burnham, Capt. John W. 65, 69, 104, 122, 140, 217, 226

Caine, Billy 36
Campbell, Baptiste 38, 194, 196, 201, 204, 205
Canada 10, 17, 45, 49, 55, 69, 104, 105, 109
Centralia 85

Chaska 185, 187, 222
Chattanooga 40, 77, 78, 79, 87, 225
Chickamauga 87, 89, 109
Chippewa 2, 26, 31, 36, 50, 52, 110, 178, 179, 181, 205
Cleburne, Gen. Patrick R. 90, 219
Cobb 40
Collins, Capt. L.W. 64, 104
Connolly, Col. A.P. 26, 34, 35, 42, 44, 46, 56, 62, 68, 70, 104, 215, 216, 224
Cook, Maj. Michael 5, 96, 115, 121, 122, 124, 125, 127, 128, 130, 132
Crooks, Col. William 37, 117, 120, 182, 193
Cut Nose 52, 53, 204

Dakota Territory 39, 45, 49, 50, 51, 53, 54, 55, 59, 60, 67, 75, 107, 109, 164, 174, 178, 179, 180, 181, 186, 221
Davis, Jefferson 8, 9, 77, 87, 88, 99, 213, 218, 219, 221, 226
Devil's Lake 55, 67, 70, 73, 74

Ebell, Adrian J. 23, 104, 188, 214, 226
Edgerton, Capt. Alonzo J. 15, 63, 104, 115, 116, 117, 118, 122, 133, 135
Edmunds, Gov. Newton 75
Eggleston, Ira 39, 57, 104, 143, 216

Fifth Minnesota Infantry Regiment 1, 2, 7, 11, 20, 53, 60, 125
fifty-eight caliber 8, 39
First Regiment of the Minnesota Mounted Rangers 21, 55, 57, 65
Flandrau, Judge (Col.) Charles E. 9, 28, 29, 30, 104, 115, 213, 214, 223
Forrest, Gen. Nathan Bedford 2, 40, 41, 53, 76, 77, 78, 79, 80, 81, 87, 88, 89, 90, 91, 92, 93, 95, 97, 104, 105, 108, 123, 124, 125, 218, 219, 225, 226
Fort Abercrombie 38, 39, 40, 59, 60, 75, 117, 120, 133, 136, 146, 148, 170, 171
Fort Blakely 98, 100
Fort Pierre 67, 73, 74
Fort Ridgley 6, 7, 11, 13, 14, 15, 16, 45, 55, 60, 68, 75, 105, 106, 108, 115, 116, 117, 121, 160, 162, 163, 165, 171, 175, 181, 182, 202, 203, 204, 213, 215, 216, 224; battle of 19–40
Fort Snelling 5, 105, 106, 115, 120, 121, 125, 131, 144, 145, 146, 147, 149, 156, 157, 161, 162, 163, 169, 170, 171, 174, 175, 204, 225, 226; in Indian war 11–76
Franklin 2, 89, 90, 91, 92, 94, 105

Galbraith, Maj. Thomas 12, 13, 14, 21, 36, 115, 191
Gall 57, 58, 105, 178, 217, 220, 225
Gere, Lt. Thomas P. 6, 7, 11, 12, 13, 19, 20, 27, 105, 213
Grand Army of the Republic (GAR) 6, 9, 102, 224
Grant, Gen. U.S. 66, 77, 87, 88, 89, 92, 93, 95, 98, 99, 100, 106, 109, 125, 220, 225

Hackett, Capt. Charles W. 115, 116, 122, 139, 173
half-breeds 45, 71, 179, 193, 204, 209, 211, 221
Halleck, Gen. Henry 53, 60, 72, 92, 184
Hart, James R. 38, 39, 40, 59, 70, 72, 73, 74, 105, 143, 215, 216, 217, 223, 224
Hatch's Battalion 10
Heard, Isaac 31, 182, 183, 215, 331, 223
Hinds, Asa 110
Hinman, Reverend 14, 16

Index

Hood, Gen. John Bell 2, 3, 77, 87, 88, 89, 90, 91, 92, 93, 94, 95, 96, 97, 98, 105, 109, 126, 129, 130, 219, 225
House, Maj. 73
Hunt, T.J. 10, 30, 47, 55, 56, 63, 76, 79, 80, 81, 82, 84, 85, 86, 91, 93, 94, 95, 96, 97, 99, 100, 105, 122, 128, 129, 135, 166, 167, 168, 177, 178, 213, 215, 216, 217, 218, 219, 221, 224

Inkpaduta 57, 69, 105, 106, 216, 220, 224

Jennison, Col. Samuel 5, 63, 77, 96, 97, 106, 115, 116, 117, 118, 119, 120, 121, 123, 124, 125, 126, 127, 128, 129, 131, 168, 211
Johnston, Gen. Joseph E. 87, 88, 130
Jones, Capt. John 25, 68, 106, 118, 119, 215

Kansas 51, 85, 121, 126, 213, 226

LaBarge, Capt. Joseph Marie 51, 66, 67, 106
Lee, Gen. Robert E. 2, 7, 32, 55, 81, 86, 87, 90, 93, 97, 98, 99, 100, 107, 110, 130, 184, 219, 223
Lester, Col. Henry C. 40, 41, 226
Le Sueur 15, 28, 45, 108, 115, 116, 141, 142, 146, 148, 154, 159, 160, 162, 163, 170, 171, 172, 175
Leyde, Private James 36
Lincoln, Abraham vii, 7, 8, 9, 11, 18, 31, 32, 41, 45, 47, 50, 53, 55, 59, 60, 76, 77, 78, 82, 83, 84, 86, 95, 99, 100, 103, 106, 131, 197, 200, 215, 216, 219, 220, 221, 222, 223, 224, 225; report to Congress 188–195; on trials 181–187
Little Crow 3, 7, 8, 10, 81, 106, 107, 109, 178, 179, 181, 182, 183, 202, 203, 204, 205, 209, 213, 214, 215, 220, 221, 223, 224; in Indian war 11–74
Lower Agency 7, 11, 12, 14, 19, 20, 21, 115, 202, 203, 220; see also Redwood Agency

Mackinaw boat 71, 72
Mankato 20, 29, 30, 31, 45, 46, 47, 50, 51, 52, 74, 103, 116, 179, 185, 187, 197, 198, 199, 207, 211, 225
Marsh, Capt. John 7, 14, 19, 20, 28, 186, 195, 202, 203
McArthur, Gen. John 2, 78, 95, 98, 127

McClellan, Gen. George B. 7, 32, 59, 184, 219
McMillen, Colonel 5, 95, 96
McPhail, Col. Samuel 31, 36
Mdewakanton 178, 179
Medal of Honor 6, 13, 27, 88, 105, 213, 220
Meeker County 16, 37, 117, 214, 221, 226
Memphis 76, 77, 78, 79, 80, 81, 100, 104, 123, 124, 125, 126, 135, 136, 139, 140, 141, 143, 144, 145, 146, 147, 148, 151, 152, 154, 156, 158, 159, 160, 163, 165, 169, 170, 171, 172, 175
Mexico 107, 216, 224
Minié 8
Minnesota Historical Society vi, 13, 14, 15, 16, 17, 18, 22, 23, 24, 25, 27, 29, 33, 37, 41, 46, 47, 48, 52, 55, 64, 66, 101, 103, 105, 107, 213, 214, 215, 216, 220, 221, 222, 223, 224, 225, 226
Minnesota River Valley 19, 20, 28, 31
Mississippi 8, 10, 24, 27, 51, 66, 67, 77, 79, 82, 83, 86, 97, 105, 106, 108, 115, 123, 124, 125, 151, 153, 170, 171, 174, 178, 214, 225
Missouri 21, 51, 55, 60, 61, 67, 69, 70, 71, 72, 73, 75, 76, 79, 82, 83, 84, 85, 86, 89, 107, 109, 117, 118, 120, 121, 122, 123, 125, 153, 170, 178, 215, 216, 217, 218, 219, 220, 223, 224, 226
Mobile 79, 98, 99, 100, 101, 102, 124, 130
Murfreesboro 40, 43, 46, 47, 53, 81, 92, 225, 226
Myrick, Andrew 12, 14, 19, 36, 214

Nashville vii, 5, 6, 27, 29, 41, 63, 86, 98, 101, 102, 105, 106, 107, 108, 109, 126, 128, 131, 132, 135, 136, 137, 138, 140, 141, 142, 143, 144, 145, 146, 148, 149, 150, 151, 152, 153, 155, 157, 159, 161, 163, 164, 165, 166, 167, 168, 169, 171, 172, 173, 176, 216, 218, 219, 224, 225, 226; battle of 87–97
Native American 2, 178, 179, 181, 213
Nebraska 51, 74, 109, 121, 216, 219, 221, 224, 225
New Ulm 8, 26, 28, 29, 30, 33, 52, 60, 74, 104, 108, 110, 115, 182, 183, 195, 196, 202, 203, 205, 215, 223
Ninth Minnesota Infantry 37, 38, 55, 76, 78, 86, 121, 211
North Dakota 60, 62, 69, 104, 105, 217, 225

Other Day, John 21, 22, 106

Patoile, Peter 21
Pettie, George C. 45, 46, 47, 69, 71, 75, 107, 109, 134, 171, 173, 216, 217, 224
Pleasonton, General 85
Pope, Gen. John 7, 32, 45, 52, 53, 54, 55, 56, 57, 59, 60, 71, 72, 107, 109, 115, 116, 121, 184, 188, 216, 217, 224
Price, Gen. Sterling 81, 82, 83, 84, 85, 86, 89, 91, 102, 107, 125, 126, 218, 223, 224

Quinn, Interpreter 11, 186, 203

Ramsey, Alexander 9, 11, 13, 20, 24, 25, 31, 32, 37, 50, 52, 53, 60, 107, 111, 112, 113, 130, 184, 214, 222
Red River 39, 79, 111
Redwood Agency 7, 11, 19, 20, 24, 26, 33; see also Lower Agency
Redwood River 56
Renville, Gabriel 21, 22, 107, 116, 214
Renville Rangers 21, 43, 116
Riggs, the Rev. Stephen R. 22, 23, 107, 108, 113, 180, 183, 200, 201, 202, 207, 213, 214, 221, 223
Ruggles, Francis H. 185, 186

St. Louis 42, 67, 76, 77, 82, 83, 84, 85, 86, 100, 106, 107, 109, 116, 121, 122, 123, 125, 126, 131, 140, 143, 144, 146, 148, 153, 155, 156, 157, 158, 159, 160, 161, 162, 163, 169, 170, 172, 175, 223
St. Paul 11, 14, 15, 16, 21, 24, 27, 31, 37, 39, 40, 50, 51, 52, 55, 86, 100, 103, 104, 105, 106, 107, 108, 131, 162, 163, 171, 188, 189, 191, 192, 194, 197, 213, 214, 216, 217, 219, 220, 221, 222, 223, 224, 225, 226
St. Peter 24, 29, 31, 156, 162, 163, 170, 198
Sanders, Capt. Edwin C. 5, 28, 29, 96, 97, 108, 115, 126, 127, 128, 129, 130, 132, 152
Santee Sioux 10, 55, 57, 178, 179, 221, 225
Schofield, Gen. John 2, 88, 89, 90, 91, 92, 96, 121, 213
Seventh Minnesota Infantry Regiment 43, 44, 47, 55, 64, 68, 69, 78, 86, 88, 116, 118, 121, 122, 198, 200, 211
Shakopee 10, 16, 17, 18, 21, 24, 45, 160, 179
Sheehan, Lt. Timothy 7, 11, 12, 13, 19, 20, 21, 25, 31, 108

Index

Sherman, Gen. William T. 76, 77, 78, 81, 87, 88, 89, 91, 92, 98, 124
Sibley, Gen. Henry Hastings vii, 2, 3, 6, 11, 15, 21, 103, 104, 105, 106, 107, 108, 115, 116, 117, 121, 164, 178, 180, 181, 182, 183, 184, 185, 186, 189, 194, 204, 206, 213, 214, 215, 216, 217, 221, 222, 223, 225, 226; in Indian war 24–75
Sioux 1, 2, 3, 5, 6, 7, 8, 9, 10, 101, 103, 104, 105, 106, 107, 108, 109, 110, 111, 112, 113, 114, 115, 116, 120, 164, 174, 178, 179, 180, 188, 191, 192, 193, 194, 197, 199, 212, 214, 215, 216, 217, 218, 219, 220, 221, 222, 223, 224, 225, 226; Indian war 11–75; trials 181–187
Sioux City 52, 67, 73, 75, 105
Sirocco 54, 61, 74, 109
Sissetons vii, 21, 33, 69, 178, 179
Sitting Bull 57, 58, 64, 66, 105, 108, 178, 225, 226
Sixth Iowa Cavalry 60, 73, 74
Sixth Minnesota Regiment 34, 36, 43, 55, 57, 64, 65, 66, 68, 104, 114, 117
sixty-nine caliber 8, 39, 60
Smith, Gen. A.J. 76, 77, 78, 79, 80, 81, 83, 84, 85, 87, 89, 95, 98, 108, 109, 123, 124, 125, 126, 130, 133
Spanish Fort 10, 99, 100, 130, 131, 153, 154, 155, 157, 165, 167, 168, 169
Spirit Lake 57, 106
Standing Buffalo 57, 58, 62, 63, 64, 65, 109, 179
Stanton, Edwin 78, 94, 122
Strout, Capt. Richard 37, 38, 39, 204

Stubbs, Milton 37, 38
Sully, Alfred 2, 55, 56, 57, 60, 66, 67, 70, 71, 72, 73, 74, 75, 109, 216, 217, 226

Tennessee 40, 77, 79, 81, 83, 86, 87, 88, 89, 90, 91, 97, 98, 99, 126, 130, 218, 225, 226
Tenth Minnesota Volunteer Regiment 1, 2, 3, 5, 6, 8, 9, 10, 14, 15, 98, 99, 100, 101, 102, 104, 105, 106, 107, 108, 109, 110, 114, 115, 116, 117, 118, 120, 121, 122, 123, 124, 125, 126, 127, 128, 129, 130, 131, 132, 135, 139, 142, 145, 148, 152, 155, 158, 161, 164, 166, 174, 175, 176, 177, 178, 197, 211, 216, 217, 220, 221, 224; Indian war 28–75; in Missouri 76–86; Nashville battle 89–97
Teton Sioux 57, 64, 66, 69, 73, 117, 178
Third Minnesota Infantry Regiment 40, 41, 42, 43, 47, 59, 81, 103, 130, 225, 226
Thomas, Gen. George H. 88, 89, 91, 92, 93, 94, 95, 96, 97, 109, 128, 219, 225
Traverse de Sioux 7, 11, 111, 112, 220, 222, 223
Tupelo 5, 10, 79, 80, 81, 84, 102, 108, 124, 125, 138, 142, 148, 149, 150, 152, 154, 165, 167, 168, 169, 176, 226
Twain, Mark 66, 67, 106, 225, 226
Two Moons 57, 58, 178

United States Colored Troops 94
Upper Sioux Agency 11, 21, 22, 24, 40, 42, 106, 107, 206, 214; *see also* Yellow Medicine Agency

Vander Horck, Capt. John 39

Wabasha 18, 115, 130, 179, 203, 206
Wacouta 18, 179
Wahpekutes 178
Wahpetons vii, 33, 178
Wakefield, Sarah 33, 185, 204, 215, 223, 226
Washington (city) 7, 8, 18, 32, 53, 55, 72, 81, 106, 109, 122, 144, 151, 160, 184, 186, 189, 192, 193, 200, 206, 216, 217, 221, 222, 223, 224, 225, 226
Welsh, Maj. Abraham E. 43
Whipple, Bishop Henry Benjamin 68, 119, 185, 221, 222, 223
White Dog 186, 194, 195, 201, 203, 222
Whiting, George C. 185, 196
Williamson, John P. 12, 14, 22, 109, 113, 203, 207, 208, 214, 224
Wilson, Gen. James 92, 94, 95, 97, 109
Winnebago 15, 26, 31, 45, 47, 50, 51, 52, 116, 117, 152, 174, 178, 181, 226
Wisconsin 9, 32, 51, 55, 105, 108, 110, 181, 216, 225
Wood, General 91, 94
Wood Lake 40, 42, 43, 45, 53, 55, 59, 81, 103, 115, 181, 202, 203, 205, 215, 216, 224
Wowinape 48, 49, 106, 109

Yankton 69, 74, 109, 178
Yanktonais 73, 178
Yellow Medicine Agency 11, 21, 33, 43, 115, 179, 205; *see also* Upper Sioux Agency

www.ingramcontent.com/pod-product-compliance
Lightning Source LLC
Chambersburg PA
CBHW081553300426
44116CB00015B/2860